Palgrave Studies in Economic History

Series Editor
Kent Deng
London School of Economics
London, United Kingdom

Palgrave Studies in Economic History is designed to illuminate and enrich our understanding of economies and economic phenomena of the past. The series covers a vast range of topics including financial history, labour history, development economics, commercialisation, urbanisation, industrialisation, modernisation, globalisation, and changes in world economic orders.

More information about this series at
http://www.springer.com/series/14632

Tirthankar Roy

The Economy of South Asia

From 1950 to the Present

palgrave
macmillan

Tirthankar Roy
LSE
London, United Kingdom

Palgrave Studies in Economic History
ISBN 978-3-319-54719-0 ISBN 978-3-319-54720-6 (eBook)
DOI 10.1007/978-3-319-54720-6

Library of Congress Control Number: 2017939568

Cover illustration: dbimages / Alamy Stock Photo

Printed on acid-free paper

This Palgrave Macmillan imprint is published by Springer Nature
The registered company is Springer International Publishing AG
The registered company address is: Gewerbestrasse 11, 6330 Cham, Switzerland

For Ashok Desai

Preface

The author of this book studied economics in India in the 1980s, when the standard curriculum was loaded with something called Indian Economics, had a decent quantity of European economic history, and barely recognized the existence of Pakistan, Bangladesh, Sri Lanka, and Nepal. In this age of globalization, economics teaching in South Asia may be less resolutely nationalistic than it was then, but the absence of good narrative histories of South Asia shows an enduring lack of readership for such works within the region. A book such as this one may help the student of economics see that we can understand every country in the region a little better if we compare it with the others.

For teachers and students outside South Asia, a history of South Asian development has a practical value. Worldwide, the teaching of area studies shows a preference for regions rather than nation states as the unit, because cultures overlap, and economic forces like trade, migration, technology, ideology, and investment cross national borders. These countries in particular share the legacy of colonialism, and geographical similarities as well. In many taught courses in economics, history, and development studies, 'South Asia' is used in the titles, but a guide to economic change in postcolonial South Asia that is comparative in scope is scarce. Such a guide should make for greater balance in courses on South Asia, which otherwise risk being hijacked by the large literature on

India, and for introducing comparisons, parallels, and differences among these countries more effectively than it is now possible to do.

More than serving as a teaching aid, the book has an intellectual agenda. Between 1950 and the present times, the region has seen two almost parallel shifts, from slow economic growth to rapid economic growth, and from a belief that nation states should manage and lead the process of economic development to a loss of that belief. It is tempting to explain the former with the latter, and say that the growth reversal happened *because* managers of the economic system – a group made up of politicians serving class interests and economist serving ideological goals – made right or wrong choices. Most country-specific accounts tend to be policy-centric and state-centric in this fashion. There is an obvious problem here, for the managers and the styles of economic management differ a lot between the larger countries of the region, and yet all experienced the two movements. The book starts from that puzzle. It shows that nation states were always less powerful and consequential than the economic managers imagined them to be. The choices made by the elite shaped economic change no doubt, but the choices were shaped by geography, history, and the world economy in turn, in ways that the people making decisions were not always aware of. A comparative history is necessary to reveal the working of these deeper forces.

Three anonymous readers offered many comments and suggestions, which helped me plan the work. While writing the book, I discussed the subject with and received helpful suggestions from Deepita Chakrabarty, Richard Gellner, Bibhas Saha, and Kunal Sen. Comments from Kent Deng led to significant improvements on an earlier draft. I am grateful to all of them.

London Tirthankar Roy

Contents

List of Figures

List of Tables

List of Boxes

List of Boxes

1

Introduction

The Question

Between the 1950s and the present times, the economy of South Asia has seen a turnaround. During 1960–1990, growth in income per head in the region fell behind the world average. In the next 25 years, South Asia was one of the fastest growing regions of the world, and catching up with the world average income (Figs. 1.1 and 1.2).[1] Many outward features of this transformation are shared between the five large countries that make up South Asia, which are, India, Pakistan, Bangladesh, Sri Lanka, and Nepal. At the same time, they are socially and politically very different countries. The aim of the book is to

[1] We have to be sure that the u-shaped line shown in Fig. 1.1 is not an outcome of population growth. With gross GDP growing at the same pace in South Asia and the world, a relatively faster rise in population in South Asia in the earlier phase and slower rise in the latter phase could produce the same outcome that we see in the chart. In fact, the population of these countries as a proportion of world population shows a more or less steady rise throughout, though the pace of the rise fell from the 1980s. The reversal was mainly a result of relative GDP growth. Figure 1.2 confirms the point.

T. Roy, *The Economy of South Asia*, Palgrave Studies in Economic History, DOI 10.1007/978-3-319-54720-6_1

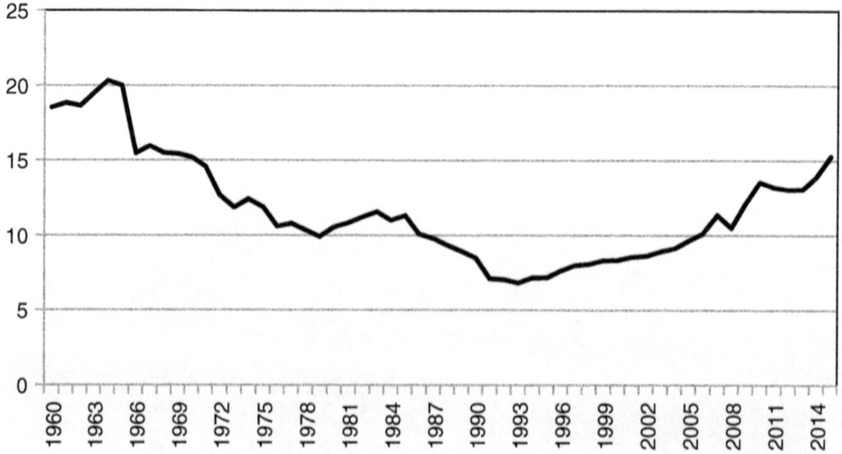

Fig. 1.1 GDP per head (current price) of South Asia to world average (%)

Source: World Bank, World Development Indicators, http://data.worldbank.org/products/wdi (accessed 16 August 2016).

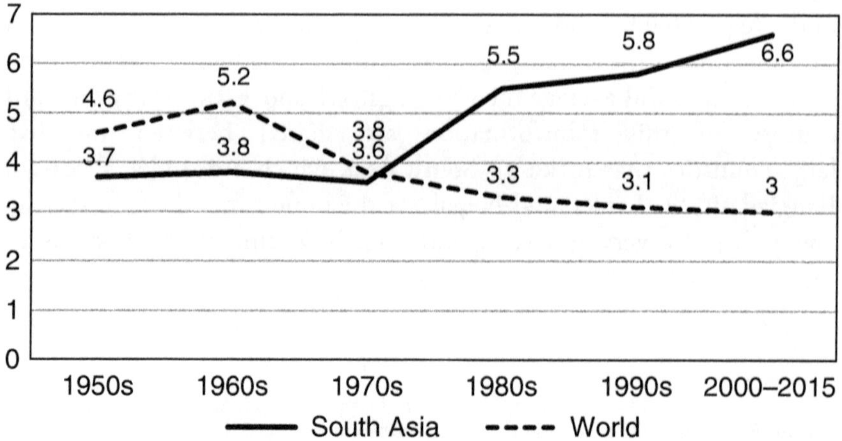

Fig. 1.2 GDP (constant price) growth rates, average annual %

Source: 1950–2000, 1990 international Geary-Khamis dollars, from http://www.ggdc.net/maddison/oriindex.htm, accessed 20 November 2016. 2000–2015, average annual growth rate for South Asia (the definition of the region differs slightly from the definition in this chapter) from World Bank, see above Fig. 1.1.

discover the overlaps and differences in the recent economic history of the region. By drawing connections, comparisons, and parallels within the region, the book attempts to find out why the five countries experienced a turnaround despite many differences in policy and the political set-up.

Why is the story of South Asia's turnaround important to know? There are three reasons why it is important. First, the recent transformation is of great significance for the world. The region contains a fifth of the world's population, and 40 per cent of the world's poor. Its rapidly increasing middle class is eager to consume more and better quality goods and services. The region sends out millions of people to labour markets abroad. It is a leading producer and exporter of textiles and information technology services. A strong growth impulse in South Asia, therefore, vibrates throughout the world, and does so with increasing force.

Second, the theory of comparative economic growth does not supply an obvious explanation for the recent convergence between South Asia and the world. The theory of economic growth in its original form explained growth with reference to accumulation of land, labour, and capital. More recently, the field has turned to world inequality. There are two distinct traditions in economic theory and history to show why countries diverge or converge in levels of income. One of these suggests that growth is 'endogenous' to the quality of politics, institutions, and human capital. The quality of these resources influences investment and innovations, and endogenous means that these qualities are home-grown and self-reinforcing. This tradition is able to explain growing international inequality with reference to initial conditions (the world became more unequal between 1820 and 1985), but it leaves convergence (possibly, the condition of the world since 1985) open to a variety of interpretations. The second tradition is the 'neoclassical' one, where innovation is exogenous, and which gives rise to a clear prediction of convergence that follows from diminishing returns to capital in the capital-rich countries. Departures from the prediction can happen if there are barriers to factor mobility. In hybrid perspectives, the absorption of mobile capital or knowledge depends upon initial conditions.[2]

If this book were written in 1990, we would ask why South Asia diverged from the world, and use lessons drawn from these traditions to answer the question. The lessons might be that poor quality of institutions and human capital, unstable politics, and government policy that obstructed capital mobility, repressed economic growth potentials here. In 2016, we would ask a different question, why South Asia converges to the world average, and it is not easy to answer this question with the help of the same lessons. The region *still* lacks institutions of good quality. Human capital is *still* of poor quality. Whereas barriers to capital mobility have come down, the growth turnaround predated the reform. And, despite capital inflow, capital is *still* expensive for the investors who rely on the domestic market. Politics is *still* unstable.

I do not suggest that comparative economic theory does not have useful lessons for the region, or that the countries in South Asia do not share anything in common with other emerging economies of our times. In the manner of the endogenous growth tradition, the book says that initial conditions matter and despite some differences, there were similarities between the South Asian countries in initial conditions; in the manner of the neoclassical tradition, mobility of capital and knowledge do make a difference. Having said that, the purpose of writing the book is to show *why* these factors matter to South Asia, rather than to use the region to illustrate theory. 'It is a capital mistake to theorise before one has data,' Sherlock Holmes said in 'A Scandal in Bohemia.' In that spirit, the book will take a look at the data and offer some reflections on divergence and convergence in a short section in the concluding chapter. The second reason for reading it, then, is that this exercise can aid our understanding of world inequality from 1950 to the present.

In the end, this is a region-bound narrative history. As such, it can and should engage with other region-bound narrative histories that do

---

[2] The literature is large. A set of useful essays that combine history and theory can be found in Philippe Aghion and Steven Durlauf, eds., *Handbook of Economic Growth*, Amsterdam: Elsevier (North-Holland), vol. 2, 2013.

offer explanations of falling behind and catching up. The book departs from the two common narratives available on these processes, which is the third reason why this book should be read. Later in the chapter, I will discuss the two accounts more fully. Briefly, one of them holds economic policy alone responsible for both the falling behind and the catching up, and the other one holds politics responsible. According to the former story, economists in the 1950s and the 1960s tried to achieve rapid development by means of state intervention. Although their heart was in the right place, the methods were not right. Too much state intervention led to over-regulation and inefficiency, and caused South Asia to fall behind. Realizing their mistakes, economists allowed markets fuller play, hence the revival of growth. According to the latter story, politicians in the 1950s and 1960s tried to achieve economic growth together with redistribution. The redistributive agenda was obstructed by the elite. Politicians came to terms with that failure by giving up on distribution, retracting the state partially, and focusing on growth instead.

The book agrees with both these paradigms that there was rise and fall of a particularly statist and redistributive developmental ideal during this time, but reads the link between the state and the economy differently. That the failure of the state stemmed from either over-regulation or failed redistribution is an Indo-centric thesis that does not work too well for the other countries of South Asia, and yet the growth turnaround was shared by all. In my reading, the problem that led to falling behind was not state intervention as such, but the fact that the nation states overestimated their ability to deal with the world economy or overcome geographical conditions. The catching up did not originate in a retraction of the state, but from a benign world economy. The emergence of a world economy that consumes more services than before is a revolution that began around 1980. After 1980, the richer world started buying a typically South Asian export in enormous quantities, labour services and labour-intensive manufactures. In my story, the biggest form of redistribution, land reform, failed because it had hit a geographical and not a political obstacle. Many other forms of redistribution remain in place. In short, South Asia's links with the world and its own resource endowments shaped the capacity of the states to make changes. The wisdom of the economists and the selfishness of the elite play a smaller role in this story than do geography and international relations.

The book claims that the story fits the five countries because they shared geographical and historical experience, and interacted with the world in similar ways. The idea that the countries in the region shared initial conditions leads us to ask, which are the countries, and how were they similar? The next chapter goes into the question in some detail, but a short description of the region is in order.

The Region

The book deals with economic change in the five larger countries, India, Pakistan, Bangladesh, Nepal, and Sri Lanka. By official definition, that is, the definition of the South Asian Association for Regional Cooperation or SAARC, 'South Asia' should include Afghanistan, Bhutan, and Maldives as well. I exclude these countries on the grounds that the scholarship on them is too thin, and the differences between the excluded nations and those included are too many. In terms of population, exclusion of Bhutan and Maldives still leaves 99 per cent of South Asia in the book. Afghanistan is a much larger entity, in fact, larger than Sri Lanka or Nepal in population. Although Afghanistan was linked to mainland South Asia through trade, and through political and military transactions in the past, its politics followed a distinct trajectory in the last 50 years, to the extent that it becomes difficult to draw direct comparisons and parallels. A similar argument applies to another excluded country, Burma, with which India was deeply engaged until the mid-twentieth century. Imposing territorial limits on a study that is comparative in ambition is always artificial. However, we need coherence too.

Although in area, population, and size of the economy India dominates the region (Table 1.1), taken together, the countries share both geographical features and historical experiences. South Asia can be divided into four geographical areas, the Himalayas, the Indo-Gangetic Basin, the arid and semi-arid interior including the Deccan Plateau, and

Table 1.1 Size of countries, 2015

	Area (000 km)^2	GDP billion US$	Population in millions
Bangladesh	144	195	160
India	3,287	2,073	1,311
Nepal	147	21	29
Pakistan	796	270	189
Sri Lanka	65	82	21

Source: World Bank, World Development Indicators, http://data.worldbank.org/products/wdi (accessed 16 August 2016).

the coasts. These zones were created by average elevation, the Tropic of Cancer, the seasonal monsoon winds, and the Himalayas. The tropical location makes South Asia one of the hottest parts of the earth. The southwest monsoon brings in enough rains, if only within a narrow time span, to enable cultivation. The monsoon gets weaker as it goes inland. In turn, the heat, the monsoon, and the Himalayas give rise to massive snowmelt rivers that sustain the Indo-Gangetic Basin, a tract of mostly alluvium spanning 700,000 square kilometres. Each one of these four zones can be found in more than one country. The Indo-Gangetic Basin, for example, straddles all countries except Sri Lanka. Chapter 2 discusses ways in which the geography of the region impinged on its economic prospects.

Two related features of political history imparted a certain unifying element over this region. One of these was British colonial rule, and the other one developmental states. The British Empire, or the Raj, ruled over mainland South Asia from the late eighteenth century until 1947–1948. Sri Lanka was a Crown colony. Nepal remained an independent country, but treaties drawn with British India integrated the economies of India and Nepal closely. How did the experience of colonialism shape the long-term economic prospects in the region? A fuller discussion of the legacy will appear in Chapter 2. A summary of that discussion should be sufficient here.

The British Empire in South Asia originated in Indian Ocean trade and eighteenth-century military contests among Indian rivals and between the French and the British in Europe. A commitment to maritime trade and a large army were the direct legacies of these processes. The operation of the East India Companies, military protection of trade, and migration of merchants from conflict zones in the interior contributed to the formation of cosmopolitan port cities on the coast. Later in the nineteenth century, migration of European investors into trade, industry, and plantations strengthened the foundations of a globally connected business world in South Asia. This global business heritage and a huge army were among the major legacies of the Raj that the South Asian countries shared, if unequally.

Industrial development in the port cities marked British India as an 'emerging' economy of the early twentieth century. British India led the contemporary developing world in two major industries of the industrial revolution, cotton textiles and iron and steel. In 1910, 55 per cent of the cotton spindles installed outside Europe, North America, and Japan were installed in India. In 1935, 50 per cent of the steel produced outside Europe, North America, and Japan was produced in India. There were by then several concentrations of factory workers in the tropics, but possibly none of these had more factory workers than Bombay and Calcutta (together nearly half a million). Although good comparative data on sources of GDP are unavailable, it is likely that in manufacturing GDP, colonial India was converging with the world.[3]

The Raj also left a negative legacy. Colonialism failed to transform the main livelihood in the region, agriculture, and therefore, failed to make a big impact on poverty, illiteracy, and malnutrition. To some extent at least, the solution to these problems would need states willing to spend vast sums of money on redistribution, transfer, and subsidies, and in order to do this, increase its fiscal capacity by new types of taxes and borrowing. The motivation to do any of this was weak throughout the career of the Raj, and partly in reaction to the inertia, the desire of the postcolonial states to grow bigger and spend on development was particularly strong in 1950. This, the formation of developmental states,

[3] Output growth rate in manufacturing in 1900–1947 was 4.3 per cent, as against 3.2 in Britain in 1856–1937, and labour input growth was more than three times the British counterpart. Based on S. Sivasubramonian, *National Income of India in the Twentieth Century*, Delhi: Oxford University Press, 2000; and C.H. Feinstein, R.C.O. Matthews, J. Odling-Smee, *British Economic Growth 1856–1973*, Oxford: Clarendon Press, 1982.

is the second of the two unifying features of the political history of the region in the recent past.

The time span of the study starts when British colonial rule ended in the region (1947–1948), and developmental states took over. No matter which country in South Asia we start from, in the 1950s and the 1960s, the states made a radical experiment that had no precedent in the region's history. They tried to manage the development process. States adopted new ideological positions, grew bigger, moved to the left, tried to redistribute and reallocate resources, and sponsored industrialization. There is little evidence that ordinary people had strong feelings about these choices. Whether they lived under democratic or despotic rules, they were subjects of the experiments. The makers of the experiment were the 'elite' consisting of nationalists in India and Sri Lanka, a reformed post-monarchic state in Nepal, and a group formed of Muslim League leaders and immigrant businesses in Pakistan. From the 1970s and the 1980s, the states backtracked from this experiment. The power of these groups had grown weaker by then. Although the retreat was not linear and met with frequent reverses, in the long run, the ideal of state-led development declined.

We need to know why this change happened. Before I offer my own answer to the question, it is necessary to consider the literature on South Asian development to see how the question is answered there.

The Field

The region is well served with research. The country-specific literature on the process of economic change is large. It consists of books, articles in journals dedicated to publishing local research such as *Pakistan Development Review*, international economic journals like the *Journal of Development Studies*, international area studies journals like *Modern Asian Studies*, cross-disciplinary vehicles like the *Economic and Political Weekly*, a string of recently launched South Asia-oriented journals, country reports of international funding agencies and donors, blogs and websites dedicated to issues such as poverty measurement, and official publications. I will cite country-specific works in particular contexts throughout the book. The whole scholarship is too large and heterogeneous to be treated either as a paradigm or as a point of departure.[4] Besides, only a small part of this big corpus compares the five countries.

However, experts on the region do often stress the need for comparison.[5] Evidence of growing economic links among these five countries has spawned a few books that try to see the region as a whole. The standard work in this set is a collection of essays surveying some aspect of economic performance, one that makes a case for a regional outlook.[6] These projects yield valuable data and new interpretations. Yet, the scale of the comparative scholarship is small, and its intellectual ambitions limited. Most contributions are technical analyses of economic policy. Many are seminar volumes, and suffer from the usual problem of seminar volumes, which is that, notwithstanding an editorial introduction that is comparative in intent, the chapters are firmly country-specific. Overall, the scholarship is meant for a limited audience of specialists on development policy. It is good on measurement, good on policy analysis,

---

[4] The interested reader should find the following short list a good start, Arvind Panagariya, *India: An Emerging Giant*, New York: Oxford University Press, 2007; Jean Drèze and Amartya Sen, *An Uncertain Glory: India and its Contradictions*, Princeton: Princeton University Press, 2013; Matthew McCartney, *Pakistan – The Political Economy of Growth, Stagnation and the State 1951- 2008*, London: Routledge, 2011; Baburam Bhattarai, *The Nature of Underdevelopment and Regional Structure of Nepal: A Marxist Analysis*, Delhi: Adroit Publishers, 2003; Prema-Chandra Athukorala and Sarath Rajapatirana, *Liberalization and Industrial Transformation: Sri Lanka in International Perspective*, New York, Oxford University Press, 2000; Willem Van Schendel, *A History of Bangladesh*, Cambridge: Cambridge University Press, 2009; and David Lewis, *Bangladesh: Politics, Economy, and Civil Society*, Cambridge: Cambridge University Press, 2011.

[5] 'There is a dearth of comparative work on the region.' Matthew McCartney, Review of Ejaz Ghani and Sadiq Ahmed, eds., *Accelerating Growth and Job Creation in South Asia*, New York: Oxford University Press, 2010, in *Pacific Affairs*, 83(4), 2010, 816–818. McCartney belongs in a small set of scholars who have studied the process of economic change in both India and Pakistan. The set should also include Stanley Kochanek on business-politics relation, and Mushtaq Khan on political economy. Three exploratory essays by Meghnad Desai try to develop a common history for South Asia, again in a mainly India-Pakistan frame. See *Development and Nationhood. Essays in the Political Economy of South Asia*, New Delhi: Oxford University Press, 2005, 269–316.

[6] Ghani and Ahmed, eds., *Accelerating Growth and Job Creation in South Asia*; Ejaz Ghani, ed., *The Service Revolution in South Asia*, New York: Oxford University Press, 2010; Md Rizwanul Islam, *Economic Integration in South Asia. Charting a Legal Roadmap*, Leiden: Martinus Nijhoff, 2012. Ejaz Ghani, ed., *The Poor Half Billion in South Asia: What is Holding the Lagging Regions*, New Delhi: Oxford University Press, 2010.

but unhelpful on history, business conditions, or political economy. Although useful for certain purposes, the comparative projects done by economists do not deliver a robust economic history, nor build on one.[7]

More promising is a scholarship that addresses the nature and role of the state. Although little of that scholarship is comparative in the way this book is, it does answer the three-part question: why did the idea of state-leadership take shape in the 1950s, why did it survive so long, even revive on certain occasion, and why did it end?

Two Stories: Adjustment in Policy and Adjustment in Politics

These works suggest broadly two ways to answer the question. One of these says that wrong policies were chosen in 1950. Many experts on India would suggest that the post-1950 development process in the country went too far trying to push protectionist industrialization, leading to over-regulation of markets and wastage of public resources on inefficient industries. When the economic managers realized that 'the main factors behind the stagnation and decline were poor policies,' they made corrections.[8] A strong form of this explanation, of which professional economists are the main advocates, gives the credit for the 1990s economic reforms in India to the economists. According to this thesis, the Indian liberalization pathway embodied 'a clear definition of the goal' and 'a deliberate choice of an extended time frame to reach it' on the part of the experts on policy.[9] Terms such as 'gradualist,' 'fitful,' or

[7] Isher J. Ahluwalia and John Williamson, ed., *The South Asian Experience with Growth*, New Delhi: Oxford University Press, 2003, does contain a discussion of economic history, all of two paragraphs of it, but otherwise conforms to the pattern of quantitative and policy-centric development analysis.

[8] The World Bank, cited in McCartney, *Pakistan – The Political Economy of Growth, Stagnation and the State*, 207.

[9] Ahluwalia and Williamson, eds., *The South Asian Experience*, 8.

'opportunistic' – applied to clarify the nature of the Indian liberalization – imply the presence of an experienced and cautious driver steering the reform car.[10] Anyone with experience of Indian traffic conditions knows that one has to be gradualist, fitful, and opportunistic to drive a car in an Indian city, which encourages many car-owners in that country to hire professional drivers. In policy-making, the driver is an academic economist hired as an adviser by the government in New Delhi.

This error-correction paradigm of retraction of the state has been criticized for ignoring the political context in which decisions were taken, and for assuming that policy and thinking about policy were somehow autonomous and dis-embedded from politics.[11] I agree with the criticism. For example, the model recognizes that the autarkic and statist policy regime in the region had created 'a set of strong vested interests,' but does not quite explain how pro-reform economists managed to defeat these vested interests.[12] In short, its politics is simplistic, and often confined to bland statements like 'the political mindset has changed' or that 'the general public . . . realized' that too much government is bad.[13]

A further problem with the error-correction model is that, if it works at all, it works for India, it does not work so well for Pakistan, Bangladesh, Nepal, and Sri Lanka, where protectionist and state-led industrialization process was present as an ideal, but pursued with different instruments, with less resolve, and for shorter time spans than in India. Throughout the region, the states grew bigger and more interventionist, but they did not all use this capacity to implement a capital-intensive industrialization as India did. Yet, there *was* something common in their development experience. There *were* elements of failure and learning that were shared. I will come back to the shared elements later.

---

[10] On the use of these adjectives, see Ahluwalia and Williamson, eds., *The South Asian Experience*.

[11] Almost all contributors to the second perspective take this line, for citations, see below.

[12] Ahluwalia and Williamson, eds., *The South Asian Experience*, 7.

[13] Saman Kelegama and Kirit S. Parikh, 'Political Economy of Growth and Reforms in South Asia,' in Ahluwalia and Williamson, eds., *The South Asian Experience*, 123.

A second view, present across India and Pakistan but again especially India, suggests that state intervention of the redistributive kind failed to deliver equity, and draws the inference that this failure forced the state to step aside, and let markets back in. The experience of the land reforms and regulation of big business are offered as examples of the failure, explained almost always with reference to entrenched local power that could thwart efforts from above to redistribute assets or regulate capitalists. One explanation of the failure proposes that the political parties were not sufficiently 'autonomous' from powerful groups.[14] Another work holds the 'embeddedness' of the bureaucracy in rural power structures responsible for failure of implementation of policy.[15] A third view suggests that the state redistribution process in India was hijacked by a coalition of industrial capitalists, rural magnates, professionals and bureaucrats.[16] A collection of essays on Pakistan shows that direct or indirect army rule was a reason behind weak development effort in Pakistan.[17] Others suggest that the political leadership was responsible for weakening of the rule of law and disregard of the constitution.

Some writings by economists explain 'growth without development' with reference to elite power to influence the distribution of state resources and public goods. The idea is that whereas markets take care of growth, 'development' – which includes access to public goods like health care and education – needs the state, and here elite power played an adverse role. William Easterly, for example, reads Pakistan as a case of 'growth without development' using such an argument.[18] Jean Drèze and Amartya Sen suggest that rich consumers in India extract more from the state, leaving little for the poor. In the last 20 years, market-led growth generated inequality, and inequality weakened the development

[14] Atul Kohli illustrates this general idea with reference to tenancy reform in left-ruled West Bengal in the 1980s, *The State and Poverty in India. The Politics of Reform*, Cambridge: Cambridge University Press, 1987.

[15] Ronald J. Herring, *Land to the Tiller. The Political Economy of Agrarian Reform in South Asia*, New Haven: Yale University Press, 1983.

[16] Pranab Bardhan, *The Political Economy of Development in India*, Oxford: Basil Blackwell, 1984.

[17] See essays in John Wilson, ed., *Pakistan: The Struggle Within*, New Delhi: Pearson-Longman, 2009.

[18] William Easterly, 'The Political Economy of Growth Without Development: A Case Study of Pakistan,' Cambridge Mass.: Harvard University (Kennedy School of Government), 2001.

effort, because the 'privileged' classes shaped the public discourse on development.[19] In this way, market-led growth compromised development and yet generated its own defence.

That states failed in implementing redistributive policies could lead us to the inference that, when the economic managers realized that statist policies could not be implemented in the way designed because local power was too strong, the states made a compromise by stepping aside, and by making market-led growth take priority over state-led development. With Pakistan, '[i]t is possible to interpret liberalization as a strategy of state withdrawal given the political failure to implement intervention efficiently.'[20] Another writer on India explains the pro-market reforms of the 1990s as the result of 'a fairly narrow ruling alliance of the political and the economic elite.'[21] The backdrop to that new alliance with the business elite is a long-term failure of the state to discipline the same elite and deliver pro-poor policy outcomes. Yet another work stresses the emergence of new lobbies in the 1980s with a stake in market-friendly policies.[22]

I find the political economy approach to be not entirely convincing. It uses keywords such as elite, privileged class, coalition, and alliance in a manner that their meaning is neither clear nor fixed. I will say a little later that the politics of the five countries is sufficiently different for a single set of meanings ever to be found for these words, making them unworkable in a historiography of South Asia. And yet, the problem we set out to explain applies to all of South Asia. Lobbying by businesses can be important, but the emergence of new lobbies alone does not tell us why politicians would feel obliged, even ready, to listen to them.

The inference that is most relevant to the present work – that the states retracted because they had to – overstates the agency of political actors

[19] Jean Drèze and Amartya Sen, *An Uncertain Glory: India and its Contradictions*, Princeton and Oxford: Princeton University Press, 2013.

[20] Mushtaq H. Khan, 'The Political Economy of Industrial Policy in Pakistan,' no date. Working Paper of the School of Oriental and African Studies, London,

[21] Atul Kohli, 'Politics of Economic Growth in India, 1980–2005. Part II: The 1990s and Beyond,' *Economic and Political Weekly*, 41(14), 2006, 1361–1370.

[22] J.B. Pedersen, 'Explaining Economic Liberalization in India: State and Society Perspectives,' *World Development*, 28(2), 2000, 265–82.

and relies on inference rather than facts. It is too country-specific, that is, explains economic change with conditions peculiar to either India or Pakistan. Or, it compares individual South Asian countries with, typically, South Korea or Japan, the gold standards of statism according to some economists. When we compare countries within the region, we should see that, whereas the broad tendency from regulation to deregulation was more or less universal, the politics was widely variable. The current territories of India, Pakistan, and Bangladesh formed of the land governed directly or indirectly by the British Empire in India until 1947. Sri Lanka was a Crown colony until 1948. Nepal was under hereditary rule, with peace and cooperation treaties with British India. After British rule ended, India and Sri Lanka remained democratic, Pakistan and Bangladesh were under military dictatorships for some of the years, while Nepal completed a transition from absolutist to democratic rule. With such variability in the political experience and yet uniformity in the trajectory of economic policy, can politics explain the trajectory?

All region experts do not share the pessimism of the political theory of reforms. Even such plainly elitist political set-up as military regimes has not been painted in black all the time. Although military rule did entail conflicts of interest between welfare of soldiers and welfare of the population, in the opinion of one political analyst, 'in some respects Pakistan's military regimes were less arbitrary than some democratically elected leaders....'[23] Not all opinions about Indian democracy are negative, or suggest that it allows class and elite power an unrestrained field of play. In the 1970s and 1980s political scientists asked why democracy survived at all when civic culture was weak, the middle class small, ethnic and regional differences marked, and traditional loyalties and patronage strong. If indeed the poor are short-changed systematically, the question is still a relevant one. Why does democracy survive?

Some of the more well-known hypotheses about the robustness of Indian democracy suggest that it survives because it refuses to be captured by the elite. These point at 'the marginality of class politics,'

[23] Parvez Hasan, 'Role of the State in Pakistan's Economy: Assessing the Past and Exploring Future Challenges,' *Economic and Political Weekly*, 42(18), 2007, 1623–1630.

which 'helps to explain centrism' in state policy, constitutional and political arrangements that allow sharing of political power, the capacity to give political voice to the marginalized, and a combination of factors from the institutionalization of civil liberty to the ability to accommodate pluralism.[24] In short, the ideas that the state is weak, that it works only for sectional interests, that it cannot deliver a pro-poor policy for these reasons, and that therefore the state gave up and invited markets back in, is simplistic even for India.

A further problem with the political economy approach is that it assumes too easily that redistributive measures like the land reforms failed because of elite resistance, and not because the policies were badly designed. In a later chapter, I suggest that the widespread failure of land reform in the region had more to do with the scarcity of land than weak resolve of the political parties to implement redistribution of land. Regulation of business, in my view, had little to do with the sentiment to reduce inequality and concentration of power. It had owed, in Jawaharlal Nehru's times, to a dislike for foreign capital, and later in Indira Gandhi's times, to a fear of capitalists as a political lobby. Because bad faith underlay regulation, it did not succeed.

On these grounds, the book does not follow a political economy approach to explain the evolution of the economic system. The book tells a different story.

A Different Story

The story revolves on the *capacity of the state* to attain economic growth and development through its own efforts alone. Certain parts of the shared historical legacy in 1950 – indigenous entrepreneurship,

---

[24] Lloyd J. Rudolph and Susanne H. Rudolph, *In Pursuit of Lakshmi. The Political Economy of the Indian State*, Chicago: Chicago University Press, 1987; Atul Kohli, *The State and Poverty in India. The Politics of Reform*, Cambridge: Cambridge University Press, 1987; Niraja G. Jayal, ed., *Democracy in India*, New Delhi: Oxford University Press, 2001; Ramachandra Guha, *India after Gandhi: The History of the World's Largest Democracy*, London: MacMillan, 2007.

bureaucracy, and the army, for example – contributed positively to this capacity. But in their desire to speed up industrialization with own resources, the states weakened, even destroyed, certain other parts of the shared legacy, including foreign enterprise and a commercial heritage that had thrived on trade openness. That disastrous choice impaired state capacity to manage development. The states also underestimated the scale of the geographical challenges of agricultural change. Let us follow these ideas further.

Just before World War II, conditions were different from what they were to become 20 years later. All of South Asia was a large trading zone in the nineteenth and early twentieth century, and the relationship between the domestic and world economies was a complementary one.[25] The entire region exported agricultural commodities, processed primary goods like tea and coffee, and labour-intensive industrial goods like cotton textiles, and exchanged these products for food, chemicals, machinery, and services of skilled people hired from abroad. Foreign firms and specialized trading firms dominated the business world of the port cities like Bombay, Calcutta, Madras, Karachi, Colombo, and Chittagong. Some of these processed the materials, others organized their export, and still others were engaged in the import of machinery and intermediate goods. A network of domestic trade and indigenous bankers stretched deep into the interior and fed the port-based trade. The Great Depression and the Partition of India disturbed the system, but did not destroy it.

After 1950, the complementary relationship between South Asia and the world, and between export and import, ended. India repressed agricultural trade, private banking, the textile industry, foreign investment, and foreign labour. Sri Lanka slowly squeezed the life out of its exporting plantations between 1950 and 1975. Both countries drove out the foreign firms that organized export businesses. They did not do this only by direct regulation or sequestration, but indirectly by restraining repatriation, investment, and hiring practices, and land reforms in

[25] Tirthankar Roy, *India in the World Economy from Antiquity to the Present*, Cambridge: Cambridge University Press, 2012.

Sri Lanka. Indian export capacity fell, just when the country started to pursue an industrialization policy, which was intensive in capital and foreign technology, and therefore, expensive in terms of foreign exchange. In Pakistan, Nepal, and Bangladesh (after 1971), export capacity had been limited to begin with, so that meeting any rise of developmental expenditure from infrastructure to food was a challenge. In Bangladesh or East Pakistan, mild repression of export added to the challenge.

Foreign aid redressed the imbalance to some extent, and the USSR offered compensatory trade deals. When the Cold War politics made any such external help politically sensitive, the imbalance in the external payments hit one country after another again and again. It is a paradox that, in the 1970s, no country was ready to backtrack and restore the compatible relationship between the world economy and the domestic economy. If anything, the crises increased a fear of the world economy and energized leftist sentiment against openness. The imbalance persisted, and macroeconomic collapse was postponed by harsher controls over foreign exchange.

The 1980s changed the equation between the domestic and the world economies due to three new developments, remittance of migrant workers who went to the Persian Gulf for work, procurers of readymade garments who sought cheap production bases in South Asia, and the Green Revolution that obviated the need for food import. The states had not planned any of this. They had little knowledge of what was happening. They were not correcting an error because they did not think they had made any. All that had happened was, a benign external balance eased pressures off foreign exchange regulation, so that the states could take risks and allow some relaxation on import controls. This small window to the world was then joined by the collapse of the USSR, pressure from IMF and World Bank, and the growing presence of international garment firms, to evolve into an endorsement of openness. As these economies reset their relationship with the world economy, they returned to the foundations that they had begun from, export of labour-intensive industry and services, which funded the capacity to import technology for domestic consumers of high-quality goods and services.

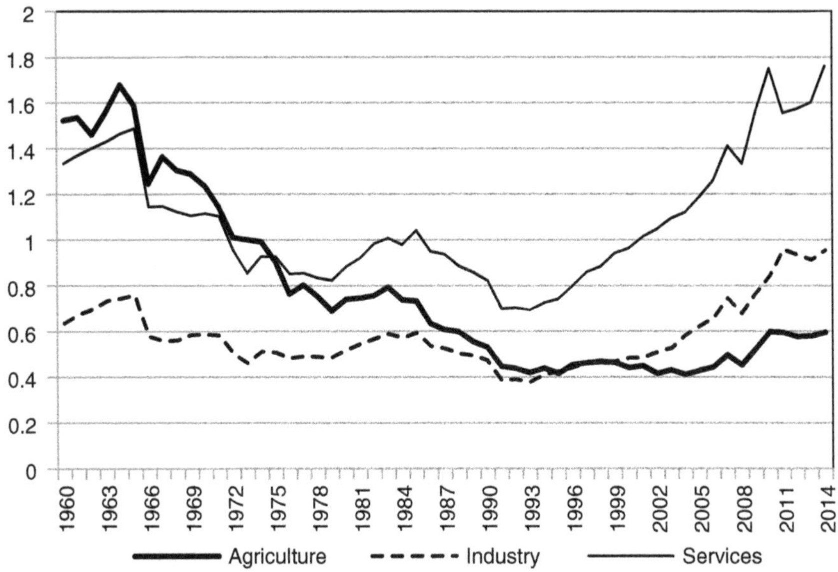

Fig. 1.3 GDP by activity in South Asia, proportion of world GDP (%)

The importance of trade in explaining the divergence and convergence between South Asia and the world shows up when we plot income generated in the three main sectors of activity measured as a proportion of world income (Fig. 1.3). Agriculture explains the falling behind of South Asia until the 1980s, but does not explain the subsequent catching up all that well. Industry explains the catching up to some extent, but not the falling behind. It is in the services that the deepest relative fall and the sharpest relative recovery can be seen. The main components of services are trade, transportation, construction, and finance. Each one of these components tells a slightly different story. One dominant narrative overriding the differences is that a major trading zone of the prewar world retreated in the mid-twentieth century, and then regained some of the lost position. I call the retreat 'trade repression.' In popular history, one encounters the view that these economies liberalized because economic managers realized their mistakes and changed their minds, or that there was a triumph of neo-liberalism since the 1990s. The book disputes that reading. The liberalization in South Asian economies did not happen because of a new 'ism' that political classes and intellectuals started to believe in, or a mistake they thought they had made. Economists did not write the script of South Asian resurgence. On many occasions in the last 20 years, the governments, politicians, and economists in the region did not know that a revolution had begun around them. They woke up late to endorse and adapt to a trend that had begun without their knowledge and was too big to control. This was true of the Green Revolution, the Gulf migration, software export, garment export, explosion of technical education to support the software boom in India, and the growth of digital media. The list is endless. Governments and their advisers *did not know* how their economies were changing.

Does this mean that the states and politics do not matter? Politics does matter, in that politicians and economists today are a lot less sure than were central planners in the 1950s about closing off the economies and putting the state in the driver's seat. Even the hard left does not campaign on hard left economic programme as they did in the 1960s. This is so because liberalization has created wealth in diverse places, destroyed the coherence and power of the older groups, and this situation makes it too dangerous for any politician or party to campaign against openness. Politics does matter, insofar as it explains why politicians hesitate to interfere.

In popular history, one also hears another simplified version of why things changed. South Asia had distanced itself from the world economy because all of the third world turned autarkic in the 1950s. Again, South Asia joined globalization in the late twentieth century because the rest of the world did. These parallels are not supported by historical evidence. There is little data to support the view that Latin American discourses on protection led the Indians towards protection in the 1950s. These were qualitatively distinct episodes in world history because the consequences of the decision were dissimilar. South Asian port cities had some of the biggest concentrations of trade, industry, and financial services in the tropical world at the end of World War II. The choice of autarky would mean an attrition of this infrastructure. It would mean destroying capital, skills, and knowledge. This was a singular act.

The long-term consequences of such attrition were enormous and specific to the region. India allowed the disappearance of the

Indo-British firms, leaving Calcutta city, one of Asia's wealthiest business centres around 1900, de-industrialized and economically depressed for generations. In the nineteenth century, this was a City of Palaces, the 'second city in the British Empire.'[26] 'A pile of shit,' the German novelist Gunter Grasse called the city in 1975. Sri Lanka destroyed European plantation firms, thereby exposing the livelihoods of Tamil tea estate workers, in turn, contributing to civil war and ethnic strife. These consequences made the South Asian movement from openness to autarky and again from autarky to openness unique episodes in world economic history.

Plan of the Book

The rest of the book has 11 chapters. Chapter 2 defines the region with reference to historical legacy and geographical conditions. Chapters 3 and 4 present a chronological history of the state-managed development process in the five countries. Chapter 5 describes the performance of the region with statistical data. Chapters 6 and 7 deal with land – first land reforms and then the Green Revolution. Chapters 8 and 9 discuss trade and industry. Chapter 10 presents a business history, and Chapter 11 deals with migration. The last chapter concludes with a few forward-looking statements.

[26] Geoffrey Moorhouse, *Calcutta*, London: Weidenfield and Nicholson, 1971, 7, 21.

2

Defining the Region: Geography and History

At any time in the past or the present, the capacity of the South Asian states to deliver growth and welfare was shaped by three endowments – structural conditions such as geography; historical experiences, such as the legacy of colonial rule; and the world economic environment. By 'endowment' I mean such administrative resources as a bureaucracy and the army, geographical resources such as agricultural land and commercial cities, and entrepreneurial resources such as traders and industrialists. What were these endowments in 1950?

Geography

The brief discussion of geography in Chapter 1, which divides the region into four main zones, the mountains, the arid lands, the coasts, and the Indo-Gangetic Basin, helps us understand five features of South Asia that matter to economic change[1].

[1] Recently, economists have introduced colonialism and geography in the discourse on the origins of economic growth and world inequality. This literature aims to explain inequality between rich

T. Roy, *The Economy of South Asia*, Palgrave Studies in Economic History, DOI 10.1007/978-3-319-54720-6_2

First, preconditions for intensive cultivation can be found in some places, but not in most. In 1950, all five countries were agricultural, and the peasants in all of them were poor. The immediate cause of their poverty was low agricultural yield. Within India, Pakistan, and Nepal, parts of the Indo-Gangetic Basin and a few river valleys and deltas had good agricultural conditions, that is, cultivators could access water from underground aquifers, and sometimes rivers, in the dry months that stretched for almost nine months in a year. The three countries also possessed immense tracts of dry lands where the monsoon was weak, and which were too poorly endowed with groundwater and loam to sustain even a secure subsistence.

Second, regional inequality was always great where agriculture was concerned. And because of regional inequality, the population displayed a high propensity to migrate. 'Nepal,' writes an anthropologist, 'is a nation forged in migration.'[2] The statement could apply to all other countries in the region with greater or lesser force. In the poorly endowed agricultural zones, livelihood could be so uncertain one year from the next that population growth induced emigration. Within South Asia, migration tended to occur from dry uplands to irrigated floodplains, which led to high density of population in parts of the Indo-Gangetic Basin. In the Bengal delta, which covers much of Bangladesh today, density was high enough to depress the average product from fertile land.

Third, the coasts formed a distinct economic world. The coasts did not always have better agricultural land. But conditions of long-distance trade were better on the coasts. The tradition of maritime trade was an old one. It received a boost during the nineteenth century when world

---

and poor nations, and simplifies the explanatory variables to fit that task. It does not attempt to explain differences among poorer nations, which is of interest in this book. Therefore, the literature will not be used in this book. The interested reader may browse John Luke Gallup, Jeffrey D. Sachs, Andrew D. Mellinger, 'Geography and Economic Development,' NBER Working Paper No. 6849, Washington, DC, 1998; and Daron Acemoglu. Simon Johnson, and James Robinson, 'The Colonial Origins of Comparative Development: An Empirical Investigation,' *American Economic Review*, 91(5), 2001, 1369–1401.

[2] David N. Gellner, 'Caste, Ethnicity and Inequality in Nepal,' *Economic and Political Weekly*, 42(20), 2007, 1823–1828.

trade expanded on an unprecedented scale. Port cities in India, the nerve centres of the power of the British Raj, were vital parts of this globalization process.

Fourth, the Himalayas made for a distinct economic situation. 'Nepal's geography,' one author writes, 'the secret of its independence from British India, has been a considerable hindrance' to economic development (see also Chapter 4).[3] Unlike the other four large countries of South Asia, Nepal is land-locked and mountainous. It is hemmed in by Tibet and China in the north, and India in the South, East, and Southwest. Nepal's access to seaports and trade routes occurs through Indian territory. The country is stretched from the West to the East, but east–west communication is difficult, because the hills are separated by numerous river valleys that run mainly in a north–south direction. The natural communication channels go towards India in the south.[4] The mountainous landscape – in Nepal or the Himalayan regions in India and Pakistan – did not offer secure livelihoods in the form of cultivation or trade. Outlying regions in Nepal were difficult of access from the seat of power, the Kathmandu Valley. Until the late twentieth century, Nepal was ruled by a state that had a limited tax base and therefore limited means to create a centralized rule. The Kathmandu valley was well endowed and well provided for, but that prosperity left few effects on the rest of the country. Moreover, natural barriers and north–south migration had divided up the population of Nepal into many language groups, castes, and communities, which would make the task of building a republic between 2008 and 2015 a particularly tortuous one (see Chapter 4). High communication and trade costs in the mountains were a feature not only of Nepal, but of the Himalayan regions in the rest of the subcontinent as well.

---

[3] 'Introduction,' in David Gellner, ed., *Resistance and the State: Nepalese Experiences*, New Delhi: Social Science Press, 2008, 9.

[4] 'There is a virtually non-existent or negligible flow [of goods] in the east-west territorial dimension,' writes Baburam Bhattarai, *The Nature of Underdevelopment and Regional structure of Nepal: A Marxist Analysis*, Delhi: Adroit Publishers, 2003, 318, in reference to contemporary times.

Fifth, the island and semi-equatorial situation made Sri Lanka distinctive in a different way. Sri Lanka combined the comparative advantage of the coastal zones in maritime trade, with a rich endowment of wet highlands ideal for tree crops. The colonial Sri Lankan economy built itself around an export-oriented plantation system. Thanks to the higher taxes per person earned, the colonial state subsidized education and health care in this country, with the result that Sri Lanka not only had higher average income, it also had higher levels of human development in 1950.

This leads us directly into the issue of shared history.

History

The history of British colonial rule in the region forms the most visible shared legacy. Perhaps nowhere is the colonial legacy more visible than in the region's politics. A striking thing about postcolonial South Asia, especially when we compare the region with contemporary Latin America and Africa, is its political stability. Despite years of military rule, unstable civilian rule, growth of Islamic fundamentalism, and insurgency, Pakistan not only escaped large-scale civil strife and economic collapse, also registered robust if fluctuating economic growth. Despite its diverse society, the Indian union stayed intact as a union, remained committed to parliamentary democracy, and grew into one of the largest and strongest economies of the world. Years of civil war did not cause a debilitating economic crisis in Sri Lanka. Bangladesh, once seen as a country chronically aid dependent, is one of the largest textile manufacturers of the world now and the original home of the microfinance revolution.

In retrospect, four institutions can be identified as sources of stability in the ex-colonial countries, bureaucracy, army, elected legislature, and the central bank. All four were created during British imperial rule in South Asia. By themselves, these institutions would not amount to much, but together they allowed for a continued influence of bureaucratic, military, and intellectual classes on economic and developmental administration, which made for effective crisis management,

Fig. 2.1 Lord Mountbatten addressing the princely rulers on 25 July 1947

In June 1947, Partition of India was announced. In this significant meeting a month later, Mountbatten, the last Governor General of India, told the princes that they had little choice but to accept merger with India or Pakistan.

and imposed checks on absolutist type of power to develop (see also 'state-making' later).

The colonial legacy had its dark sides. In mainland South Asia, the Raj made limited efforts to create public goods, such as roads, schools, and hospitals. The majority of the population lived in villages and cultivated land. If the village was located in an arid or upland district, the land produced too little even for a comfortable subsistence. The colonial rulers never seriously considered a policy to overcome the geographical constraints upon intensive cultivation in dry lands. In 1950, the formerly colonial territories in mainland South Asia had some of the lowest literacy rates and highest infant mortality rates of the world. Why was the rule indifferent to 'development'? An answer is that, ideologically speaking, it was wedded to a small government. In turn, ideology may well have been an excuse for a structural weakness. The Raj was a poor state. Tax per head in British India was among the smallest not only in the world, but also within the imperial domain.[5] The state earned too little money because it relied on land tax, and land yielded little.[6] It was not a weak state; it was militaristic. It spent enough to maintain a large army. It never had much money left over from military expenditure to spend on public good.

Apart from small government, the Empire was also committed to keeping borders relatively open to trade, migration, and investment. In this latter role, the power of the Raj was an instrument to forge close interdependence between South Asia and the world economy of the nineteenth century, which brings us to the third of the three endowments.

Markets and Enterprise

For hundreds of years, settlements on the Indian Ocean littoral traded with each other, exchanging Indian textiles for horses, armaments, pearls, and ivory. In the seventeenth and eighteenth centuries, Indian textiles were passed on to the Atlantic slave trade in Africa as a medium of exchange, or sent overland to European markets. Coastal merchants who engaged in maritime and overland trade had developed sophisticated systems of banking and shipbuilding. In the seventeenth century, the Arabian Sea trade flourished thanks to the sponsorship of three powerful empires – the Ottoman in Turkey, the Safavid in Iran, and the Mughal in India. While these empires declined and trade between them declined too, the European merchant companies consolidated their position on the coasts.

The British Empire in South Asia was established by the East India Company. It was a 'maritime empire,' one that emerged from Indian Ocean trade and financed its military enterprise initially by commercial income, as opposed to the land-based empires, or states that depended on agricultural taxes. As the Company acquired territorial states, it changed

[5] Ewout Frankema, 'Raising Revenue in the British Empire, 1870–1940: How Extractive were Colonial Taxes?,' *Journal of Global History*, 5(3), 2010, 447–477.

[6] In 1950, Indian grain yield per hectare was about one-third that of Europe excluding Russia. For the world figure, see Giovanni Federico, *Feeding the World: An Economic History of Agriculture, 1800–2000*, Princeton: Princeton University Press, 2010, 70.

itself from a maritime into an agrarian state. In the course of doing this, the Company state in India became distinct from its rival or partner Indian princely states, in two ways. It created a standing army financed by the central treasury, as opposed to armies contributed by feudal land grantees. This move made it militarily more powerful in relation to rivals like the Marathas. To achieve this end, the Company brought land taxation under closer central control, partly by means of interventions in landed property rights. In the process of the reforms, many old feudal and military elements either lost their hold on land or had to reinvent themselves as a landlord as opposed to a warlord. Through these two changes, the bureaucracy and the army greatly expanded in scale and capability.

After the Company's possessions came into the hands of the British Crown (1858), the state retained a strong interest in commerce. Although the textile export trade had much reduced after 1810, trading in food and cotton grew, and South Asia emerged as a field of employment for European artisans, workers, and entrepreneurs. The Empire was keen to maintain freedom of transaction in commodities, capital, and labour within its sphere of influence, and sustained the freedom by the use of military power if necessary. Until the 1920s, tariff barriers were low in South Asia, barriers to capital and labour transactions low, and the Empire functioned as a giant customs union.

During the years of Crown rule, in colonial India and in Sri Lanka, two particularly prominent clusters of capitalist enterprise emerged – textile-based industrial complexes in Bombay, Calcutta, and Madras on the one hand, and plantations in Sri Lanka and Assam. Although some of these clusters the Europeans dominated, Indian merchants dominated the others, and almost all of the coastal and overland trade linked to these new industries were in the hands of indigenous merchants and bankers. The trades extended out to East Asia, East Africa, and West Asia, where British-held ports like Aden, Hong Kong, and Singapore offered opportunities to South Asian business groups to expand trade and migration. The South Asians set up overseas bases, shared information and resources, built associations, and negotiated with political actors. Business institutions, from company and contract law to chambers of commerce, were well developed in South Asia. The port cities were cosmopolitan, offered diverse opportunities, and gained from the considerable investment the rich capitalists made in schools, hospitals, colleges, and associations. At the turn of the twentieth century, city management was a field where the idea of self-government was being tried, and wealthy Indians took the lead in urban politics.

As the Empire fostered new types of enterprise, millions of South Asians went to British colonies in search of wage work. At the same time, businesses in the region hired from the imperial labour market. For example, Bombay's cotton merchants hired Manchester engineers to work their cotton textile mills in the nineteenth century. Indian railways and manufacturing industry were a destination for British capital and European artisans from the mid-nineteenth century.

These three elements – geography, history, and the world market – were both exploited and reshaped by the states after 1950.

State-Making in 1950

At the time modern nation states emerged in South Asia, 1947–1951, there were two immediate problems to be solved, to create the state apparatus where it was weak, and to set an aim before the states.

The first process, state-making, was carried out with the bureaucratic and military infrastructure the colonial rulers had left behind. The legacy was substantial and diverse. 'Many of the basic institutional rearrangements . . . that made Britain the forcing house of nineteenth-century globalization were almost immediately reproduced in India.'[7] India inherited the bureaucratic setup of the Raj more or less intact. Almost all of the commercial law and a part of property rights adopted by the new state had been modelled after British precedence. The last years of the Empire had seen parliamentary democracy take roots. The Constitutional Act of 1935 in British India created elected legislatures, and the first Congress government in the provinces. In Sri Lanka,

[7] Morris D. Morris, Review of Mahbub ul Haq, *Human Development in South Asia, 1997*, New York: Oxford University Press, 1997, in *Economic Development and Cultural Change*, 48(2), 2000, 433–439.

the Donoughmore Commission (1927–1931) converted communal electorates into universal adult franchise. An elected legislature was established, even though some executive functions were left to a council headed by the Governor.

Central banking was another inherited institution. The Reserve Bank of India (RBI) was established in 1935. Until then the debt part of the monetary system of British India was managed by the India Office in London, whereas the currency part as well as the fiscal system were managed from India. The RBI integrated the debt and monetary operations. The prehistory of the Bank was very old, in fact, the first proposal of a banker to the government was introduced in the late eighteenth century. The State Bank of Pakistan was formally started in 1956. It had originated in a bifurcation of the RBI soon after independence. The Bangladesh Bank evolved from the Dhaka branch of the State Bank of Pakistan. The Central Bank of Ceylon formed in 1950 out of the colonial Currency Board. Central banking function in Nepal was shared between the RBI and the Ministry of Finance in Nepal until 1956, when the Nepal Rastra Bank was established.

Pakistan had a harder challenge than did India and Sri Lanka constructing the state apparatus, and in one interpretation, the scale of the challenge made the process of state formation authoritarian.[8] Other writers, however, stress areas of continuity between the colonial and the postcolonial, and similarity between India and Pakistan. 'In the formative years after independence fifty British I.C.S. (Indian Civil Service)-I.P.S. (Indian Political Service) officers who entered the Pakistan service on contract helped stabilize the administrative system.'[9] Other experts see the colonial legacy to be not only strong but also persist for decades. 'After four decades of independent existence, .. [t]he viceregal system with a dominant executive and powerful bureaucracy

[8] Ayesha Jalal, *Democracy and Authoritarianism in South Asia: A Comparative and Historical Perspective*, New York: Cambridge University Press, 1995.

[9] Talukder Maniruzzaman, 'Development Administration in Pakistan,' *Public Administration*, 46(2), 1968, 171–184.

has continued to govern the country.'[10] Experts on the economy of Pakistan place some weight upon bureaucratic depth and continuity. Thanks to the element of bureaucratic continuity, the first military regime in Pakistan (1958–1969) could precisely define the goal of the bureaucracy. In the process, 'Pakistan has succeeded in evolving a fairly effective system of development administration.'[11] 'The government and civil service,' another expert writes, were 'able to maintain law and order, to prevent massive capital flight, to enforce import controls, and to provide reasonably adequate overhead facilities.'[12]

Like the civil service, the army was another one of the Raj's legacies. In this area too, substantial continuity was maintained. India inherited the major part of the military infrastructure. Pakistan could recreate the shared tradition quite easily. After Partition, 'virtually all the Muslim officers and soldiers trained by Britain joined the armed forces of the Islamic State of Pakistan.'[13] Military politics, despite allegations of cronyism, is seen by some to have delivered an element of economic stability in Pakistan and Bangladesh.

In this way, in the 1950s, mainland South Asia and Sri Lanka could count on a solid administrative structure inherited from British colonial rule, a basic legislative framework, and a robust cosmopolitan capitalist tradition. The major ports and businesses were based in the Indian Union. A number of trading firms owned by Muslim merchants shifted base from the Indian ports to Pakistan. These groups were to play the supporting role for a new industrialization strategy.

If in state-making, the new countries made use of the colonial tradition, they tended to depart from it when setting a goal for the state. Who defined this goal?

---

[10] Nasir Islam, 'Colonial legacy, administrative reform and politics: Pakistan 1947–1987,' *Public Administration and Development*, 9(3), 1989, 271–285.

[11] Maniruzzaman, 'Development Administration in Pakistan'.

[12] Gustav Papanek, 'The Development of Entrepreneurship,' *American Economic Review*, 52(2), 1962, 46–58.

[13] Alan Lindquist, 'Military and Development in Bangladesh,' *IDS Bulletin*, 9(1), 1977, 10–18.

The Pursuit of Economic Development

In India, Pakistan, and Sri Lanka or Ceylon, the political leadership was in some sense a colonial creation, and had no problem with the bureaucratic and military set-up the British left behind. British India took wealthy, aristocratic, and educated people seriously, as long as they did not challenge authority. It was an elitist rule until the interwar period, when elected Indians were inducted on a limited scale into governance. The leading political parties in the last days of the Raj were led by the educated and propertied Indians. When India, Pakistan, and Sri Lanka became independent, in the business of governance, a degree of elite influence carried over, where the elite formed of bureaucrats, technocrats, army officers, academics, and capitalists. In 1947, power shifted from British hands to the hands of foreign-educated lawyers, landlords, industrialists, army bosses, and intellectuals.

Some of these people believed that they could use the administrative experience and influence to address poverty and inequality, which was a justifiable goal given that the British rule had neglected poverty and inequality for so long. The received wisdom was that the governments should manage the development process by two sets of policies, one set should deliver import-substituting industrialization, and the other set should deliver rural development. The states grew bigger in size in order to achieve these goals. The principal tool in the first set was protection, and the principal tool in the second set was land reform.

Where did these ideas come from? Along with external influences – such as the example of socialist USSR, and the collapse of world trade during the Great Depression – the politics of nationalism in India played a role in the choice. Indian nationalists criticized the economic liberalism of the Raj that had long justified small government and free markets. They claimed that these two things had reduced India from a rich to a poor country. This was a specifically Congress party narrative, though a few ambitious and politically connected Indian business groups that hoped to gain from protectionism rallied behind this narrative.[14] The power of the narrative was weaker in Pakistan or Sri Lanka which did not share the same tradition of economic nationalism as did India. Compared with the sentiment against openness, the ideological impetus behind land reform was less political and formed of a complex economic argument. Although initially redistribution of land was seen as a step to redress rural inequality, later it was also endorsed as a means to achieve agricultural growth.

Despite these goals, the elite misused or misread the quality of the endowment in their command. The late 1960s revealed tensions that resulted from this misuse. How did they misuse the legacy?

Adversities

All five countries, in their eagerness to jump into a home-grown industrial capitalism, favoured indigenous over international business. In the process, they destroyed a part of the business tradition that had been built up over the previous century, the part represented by foreign firms and trading firms. The Congress legacy in India was deliberate repression of trade to favour industry, resulting in a disengagement from foreign trade, nationalization of domestic trade, and a fall in intra-regional cross-border trade. Both India and Sri Lanka, in this way, set out to dismantle and destroy a cosmopolitan capitalist tradition.

Between 1965 and 1975, land reforms failed in India to significantly improve either equity or efficiency (it was never seriously implemented in Pakistan). It did little to redress the problem of low yield of land, and consequently, low wage and mass poverty in agriculture. The states clearly misread the geographical constraint on transforming agricultural productivity. Food shortages became acute. The oil shock upset the balance of payments. Domestic politics became polarized. Indigenous entrepreneurship did play a supporting role to the state, but only for a few years before protectionist industrialization exhausted itself. A violent

[14] On the articulation of this critique, see Tirthankar Roy, 'The Rise and Fall of Indian Economic History,' *Economic History of Developing Regions*, 29(1), 2014, 15–41.

left movement grew in strength. In varying degrees, this set of conditions threatened to derail state-led development in India, Pakistan, Bangladesh, and Sri Lanka. The gloom was relieved somewhat by the Green Revolution, but the geographical reach of the revolution was limited.

The countries did not simply backtrack realizing that they had made a bad choice. On the contrary, the adverse conditions led to a heated contest between a liberal and a leftist solution to the crises. The contest was intense in India, Sri Lanka, and newly independent Bangladesh. In a more muted form it was present in Pakistan and Nepal. The liberals wanted to restore openness, the left wanted more regulation. In the first half of the 1970s, the leftists prevailed, in a remarkable convergence of policy across the region. All countries responded to the crises by means of tighter control over foreign exchange markets. In 1973, foreign capital was regulated by new laws in India. Land reform was reinforced in Sri Lanka. Businesses were nationalized in Pakistan and Bangladesh, and ailing industries nationalized in India.

Why was the liberal option rejected so decisively? In the 1970s, world economic growth was depressed, leftist trade union movements were in ascendance in Western Europe, and USSR was ready to help countries in transition from capitalism to socialism. Constrained or enabled by these conditions, South Asian leaders undertook to solve problems by more regulation rather than less. They did not choose to become more socialist, they were forced into that choice by a combination of domestic failures and external adversities. The only limited freedom to maintain status quo came from Soviet help.

These conditions started to change from the end of the 1970s.

South Asia and The World After 1980: How the Link Was Reset

The oil shock had contributed to the exchange crisis, the oil boom solved it. By the turn of the 1980s, emigration to the Persian Gulf countries was beginning to pay off in the shape of a large remittance inflow into South Asia. The continuing success of the Green Revolution in parts of the Indo-Gangetic Basin made food import less critical. Population growth rate, which accelerated in the 1950s, was starting to fall in the 1980s. These circumstances enabled the policy regime to relax. The flow of remittance money allowed the governments to reduce exchange rationing and to let the currencies float, a measure that had an immediate and dramatic effect on export of labour-intensive manufactures. What started as a few isolated steps from around 1980 joined together into a coherent reform movement, and led to full-fledged deregulation in the 1990s. The game-changer was South Asian migration to West Asia, one of the largest market-driven migration flows the post-war world has seen.

The liberalization that followed was not yet the outcome of a definite change in ideology. In Pakistan and Bangladesh donor pressure and military politics created a push for reforms, but these groups did not represent the political mainstream. In India, the first hesitant moves to liberalize were no more than a risk worth taking because remittance earnings made the economic managers less worried about foreign exchange. The public discourse changed much later. When in the 1970s, land reforms failed, industrial stagnation set in, and socialist nationalization of business went wrong in Pakistan and Bangladesh, the politicians and economists blamed interest groups and 'foreign hands,' but not their own beliefs. By 2015, faith in managed development had receded. In place of ideological debates and positioning, there emerged an informal agreement that liberalism cannot be reversed. Even the Maoist political parties in Nepal talked about being pragmatic on economic policy, and the polarized politics of Sri Lanka gave way to a 'convergence' of views.[15] Whether home-grown or induced by advice from foreigners, ideological shifts had a limited role to play. External and internal conditions reshaped the capacity of the states to make new choices and enabled liberalism in the 1980s.

[15] Prema-chandra Athukorala and Sisira Jayasuriya, 'Liberalisation and Industrial Growth: lessons from Sri Lanka,' in Raghbendra Jha, ed., *Economic Growth, Economic Performance, and Welfare in South Asia*, Basingstoke: Palgrave Macmillan, 2005, 102–118.

Conclusion

I suggest in this chapter that whereas the economists and politicians did make a radical choice to break with the past in the 1950s, the effects of their actions were shaped also by forces of geography and history, on which the states had little control.

In the 1950s, the leaders believed that being free nations meant that the states should act to speed up development. Confidence in their ability to do so was predicated on such inherited resources as bureaucratic, institutional, and military infrastructures, plenty of land, and a pool of indigenous entrepreneurship. The states, however, also changed these inheritances. In India and Sri Lanka, they weakened globally connected commercial enterprise that had flourished in the nineteenth century. The reaction to the exchange crisis that followed was conservative to begin with. As international migration improved the balance of payments position of South Asia, the states could take the risk of opening doors elsewhere.

Having completed an overview, let us return to a key element in it, the state and development policy in Chapters 3 and 4.

3

The State and the Economy I: India, Pakistan, Bangladesh

Chapters 1 and 2 discussed why countries of South Asia tried socialism first, some tightened and some gave up the ideal under a variety of pressure, finally returning to liberalism. Chapters 3 and 4 will complicate the story by showing that there were differences between countries in the way this transition occurred.

Acting on a belief that they had a mission to manage and speed up the process of economic development, nation states grew bigger in size in order to make larger investment commitments. Investments went into irrigation projects, infrastructure, public administration, and manufacturing industry. Industrialization and industrial diversification were the ultimate goals of the new development policy. Of the five countries discussed in the book, India went further than the others in pursuing industrialization by using protection, regulation, and public investment. The statist model was qualified by pragmatism and realpolitik in Pakistan. It was a field of contestation in Sri Lanka. And given Nepal's trade treaty with India, it could not act as a tool in Nepal in quite the same way it could in the rest of South Asia.

T. Roy, *The Economy of South Asia*, Palgrave Studies in Economic History, DOI 10.1007/978-3-319-54720-6_3

India took the protectionist road because economic nationalism was influential here (see Box 3.1). Economic nationalism justified itself by using a model of economic history, which suggested that trade openness had damaged the Indian economy during the colonial times. The narrative was a specific legacy of the Indian National Congress, reinforced by a partnership between nationalist politicians and indigenous industrialists. Neither was politics so nationalist nor indigenous capitalists so wealthy or powerful outside the Indian Union in the 1950s. Opinions on policy were polarized in Sri Lanka, Pakistan, and Bangladesh. Nepal did not have a colonial experience.

Because of these differences, the return to liberalism was a dramatic change only in India. In the rest of the region, there was no one decisive break with the past. There were episodes of hard socialism followed by liberalization in Pakistan, Bangladesh, and Sri Lanka. GDP growth rates and trade-GDP ratios in these countries reveal a fluctuating pattern, whereas India's record can be read as a sequence of three neatly distinguishable stages: growth with protection (1950–1965), slowdown with protection (1965–c.1985), and growth with openness (1985).

India

Partition

In 1947–1948, British colonial rule in South Asia ended, and the region saw the creation of several independent nations, principally India, Pakistan, and Ceylon (Sri Lanka). The map of the region was redrawn in 1971 with the birth of Bangladesh. The Partition of India had been a traumatic episode, involving the largest forced migration the world had seen. On the Bengal frontier, the population exchange continued sporadically for many years. Those who moved included many merchants, artisans, and peasants. Some of them had lost their lands, assets, and customers. The new borders were drawn in a hurry, without due regard to economic geography. Mass migration created conflicts and competition between the older settlers and the new, and led to the fashioning of

Fig. 3.1. Socialist demonstration in Delhi, 1964

Even before a bad harvest caused a near-famine in 1965–66, shortage of food had become a politically charged issue in India. This gathering of villagers in the capital New Delhi demanded a remedy.

Source: Author's collection

new interest groups. The most visible impact fell upon towns and cities affected by migration.[1]

A full economic history of the Partition is yet to be written. It is clear that Partition made heavy demands upon the financial and administrative resources of the new nation states, at a time when the enforced division of offices between the national capitals had weakened state capacity.

[1] On political and social history, historiography, and the aftermath, see Tai Yong Tan and Gyanesh Kudaisya, *The Aftermath of Partition in South Asia*, Abington and New York: Routledge, 2000; and Ian Talbot and Gurharpal Singh, *The Partition of India*, Cambridge: Cambridge University Press, 2009.

In comparison with the Partition, another managed territorial restructuring, the incorporation of the princely states into the larger unions, was handled with more firmness and planning, even though few among the rulers of the larger princely states took part in the project (see also Fig. 2.1).[2]

Despite continuing differences and disagreements among politicians about the future shape of economic policy, there was a consensus over choice of import-substituting industrialization or ISI with a leading role for the state. Where did this idea come from?

Import-Substituting Industrialization

Publicists affiliated to the nationalist movement alleged that openness had damaged Indian development, obstructed industrialization, killed the handicraft industries, and that protection was necessary for rapid industrialization. Like many politicized accounts, this economic history was a constructed narrative and not one based on serious research with facts. Facts suggest a different economic history. Between 1900 and 1946, private enterprise (including trade, transportation, manufacturing, and small industry) grew substantially (Fig. 3.2), whereas agricultural

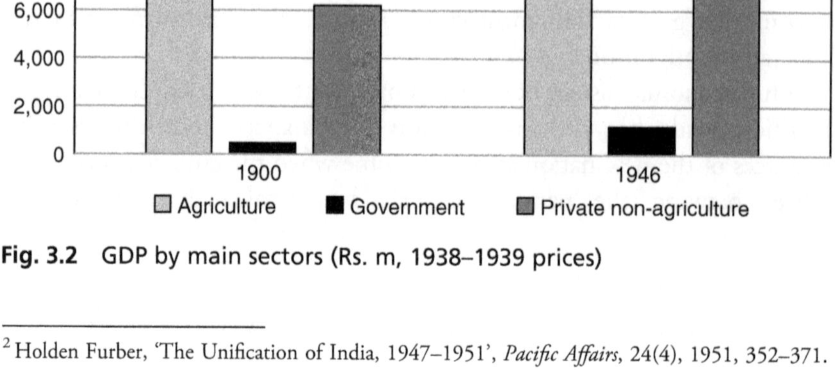

Fig. 3.2 GDP by main sectors (Rs. m, 1938–1939 prices)

[2] Holden Furber, 'The Unification of India, 1947–1951', *Pacific Affairs*, 24(4), 1951, 352–371.

production was stagnant and the government stayed small. The colonial open economy, far from hurting trade and industry, helped them grow. Agricultural productivity, being shaped by geographical conditions, was not responsive to the open economy. Whether real or imagined, the narrative inspired anti-colonial movements, and it had the support of a section of big business that wanted protection. There were a large number of trading firms, as well as foreign companies, who might not have wanted protection, but they did not carry political weight. On the other hand, for a leading Indian industrialist group, Birla, which was politically connected and had sufficient resources to make good use of protection, import substitution might seem like an entitlement.

By 1963, average tariff rates on manufactured consumer goods in India were among the highest in the world, above 70 per cent. While average tariff rates on capital and intermediate goods were low, their imports were regulated by state procurement and the licensing system.[3] Just before the economic reforms of 1992, unweighted average tariff rate in India, at over 100 per cent, was likely the highest among large countries in the developing world. And it had been reinforced by nontariff barriers, restraints on foreign investment, nationalization of financial services, and regulation of private investment.

ISI was not unique in the developing world in the 1940s and 1950s. In fact, the average level of protection in the world had risen in the interwar period, though considerable international variation has been found to exist behind this rise.[4] However, a clear connection between tariff protection and industrialization was not established until 1950. In the larger Latin American countries economists working for the Economic Commission for Latin America around 1950 drew the link by arguing that trade-dependence and the dependence of exports upon primary commodities had hurt the long-term development prospects

[3] V.R. Panchamukhi, *Trade Policies of India*, Delhi: Concept. 1977. The averages do not account for the ad valorem duties.

[4] M.A. Clemens and J.G. Williamson, 'Why Did the Tariff-Growth Correlation Reverse After 1950?,' NBER Working Paper No. 9181. 2002. B. Eichengreen and D.A. Irwin. 'The Slide to Protectionism in the Great Depression: Who Succumbed and Why?' NBER Working Paper No. 15142. Cambridge MA: NBER. 2009.

of these countries.[5] ISI was the solution to the problem. India was not Latin America. Neither was India as trade-dependent as Latin America nor was its export composition dominated by primary products around 1947. In fact, primary commodities accounted for less than a quarter of India's exports at the end of the War.[6] There is no evidence that Indian politicians of the 1950s learnt their economics by observing Latin America. The Indian ISI was home-grown, a legacy of economic nationalism nurtured by the Congress and a section of capital (see Box 3.1).

Box 3.1 Economic nationalism

With reference to its nineteenth-century European origin, economic nationalism can be defined as a worldview that sees economic growth as a nation-building process. In this broad sense, economic nationalism can accommodate a variety of economic systems (see Helleiner). The term began to mean a specific type of economic system during the post-war era of development policy. In particular, it meant a statist economy. This idea, in turn, was rooted in another older tradition in political thought, where 'economic activities are...*subordinate* to the goal of state-building' (Gilpin, emphasis added).

Protectionism as an instrument to meet these aims was long familiar to the world. The infant industry argument provided the theoretical justification, though countries varied in the application of the rule. Friedrich List, one of the architects of the argument, was introduced to the Indian readers by M.G. Ranade. Judge and public intellectual, Ranade believed that the state should play a role in economic development. The role should not be that of a regulator of business. Instead the state should create favourable conditions for business, if necessary by means of protection. In Ranade's own time, protection was seen as a mixed blessing, a step that could encourage corruption, monopolistic combination, and inefficiency, unless applied with discrimination.

In India, economic nationalism did contain the classical idea of a nation in full control over its economic system. It contained another more specific element. Having started as a criticism of the British colonial regime, it had an element of reaction against the open economy that the Empire was so

[5] W. Baer, 'Import Substitution and Industrialization in Latin America: Experiences and Interpretations,' *Latin American Research Review*, 7(1), 1972, 95–122.

[6] In South Asia, only Sri Lanka resembles the Latin American commodity exporting type, and in Sri Lanka, the reaction to commodity price issue was muted, possibly because it relied on tea, which did not suffer the shock.

keen on. The Empire tried to protect British interests abroad. Fighting for political liberty, therefore, became synonymous with fighting foreign capital. Because of this sentiment, discriminatory protection evolved into indiscriminate protection for industries domiciled in India.

Readings: Bipan Chandra, *The Rise and Growth of Economic Nationalism in India: Economic Policies of Indian National Leadership, 1880–1905*, Delhi: Har-Anand Publications, 2010; E. Helleiner, 'Economic Nationalism as a Challenge to Economic Liberalism? Lessons from the nineteenth Century,' *International Studies Quarterly*, 46(4), 2002, 307–29; R. Gilpin, *Global Political Economy*, Princeton, NJ: Princeton University Press, 2001; J. Adams, 'The Institutional Economics of Mahadev Govinda Ranade,' *Journal of Economic Issues*, 5(1), 1971, 80–92; Tirthankar Roy, 'The Origins of Import-Substituting Industrialization in India,' *Economic History of Developing Regions*, 32(1), 2017, 71–95.

State Leadership

A second idea to emerge during India's nationalist movement was enlargement of the state. In 1938, a document of the Congress-affiliated National Planning Committee set out socialist planning as the principal means for managing development and industrialization. The famous document called Bombay Plan, drafted by a group of Indian businesses of Bombay, proposed a deregulated domestic economy, but allowed scope for public investment in capital-intensive industries and industries of strategic importance.[7] Another strand within the Congress, inspired by M.K. Gandhi, while accepting state leadership, considered that rural development should be the main aim of state intervention. Internal debates on policy leading up to the First Five-Year Plan in 1950 saw conflicts and compromise between these visions.[8]

Besides expenditure plans and regulation of foreign trade, the state wanted to regulate domestic markets, ostensibly to protect the poor from

[7] On the early history of planning, Vivek Chibber, *Locked in Place: State-building and Late Industrialization in India*, Princeton: Princeton University Press, 2003.

[8] Bidyut Chakrabarty, 'Jawaharlal Nehru and Planning, 1938–41: India at the Crossroads', *Modern Asian Studies*, 26(2), 1992, 275–28.

exploitation and the risk of fluctuations in the market. A series of measures were taken to reduce private trade and moneylending in agriculture. The decision to make at home goods necessarily intensive in foreign technology implied reliance on imports. The government became the principal approved channel for these imports, including import of technology, essential raw materials, and food. To reduce the fiscal burden, exchange rates were fixed, rationed, and overvalued, which tended to crowd out private import of technology.

Between 1950 and 1955, the Industrial Policy Resolutions of 1948 and 1951 defined the goals of policy, and the Industries (Development and Regulation) Act of 1951 created the instruments of implementation. The principal instruments designed to manage a desired pattern of investment were tariffs, industrial licensing, and public investment. The Industrial Disputes Act (1947) sought to protect jobs of factory workers, and enabled a formal role for the government in collective bargaining and dispute settlement. The principle of job protection was subsumed under the pursuit of 'social justice', and while it was in some way a reward to the politically affiliated trade unions for their contribution to the nationalist movement, it was also in the logic of the new system being erected. The state gave employers protection from imports, and in exchange, made them accept laws that gave workers protection.

India's Second Five-Year Plan (1956–1960) defined the role of the state more precisely. It was to be public sector production of capital and intermediate goods. This element was framed within the so-called Mahalanobis-Feldman growth model, designed by the statistician P.C. Mahalanobis (Box 3.2). The legacy of the model was an industrial policy that identified several capital-intensive industries in which new capacity was to be reserved for the government sector. These included iron and steel, heavy plant and machinery, telecommunications and telecom equipment, minerals, oil, mining, air transport services, and electricity generation and distribution. Domestic production of capital-intensive goods in a capital-scarce economy required average tariffs to be raised to levels much higher than otherwise necessary. Furthermore, capital needed to be rationed by making it mandatory for private investment to take out a license before implementing projects.

There was little complaint from private capitalists to these measures. Tariffs helped them. Private entrepreneurs did not necessarily want to move into the fields where the government was to assume 'commanding heights'. And a growing public sector created demand for the consumer goods manufactured in private factories. How would the government fund an expensive industrialization?

Box 3.2 The Mahalanobis model and the accent on capital goods

Development economics in the 1950s was obsessed with the idea of investment planning. The pioneers of the field behaved as if trade, markets, capitalism, and entrepreneurship did not exist in the underdeveloped world (see also Box 3.3), and the task of managed development boiled down to choosing the most effective design for investment, presuming a socialistic state that will make the investment. Ragnar Nurkse and Paul Rosenstein-Rodan are the two names most closely associated with the emergence of development economics as a theoretical field. Both worked on capital formation. The exchanges that followed these early writings, which owed to Albert Hirschman and Paul Streeten among others, turned into debates on the correct application of investment, rather like a team of doctors debating the dosage of a medicine to be given to a sick patient.

In India, the preoccupation with investment had a deep effect. P.C. Mahalanobis was the bridge between theory and policy. His model showed that economic growth depended on the proportion of investment between capital goods and consumer goods, and showed that the rate of growth depended on the composition of output between these two sectors. Since the private sector did not yet make a lot of machines and intermediate goods, the government must do so.

Mahalanobis left the supply of consumer goods unexplained, assuming that small firms and rural industry would meet the need. This was a clever way to accommodate two distinct visions of industrialization, one represented by Gandhi's accent on rural regeneration and the other by Jawaharlal Nehru's fondness for Soviet industrialization. From the former root, there emerged a further element of India's industrial policy, protection for small firms and handicrafts. Small was defined with reference to a nominal level of investment in plant and machinery, which level needed resetting from time to time. Handicrafts were defined with reference to antiquity and location.

The Mahalanobis model did not acknowledge the most important forms of Indian large-scale enterprise at that time, cotton mills, jute mills, and tea plantations. These businesses fell between the two stools of heavy industry and rural industry, and were given no specific role in the development process. All three declined soon after.

Foreign Aid

Foreign aid was critical to the enterprise. Import-substitution in capital goods would require the purchase of foreign know-how and equipment. Agriculture was monsoon-dependent and prone to harvest failures. The avoidance of food crises again needed foreign assistance. In contemporary development literature, foreign aid was seen as the answer to two types of shortage at the same time, shortage of savings and that of foreign exchange.[9] Even if the gap between saving and potential investment was small, there was a point in raising resources abroad, because foreign exchange created access to machinery and intermediates not available at home, and therefore had higher productivity than domestic saving. India, like any developing country in the 1950s, was believed to 'suffer from a structural balance of payments problem. Its current export earnings are not adequate to meet its requirements for maintenance of imports.'[10] The 'two-gap' model did not ask why foreign aid was better than foreign investment. Implicitly, the primacy of the state was assumed, consistent with the prevailing sentiment among development economists in the 1950s.

Western governments and multilateral agencies were keen to fund projects in both India and Pakistan in the 1950s. So was the Soviet Union, which established a small but growing presence as a partner in Indian development. In March 1965, three-quarters of cheap loans from the USSR flowed into the public sector, whereas three-quarters of cheap loans from the USA for industrial development flowed into the private sector. In key publicly owned industries such as oil refinery and steel, the government found partnerships with western firms and governments

[9] For general statements on the 'theory of aid', see H.B. Chenery and A. Strout, 'Foreign Assistance and Economic Development', *American Economic Review*, 56(4), 1966, 679–733; I. M.D. Little and J.M. Clifford, *International Aid: A Discussion of the Flow of Public Resources from Rich to Poor Countries with particular reference to British Policy*, London: George Allen and Unwin, 1965; V. Joshi, 'Savings and Foreign exchange Constraints', in P. Streeten, ed., *Unfashionable Economics: Essays in honour of Thomas Balogh*, London: Weidenfield and Nicholson, 1970; A.O. Krueger, C. Michalopoulos, and V.W. Ruttan, *Aid and Development*, Baltimore MD: Johns Hopkins University Press, 1989.

[10] M. Balasubramanian in Indian Council of Current Affairs, *Foreign Aid: A Symposium, a Survey and an Appraisal*, Calcutta: Oxford Book and Stationery, 1968, 373.

difficult to sustain. In the 1950s, negotiations with the oil multinationals on profit margins and exploration rights often broke down. The major new factor in the world oil industry in the 1950s was the emergence of USSR as a source of supply. India welcomed this development. Soviet aid began to enter from the late 1950s into refinery projects. India by then was dependent on Russian oil. Simultaneously, restrictions on refinery expansion were imposed on the private companies. Cold War politics would not let the peaceful coexistence of the West and the East go on for long. In the backdrop of friendship with the USSR, the West's support for Indian industrial policy became hesitant. American refusal to support a large steel project, Bokaro, after pondering on the proposal for years, became a minor scandal.

After a 1965 war between India and Pakistan, South Asia was a major theatre of the Cold War. In the first half of the 1960s, Sino-Indian and Sino-Soviet conflicts had brought Indian and Soviet military interests in the region in line. After the Indo-Pakistan war of 1965, which Pakistan fought with American and Chinese weapons, India's dependence on Soviet arms increased. Soviet commitment survived the death of two Indian prime ministers in quick succession and the removal of pro-India Nikita Khrushchev.[11] After the Indo-Pakistan conflict of 1971, and the Indo-Soviet arms treaty of the same year, the foreign policy stance of the United States under Richard Nixon's administration turned against India.[12]

The politicization of foreign aid raised a fierce reaction among both donors and receivers. After a 1965 harvest failure, the Aid India Consortium (a body of Western nations started in 1958) extended aid on condition that India devalued its currency. USA insisted that India refrained from criticizing its foreign policy in Southeast Asia, and on tying aid to diplomatic initiative on Kashmir, which India's stand on the Kashmir issue did not permit. A turning point in Indo-US relations had been reached, which showed up in the increasing dependence of India on

---

[11] For a survey of the turn in Indo-Soviet relations, see Dietmar Rothermund, 'India and the Soviet Union', *Annals of the American Academy of Political and Social Science*, 386, 1969, 78–88.

[12] On the souring of Indo-US relations, see Baldev Raj Nayar, 'Treat India Seriously', *Foreign Policy*, 18, 1975, 133–154; William J. Barnds, 'India and America at Odds', *International Affairs*, 49(3), 1973, 371–384.

Soviet arms. Devaluation was adopted in 1966, and raised a political storm in the Indian Parliament and media.[13] Aid now began to be seen as a price paid for political compliance. With so much sentiment informing choices, the devaluation had no chance of becoming the first step to a liberal reform, as some economists had hoped it would. Political leadership, big business and trade unions, all lobbies proved unwilling to accept an open trade regime.[14] Since foreign aid was a route through which foreign capital entered India, it was never totally acceptable to the left. In the 1970s, Maoist groups grew in influence in some regions. Maoist critiques of Indian policy placed the USA, the USSR, private capital, and military aid all in one basket, though Japan seemed to be a misfit.[15] Some of this sentiment, fed by a tilt to the Eastern bloc by choice or by compulsion, evolved into an intense anti-World Bank campaign in the 1980s.

Amidst the fuss over industry, agriculture was not forgotten.

Agriculture

In the 1950s, redistributive land reforms were seen to be the solution to two problems in agriculture, inequality that stemmed from power of landlords over tenants and small peasants, and poor productivity. It was thought then that redistribution of land to smaller farms would encourage intensive cultivation and solve the productivity problem at the same time (see Chapter 6). The land reforms, however, did not deliver benefits large enough to reduce India's dependence on food aid. From the late 1960s, a

[13]When asked by the US Secretary of State what questions she expected to face in Parliament on famine relief, the new Prime Minister of India answered, 'Have I sold the country?' United States, Foreign Relations of the United States 1964–1968, Volume XXV.

South Asia. Available at http://www.state.gov/www/about_state/history/vol_xxv/zb.html. Later reassessments of the macroeconomic history of this time suggest that the devaluation did not contribute to the economic recovery, so that some of the scepticism was perhaps justified, Pronab Sen, 'The 1966 Devaluation in India: A Reappraisal', *Economic and Political Weekly*, 21 (30), 1986, 1322–1329.

[14]Rahul Mukherji, 'India's Aborted Liberalization-1966', *Pacific Affairs*, 73(3), 2000, 375–392.

[15]Nirmal Chandra, 'Western Imperialism and India Today, I and II', *Economic and Political Weekly*, 17, 1973, 221–44, 403–8; A.G. Frank, 'The Development of Underdevelopment', *Monthly Review*, 18(4), 1966, 17–31.

different strategy took shape. The US government that had made a large food loan in the mid-1960s had some stake in India's long-term agricultural prospect. Although foreign policy made open cooperation between the two governments difficult, a few bureaucrats encouraged research collaboration between Indian scientists and land grant universities in the USA, where dwarf varieties of wheat were being promoted. The seeds worked wonders together with water and nitrogenous fertilizers. The strategy succeeded in wheat-growing Punjab where British engineers had earlier constructed canals out of Himalayan rivers. In the same region, major canal projects were taken up soon after 1947 to resettle migrant farmers from Pakistan. Later, the revolution spread to rice-growing deltas where peasants erected tube wells to extract groundwater. Overall, the package raised farm output, yield, and wages above historical levels.

Outside agriculture, the statist and autarkic policy was beginning to unravel from the 1970s. Industrial growth rate fell after 1965. Foreign exchange threatened to run out in 1967 and 1973. Poverty, inequality, and malnutrition failed to respond to the development effort; and corrupt politicians were often blamed for the failure (see Figs. 3.1 and 3.3). The domestic currency was overvalued, despite a devaluation forced on the government in 1967. Organized trade unions were restless.

Crisis and Response: 1970–1985

The Congress stalwart Jawaharlal Nehru was prime minister until his death in 1964. In 1966 a new prime minister, Indira Gandhi, took over power. A harvest failure the same year showed that the rural poor who had voted her to power were in terrible economic shape. It was her turn to do them a favour. Under a *garibi hatao* (remove poverty) campaign, roads, schools, bank branches, and electricity connection in the villages grew.[16] Decentralization of politics enabled the poor to articulate their demands better.[17] Gandhi's

---

[16] The campaign was launched in 1971, much of the actual results occurred after Gandhi's re-election in 1972.

[17] Abhijit Banerjee and Rohini Somanathan, 'The Political Economy of Public Goods: Some Evidence from India', *Journal of Development Economics*, 82(3), 2007, 287–314, draws a

Fig. 3.3. Uplift of the Poor

Poverty became a politically charged issue in India from the 1970s. Some thought that instead of providing solutions, politicians used the slogan 'uplift of the poor' to promote corrupt uses of public money. Here, a noted historian and cartoonist takes a scathing view of the 'uplift.'

first term as head of state came to an end in 1971, the year of the Bangladesh war of liberation. During the later stages of the Bangladesh war, India had joined as an ally of the Bangladeshi nationalists. In the elections of 1972, Gandhi won an overwhelming majority thanks to her role in the war.

connection between the increased supply of rural public goods and the increased political representation of scheduled castes in this second phase.

But the war had been expensive. A harvest failure in 1972 added to the financial crisis. In 1973, the oil shock dealt another blow to the balance of payments. The government responded to the crises by tightening exchange, and more control over domestic saving. In 1969, leading private banks had been nationalized. Insurance companies followed suit in 1972. Public development banks were established to supply long-term loans to industry, whereas the nationalized banks were pushed to providing rural lending. The number of rural and semi-urban branches of nationalized banks increased fourfold between 1969 and 1981. Upon nationalization, interest rates were controlled, not allowed to rise often, and eventually the real rates turned negative. As bank deposits became unattractive to the savers, government securities that offered tax concessions became more acceptable, again channelling money to the state.[18] This set of intervention did not have an effect on investment rates. But it compromised efficiency and employment growth. By controlling the banks and interest rates the government drove the market price for capital below the 'shadow price' or true price, and by strong job protection laws, the government drove the price of labour above the shadow price, thus biasing the choice of technology in the private sector against job creation.

There had been an anxiety among the political classes over the rising power of the industrialists in the first two decades of independence. Protection and licensing had contributed to industrial concentration in the hands of a few conglomerates, or 'monopoly' houses in India. Private enterprise in banking was believed to be a factor behind rising concentration of economic power. Indira Gandhi (like Zulfikar Ali Bhutto, who assumed power in Pakistan in 1972) guessed that the latter would be unlikely partners of a socialistic state for too long. Gandhi, who had suffered an attempt to marginalize her in politics, doubted their loyalty. Using new anti-monopoly laws, expansion projects of several large firms

[18] Clive Bell and Peter L. Rousseau, 'Post-independence India: A Case of Finance-led Industrialization?', *Journal of Development Economics*, 65(2), 2001, 153–175.
P.O. Demetriades and K.B. Luintel, 'The Direct Costs of Financial Repression: Evidence from India, *Review of Economics and Statistics*, 79(3), 1997, 311–320.

were rejected, on the grounds of potential competition with government enterprises.[19]

These were desperate measures. The economy was slowing down, industries were in a bad shape since the late 1960s, and by 1977, India's neighbours were liberalizing their economies. Why did India not follow them in the late 1970s? By 1980, a bilateral trade agreement with the USSR on a barter basis (called rupee trade) cushioned the government somewhat from the adverse effects of reduced trade with the West. It was no substitute for the trade lost with the rest of the world because of overvalued exchange and curbs on imports.

Liberalization

Indira Gandhi was prime minister on three occasions, 1966–1971, 1972–77, and 1980–1984, until her assassination. It was during the third of these terms that a liberalization began. Nothing was announced. Only the exchange rate was allowed to creep back to its market value over a period of a few years. There was, by then, considerable criticism of the policy within India. Assessments of the regulatory regime revealed that protection had taken a toll on efficiency and productivity. Total factor productivity growth fell between the 1950s and the early 1980s.[20] Restraints upon the textile industry in order to help the handicrafts did not actually help the handicrafts but succeeded in weakening otherwise healthy cotton mills.[21] In 1985, the policy was reformed. External circumstances added to the pressure. An opinion in Japan and Southeast Asia argued that low effective rate of protection enabled East Asia to industrialize by importing knowhow

[19] Nirmal Chandra, 'Monopoly Legislation and Policy in India', *Economic and Political Weekly*, 12 (33–34), 1977, 1405–1418.

[20] I.J. Ahluwalia, *Industrial Growth in India: Stagnation since the Mid-sixties*, New Delhi: Oxford University Press, 1985; and I.J. Ahluwalia, *Productivity and Growth in Indian Manufacturing*, New Delhi: Oxford University Press, 1991.

[21] Omkar Goswami, 'The Indian Textile Industry, 1970–84: an Analysis of Supply and Demand', *Economic and Political Weekly*, 20(38), 1985, 1603–1614; and Omkar Goswami, 'Sickness and Growth in India's Textile Industry', *Economic and Political Weekly*, 25(44–45), 1990, 2429–40, 2497–2506.

and exporting labour-intensive manufactures. While Southeast Asia was beginning to adopt that strategy, the still closed South Asia risked missing the opportunity.[22] By 1985, the USSR was in the throes of its own collapse. The imminent end of the rupee trade, 'profoundly consequential' in one view, would mean that import capacity would have to be funded with export receipts.[23]

These criticisms of insular economic policy had been voiced before, during the 1967 devaluation.[24] The government did not listen then. Why would it listen now? We can find a clue to this puzzle in the remittance from the Gulf, which was growing rapidly from the late 1970s. The government, whether or not it was persuaded by the capitalist alternative, was able to take chances with a freer trade regime. The remittance would provide a cushion against sustained deficit in the balance of trade.

In 1991 and 1992, a further package of reforms was announced quite similar to the 'structural adjustment' programme advocated by the International Monetary Fund elsewhere. Along with decontrol of exchange rates, there was reduction in tariffs, easing of industrial regulation, and rollback of state investment. In the second half of the 1990s, the reforms extended to financial deregulation, privatization of nationalized firms, removing price controls, privatization of the services provided by the utilities, and easing employment laws. Long-standing restrictions on foreign private investment were reduced early in the 1990s, in a piecemeal way.

Another field of reform concerned the relationship between the central bank and the government. Earlier the bank had little autonomy in respect of the government's financial demands made on it. The relation was made contractual, and the autonomy of the bank reaffirmed in the 1990s. About 1995, the easing of quantitative trade restrictions followed the Uruguay

---

[22] William James, Seiji Naya and Gerald M. Meier, Asian Development: Economic Success and Policy Lessons, Madison, WI: University of Wisconsin Press, 1989.

[23] Cited text from Atul Kohli, 'Politics of Economic Growth in India, 1980–2005. Part II: The 1990s and Beyond', *Economic and Political Weekly*, 2006, 1361–1370.

[24] J.N. Bhagwati and Padma Desai, *India: Planning for Industrialization*, Oxford and New York: Oxford University Press, 1970.

round of trade agreements. Foreign investment flows increased more than 20 times over between 1990 and 2008, and its character changed from investment in firm ownership to technological collaboration. With exchange deregulation, exports of three light industries, clothing, leather goods, and cut gems, rose. GDP growth rate accelerated, led by huge rise in manufacturing and services exports. In the 2000s, service export forged ahead. This is sometimes seen as a distinctively Indian success story, and will be discussed in detail in Chapter 7.

The liberalization created strains. During Indira Gandhi's rule, rural infrastructure and farming-related subsidies received state funding. As subsidies paid out to Green Revolution farmers increased, the rural bias in government transfers led to a neglect of urban infrastructure, from roads to railways, ports, electricity, telecommunication, financial services, schools, and hospitals. Much of this infrastructure was in charge of the states (provinces) who faced fiscal pressures. Industrial investment by the public sector favoured 'backward' regions, private investment had no such compulsion. The major part of the states' own tax income was derived from the sales taxes, which were often waived in a competitive bid to attract industry. The states' power to borrow was limited. The division of central assistance was based upon distributional rules that gave greater weight to poverty, in effect discriminating against efficient financial management. Some states paid a price for nationalization of bankrupt enterprises, and expansion in public undertakings, that they had indulged in. The rate of return on investment in state-owned businesses was low.[25] To this burden were added waived farm income taxes and lost taxes from alcohol in states that prohibited its consumption. Given that changes in labour regulation were variable regionally, 'delicensing resulted in a sizeable reallocation of industrial production from states with pro-worker labor institutions to states with pro-employer labor institutions.'[26]

[25] The dividend to equity ratio in 1994 worked out to 3 per cent. The losses sustained by 514 state companies (out of a total of 840) were staggering. The rate of return on net fixed assets generated by the electricity undertakings was –13 per cent in 1993–1994. The transport corporations' combined losses amount to Rs 2.85 billion in 1993–1994.

[26] Philippe Aghion, Robin Burgess, Stephen J. Redding and Fabrizio Zilibotti, 'The Unequal Effects of Liberalization: Evidence from Dismantling the License Raj in India', *American Economic Review*, 98(4), 2008, 1397–1412.

The Indian states remained funds-constrained and dependent on loans from the central government until about 2004, when reforms in federal finance allowed them to borrow from the market. This move, along with higher inflow of taxes from tax on consumption and trade led the majority out of crises. Their ability to draw in private investment in industry still varies considerably.

Box 3.3 Quality of capitalism and South Asian history

The idea that economic development in the poorer countries can be and should be managed by the state was common in the immediate post-war years. What about markets? What role would capitalism play in the development process?

While economists concentrated on the design of investment plans (see Box 3.2), the question of capitalism was left to the sociologists to explore. The American 'modernization' theorists proposed that industrialization required entrepreneurs, and entrepreneurship was a scarce resource in the poorer world. Individual authors attributed deficient entrepreneurship to different sources, strength of traditional forms of power (Everett Hagen), weak motivation to achieve (David McClelland), lack of freedom of decision-making (Albert Hirschman), small size of the middle class (Ragnar Nurkse and J.J. Spengler), insufficient 'capitalist culture' (Walt Rostow), and 'national character' (Alex Inkeles), among other factors. Two types of policy lessons followed from this reading. First, development needed social planning along with investment planning. That idea never took off. Second, development required government regulation of markets because market incentives would fail in the absence of entrepreneurship. The second idea became a canon.

The modernization theory was criticized. The more famous criticism came from the Dependency school writers, who argued that underdevelopment was an outcome of western exploitation rather than social backwardness. The Dependency school did not challenge the assumption that capitalism was indeed weak in the poorer world. All it did was to substitute the myth of undeveloped capitalism by the myth of dependent capitalism. The second challenge came from economists who did field research in South Asia. Morris David Morris, pointing out that the fourth largest cotton mill in the world emerged in the unlikely setting of India, rejected the premise of undeveloped entrepreneurship and deficient culture. Gustav Papanek drew a similar lesson from Pakistan, 'there is considerable evidence of a rapid development of industrial entrepreneurship in response to powerful economic incentives,' and therefore, 'Pakistan does not lend support to the propositions' of the sociological approach.

The idea that 'culture' matters to the quality of capitalism lives on in applied economic theory. One view is that caste-like groups, which make conformity to norm a positive moral value and breach of norm a sin, can suppress individual enterprise. Another view is that associational culture was more advanced in Western Europe than in Asia and Africa, and this difference accounts for different trajectories in institutional development. These arguments suggest, like modernization theory, that South Asia is not likely to see flourishing capitalism.

Readings: Morris D. Morris, 'Values as an Obstacle to Economic Growth in South Asia: An Historical Survey', *Journal of Economic History*, 27(4), 1967, 588–607; Bert Hoselitz, *Sociological Aspects of Economic Growth*, Glencoe: The Free Press, 1960; Gustav F. Papanek, 'The Development of Entrepreneurship,' *American Economic Review*, 52(2), 1962, 46–58; Avner Greif, *Institutions and the Path to the Modern Economy: Lessons from Medieval Trade*, Cambridge: Cambridge University Press, 2006

Pakistan

Partition and State-Making

If India in some sense inherited the administrative infrastructure from the British, state formation in Pakistan was a tortuous process. The leading political party, Muslim League, did not have deep organizational roots in West Pakistan. Its educated middle-class leadership had been based in India, whereas in Pakistan its leadership was influenced by landlords and rulers of princely states. Landlord power posed a thorny issue, since many economic reformers wanted their power to end and demanded land reforms. The bureaucracy being small in relation to the huge internal security challenges and a fragile federal union, it tended to concentrate powers. With the bitter experience of communal conflict in the recent past, co-opting minorities became a priority for the new state.[27] The death of M. A. Jinnah and the Prime Minister Liaquat Ali Khan within a few years of independence disturbed the process of succession of power, which in turn contributed to the growing power of bureaucrats and the military.

[27] Richard Symonds, 'State-Making in Pakistan,' *Far Eastern Survey*, 19(5), 1950, 45–50.

Pakistan had few large-scale industries, banks, and other businesses. The Partition caused enormous difficulties for industry, especially the jute and cotton textile industries. Before Partition, the manufacturing facilities for the two industries was mainly located in India and raw material production in Pakistan territory. The textile industry needed urgent help because of the Partition. A functioning state machine was several years in the making. Agriculture, the main source of livelihood by far, suffered due to loss of industrial markets in India. A trade war with India further added to the problem. By comparison, integration of the princely states was a less important problem for Pakistan. The states formed less than 4 per cent of the population in Pakistan, whereas in India, they formed a quarter of the population.

A complex issue of negotiation was water sharing. India and Pakistan relied on the five major rivers of the Indus River basin for irrigation and power. All of these rivers originated inside India and four of them flowed inside Pakistan. Pakistan was the potential loser from the new border, which had made some districts in Punjab lose access to the so-called Eastern rivers. Under World Bank mediation, the Indus Waters Treaty was drawn in 1960 between the two countries, which allowed Pakistan to exploit the Western rivers more intensively in future, while allowing India rights to the Eastern rivers.[28] The Treaty was hailed as a successful example of international mediation when it was signed, and survived strained relations and three wars between the two countries fought since 1960.[29]

In the area of industrialization, realism dictated a less radical strategy than India's. In Pakistan, protectionist sentiment was weaker than in India, the economy more open, and labour law a less sensitive issue. Pakistan's commitment to state leadership and capital-intensive industry

[28] One of the major projects designed to make fuller use of the western rivers, the Tarbela Dam, took 17 years to be ready.

[29] Between 2002 and 2012, however, threatening voices were heard on both sides about the Treaty, and it is not unthinkable that increasing water scarcity in the region and in some cases falling water level in the rivers could unleash a conflict over the Treaty. Ramaswamy R. Iyer, 'Indus Waters Treaty 1960: An Indian Perspective,' 16 March 2014, available at https://www.boell.de/en/2014/03/16/indus-waters-treaty-1960-indian-perspective (accessed 2 August 2016); and 'The Indus Waters Treaty', http://www.stimson.org/the-indus-waters-treaty (accessed 2 August 2016), provide different perspectives on the recent uneasiness. The latter resource supplies the full text of the treaty.

was weaker than India's too. The market and labour-intensive industry were allowed to play a larger role. The early 1950s saw little government regulation of trade or investment. Whereas in the late 1950s import and exchange controls came into existence, the private sector was left less regulated by Indian standards. Import-substituting industrialization was present, but it did not involve, as it did in India, redirection of investment into heavy industry. By contrast, in Pakistan, 'the import substitution strategy…encouraged the emergence of a consumer goods-dominated industrial structure.'[30] Both countries had a meritocratic civil service in the British Indian model, and a university system that churned out bureaucrats. Probably because India was committed to building domestic capability in technology, the country went further than Pakistan in expanding the university system, reduction of barriers to entry into high-quality technical education, and the addition of science and technology instruction. Later in the twentieth century, the difference explained to some extent the differential composition of service export from South Asia.

Foreign aid was more important to Pakistan than to India. Between 1955 and 1970, foreign aid formed 2.5–4 per cent of GDP on average, and well over a third of gross investment in Pakistan. The percentages for India in the same time were 1.1–2.2 and 6–14 per cent respectively. Pakistan entered a strategic alliance with the USA in the mid-1950s, and a large part of foreign assistance came in the form of military aid. The army was empowered first by the uncertainty surrounding civilian rule and Partition, and further empowered in its political ambitions by US involvement during the Cold War years. Although the involvement had an economic dimension, US interest was dominated by security concerns. The Pakistan army, and not the state, was the key ally of America (see Fig. 3.4).

Although manufacturing grew rapidly, led by cotton textiles, overall economic growth in the 1950s was of limited order. In the 1950s agriculture grew at a rate that was on average well below the rate of population growth. Food needed to be imported on several occasions. There was land

[30] Masood Ahmed, 'Import Substitution as a Strategy of Industrialization in Pakistan – A Review,' *Pakistan Economic and Social Review*, 18(1/2), 1980, 56–64.

Fig. 3.4. President Lyndon Johnson meets with President Ayub Khan in Karachi, December 1967

Wars in South and Southeast Asia saw new political alliances being drawn in the region, with implications for foreign investment and trade openness.

reform, but the land ceiling had been set so high as to make little difference to asset distribution. The 1958 coup d'état that followed a period of instability and brought General Muhammad Ayub Khan to power was in some sense anticipated by the poor economic record.[31]

[31] Since 1958, Pakistan has seen shifts between elected governments and military dictatorship. The switch of control meant that, unlike India, Pakistan witnessed radical shifts in the policy environment. An assessment of Ayub Khan's regime states, 'most descriptions of the Pakistani political system since 1958 have emphasized the personal nature of executive rule.' Robert LaPorte, Jr., 'Succession in Pakistan: Continuity and Change in a Garrison State,' *Asian Survey*, 9(11), 1969, 842–861. Personal nature of rule was more contested in the 2000s than it was in the 1960s. The controversial legacy includes subversion of institutions. Because of the personal element, Pakistan analysts often discuss the past in the style of dynastic histories, 'Ayub Khan era', 'Bhutto era', 'Musharraf era', and so on. Such a period division may be appropriate for Pakistan, but it makes comparative history a rather difficult task, and is avoided here.

The First Military Regime (1958–1969)

Ayub Khan's was to be the first of several military regimes to rule Pakistan. Why did military politics play a prominent role in the country's political history whereas in India it did not? The military-political elite in Pakistan was formed of migrants from India, who were a minority and anxious about losing power. The electorate was dominated by the population of East Pakistan, whereas the elites were based in West Pakistan. This anomaly created a tendency for the elite to grab power. Unlike the first prime minister of India, Jawaharlal Nehru, who lived long enough to secure secular and democratic rule in India, Muhammad Ali Jinnah, the founder of Pakistan, died too soon after independence to have such an impact. The Indian political class turned its back on the landlords, already much reduced in power, whereas in Pakistan, their power was left intact until the Green Revolution. Compared to such a power base that was suspicious of democracy, in India, the political mainstream had a significant place for the more pro-democratic capitalists and workers. In Pakistan, these lobbies were weaker because the indigenous business and worker classes were smaller in size. The landlords, bureaucrats, and the army dominated politics and retained hold of it despite the return of democratic governments thanks to the entrenchment of a range of 'bureaucratic and hierarchical non-democratic organisations and institutions,' some of which the military created and maintained.[32]

The economic environment improved in the 1960s. In the early 1960s, trade policy eased, though it was tightened again in the late 1960s. Foreign aid softened the impact of 'import liberalization in 1963–1964 as well as in the relaxation of controls over food grain prices and distribution in the early sixties.'[33] Business groups received a variety of privileges and were encouraged to diversify. Export subsidy and a relaxed implementation of import licenses saw industries with significant

[32] S. Akbar Zaidi, 'State, Military and Social Transition. Improbable Future of Democracy in Pakistan,' *Economic and Political Weekly*, 2005, 5173–5181; Anatol Lieven, *Pakistan: A Hard Country*, New York: Public Affairs, 2011.

[33] Nurul Islam, 'Foreign Assistance and Economic Development: The Case of Pakistan,' *Economic Journal*, 82(325), 1972, 502–530.

import content (such as metals) expand capacity. Among these privileges, a crucial one was a distorted price policy that subsidized agricultural raw materials. Restrictions of agricultural exports kept prices of agricultural goods low for domestic users.[34] Further, the rupee was overvalued. Foreign exchange earned by the export of agricultural goods by state agencies helped the government to import the goods it needed. Transfer of surplus from agriculture to industry by the operation of trade and exchange controls was normal in the region. The issue became politically sensitive because East Pakistan, which produced a lot of the raw material and foreign exchange, did not receive its share of investment in public goods.[35]

Aid and foreign investment both flowed in on a larger scale in Pakistan than in the rest of South Asia in these years. In the 1960s, per capita aid and aid share in GDP were higher in Pakistan than in the developing world on average. Both India and Pakistan needed foreign aid to meet food shortage. In India, non-food aid went to meet shortage of machinery, oil, and chemicals. In Pakistan, non-food aid went into public infrastructure programmes such as irrigation, healthcare, and education. Aid in this way contributed to economic growth. It also made governments more relaxed about generation of resources.[36] Behind the aid flow, there was a perception that Pakistan, being more market-friendly than India and in possession of a stronger agriculture, was a good horse to back. Between 1960 and 1970, books written by western scholars and World Bank reports celebrated the impressive growth of the Pakistan economy.

[34] Stephen R. Lewis, *Economic Policy and Industrial Growth in Pakistan*, London: George Allen and Unwin, 1969.

[35] See, for a discussion of the implicit transfer of surplus from the East to the West Pakistan, David Lewis, *Bangladesh: Politics, Economy and Civil Society*, Cambridge: Cambridge University Press, 2011. Interestingly, the same mechanism was at work on the Indian side of the border. The West Bengal state, which produced and traded a lot of the exportable goods, mainly jute and tea, implicitly subsidized New Delhi's budget thanks to overvalued exchange. The Bengali Marxists who protested New Delhi's neglect of West Bengal, did not somehow base their campaign on this issue. Many of them came from the small towns and Eastern Bengal, later Bangladesh, and were even more hostile to Calcutta's corporates than they were to the government at the centre.

[36] Azhar Mahmood, 'The Role of Foreign Aid in Economic Development of Pakistan (1960–61 to 1994–95),' *Pakistan Economic and Social Review*, 35(1), 1997, 57–90.

From late in the 1960s, agriculture turned around. The aid-funded expansion in rural roads and irrigation projects between 1955 and 1965 paid off. The new infrastructure made access to input and product markets easier, contributed to extension of the land frontier, and induced complementary private investment in tube wells. Unlike India, West Pakistan was not constrained by shortage of land. The existing cultivated land in Punjab and Sind had an irrigation ratio higher than that in the rest of South Asia. Land, therefore, was more abundant and of better quality. In principle, land could play a relatively larger role in the pattern of economic growth to follow in West Pakistan compared with the rest of South Asia. Furthermore, fertilizer usage, rising fivefold between 1958 and 1965 even before the dwarf wheat plant had come in, made a major contribution to the growth in production. When the new plants of the Green Revolution did come, landlords and middle peasants had already grown capitalistic enough and in possession of capital to respond to the opportunity quickly.

The 1965 war and economic dislocation due to drought and exchange crisis pushed Pakistan to the brink of economic crisis. Unrestricted pursuit of private enterprise in agriculture and manufacturing increased inequalities between regions, and between persons. Industrial concentration was high; about 20 business groups commanded a substantial share of the assets. Improvements in social indicators between 1950 and 1970 had been slow, even imperceptible. Deep gender inequalities persisted. Between half and two-thirds of total government expenditure in 1950–1966 went into defence.[37] It tended to crowd out everything that was not aid-funded, including education and healthcare. Rates of economic growth had a negative association with democratic regimes, suggesting a failure of democratic regimes to build strong economic institutions. The Bangladesh war in 1971 created a political crisis and loss of credibility for the ruling military leader General Yahya Khan.

Ayub Khan's rule set in motion a new style of governance by codifying 'a set of economic favors for members of the armed forces: transfer of ownership of state land; "perks and privileges" for retirees,

[37] LaPorte, Jr., 'Succession in Pakistan.'

including living allowances and memberships at private clubs; state shouldering of the cost of training personnel who then seek employment in the private sector; and a revolving door between private industry and government for these ex-military men.'[38] When military politics returned, and military aid rose, these leakages of public resources increased.[39] This was surely not the main axis of inequality in Pakistan society, but it sanctioned a culture of disbursing privilege at the taxpayers' expense that caused widespread resentment against the political class. Politics of patronage was not confined to the military. State aid to industry was also conditional on connections. 'The possibility of monitoring and imposing discipline on the established capitalists steeply declined.'[40]

A socialist turn in 1972 was a reaction to these inequalities.

Socialism: 1970s

A new government under Zulfikar Ali Bhutto (president 1971–1973 and prime minister 1973–1977) took over power in 1971. The Pakistan Peoples' Party, which he led, was socialistic in leaning and dynastic in leadership. Neither of the two qualities served Bhutto nor his daughter Benazir Bhutto (prime minister 1988–1990 and 1993–1996) well. When in power, Bhutto initiated a move to turn the economic system more socialist. Socialism was a response to a popular anxiety over inequality and corruption. Further, 'Bhutto's socialistic interventions on the surface may have stemmed from "feudal" concerns over a rapidly emerging industrial class.'[41]

---

[38] Sameer Dossani, 'Power and Patronage: The Political Economy of Pakistan,' *Middle East Report*, 246, 2008, 16–21.

[39] Matthew McCartney, *Pakistan – The Political Economy of Growth, Stagnation and the State 1951–2008*, London: Routledge, 2011, 204.

[40] Mushtaq H. Khan, 'The Political Economy of Industrial Policy in Pakistan,' Working Paper of the School of Oriental and African Studies, London, no date, https://www.soas.ac.uk/economics/research/workingpapers/file28876.pdf (accessed 1 September 2016).

[41] Imran Ali and Adeel Malik, 'The Political Economy of Industrial Development in Pakistan: A Long-Term Perspective,' *The Lahore Journal of Economics*, 14(1), 2009, 29–50.

Businesses were nationalized. The share of the state in total investment increased. For the first time, capital-intensive industrialization was made a priority. One public sector factory absorbed a great deal of public savings. 'Karachi Steel Mill became the single most important development project claiming, in real terms, more resources during the 1970s, than did the entire public sector in the 1970s.'[42] Social reconstruction and equity were made explicit priorities of state intervention. Banks were nationalized, and education and health care were partially brought under the direction of the state. By this time, a substantial body of industrialists had emerged in Pakistan. They tended to shift money from industry to construction, and sought avenues abroad. Some turned towards the Persian Gulf states for this purpose.

The results of the socialist policy were disastrous. Agricultural growth fell, forcing food imports in 1978–1979. While import commitments remained high, export earnings fell because the main exporting industry, cotton textiles, suffered under the restrictive business policy. Textiles, incidentally, were not nationalized, but suffered due to reduced access to technology. Balance of payments problems led to heavy external borrowing.

In 1977 a military coup led by Muhammad Ziaul Haq changed government. Almost immediately, a new Cold War chapter opened with Soviet invasion of Afghanistan (1979–1989). The invasion turned Pakistan into a key American ally, which translated into large-scale inflow of military aid. In some accounts, the aid revived the flagging Pakistan economy, though that claim may be exaggerated.

Liberalization

In common with India and Bangladesh, capital inflow, remittances from the Middle East, and decline in population growth rates, kept investment and GDP growth rates comfortably high from the end of the 1970s until the end of the 1980s. The government seemed happy enough with the windfall to avoid tough reforms. In terms of institutional and policy

[42] Shahid Javed Burki, 'Pakistan's Development: An Overview,' *World Development*, 9(3), 1981, 301–14.

changes, despite being the longest in Pakistan's history under a single ruler, Haq's government (1977–1988) was noted for being 'the least innovative.'[43] It was also 'the least ideological.'

In August 1988, Ziaul Haq died in a plane crash. Between November 1988 and October 1999, Pakistan was under civilian rule. The Pakistan People's Party and the Pakistan Muslim League formed governments in this time. The former leaned towards socialism and the latter towards liberal reforms. Both rules suffered from corruption scandals and were dismissed under military pressure. Despite erratic politics, the liberal economic stance continued.

During civilian rule, the International Monetary Fund and the World Bank were involved in implementing a reform process, in the backdrop of a large build-up of foreign debts. Deregulation of banks, privatization, and easier foreign exchange system were key elements of the package. Private banks were allowed entry, a few smaller banks were privatized, interest rate caps were removed, and the central bank (the State Bank of Pakistan) was granted formal autonomy of operation. Commitment to liberal reform was reaffirmed in 1991 with reduction in tariff and non-tariff barriers to import. On the other hand, defence spending remained large, on average 6.5 per cent in the 1980s, and kept deficit and debt large too. International sanctions after nuclear tests in 1998 and a small-scale war with India in the next year added to the problem of debt.

Between October 1999 and the parliamentary elections of March 2008, Pakistan was back to military rule under General Pervez Musharraf. The regime's pro-US stand in the war on terror eased international relations. The liberalization was also starting to pay off. Economic growth was sustained by revival of private investment and exports. External debt came down from 250 to 110 per cent of exports between 2000 and 2006, and public debt from 90 to 55 per cent of GDP in the same period. The regime registered significant success with privatization and foreign investment inflow. Since 2008, when Musharraf

[43] Parvez Hasan, 'Role of the State in Pakistan's Economy: Assessing the Past and Exploring Future Challenges,' *Economic and Political Weekly*, 42(18), 2007, 1623–1630.

resigned, Pakistan has been under civilian rule, and though complications arising from terrorism and fundamentalist revival made the relationship between the military and the government uneasy at times, civilian rule survived.

Bangladesh

The East Pakistan Era: 1950–1971

The Bengal delta had a population density of over 600 persons per square mile at the time of independence. Population pressure on land was acute, with the result that there was land degradation and fragmentation of holdings. Most peasants lived on subsistence and did not have access to enough capital. In the monsoon-dependent rice cultivation system crop choice options were limited. Still, land was more fertile on average in the East. When an international border was drawn in the region in 1947, the East had a higher gross income than the West, but a much smaller average income. The West was better endowed with irrigation, had more commercial and technical manpower, and received a bigger share of the foreign aid. The East was located in the flood-plains, exposed to natural disasters, and dependent on the cultivation of labour-intensive crops, such as rice and jute, upon lands that seemed to have reached their potential levels of production.

Agricultural improvement, therefore, was a priority for the East. The first major step taken to improve agriculture was to abolish 'zamindari' rights. The zamindari property right was created by a 1793 law, known as Permanent Settlement. The law defined property right in land as a pure ownership right, as opposed to a pre-colonial property right that combined the right of the peasant to use a plot of land and the right of the tax collector to collect a revenue from it on behalf of the government. The zamindari reform defined property as ownership and gave it away to the former tax collecting nobles and merchants, known as zamindars, rather than to the peasant cultivators. Long criticized as a move that reduced the incentive of the peasant to improve land, zamindari abolition was on the cards even before independence. For well over

60 years before this move, tenancy legislation had restricted the zamindar's powers, the zamindars had experienced either a steady decline of fortunes or transformed into cultivators, and economic as well as political power on the ground had shifted to large tenant farmers. The formal abolition of zamindari, therefore, served little purpose.

Industrialization on a limited scale occurred under the leadership of trading groups that had migrated from India. A programme designed to provide employment to the seasonally unemployed rural labour became moderately successful. However, no radical change in the pattern of economic growth took place, when compared with the vigorous industrialization under way in both India and West Pakistan.

The mainstay of the non-agricultural economy was trade instead. East Pakistan produced jute, rice, and tea, which were exportable goods and foreign exchange earners. The fact that the East exported more created an awkwardness in the relationship between the two parts. Overvalued exchange rates would mean an implicit subsidy the East delivered to the West. The union was an awkward one also in political terms. The East had more people than the West, but the West did not seem ready to be ruled by a leader from the East, especially if the leader happened to espouse Bengali nationalism. During Ayub Khan's presidency, the relationship between the two units was uneasily held in balance. His successors Yahya Khan and Zulfikar Ali Bhutto precipitated a crisis by refusing to endorse the eastern party Awami League's right to form a government after an election in 1970. During the violent war that followed (from 26 March to 16 December 1971, when Bangladesh was born), around 8 to 10 million refugees crossed the border into India. Although many of them did not return, those who did return to the war-torn nation created an enormous resettlement problem for the government.

Bangladesh: The Foundations

Bangladesh began with a chaotic economic situation. The few large-scale industries that did work had been abandoned by their original owners during the war and the government had little choice but to take these over. The war had seen groups with diverse economic interests come together, but with the end of the war, the demand for a return of favours grew to unmanageable scale. While the state was forced by the circumstances to assume greater powers over the economy, the tendency was reinforced by ideological battles. Some of the leftist parties had projected the war of liberation from Pakistan as a revolutionary war in the making, truncated due to Indian intervention. The ruling Awami League hoped to steal some popularity away from the radical left movement. To placate those who saw things this way, the state nationalized foreign trade, banks, insurance companies, jute, textile and sugar mills, a large part of inland and coastal shipping, and airways. Investment licensing was introduced, and distribution of food came to be state controlled.

In the next 4 years, the manner in which the government managed and regulated the economic system raised charges of corruption. Import licenses were given to party workers, and nationalized industries were headed by party workers, who enriched themselves, and secretly sold some of the machinery and material to Indian buyers.[44] Overvalued exchange drove foreign trade to the underground market. Price regulations in the main industrial raw material, jute, meant that the price of raw jute in India was several times that in Bangladesh. Just when industries needed raw material to recover, jute was smuggled across the border. By the middle of 1974, the government was bankrupt and inflation ran in triple digits. Foreign aid inflow, which was initially high on account of resettlement of refugees, fell in the same year as the programme ended. Devastating floods in the monsoon months forced the government to seek relief aid abroad. By November 1974 famine conditions existed in parts of the country and starvation deaths exceeded a hundred thousand.

In the winter of 1974–1975, conflicts between the left and the centrists within the ruling party was out in the open. The main issue in contention was not domestic policy but foreign policy, rather, the desired level of collaboration with the West, the Soviet Union, and

[44] Talukder Maniruzzaman, 'Bangladesh in 1974: Economic Crisis and Political Polarization,' *Asian Survey*, 15(2), 1975, 117–128.

India. Although relations with the Arab states and even Pakistan had improved in 1973, a serious discord with India opened up over India's plans to divert a quantity of the Ganges water to its own uses. The contentious project, Farakka barrage, was commissioned in 1974 despite protests and negotiations. The anxiety that Bangladesh was at risk of a colonial relationship with India was widespread not only among nationalists, but also in the military.

On 15 August 1975, a group of army officers assassinated Prime Minister Mujibur Rahman, and installed a new government. During the next 2 years, there were several other assassinations and coups. The cycle ended in 1977 with a coup that brought General Ziaur Rahman to power. If in Pakistan, the process of state-making made the military a powerful factor, in Bangladesh, the formation of military regimes is seen as an inheritance of Pakistan, or rather as a British colonial legacy that the Pakistan state bestowed on East Pakistan. That power, however, was reinforced by the war of liberation.[45] For the next 13 years, military control over politics would continue.

Liberalization

Well before the political turmoil of 1975–1977, the pace of socialist reform had slowed. In 1974, licensing was relaxed, foreign investors invited in, with little success, and private trade was reintroduced, notably in agricultural commodities, inputs, and equipment. Ziaur Rahman's regime freed markets further. In 1981, Rahman was assassinated, and the next year Hussain Muhammad Ershad became the president of the republic after yet another military coup. Thereafter, a radical retraction from socialism began. State companies were privatized, and investment licensing withdrawn. The privatization was carried out with remarkable speed so that organized labour and the bureaucracy had little chance to resist the move. Units were sold at a discount with unpaid liabilities. Although these steps did signal a new incentive structure for private enterprise, it was a messy

[45] Willem van Schendel, *Bangladesh; A History*, Cambridge: Cambridge University Press, 2009.

process. Trade policy remained regulated until well into the 1990s. Thereafter, tariffs were lowered, and exchange controls and trade licenses removed. Between 1990 and 2000, the maximum tariff rate came down from over 300 per cent to 37.5, and the average tariff rate from 89 to 17 per cent. There was a de-industrialization of consumer goods, especially processed food items as a result. Agricultural trade, both input and output, had been more or less state regulated in Bangladesh in the 1970s. The 1990s' reforms freed up the trades.

The liberalization had darker sides. The provision of easy government loans to private entrepreneurs and private control of banking led to poor quality debt, and concentration of economic power in what some authors saw as an undeserving group of capitalists. Foreign aid continued to be an important source of money. Cheap and plentiful aid in the 1980s led to wastage and scramble for a share of the money. Measures of inequality show a definite and significant increase in the 1990s.[46] On the other hand, the reforms had begun to deliver a game-changing development. Export of clothing, which had begun in the 1980s, experienced dramatic expansion.

The late 1970s had seen the beginnings of a Green Revolution. The impetus to invest in land improvement and adoption of high-yielding seeds in rice came from the agricultural deregulation policies, and the retreat of the state from agricultural trade. In the 1980s, changes in the production regime followed a path that was also producing dramatic results in West Bengal, a combination of dwarf winter rice, high-yielding seeds, and shallow tube wells. The resultant rise in the gross area sown and total factor productivity in agriculture was large. Rural livelihoods diversified, and nonfarm activities increased. Interestingly, West Bengal in India and Bangladesh experienced a similar pattern of agrarian transformation, about the same time, but under different institutional and political arrangements.

Along with the agricultural revolution, and export-oriented industrialization, a third transformative factor was the decline in fertility.

[46] Mohammed Nuruzzaman, 'Neoliberal Economic Reforms, the Rich and the Poor in Bangladesh,' *Journal of Contemporary Asia*, 34(1), 2007, 33–54.

Bangladesh, which spent far higher share of the budget on social expenditure than the other nations of South Asia, reaped the benefits in an earlier and deeper demographic transition. The process of public and foreign funding of social sectors allowed non-governmental organizations a large role in the implementation of population policy. The partnership led to a flourishing NGO sector engaged in health, education, micro-finance and empowerment, the scale and effectiveness of which had few parallels in the developing world.

The advisory role of foreign donors was a powerful force in Pakistan and Bangladesh (and as we shall see, Nepal). For Bangladesh, there is a debate on the significance of such influence. 'Despite changes in political power and governance and the bloody conflicts among groups wishing to govern,' one analyst explains, 'the economic front experienced a continuity of policy and ideology. One of the major factors behind this continuity could be the increasing authority of the global institutions that have been operating in Bangladesh,' including the World Bank.[47] The explanation, although credible, may seem to place too much weight upon external influence. Another emergent political axis was a home-grown one, the rise of a middle class with its economic interest tied to businesses like clothing exports. No matter where the support for openness came from, neither the international institutions nor the capitalists would want politics to upset the process of rebuilding ties with the world economy. That process continued without significant obstacles.

Conclusion

While the states made definite choices, for example, in 1950, 1972, or 1992, it is difficult to write the economic history of the three countries in terms of the intentions of the political actors behind these choices. The choice of a more or less state-led industrialization strategy in 1950

[47] Anu Muhammad, 'Globalisation and Economic Transformation in a Peripheral Economy: The Bangladesh Experience,' *Economic and Political Weekly*, 41(15), 2006, 1459–1464.

was predicated on business support and administrative capacity. The socialist turn in the 1970s was not invented by an individual leader. Indira Gandhi in India, Mujibur Rahman in Bangladesh, Zulfikar Ali Bhutto in Pakistan, and Sirimavo Bandaranaike of Sri Lanka (see Chapter 4), all opted for the path from 1972. There was an element of defensive reaction to a similar type of external shock behind that apparently coordinated move, a reaction to persistent foreign exchange crisis, to be specific. The backtrack in the 1980s may have been influenced by donor pressure, business pressure, and the predilections of military rulers, but the fact that it occurred across the board suggests that the external constraints eased too. I will suggest that Gulf remittance and clothing export eased the exchange constraint from the late 1970s (see Chapters 5 and 11).

Even as the state tried to steer the economy in particular directions, some of the most dramatic examples of change post- or pre-liberalization happened in a manner that the state neither predicted nor was prepared for. The examples include, mass migration to the Persian Gulf states, the Green Revolution, or the export of readymade garments. These developments happened without the state playing either a formal or an informal role in making them happen. Once they happened, they created lobbies protecting the interests of those who had gained from them.

These conclusions hold in a general sense in Sri Lanka and Nepal too, with the qualification that both countries faced a different set of constraints, as we see in the next chapter.

4

The State and the Economy II: Sri Lanka and Nepal

The initial conditions of Sri Lanka and Nepal were different from those of the mainland South Asia at the start of the period. The differences were in their geographical situation and the nature of the political legacy. In common with the rest of the region, both countries went through a stage of state-managed development, with different capacities and consequences. A particular consequence was that regional inequality in both countries acquired an ethnic dimension. The present chapter will discuss the path of statist development in Sri Lanka and Nepal and suggest why the trajectory of economic change could produce this outcome.

Sri Lanka

Towards Independence

Although the maritime provinces of the island had been ruled by the Portuguese and the Dutch before 1800, British rule (1796–1948) was the first time that a coastal state had established control over the entire island. The control was obtained after annexation of the Kandyan

T. Roy, *The Economy of South Asia*, Palgrave Studies in Economic History, DOI 10.1007/978-3-319-54720-6_4

Kingdom (1818) after nearly 20 years of intrigue, diplomacy, and warfare.[1] By the mid-1800s, the state was starting to encourage plantations to increase revenue and as an opportunity to British capitalists. Wasteland development laws were introduced (Crown lands (encroachment) Ordinance No 12 of 1840), and the highlands were settled with Europeans interested in making tea or coffee (see Chapter 10 on the rise and fall of the plantations). The workers came from Madras State or Tamil Nadu in India. Between 1840 and 1940 the highlands had been transformed from forests into extensive tea estates, and Sri Lanka was one of the world's leading producers and exporters of tea. Other plantations that flourished in this time, but with smaller contribution of European capital, were rubber, coffee, and coconut.

When Sri Lanka became independent in 1948, the mainstay of its economy was the plantation sector. The industry was export-oriented, and earned 90 per cent of the foreign exchange for the country. Trade-GDP ratio was well above the South Asian average. The plantations also provided valuable revenue. Nearly half of the government revenues came from taxing trade. Trade value per head was three to five times that of British India in the 1920s, and total public expenditure per head three times that in British India. The export orientation of the economy, in this way, translated into greater capacity to finance public expenditure than in British India. The larger size of state helped maintain a high level of spending on public goods and on imports. In 1920, both British India and Ceylon spent about 5 per cent of the government budget on education, but the proportion translated into more than double the amount of money per head in Sri Lanka.[2] The capacity to import was an asset during shortages of food, whereas India experienced periodic famines in the nineteenth century.

High level of social development was a distinct feature of Sri Lanka. In 1920, the school enrolment rate, and female enrolment in schools, in

---

[1] The process of state making in the early nineteenth century is described in Sujit Sivasundaram, 'Ethnicity, Indigeneity, and Migration in the Advent of British Rule to Sri Lanka,' *American Historical Review*, 115(2), 2010, 428–452.

[2] Tirthankar Roy, 'The Role of the State in Initiating Development: A Study of Interwar South and Southeast Asia,' *Indian Economic and Social History Review*, 33(4), 1996, 374–401.

Ceylon were several times higher than in British India. The Education Act of 1945, formation of the department of social services in 1948, and the Health Act of 1953 laid the legal basis for a policy to supply subsidized rice, compulsory primary education, free secondary and tertiary education, and free health care to the majority of the population.

The Sri Lankan nationalist movement emerged, much as in India, through a process of dialogue with the colonial authorities on representation. In 1931, colonial Ceylon was the first country in Asia to have elections held under universal adult suffrage. The transfer of power was peaceful compared with the mainland, and led to the United National Party (UNP) under the leadership of D.S. Senanayake take over power. The UNP is often described as 'conservative,' and it was liberal in its economic ideology, though inside the party a contest had begun over leadership and economic ideology at the same time. The outcome was the split in 1951, when a breakaway group under S.W.R.D. Bandaranaike, a British-educated lawyer and Sinhala nationalist, formed the Sri Lanka Freedom Party (SLFP). The SLFP won the election in 1956 in dramatic fashion, inaugurating a socialist era.

Sri Lanka and India share the distinction in South Asia of maintaining a democratic political system throughout their postcolonial history. The way politics shaped economic policy differed between Sri Lanka and India. In Sri Lanka, power was more contested between parties that held quite different views on how economic policies should be framed. In India, Congress dominance was more or less intact until 1977. This difference accounts for an element of instability in economic development regimes in Sri Lanka from the beginning, whereas in India, the Congress brand of socialism ruled without a serious contest for a significant length of time.

The Land Question

Unlike in India, where the dominant nationalist position lobbied for industrialization as well as land reform, the prominent issue for the nationalists in Sri Lanka was land reform alone. The plantation experience coloured the land question. The nationalist criticism of the colonial economic system blamed expatriate planters for perpetuating inequality, which they did allegedly by preferential access to land, repatriating profits, and creating jobs for migrants rather than locals. Since the plantation system, at least the tea and coffee plantations if not rubber, employed migrant Tamil workers, and the latter wanted to possess private landholding outside the estate areas, they became a target for the critics of the land system. In this way, the discourse on economic policy became entangled with a parallel discussion on exclusion and inclusion of ethnic communities.

The economic structure that evolved during British rule is sometimes seen to lend itself to 'dualism,' consisting of an export-dependent plantation enclave, and a small-holding peasant agriculture, the interaction between the two being neither deep nor direct. Dualism suggests a parallel between Sri Lanka and other tropical export economies. The elitist nature of capitalist development, the interpretation goes, spawned a leftist and nationalist movement, which fought for the interests of the peasants. The dualism narrative is simplistic, however. As we have seen, capitalist prosperity in Sri Lanka enabled welfare spending that benefited ordinary people. The colony's welfare system was embedded in the so-called enclave economy. Further, dualism overlooks the entanglement of ethnicity and livelihood that was peculiar to Sri Lanka. 'Social pluralism [as opposed to dualism] has been an almost inevitable legacy of plantation agriculture in the Third World.'[3]

The nationalist preoccupation with land meant that the political mainstream was less interested in industrialization or socialist control of non-agricultural capital. In fact, support for capitalism remained in place even as Marxist political parties emerged late in the interwar period, which campaigned for socialist industrialization and attacked European investment. Although initially distanced from the SLFP, the main Marxist party, the Lanka Sama Samaja Party, later joined

[3] Vijaya Samaraweera, 'Land, Labour, Capital and Sectional Interests in the National Politics of Sri Lanka,' *Modern Asian Studies*, 15(1), 1981, 127–162. An earlier critique of dualism can be found in Asoka Bandarage, *Colonialism in Sri Lanka: The Political Economy of the Kandyan Highlands, 1833–1886*, Berlin: Mouton, 1983. The term 'plural society' in the south and south-east Asian context was apparently first used by J.S Furnivall.

coalitions with the former (1964). Sri Lankan politics since then was torn between a liberal drive and a leftist drive.

Socialism

The socialist phase in Sri Lanka's postcolonial history was to last between 1956 and 1977, when the SLFP-led coalition was defeated by the UNP, and liberal economic policies were reinstituted. The SLFP regime adopted an import-substituting industrialization policy. Tariffs were raised, and supported with quotas. New incentives were created to encourage diversification and capital intensive investment. The policy delivered good growth rates in manufacturing in the 1960s (6 per cent), which then declined to less than 2 per cent in 1970–77. The state also increased its commitment towards food, education, and health care. Finally, land reforms were vigorously implemented in the 1970s. 'By the mid-1970s the Sri Lankan economy was one of the most inward-oriented and regulated economies outside the communist block.'[4] Towards the end of this phase, economic growth rate was near zero, the government had gone bankrupt, and high unemployment among middle class youth fed widespread discontent. The state licensing system had not only erected regulations on investment but also exposed itself to charges of corruption and patronage.

The socialist era was not an unmitigated disaster. As in India, the system did encourage some domestic entrepreneurs without a strong prior base in industry to accumulate capital. Socialism was good for welfare spending, though that claim is disputed. Amartya Sen has argued that socialism was successful in achieving high levels of human development.[5] In the absence of direct state intervention and the prevailing low growth of average income (2 per cent), Sen's estimates show, economic

[4] Prema-chandra Athukorala and Sisira Jayasuriya, 'Liberalisation and Industrial Growth: lessons from Sri Lanka,' in Raghbendra Jha, ed., *Economic Growth, Economic Performance, and Welfare in South Asia*, Basingstoke: Palgrave Macmillan, 2005, 102–118.

[5] A.K. Sen, 'Public Action and the Quality of Life in Developing Countries,' *Oxford Bulletin of Economics and Statistics*, 43(4), 1981, 287–319.

growth alone would need 152 years to accomplish the high level of development that there was. A critique of Sen disputed the conclusion by pointing out that the roots of the welfare system and high levels of development were colonial, and not the socialism of the 1960s. Taking these initial conditions into account, the development record in 1956–1977 turned out to be a poor one.[6] A later assessment of 'the Sri Lankan equity and growth debate' argued that the debate underestimated the value of welfarism 'in maintaining social cohesion and political stability' suggesting that, after 1977, compromises made on the welfare front contributed to the ethnic conflict.[7]

The deeper problem with the welfare system was not what the politicians wanted but whether the capacity to deliver welfare was sustainable or not. And this capacity had been reduced due to state intervention in plantation agriculture. The possession of a strong export economy – Sri Lanka's plantations were 'one of the best-run commercial enterprises in the third world' in 1948 – was a useful resource for a poor country that needed to make new investments and diversify its economy.[8] It had sustained the head start on public goods, and could continue doing so. That trajectory did not materialize though. The mainstay of Sri Lankan revenue was the export of tea, coffee, rubber, and coconut. That dominance of export crops in trade and revenue was to remain more or less intact. But new taxation and repatriation policy targeting foreign owners pushed capital out of Sri Lanka, and reduced profitability and productivity in the plantation sector. Without new sources of revenue and foreign exchange, the attrition of the plantations created a fiscal crisis.

In the late 1960s, the state set up enterprises in heavy industry in the Indian pattern, including in steel, fertilizers, tyres, petroleum, and cement. State investment in consumer goods, utilities, and aviation also increased. Such industrialization increased import dependence and

[6] Surjit S. Bhalla and Paul Glewwe, 'Growth and Equity in Developing Countries: A Reinterpretation of the Sri Lankan Experience, '*World Bank Economic Review*, 1(1), 1986, 35–63.

[7] David Dunham and Sisira Jayasuriya, 'Equity, Growth and Insurrection: Liberalization and the Welfare Debate in Contemporary Sri Lanka,' *Oxford Development Studies*, 28(1), 2000, 97–110.

[8] Cited text from Saman Kelegama, 'Development in Independent Sri Lanka: What Went Wrong?' *Economic and Political Weekly*, 35(17), 2000, 1477–1490.

reduced export capacity. 'By the mid-1970s, total earnings from manufactured exports covered only 6% of the total import requirements of the industrial sector. Poor performance was seen in all other sectors as well, resulting in economic stagnation in the country.'[9] Trade-GDP ratio fell (see also Fig. 5.13 in Chapter 5).

The second half of the 1960s, when the UNP ran a government, is sometimes called 'partial liberalization.' Import-substituting industrialization receded somewhat from priority and self-sufficiency in agriculture became the focus of government policy instead. In 1970, SLFP returned to power and affirmed commitment to socialist policy. The capacity of industry or the plantations to earn foreign exchange fell further, and the first oil shock delivered another blow to the balance of payments. For political reasons, Sri Lankan rulers did not consider going for foreign aid. Nor was Sri Lanka sufficiently central to the Cold War calculations as were India and Pakistan. The World Bank and IMF were engaged with the country from the 1950s, but on a smaller scale than elsewhere.[10]

In common with India, Pakistan, and Bangladesh, the response to the gathering crisis was a larger dose of state control. During its second government, the SLFP targeted private enterprise in the plantations for acquisition and redistribution of their land, and partial nationalization of the companies (see also Chapters 6 and 10).

Liberalization

Elections in 1977 saw the UNP come back to form a government. A liberalization package was pushed through, despite opposition from many sides, including the bureaucracy. Food subsidy was an immediate focus of the reforms. Sri Lanka was the least self-sufficient of the five countries in cereal production throughout (see Fig. 5.11 in Chapter 5), which had

---

[9] Sriyani Dias, 'Economic Liberalization and the Development of Manufacturing in Sri Lanka,' *Asian Survey*, 31(7), 1991, 613–629.

[10] See, for example, W.D. Lakshman, 'The IMF-World Bank Intervention in Sri Lankan Economic Policy: Historical Trends and Patterns,' *Social Scientist*, 13(2), 1985, 3–29.

made it invest in an expensive subsidy programme in the first place. The reformist government wanted to reduce food subsidy because it was doubly burdensome, as a drain on the budget and as a drain on foreign exchange reserves. A withdrawal of the subsidy would not be an easy step to take given that consumption was import-dependent. The compromise was a targeted food stamp programme that worked well in maintaining the calorie status of poorer households.[11]

Food had grown to be a problem to a large extent because of population growth. Not only food, agricultural livelihoods were also under pressure because much of the increase of population had happened in the 'wet' or irrigated zones. To address this issue, the outgoing government had designed plans for development of the dry zones. The new government revived it with the help of foreign aid and technical assistance. The core part of the agricultural programme was resettlement of surplus population from the irrigated or wet zones to the dry zones, with investment in small and medium irrigation projects. The programme did deliver on two of its aims, rise in output of grain and resettlement of population. The success was compromised by an ethnic-religious rhetoric, which projected the resettlement plan as a step to regain an ancient homeland. The memory of the dry zone as an ancient Buddhist homeland that later depopulated infused 'Sinhalese nationalism with the vision that the colonisation of the Dry Zone was a return to the heartland of the ancient irrigation civilization of the Sinhalese.'[12] The programme did transform 'the Dry Zone,' from 'a sparsely populated and unhealthy but ethnically diverse region to a rapidly growing and *almost exclusively Sinhalese and Buddhist* one.'[13]

In the 1980s, Sri Lanka deregulated trade and investment.[14] Foreign direct investment was encouraged with considerable success. Domestic

---

[11] Neville Edirisinghe, *The Food Stamp Scheme in Sri Lanka: Costs, Benefits, and Options for Modification*, Washington D.C.: International Food Policy Research Institute, 1987.

[12] Mick Moore, cited by Patrick Peebles, 'Colonization and Ethnic Conflict in the Dry Zone of Sri Lanka,' *Journal of Asian Studies*, 49(1), 1990, 30–55.

[13] Peebles, 'Colonization and Ethnic Conflict in the Dry Zone of Sri Lanka'. Emphasis added.

[14] Prema-Chandra Athukorala, 'Outward-Oriented Policy Reforms and Industrialisation in Sri Lanka,' *Economic Papers,* 26(4), 2007, 372–391.

investment could access the machines that were needed for export production. The re-integration with the world economy happened at a time when European garment traders were looking to sources of garments outside East Asia. Sri Lanka seemed an attractive alternative. The state responded to this demand with first one, then another, Export Processing Zone. After the fall of the plantation complex, the 1980s again yielded substantial export earnings, now on the back of manufacturing. Import controls were done away with, raising consumption and trading activity. Reduction in tariffs and controls enabled domestic industry to access imported inputs and machinery, which was a critical help to the nascent garment industry. Banks began to make loans, though much of it went to speculative real estate development.

Rise in private investment delivered per capita income growth of around 5 per cent on average (1977–1995), whereas in 1960–1977, per capita income grew at 0.8 per cent on average.[15] Foreign capital inflow combined with another bonus, remittance sent back home by expatriate workers to the Gulf. For a brief few years in the early 1980s, Sri Lanka also emerged as a popular tourist destination in Asia.

Amidst many good news on the economic front, there was bad news as well. The government managed to reduce welfare expenditure, but did not privatize loss-making public enterprises. As we shall see, tardiness with privatization was a common feature in reformist South Asia. Import liberalization hurt some of these enterprises. The land reforms were not reversed, nor was there a serious move to revive the plantation business. And whereas the overstretched SLFP regime did reduce its dependence on the world economy, the liberalized regime increased dependence on debt, beginning with World Bank and IMF loans. Levels of inequality, kept low by public spending in the earlier regime, increased.[16]

---

[15] Prema-Chandra Athukorala and Sarath Rajapatirana, 'Liberalization and Industrial Transformation: Lessons from the Sri Lankan Experience,' *Economic Development and Cultural Change*, 48(3), 2000, 543–572.

[16] Ronald J. Herring, 'Economic Liberalisation Policies in Sri Lanka: International Pressures, Constraints and Supports,' *Economic and Political Weekly*, 22(8), 1987, 325–333.

Civil War and Beyond

Years 1983–1984 marked a transition point. From then on, eruption of ethnic conflict started to take a toll on economic growth. A few foreign investors suspended expansion plans, and prospective entrants stayed away. Defence expenditure increased as a proportion of public spending. Unstable economic growth added to youth unemployment, and in turn, middle class disaffection. Growth recovered whenever the intensity of the ethnic conflict fell. Peace rarely lasted more than a few consecutive years.

The origin of Tamil discontent had owed, it is said, to the attempt by both political parties to assert Sinhala identity at different times. The Tamils, both Sri Lankan indigenous Tamils concentrated in Jaffna in the north and migrants from India in the upland tea areas, formed 22 per cent of the population in 1948, and as such, were not a small minority. Having to deal with an anxiety among the Sinhala population that they were the real minority in the subcontinent, the Tamils grew defensive.[17] The land reform that destroyed the European plantations, and colonization of the dry lands driven by the notion of an ancient Sinhalese homeland, encouraged a parallel notion of a Tamil homeland.

Sections among the Tamil political leadership felt that Tamil cultural identity would be best protected in a separate state. The demand for a separate state was first articulated in 1976. In the 1977 elections, the main political party Tamil United Liberation Front did well enough to negotiate concessions. The movement was already divided, the leadership aging, and many younger members differed on whether to collaborate with Colombo or seek a different settlement. Violent clashes broke out between the underground Tamil Tigers cadre and the military from about 1982. The military was often accused of being partisans. The clashes claimed hundreds of lives caught up in the battle.

In the 1990s, and until the final end of the conflict in 2009, the surviving militant front the Liberation Tigers of Tamil Eelam or LTTE ran a parallel state and economic system. The area under the control of

---

[17] Robert N. Kearney, 'Ethnic Conflict and the Tamil Separatist Movement in Sri Lanka,' *Asian Survey*, 25(9), 1985, 898–917.

the separatists formed a third of the land area of the island. The economy of this area had a thriving informal sector, built connections with Tamil Nadu and the Tamil diaspora worldwide, and earned revenue by taxation and smuggling.[18] It was a kind of command-and-control system, whereas the rest of the country went ahead with pro-market economic reforms. Even as the ethnic conflict became worse, and outbursts of violence were more frequent than before, the state did not retract the reform agenda. A further round of liberalization was initiated in the early 1990s, focusing on privatization and openness to investment and trade.

The conflict in Sri Lanka lasted 26 years (1983–2009), with brief moments of peace in between. The war extracted enormous cost and many types of cost, from brain drain to fiscal drain. However, the main site of the conflict was confined to the north and the east. Effectively, the country divided up, and outside the war zone it was business as usual. During these years, privatization of state-owned units proceeded fast and provided much needed revenue for the otherwise overstretched state. Foreign firms were invited in with attractive concessions. The garment industry expanded, and industry diversified into export-oriented labour-intensive fields. Years of welfare expenditure had improved life expectancy enough to induce a sharp fall in birth rates, and population growth came close to zero in the late 1990s. In the 6 years since the war ended, the rebound of the economy has been spectacular. Per capita income has increased rapidly, possibly with some rise in inequality.

Nepal

The Making of the Modern State

The modern Nepal state formed of conquests by the Gorkha aristocracy at the turn of the nineteenth century. An inevitable confrontation with the British East India Company in the south of the country came to an

[18] Saman Kelegama, 'Sri Lankan Economy of War and Peace,' *Economic and Political Weekly*, 37(47), 2002, 4678–4685.

end with the Treaty of Sugauli in 1816. Following the treaty, the borders of the state were determined, but Nepal lost some of the border zones including the forested but fertile Terai in the south of the country. The state was right to be worried that the conditions of the Treaty were a prelude to annexation of all of Nepal. British experience with governing the Terai, the sub-Himalayan lowlands, was not a happy one. The area was difficult of access and suffered from outbreak of malaria. Terai raised doubts about the wisdom of acquiring any part of Nepal. Eventually, Nepal stayed free, and Terai was returned.

Instead of proceeding with territorial acquisition, the Company formed an understanding with the king, guaranteed sovereignty, in exchange of open borders to trade and labour flows. The move turned out to be prescient when later in the nineteenth century, the enormous timber resource of Nepal supported railway expansion in India, and Nepalese soldiers were recruited *en masse* into the British Indian army. Railways more than carried trade, they connected the southern border zones of Nepal with the Indian ports. Railways, in short, enabled a geographical integration of Terai with India, which encouraged settlement and agricultural exploitation of the lowlands. The free trade arrangement with India, however, had an adverse effect on some handicraft industries in Nepal.

After Indian independence, India and Nepal made a pledge to carry on the special relationship. The Indo-Nepal Treaty of 1950 established the 800-mile border between India and Nepal as more or less open to trade, migration, and investment. Although border restrictions were imposed and relaxed from time to time, the spirit of the treaty survived. The threat to the treaty came not so much from economic anxieties, but from Nepal's desire to maintain neutrality between India and China.

In 1845, the Prime Ministers, the Rana, established hereditary rule after a palace revolution. Rana rule was modernizing in a limited sense, having initiated social reforms and brought higher education under a modern curriculum. This impulse was restricted to the Kathmandu valley, and to the military and courtly elite. The elite became more politicized than before. Members of the aristocratic and wealthy families sent children to study in India, where they were exposed to Indian nationalism in the 1940s. Upon return to Nepal, some of them wished to abolish elitist rule and fight for a republic. Rana rule discouraged access of foreigners to the court, but it could not stop the emergence of political parties and movements based in India. In this way, the Nepali Congress came into existence (after merger of two parties formed in 1947–1948), and so did the Communist Party (1949). Through their efforts, the first major watershed in the post-war political history took shape. This was the 'democratic revolution' of 1951. Rana rule was abolished. The exit of the British from India had weakened the Ranas. The movement succeeded also because of a prehistory of student and worker mobilization.

The revolution was short-lived. Because the democratic movement was divided within, Nepal did not see a strong and stable rule thereafter. Instead, the state was almost forced to introduce a constitutional monarchy and to deliver significant powers over to the king. In 1960, in a coup engineered by the King Mahendra with the help of the army, the elected government was removed. The absolutist rule of the monarchy thus established lasted until 1990.

At the time of the first democratic revolution in 1951, Nepal was an unequal country. It was agricultural, with 85 per cent of the labour force and income coming from land, 1 per cent engaged in industry, and 14 per cent in services. The government appeared to have limited capacity to govern, and its administrative oversight was limited to the Kathmandu valley, the rest of the country being ruled by land grantees. The state spent nearly all of its earning on maintaining itself. The state looked after the education and health care of only the population directly dependent on it, with the result that literacy rate was 2 per cent. Railways, long-distance roads, telegraph, electricity, and the postal services reached a tiny portion of the population.

The economy was by no means stagnant. The Indo-Nepal Treaty, the timber trade, the grain trade in Terai, and the wealth of the Kathmandu Valley contributed to the growth of commerce. Late in the interwar period, jute mills were established, the largest of which was the Biratnagar Jute Mill (1936–1937), set up in Kathmandu under the direct sponsorship of the court. Indian trading firms set up branches in Nepal. The Newar people of Kathmandu had accumulated wealth from trade and industry, especially from controlling the Tibet-India

Fig. 4.1. Maoist insurgents visit a local shop in Rukum district, Nepal (April 2004)

Located in western-central Nepal, the relatively remote Rukum district was a centre of insurgent activity during the civil war.

transit trade, in which Indian groups did not take a major part. Still, the desire for economic development was an impulse behind the democratic movement.

Towards Development

In common with the rest of the region, a developmental discourse took shape in Nepal around 1950. A development plan had been drafted in the 1940s, and laid emphasis on agricultural development, including irrigation and roads. Nepal adopted planning in the 1950s, as in the rest of the region, but the effort was compromised by a lack of economic data. The First Five-Year Plan announced in 1956 was little more than a collection of projects. The proceedings of an agricultural conference held in 1958 identified a series of structural obstacles to economic growth, for example, low and falling land yield in a number of areas of the hills. There were endemic food shortages, worsened by drought and earthquake. With this discourse forming the backdrop, the Second Plan (there was a shorter duration plan before this one) announced in 1965 projected a vision for development based on agricultural improvement and decentralization of administration. Industrialization was still a distant prospect.

The state under restored monarchy had few means to embark on an ambitious development programme. Its major commitment was a policy of local development, with an added rhetoric of political decentralization. Tariffs were raised in the 1970s, as in the rest of the region, but it yielded little industrialization. The free trade arrangement with India neutralized the effects of tariffs. The state became aid-dependent, and the projects undertaken by it reflected to some extent the priorities of the donors. The implementation of the projects also entailed corruption and wastage of resources. While the state thus lacked capacity and will, population began to grow. Between 1960 and 1990, population doubled from 9 to 18 million, and showed no sign of slowing down (not until 2006–2007). Much of the population was rural and agricultural. Arable area per person was small, unchanging, and poor in quality. Regional inequality and geographical distances were wide. Overall, the pace of positive change was so slow, inequality so extreme, and daily life so harsh that the main livelihood option for a large number of people was migration to India.

Between 1960 and 2015, three things shaped the pace and pattern of economic change in Nepal, foreign aid, emigration, and relations with India. Each one of these acted as a mixed blessing, and each one constrained the capacity of the state to pursue an ambitious development plan of its own. Consequently, there was little drive or progress with a radical restructuring of the economy, the treasured goal in the rest of South Asia. Let us consider these three factors in turn.

It is sometimes said that the open borders with India restricted Nepal's choice of policy in the sense that a broad consistency with Indian policy became the default option. In any case, when the rest of South Asia raised protectionist barriers in the 1970s, Nepal followed suit. Again in the 1990s, in common with the rest of the region, tariff rates came down. Between 1991 and 2000, peak tariff rates in Nepal declined from 245 per cent to 40. The average rates after the reforms were in the range 10–20.

In addition to the India factor, the wishes of foreign donors also mattered in the aid-dependent economy. Its strategic situation between India and China, and interest of Cold War contestants in South Asia, ensured a steady and large flow of foreign aid to Nepal. Foreign aid formed more than 10 per cent of GDP and over 90 per cent of the budget in the 1980s and the 1990s. With the end of the Cold War the percentages fell, to something around 6.5 and 60 per cent respectively. These proportions were still high. Although a certain share of aid went to import-substituting industry and agriculture, a larger share, usually 40–50 per cent, went to infrastructure projects such as road building and education.

Nepal is an ideal case to test general propositions on whether foreign aid helps or hinders development in a poor country. The argument for a positive association either draws a direct causal link between aid and growth, or suggests a conditional link, aid promotes growth in the present of right institutions. The argument against suggests that aid creates moral hazard, that is, encourages the recipients to spare less effort on raising money than otherwise. Most studies on the relationship conduct cross-country regressions, which offer contradictory results. A recent case study of Nepal sides with the pessimistic viewpoint in the debate, that is, aid works in the presence of right institutions, just what Nepal lacked.[19] When foreign aid is seen by components, the effects can look quite different. From the time that Nepal started to welcome foreign involvement in development, 1951, there has been an accent on using aid to support universal free primary education in the country. In the 1990s, the World Bank and other agencies became involved in a revived policy for universal education, as well as more enrolment in secondary and tertiary education.[20]

The state did not succeed in pursuing an effective course of development. And yet, as it globalized and opened doors to foreign aid and world tourism, the cities became more cosmopolitan, and a certain liberalism took roots in the main cities. The importance of Himalayan

[19] Kishor Sharma and Badri Bhattarai, 'Aid, Policy, and Growth: The Case of Nepal,' *Journal of Economic Issues*, 47(4), 2013, 895–910.

[20] Pramod Bhatta, 'Aid Agency Influence in National Education Policymaking: A Case from Nepal's 'Education For All' Movement,' *Globalisation, Societies and Education*, 9(1), 2011, 11–26.

tourism, which is truly international in participation, further strengthened the global links of Kathmandu city.

The impact of the positive changes was regionally uneven, and ethnically biased. As late as in 1990, two Hindu upper castes were dominant in asset ownership and public life. And they had been dominant for a long time past. Such persistent inequality boiled over into a radical left movement.

Left Radicalism

The Maoist movement of Nepal had originated in India and maintained ties with the Indian left parties. By 1990, it represented issues, such as the establishment of indigenous rights, which concerned the Nepalese poor in particular. By then it had splintered into groups that held different views on participating in Parliamentary democracy. Despite the split, the movement as a whole was growing strong enough to shape national politics (see Fig. 4.1).

In 1990, widespread pro-democracy protests forced the king to restore multi-party democracy under a new constitution. Between 1990 and 2008, the political system was a parliamentary monarchy. Whether before this experiment or during it, power remained concentrated, accountability for government spending limited, and allegations of corruption were rife. From the late 1990s, the Maoist insurgency fought the state armies more or less on these grounds. This civil war did not disturb life in the valley too much, but exposed the limited reach of the state, and underscored the deep inequalities and divisions within the society. In 2008 the king was forced to abdicate and a republic was established.

Maoist insurgency, like the Sri Lankan civil war, diverted the attention of the government from development to fighting battles, and was in that respect bad for economic growth. At the same time, the insurgency pushed more people to seek jobs abroad, mainly in Southeast Asia and the Gulf, and thus helped remittance flow in. Some wealthy Nepali left home country to buy assets in the rest of South Asia. Again, the parallel with the Sri Lankan civil war is significant.

Towards a New Political Economy

Since 2008, Nepal has seen several changes in government. Economic policy stance has been less sensitive to these changes. Whatever point they started from, the Maoists did not represent a rigid economic agenda, let alone a radical redistributive one. Instead, announcements hinted at pragmatism, and a willingness to compromise with the great forces of change, such as emigration, foreign investment, foreign aid, and trade with India. The state-making process continued. In 2008, a Constituent Assembly acting as the Parliament was created, and was entrusted with the task of drafting a new constitution, which would take until 2015.

2015 was a turbulent and tragic year in Nepal. On 25 April, the Kathmandu valley suffered a massive earthquake. The Nepali Congress government was criticized for the handling of relief. In 2015, efforts to draft a new constitution replacing an interim one in place were renewed. It came in force under one of the communist successor parties to the Nepali Congress, when the latter lost support in the assembly. The problem before those who drafted the document was to create a federal structure acceptable to all of the many communities and regions of the country. The project ran into a series of difficulties. Some groups protested a reduced proportional representation in the Parliament, and others the new proposed provincial boundaries that would have the effect of dividing up some communities. The more complicated and long-standing problem concerned the lowlanders living on the borders of Bihar state in India and Terai. They had deep social and economic connections with Bihar and India. This group of the Eastern Terai, known as the Madhesi, had a strong presence in the Nepalese assembly. They were affected by a law that children of certain mixed marriages lost Nepali citizenship. Around August, the aggrieved groups started an agitation, the effect of which was disruption of India-Nepal trade along all of the corridors. The devastating impact of the blockade was felt in all areas of life, from fuel to food to medicine. Small industrial firms in Terai closed down.

India's own role in the blockade was controversial. In official statements, the Indian government held the Madhesi agitation alone responsible for the embargo. Trade was disrupted even in areas where the

Madhesis were not strong. It was rumoured that India was unhappy with the new Maoist government because it tried to build closer cooperation with China. Sections within the Indian political establishment identified with the Madhesi interests. The agitation ended when the main Maoist party took over charge.

The episode highlights three things that makes Nepal's political and economic transition a complicated process. These are, the challenges of building a federal framework, the tensions between the lowlanders and highlanders, and the delicate geopolitics of the region, with China and India breathing down Nepal's neck. Nepal stands out as a state still in the making.

Conclusion

There were obvious similarities in the way import-substitution and state regulation were experienced in all countries of South Asia. While encouraging indigenous entrepreneurship, the strategy overstretched the state, compromised export competitiveness, and made politics unstable. Sri Lanka and Nepal illustrate the political consequences of slow and biased development better than the other countries. In the former, slow employment growth fuelled resentment among urban youth, agricultural policy fed Sinhala nationalism, and the squeeze upon the plantations hurt the future of migrant Tamils. In Nepal, while the state assumed the role of the agent of development, it could deliver little benefit outside the Green Revolution zones and the urbanized Kathmandu Valley. The sentiment that the state worked for a few, dominant landholding castes included, contributed to insurgency.

Having finished a country-by-county overview, it is useful to be comparative again, and review the evidence on how the countries performed by various benchmarks of growth and development in the long run.

5

Growth and Development

It was mentioned before that country experiences often overlapped in ways that suggest similarities in structure, history, and patterns of engagement with the world economy. This chapter explores the point with statistical data on growth and development. The major sources are the World Bank and United Nations databases. These sources start from relatively recent times. The World Bank data, for example, usually start from 1960, and in some case, much more recently. The first 12 years after the World War II ended, therefore, are not represented in this comparative study, even though the inference can be drawn that 1960 reflected initial conditions well enough.

The chapter begins with the demographic and employment transition. People in South Asia are living longer than before, and some of them seem to work harder than workers in the rest of the world. Why did this change come about?

The Demographic and Employment Transition

Data quality on demographic change for periods before 1960 is uneven. In undivided India, mortality decline had begun in the 1920s. In Sri Lanka, the fall started earlier. It is believed that mortality decline began in Nepal

T. Roy, *The Economy of South Asia*, Palgrave Studies in Economic History, DOI 10.1007/978-3-319-54720-6_5

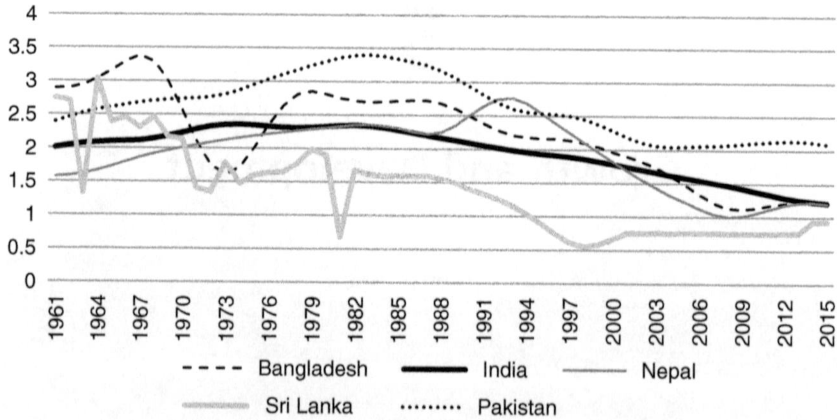

Fig. 5.1 Population growth (over previous year) %

around 1930.[1] In all cases except Sri Lanka, epidemic disease control played an important part in initiating the decline, whereas in Sri Lanka, food and nutrition also played a part. Since mortality decline more or less coincided in the interwar period, divergent patterns of population growth in the twentieth century (Fig. 5.1) was a matter of fertility transition.

The smooth fall in total fertility (Fig. 5.2) is part of a 'global fertility transition' that began or ended in slightly different time spans in different regions of the world. When voluntary, it was everywhere associated with more schooling, more health care so that children survived the early years, more wage earning opportunities, more women marrying late, and more mothers attended by health care professionals. Along with these variables, easy access to contraception and openness to contraceptive choice were also important. This last factor is called 'diffusion.' Diffusion can happen naturally via the market place or neighbourhood social networks, or through campaign by health workers and volunteers.[2]

---

[1] Griffith Feeney, Shyam Thapa, and Keshav R. Sharma, 'One and a Half Centuries of Demographic Transition in Nepal,' *Journal of Health, Population, and Nutrition*, 19(3), 2001, 160–66.

[2] John Caldwell, 'The Global Fertility Transition and Nepal,' The Tibetan Himalayan Library (online resource), 1998, http://www.thlib.org/static/reprints/contributions/CNAS_25_sp_01.pdf (accessed 9 September 2016).

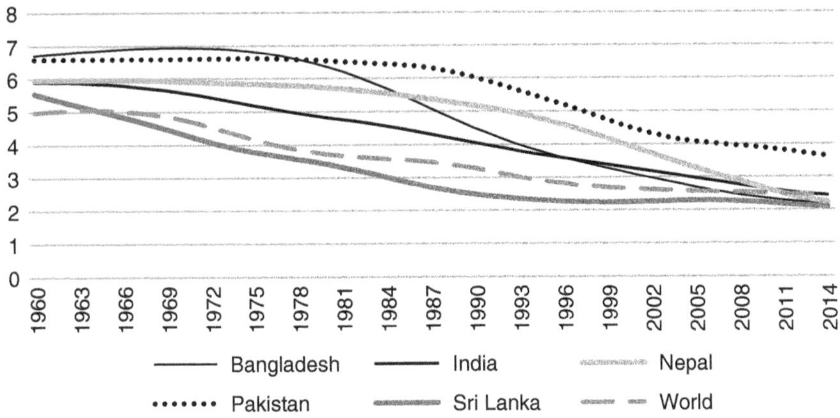

Fig. 5.2 Fertility rate (births per woman)

Fig. 5.3 Indian school children having lunch

The midday meal scheme was started between 1995 and 2001 as a measure to improve nutrition of children, attract children to school, and put idle grain stocks in state warehouses to good use. Studies find that these aims were met to some extent, despite occasional corruption scandals. © Edwin Toone / Alamy Stock Photo

The two extreme scenarios in South Asia were Bangladesh and Nepal, the former an early and sharp drop in the total fertility rate from a high level, and the latter a late and slower drop from a high level. The Bangladesh success story cannot be attributed to a natural diffusion process, rural women whose response mattered did not belong in networks where fertility decline was already a positive value, and is attributed instead to a highly motivated group of extension workers who started on their campaign in the 1960s. The secret of their success was that the extension workers believed in the message they delivered on behalf of the government. In Nepal, geographical obstacles to diffusion were enormous, and whereas the valleys that were linked up with the world through good communication and transport did join the global fertility transition in the 1970s, the remoter regions did not. The higher value of children as workers in the self-employed families in the remote areas joined with the absence of sufficient health care intervention in these regions to keep fertility rate high.[3]

Pakistan was one of the first countries to start a population control programme. Although the campaign produced results in the East, the West was one of the last regions to show significant fertility transition. Reports of what went wrong point at failures of the state-aided diffusion mechanisms, as well as the persistence of fertility norms among women that set a floor of some kind to total fertility.[4] In turn, the persistence of the norm may have had something to do with employment and education trends among rural women. These chains of causality at the family level are not easy to identify. The early and quite decisive fall in fertility rate in Sri Lanka is explained with cultural factors, including high average age at marriage of women, diffusion of family planning, and employment of women. The Indian case is a combination of distinct regional trends, and harder to generalize. It would be fair to say that at one extreme, Kerala or Goa conform to the Sri Lankan pattern, and Bihar or Uttar Pradesh the Pakistan one.

No matter which country we look at, total fertility rate was set at a high average level at the start of the period. In other words, the 1960s and the 1970s, when GDP growth was relatively low, were also the decades when

[3] Caldwell, 'Global Fertility Transition.'

[4] Family Planning Association of Pakistan, *Demographic Transition in Pakistan*, Lahore, c. 2006.

population growth was high, sometimes as high as 3–3.5 per cent (Bangladesh, Pakistan, briefly Nepal). In an accounting sense, the situation would mean low rise in average income and intense pressure on food and basic public goods. Near-famine situations in the 1970s revealed how stressful these years were. From the 1980s, in all regions, the pressures eased off.

High fertility rate can contribute to inequality. Wealthier families can educate their children better than the poorer ones because they have more wealth, but if they also have fewer children, they can educate their children even better. These inequalities are hard to measure because they often work through quality of education. That is, good schools are also the expensive private schools. It is not all bad news, however. The huge population of South Asia, which is mostly young and still growing at 1–2 per cent per year, appears less as a burden as it did to economists in the 1970s and 1980s. It is now seen more as an asset, a 'demographic dividend.' The Indian media loves to use this expression to reassure the world that India is doing alright, but what does the expression mean really?

There are two distinct senses in which a young population can aid economic growth. One of these works through wages, and another through savings. The wage effect may be present in South Asia, the saving effect is uncertain. The wage effect occurred in the early stages of modern economic growth in Western Europe. Demand for workers increased in modern industry, but the supply increased faster – because of decline in the crafts or population growth – so that the average wage remained flat for quite a while. Inequality increased as a result, but employers gained from cheap labour and made investments. In short, a young population can be a business asset.

A young population can be a business asset in a very different sense. This depends on the skill level of the young workers. The excitement about demographic dividend stems also from the belief that the labour force is made up of skilled and high-wage workers, who can afford to make savings, which savings are converted into investment and economic growth. A young work-force means many unmarried workers with low dependency, which is good for savings.

Which one of these scenarios justifies calling the young population a dividend? It is hard to construct a single wage series for India, but impressions will tell us that most labour markets in South Asia do not demand high skills and do not pay high wages. Women workers still marry early on average and bear dependents at a young age. The population is young no doubt, but they are not highly skilled. This impression is confirmed by evidence on quality of labour. 'In Pakistan currently [2009], only about half the population is literate, and only 2.6% educated up to graduate level.'[5] A Delhi and Boston organization, Aspiring Minds, reports that half of India's graduates are deemed unemployable by most knowledge industry firms, not because they lack specific skills, but they lack even generic skills like writing a grammatically correct sentence or solving simple arithmetical problems.[6] In short, if the young population is a business asset, it is asset as cheap workers, not an asset as savers. They may be an asset for the employers, being cheap, but not for themselves. It will take another generation, if not longer, for the work-force to earn enough to save early and have a decent life as young people.

Overall, the labour markets in South Asia are characterized by low levels of open unemployment, between 2 and 4 per cent of male working age population whereas the world average was 6, in 2014. These figures do not show a long-term trend, except for Sri Lanka, where unemployment was above 10 per cent in the early 1990s and fell steadily thereafter. Female unemployment rates follow a similar pattern. These numbers reflect other features that are present in many emerging economies. For example, they depend on women's participation in paid work, and the proportion of the younger adult population that do or do not go to college and take training. A broad measure of these effects is the employment to population ratio. Figure 5.4 suggests that in Nepal and Bangladesh a higher proportion of the population compared with world average join employment. In India, the proportion has fallen marginally. In Sri Lanka and Pakistan the proportion has increased. In Pakistan it has increased in response to participation of women.

[5] Mathew McCartney, *Pakistan – The Political Economy of Growth, Stagnation, and the State 1951–2009*, London: Routledge, 2011, 201.

[6] http://www.aspiringminds.com/research-reports?page=1 (accessed 9 September 2016).

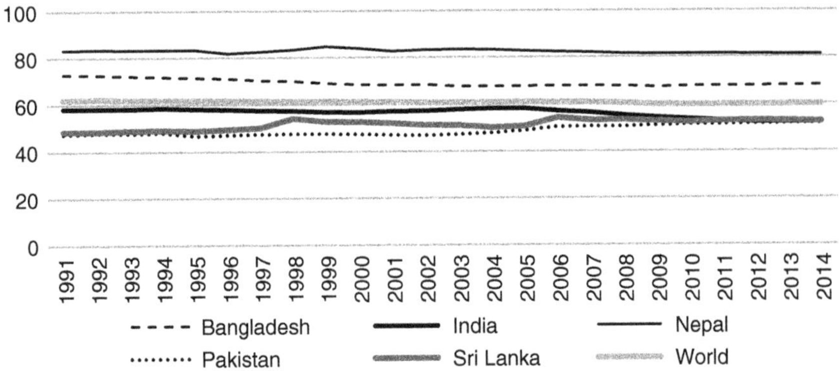

Fig. 5.4 Employment to population ratio (% of population above 15 working)

Growth and Development

The recent (post-1990) acceleration in economic growth has indeed been universal in the region. India and Sri Lanka were falling behind the world average income between 1960 and 1980, but since then catching up with the world (Table 5.1). It took India 35 years (1960–1995) to double its per capita income for the first time, 14 years (1995–2009) to double it the second time, and if it can maintain a 7 per cent annual growth rate in average income, it will take India 10 years (2009–2019) to double it a third time. If the current pace of economic growth holds, India should be a high income nation by 2035. Similar stories of falling behind and catching up can be told, if with less dramatic numbers, for Nepal and Bangladesh. Pakistan had a somewhat different trajectory. It had a better record between 1960 and 1990, and a worse economic performance in the next quarter century, though the differences are not significant.

Before 1990, there was considerable divergence among the nations in South Asia. Sri Lanka differed from the rest of the region in initial conditions. GDP per head was well above the regional average in 1960. Thereafter, there was further divergence (Fig. 5.5). There was divergence also among the other four countries. An immediate reason for better

Table 5.1 Per capita income of South Asian countries in relation to world average (%)

	World average	Bangladesh	India	Nepal	Pakistan	Sri Lanka
1960	100	10	9	7	8	16
1970	100	8	7	6	9	14
1980	100	6	7	5	9	15
1990	100	6	8	5	10	17
2000	100	6	10	6	10	23
2010	100	8	15	6	11	30
2015	100	10	18	7	11	36

Source of all tables and graphs in this chapter is World Bank, World Development Indicators, http://data.worldbank.org/products/wdi (accessed 16 August 2016), unless otherwise indicated

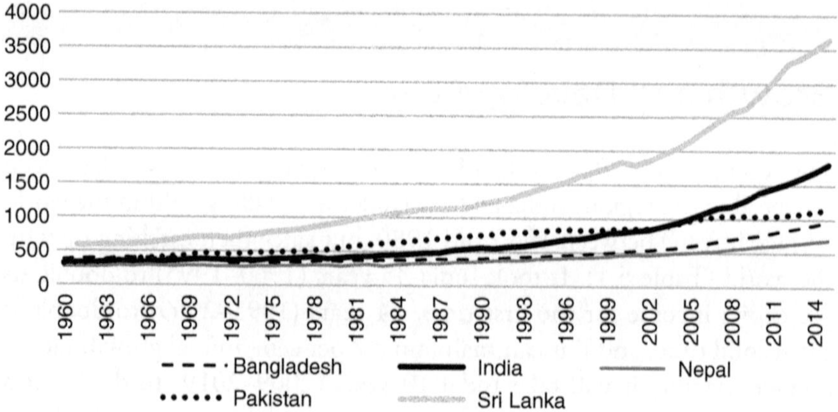

Fig. 5.5 GDP per head (2010 US$) 1960–2014

performance in average income in the earlier decades was the rate of population growth (Fig. 5.1). The population growth rates converged more recently.

GDP, it is well known, does not directly measure the quality and delivery of public goods. As Amartya Sen and others have suggested, if GDP measures economic growth narrowly conceived, the broader concept, 'development,' should be measured by an index that captures human capability, availability of choice, and the quality of life.[7] The Human Development Index or HDI, which includes measures for literacy and health along with income, reflects these other dimensions better.

The relationship between growth, as measured by GDP, and development, as measured by HDI, remains open to interpretation. The interpretation needs to use knowledge of the society for which these measures are estimated. Education and health care are private goods to some extent. So far as they are, we should expect earning capacity, or GDP growth, to shape human development. Income elasticity of demand for education and health care tends to be positive, that is, as individuals earn more, they spend proportionately more on the education and welfare of their children. We, then, may expect a proportionately larger improvement in HDI from a given increase in income. South Asia appears as a puzzle on this point. Rapid GDP growth does not seem to have translated into equally rapid improvement in HDI in the recent times, even though education and health care are partly private goods. This anomaly may suggest that some aspects of education and health care, which cannot be supplied privately, such as immunization and control of communicable diseases, have fallen short because the governments have not made these areas a priority. I will return to this issue later.

Mahbub ul Haq, the architect of the Human Development Index in the United Nations Development Programme, popularized the idea that there was a peculiarly South Asian problem with respect to development. 'The South Asia Region,' Haq observed in 1995, 'has been sinking fast into a quagmire of human deprivation and despair, emerging as the most deprived region in the world.'[8] This is also one of the theses of a series of books and articles jointly written by Jean Drèze and Amartya Sen, who show that India stands rather badly on multidimensional development indicators in relation to the poorer nations of the world, large emerging economies, and even South Asian neighbours like Bangladesh and Sri

[7] Thomas Wells, 'Sen's Capability Approach,' The Internet Encyclopedia of Philosophy, http://www.iep.utm.edu/sen-cap/ (accessed 9 September 2016).

[8] Cited by Morris D. Morris, Review of Mahbub ul Haq, *Human Development in South Asia, 1997*, New York: Oxford University Press, 1997, in *Economic Development and Cultural Change*, 48(2), 2000, 433–439.

Lanka. Comparisons of India on achievements in education, health care, and poverty reveal two interrelated failures – limited quantity of essential public services available and 'the near-absence of public discussion of this inadequacy.'[9]

Haq's dramatic statement was controversial when it was made. Challenging his reading of the numbers, Morris D. Morris claimed in a review that 'South Asia is not "sinking fast" [into a quagmire, see the above quote] . . . in fact, . . . it is not sinking at all. Between 1960 and 1994 . . . there have . . . been significant improvements in basic welfare levels.'[10] Morris had devised one of the pioneering indices of development, called Physical Quality of Life. It was based on three non-income measures, infant mortality, life expectancy at age one, and basic literacy performance on a scale from 0 to 100. This index, the PQLI, confirmed development gains, if modest ones, in South Asia. More recently, some economists have started advocating the use of multidimensional poverty and inequality measurements (see Box 5.1), which too do not include income but include an array of non-income indicators. The latter calculations seem to validate Haq's despairing assessment of South Asia and Drèze and Sen's criticism of India's record.

As these examples will suggest, Haq's statement is hard to test. The result of measurements of human development in the region are sensitive to the inclusion or otherwise of per capita income in the measure. Until the early 1990s, inclusion of average income would have depressed HDI in South Asia because income in these countries grew slowly, in comparison with the industrializing economies in East and Southeast Asia. Haq frequently made this comparison. After 2000, inclusion of average income would exaggerate the development gains, because the region is growing fast in terms of income per head and has fallen behind other emerging economies in respect of education, health care, and

---

[9] Jean Drèze and Amartya Sen, *An Uncertain Glory: India and its Contradictions*, Princeton and Oxford: Princeton University Press, 2013, 148.

[10] Morris, Review of Mahbub ul Haque.

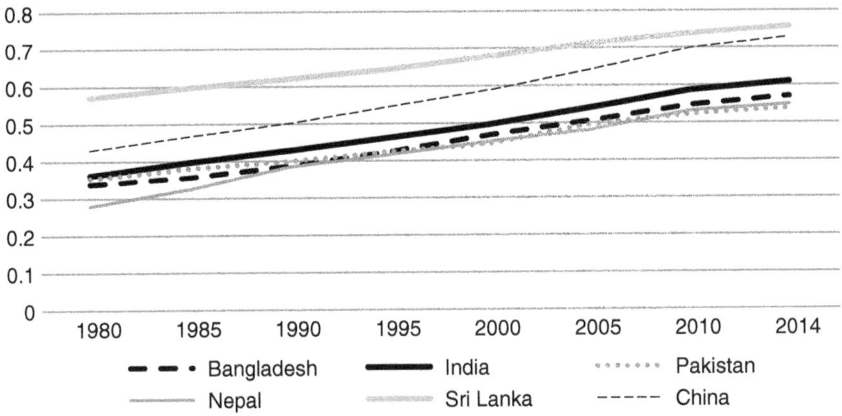

Fig. 5.6 Human development index 1980–2014

Source: http://hdr.undp.org/en/data (accessed 18 July 2016).

infrastructure. This anomaly creates unbalanced impressions of the performance of the region.

Returning to the HDI, the record of the last 20 years shows improvement (Fig. 5.6, see also Fig. 5.3), more or less at the same pace as the whole world in this time. South Asia is not lagging behind. Of course, Sri Lanka was exceptional to begin with and stayed exceptional throughout. If Sri Lanka is excluded, levels of HDI in South Asia in 1980 were low and comparable to those in the poorest regions of the world, such as sub-Saharan Africa. From that position it has improved, especially in relation to sub-Saharan Africa. However, the majority of the countries in the world experienced similar orders of improvement since 1980. The South Asia average was 71 per cent of the midpoint between the highest and the lowest scores in 1980. In 2014, the average was 73 per cent of the midpoint. Country experiences again vary, for example, the ratio for India improved from 67 to 74 per cent, but these are minor variations. The data show that compared with the fastest growing emerging economies, especially China, South Asia has indeed done rather poorly (Fig. 5.6).

How far can we explain the HDI as a government failure? Several studies show that the social returns to education are high in South Asia.

This should mean a strong demand for education. Persistent under-performance in education, then, can be laid at the door of the state. Except Sri Lanka, and a few exceptional regions like Kerala, in South Asia as a whole, the effort to deliver public education was indeed quite weak until the 1980s. For example, expenditure on education as a proportion of GDP was less than 2 per cent in Pakistan until 1982. While public delivery of schooling was inadequate, the university system expanded rapidly and was heavily subsidized. Those who completed schooling could expect to get automatic admission into the university and receive a practically free tertiary education. Thus, any inequality in school admission was likely to harden further because the insiders finished college and had access to, say, government jobs.

Why was public delivery of schooling insufficient? There can be two types of explanation for this deficiency. The mainstream explanation follows a 'political economy' approach, that is, accounts for low public effort with reference to the motivation felt by the wealthy and powerful classes, the 'elite,' to push the government in that direction. An economist attributes poor public goods delivery in Pakistan to the fact that 'each segment of the elite is powerful enough by itself to exclude the majority from power.'[11] In Pakistan, 'the dominance of the feudal class in the political system has probably meant the suppression of demands for more education on the grounds that this could threaten the existing power structure. This is one factor which not only explains the large urban-rural differentials in primary enrolment rates but also the spatial differences between areas where the feudal system still dominates like rural Sindh and the more progressive regions of Punjab and NWFP.'[12]

The second explanation would look at competing claims on government budget. 'It is interesting,' Easterly writes apropos Pakistan and comparing the country with other developing nations at similar level, 'that the overspending on defense is roughly equal to the sum of the

[11] William Easterly, 'The Political Economy of Growth Without Development: A Case Study of Pakistan,' Cambridge Mass.: Harvard University (Kennedy School of Government), 2001.

[12] Hafiz A. Pasha, 'Political Economy of Higher Education: A Study of Pakistan,' *Pakistan Economic and Social Review*, 33(1/2), 1995, 19–36.

underspending on health and education as percent of GDP.'[13] It is certain that India's expenditure on defence, agricultural subsidies, and food subsidies crowd out education and health care to some extent. Further, 80 per cent of public spending on education in India comes from the states. From the 1990s, states in India are competing hard to attract private investment, and those losing the game are heavily indebted.

These approaches focus on spending. An expenditure-centric explanation overlooks two dimensions of poor HDI scores that are societal. Behind poor HDI scores lies a sordid story of discrimination against girls. For example, until the 1980s, the relative backwardness of Pakistan in enrolment rates in comparison with other countries of similar income level was almost wholly due to poor enrolment of girls.[14] Gender discrimination was built into the average age at marriage of girls, which tended to be low in South Asia. Child marriage is still reported to be practiced extensively in India. Low average age of marriage of girls makes it highly likely that girls will be poorly educated on average, receive inadequate health care, suffer from health problems that arise from early childbirth, and be undernourished on average. Migration is historically male-biased in South Asia, which means that women are excluded from lucrative labour markets.[15]

Such biases are weakening throughout the region. The emergence of an urban and rural middle class changed the perceived value of children. '[T]he emerging rural middle class [in Pakistan], . . . like their urban counterparts, has shifted to a pattern of consumption dominated by durable items and educational expenditures and which no longer relies on children's productive and protective contributions.'[16] Whereas

[13] Easterly, 'Political Economy.'

[14] Easterly, 'Political Economy.'

[15] Tirthankar Roy, *Rethinking Economic Change in India: Labour and Livelihood*, London: Routledge, 2005. Ecology compounds the effect. The Barani region of Pakistan, for example, has dryland rainfed agriculture but towns and cities where many jobs are available. Historically, Barani agricultural households tended to be migration dependent, and migration was male-biased, thus reinforcing the bias for males to be educated and females to stay at home.

[16] Samuel S. Lieberman, 'Demographic Perspectives on Pakistan's Development,' *Population and Development Review*, 8(1), 1982, 85–120.

import substituting industrialization was bad for women's employment (because machines, metals, and chemical factories traditionally employ few women), liberalization changed the scenario dramatically. In the last 20 years, only two export-oriented businesses (clothing and information technology) created possibly 5 to 10 million jobs for women throughout South Asia.

The education problem is an outcome partly of the quality of education. From the demand side, government primary and secondary schools offer such poor quality that the demand for private education, even at a premium paid for quality, has grown steadily. The statement applies to university and technical education too. Consumers, if they can, reject state education. More public spending would not make for better HDI in that case, financial support to private education might. 'The strength of the case for increasing spending levels in health and education, and indeed infrastructure, depends on the extent to which quality can be improved.'[17] The argument holds for health care too, but with qualifications. The case for public spending remains unambiguously strong in areas where exclusion can have serious externalities for the whole population, such as immunization and the prevention of communicable diseases.

The Haq-Drèze-Sen critique of HDI performance of South Asia usefully points out uneven performance *within* the region. The advances made by the Indian state of Kerala and by Sri Lanka were outstanding, in comparison with the rest of the region. In both cases, a history of state activism played a role. With Kerala, the activism owed to the progressive stance of a princely state. With Sri Lanka, it originated in welfare measures undertaken by the British state. Both Travancore-Cochin and Ceylon may well have had higher state capacity because they could tax rich plantations. Their head-start in social development predates the post-war development discourse. We should not confuse these examples with what economists call 'developmental' states, a concept that emphasizes the intention rather than the capacity of states.

[17] Stephen Howes, Rinku Murgai and Marina Wes, 'Expenditure Implications of India's State-Level Fiscal Crisis.' In Raghbendra Jha, ed., *Economic Growth, Economic Performance, and Welfare in South Asia*, Basingstoke: Palgrave Macmillan, 2005, 185–206.

From the 1970s, in both Kerala and Sri Lanka, the sustainability of the effort to educate and buy better health care owed increasingly to the remittances from the Gulf. 'A vast amount of economic capital earned abroad used by the migrant families are invested in the education, health and in the progress of second generation' in these regions.[18] With Nepal, again, remittances are found to be correlated with increased expenditure on education.[19] Migration does have a significant positive effect on HDI. Of course, in countries like Nepal that started with low human development levels, migration does not provide a sufficient solution to the problem. Further, remittance has to work within the quality constraint. If universities are generally of bad quality and subsidized, remittance alone can make little difference. In any case, the effect of remittance on education tends to be underestimated in the HDI scholarship.

Poverty

If GDP and HDI are controversial measures of performance, none is more so than poverty (see Box 5.1). Poverty ratios measure two things, how severe the problem of poverty is (measured by level), and whether poverty is decreasing, increasing, or just persistent (measured by trend). The level suggests how far governments have to go to tackle serious levels of deprivation, and the trend suggests whether the type of policy currently pursued is working or not. Market-friendly policy is expected to work on poverty by enabling individual earners to buy more basic goods. In the presence of growing inequality, that solution may not be reliable. The alternative is redistribution and transfer. These numbers, therefore, lead to types of judgement on development policy.

[18] Ginu Zacharia Oommen, 'South Asia–Gulf Migratory Corridor: Emerging Patterns, Prospects and Challenges,' *Migration and Development*, 2015, 1–19.

[19] Apsara Karki Nepal, 'The Impact of International Remittances on Child Outcomes and Household Expenditures in Nepal,' *Journal of Development Studies*, 52(6), 2016, 838–853,

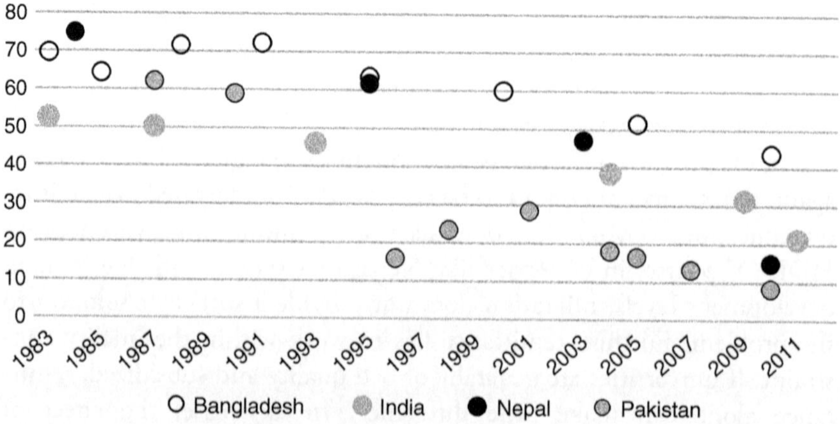

Fig. 5.7 Poverty (headcount ratio) 1983–2012

The poverty headcount ratio (percentage of population earning less than US$1.9 a day) maintained by the World Bank is the handiest measure now available, and therefore, the most popular one. According to this measure, South Asia achieved a remarkable reduction in poverty since the early 1980s (Fig. 5.7). The values vary within the region quite widely, but the median values show a declining trend (Fig. 5.8). Sri Lanka is excluded from the picture because poverty in the way defined here has long disappeared from the country. The fall should be qualified by the fact that there is a systematic difference between urban and rural poverty in the region, the former fell more rapidly than the latter.[20]

[20] For Bangladesh, see Mohammad Alauddin, 'Recent Developments in the Bangladesh Economy,' In Raghbendra Jha, ed., *Economic Growth, Economic Performance, and Welfare in South Asia*, Basingstoke: Palgrave Macmillan, 2005, 11–27; for Nepal, see Prem Jung Thapa and Shyamal Krishna Shrestha, 'Economic Reforms in Nepal: Performance and Prospects,' in Jha, ed., *Economic Growth*, 52–75; for Pakistan, Talat Anwar, 'Recent Macroeconomic Developments and Implications for Poverty and Employment in Pakistan, in Jha, ed., *Economic Growth*, 76–101; for India, Peter Warr, 'Poverty, Inequality and Economic Growth: India, 1957–1997,' in Jha, *Economic Growth*, 343–368.

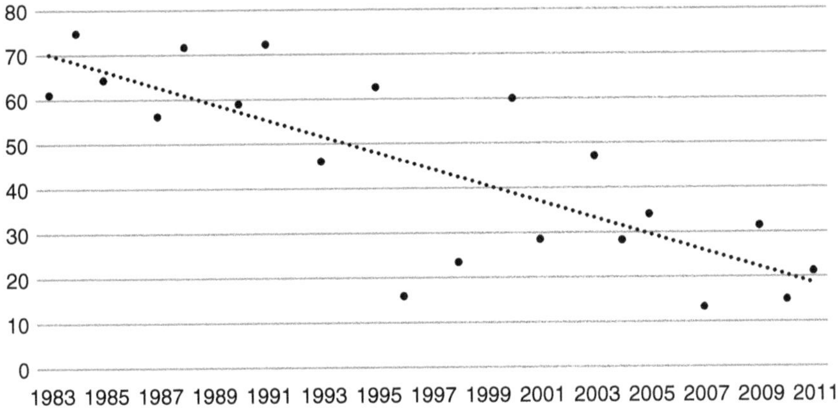

Fig. 5.8 Poverty (headcount ratio) median values 1983–2012

The picture is more complex than it looks. First of all, attempts to derive alternative headcounts based on country-specific datasets often produce contrary results. As a debate on poverty in India during the 1990s showed, official statistics on size and distribution of expenditure, which can be used for the purpose of constructing alternative headcounts, produce different conclusions because of changes in data collection and reporting methods.[21] No perfect way to reconcile these differences exists. A measured conclusion is that there is 'no support for sweeping claims that the nineties have been a period of unprecedented improvement or widespread impoverishment,' in India.[22] When the dataset is extended to surveys done in the mid-2000s, however, the case for 'unprecedented improvement' appears to be stronger.[23] Of course, this debate on method is about Indian data and not necessarily relevant to the task at hand. For useful comparative statements, we have to fall back on the World Bank headcount.

[21] For a good review of the scholarship, see Arvind Panagariya, *India: The Emerging Giant*, New York: Oxford University Press, 2008.

[22] Angus Deaton and Jean Drèze, 'Poverty and Inequality in India: A Re-examination,' *Economic and Political Weekly*, 37(36), 2002, 3729–3748.

[23] See Panagariya, *India: The Emerging Giant*, 144.

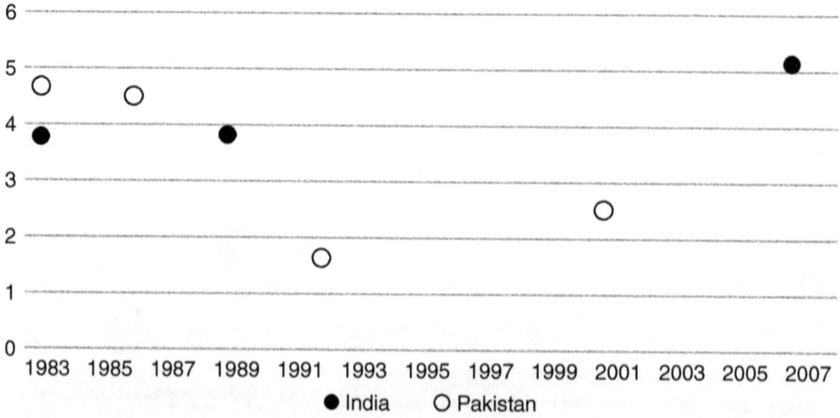

Fig. 5.9 Poverty – Country/world ratio 1983–2010

Even when we confine ourselves to the World Bank data, there is room for concern with the recent trends. There is still a staggeringly large number of very poor people in South Asia. Further, the region excluding Sri Lanka has not done remarkably well by world standards. The ratio of country poverty and world average in India and Pakistan, for example, has moved up and down, but not definitely down (Fig. 5.9). More recently, economists have argued in favour of alternatives to income poverty, such as multidimensional poverty and inequality. These measures do tell a different story about South Asia. Income poverty shows a smaller proportion of the poor compared with the multidimensional index. In terms of trend, income poverty shows a sharp fall in the 2000s, which can be seen as evidence that market-friendly policy contributes to reduction of poverty. HDI shows a modest rise and no identifiable break when economies started liberalizing. Multidimensional poverty, as far as one can see, does not yet offer a time series, but the levels suggest that the governments do need to intervene more, not less.

Why does growth in income have uncertain or little effect on poverty? We can answer this question tentatively by looking at the profile of inequality (Fig. 5.10). Levels of inequality are not particularly high in South Asia, but the levels have not changed at all, if anything, they have increased slightly. In India, the level of inequality has not changed compared with the

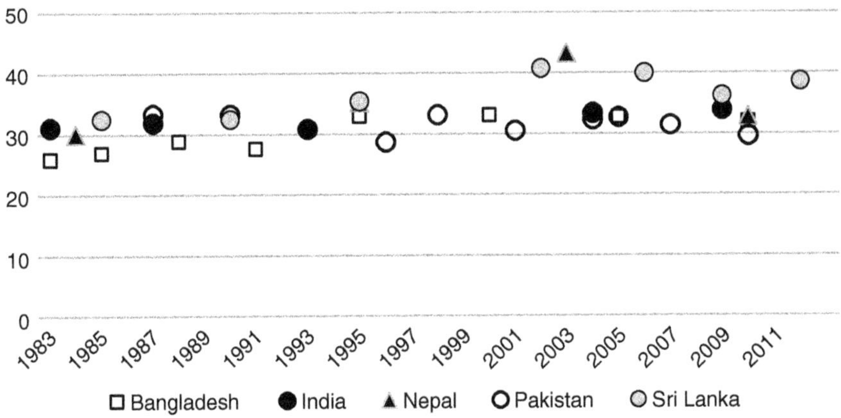

Fig. 5.10 Inequality (Gini Coefficient) 1982–2010

levels observed in 1957. The Gini coefficient was 0.34 in 1957, fell slightly to 0.30–0.31 in the first half of the 1970s, increased slightly to nearer 0.35 at the end of the 1990s and has remained there since.[24] The increase is uncertain, for there is a great deal of noise in the data, but it is likely that the acceleration in economic growth has not been shared widely enough to have an impact upon poverty. Or, growth has not 'trickled down' sufficiently.

Does this vindicate critics of market-friendly economic policy? Not necessarily. A return to openness can be expected to increase inequality, at any rate, exert an upward pressure on the graph because growth of trade should reward skills more in demand in the world market, and reduce demand for goods produced by the formerly protected segments. In South Asia, inequality also derives from a structural factor, regions within South Asia are simply unable to make use of trade enough either because the costs of trade are high, or they do not have much goods to sell.

While standard of living presents a mixed picture, the structure of livelihoods shows a clearer pattern.

[24] Peter Warr, 'Poverty, Inequality and Economic Growth: India, 1957–1997,' in Raghbendra Jha, ed., *Economic Growth, Economic Performance, and Welfare in South Asia*, Basingstoke: Palgrave Macmillan, 2005, 343–368, and World Bank data.

Box 5.1 The poverty measurement debate

The proportion of population who can be called 'poor' has long been used as a metric by development-oriented states to measure the success or failure of public policy. The standard procedure is to define a numerical benchmark, and count the number of people below the benchmark. This 'headcount' approach can fail to give reliable figures if there are a large number of people whose circumstances are usually unstable (see Krishna, 2010). Subject to that criticism, headcount can be implemented in a variety of ways depending on what the benchmark stands for. The most widely used benchmark is income. The world dataset corresponding to this benchmark is maintained by the World Bank. The benchmark is revised from time to time, currently it is US$1.9/day, and the numbers recalculated retrospectively. This gives headcount ratios from at least the early 1980s.

Economists express dissatisfaction with a pure income measure for poverty. The measure does not capture access to public goods, such as education and health care. Around 1970, the economic historian Morris David Morris constructed a Physical Quality of Life Index (PQLI) to address this problem. Later, the United Nations Development Programme introduced the Human Development Index (HDI). This is a number indicating the level of 'human development' of a country. It is not a headcount. HDI is a derived version of PQLI. HDI includes income, along with life expectancy and education. The dataset is available from 1975 on the UN website. More recently, the UN has also developed measures that capture other dimensions of the quality of life, including Gender Development Index.

Another criticism of income derives from Amartya Sen's concept of development with reference to an individual's capability of living the lives that he or she wants. One initiative that emerged from this idea is the Multidimensional Poverty Index (MPI, both United Nations and the Oxford Poverty and Human Development Initiative maintain a dataset). The index is based on a variety of direct and indirect indices of 'capability' – including schooling, child mortality, nutrition, electricity, sanitation, drinking water, and cooking fuel – but does not include income.

Readings: Anirudh Krishna, *One Illness Away: Why People Become Poor and How They Escape Poverty?*, Oxford: Oxford University Press, 2010; Morris D. Morris, 'The Physical Quality of Life Index (PQLI),' *Development digest*, 18 (1), 1980, 95–109; http://www.ophi.org.uk/wp-content/uploads/OPHI-MPI-Brief.pdf; http://hdr.undp.org/en/data; http://data.worldbank.org/topic/poverty

Structural Change

Around 1950, nations in the mainland South Asia were mainly agricultural, with half or more of national income coming in from land, and a somewhat larger percentage of the work-force engaged in cultivation. Throughout the region, economists and politicians shared a strong desire to industrialize. Table 5.2 shows that the strategy worked in India, Bangladesh, and Sri Lanka, and did not work in Pakistan and Nepal. In Pakistan, good quality land was more plentiful to begin with, in Nepal, neither agricultural nor industrialization strategy was likely to succeed given high trade and resource costs and the attraction of migration as a choice. Underlying the Table 5.2, there is a chronology of industrialization. In India, protection and public investment in capital goods delivered 7 per cent per year manufacturing growth between 1955 and 1965. The rate was less than 5 in the next 10 years. The industrial stagnation depressed overall growth rates.

Agricultural conditions vary by region. In all countries agricultural performance was unimpressive in the 1950s, and much better during the Green Revolution. Because local geography matters so much to growth, agriculture alone did not lead the South Asian countries either to a high-growth trajectory or to converge on levels of living. Countries that enjoyed relatively higher agricultural productivity in 1960 had higher productivity in 2015 as well, and similarly for the low-productivity countries. As Figs. 5.11 and 5.12 show, while cereal production responded to the Green Revolution, in the region as a whole, and especially India, Nepal, and Pakistan, agricultural productivity

Table 5.2 Structural change 2000–2014 (percentage of GDP at current prices)

	Agriculture		Industry		Services	
	2000	2014	2000	2014	2000	2014
Bangladesh	24	16	23	28	53	56
India	23	17	26	30	51	53
Nepal	41	34	22	16	37	51
Pakistan	26	25	23	21	51	54
Sri Lanka	20	9	27	31	53	61

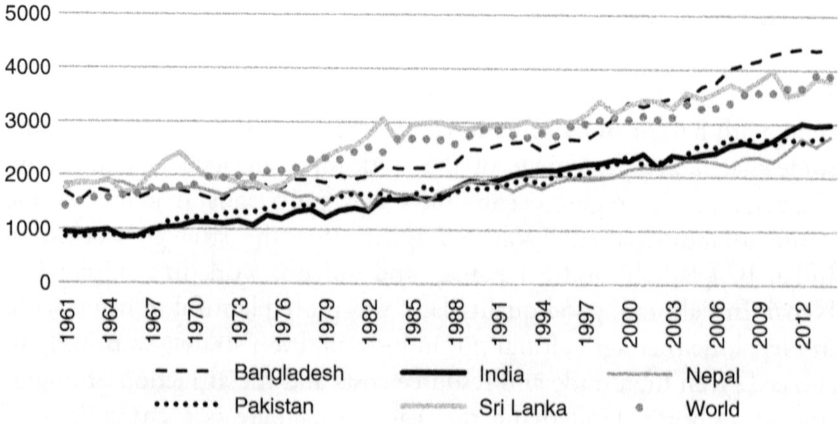

Fig. 5.11 Cereal production, Kg/Hectare

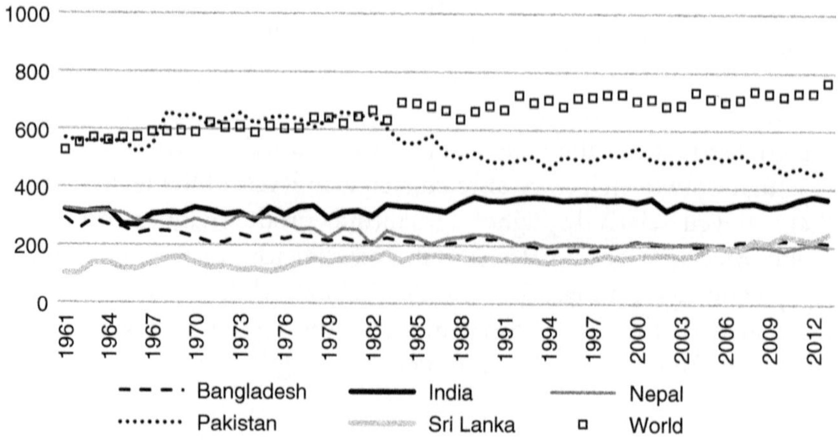

Fig. 5.12 Cereal production (Kg) per person 1961–2013

remained consistently below the world average. In Pakistan, yield decelerated in the 2000s. When population growth is added to these numbers, South Asia excluding Pakistan barely maintained equilibrium in cereal supplies per head (Fig. 5.12). In Pakistan there was a fall. The same trend appears in Sri Lanka, but the level of cereal supplies is the lowest in this region. The limited supply of arable land in Sri Lanka and the consequent need to import food have been an argument for a food subsidy before 1979 and an argument for an export-oriented policy more recently.

When we combine these trends, the share of agricultural income in GDP (Table 5.2) did fall everywhere. The composition of the gainers differed. Industry gained in Bangladesh, India, and Sri Lanka. Services gained in all five countries. In Pakistan, the extent of structural change was moderate. The universal shift from agriculture to non-agriculture is reflected in urbanization data (Fig. 5.13). All five countries are urbanizing, but not any faster than the world. Within the region, Nepal has the least urban population and the highest agricultural one. Sri Lanka too has a low urban population, but this reflects a classification issue. Sri Lankan coastal settlement pattern defies easy demarcation between the village and the city.

The service sector did remarkably well everywhere. This is a mixed basket. Throughout the region, income from labour export made a contribution. In India, expansion in export of software services was a key variable. Whereas the IT service export is a particularly Indian phenomenon, the greatly increased labour circulation is a pan-South-Asia story. I will return to the remittances in a moment. The services

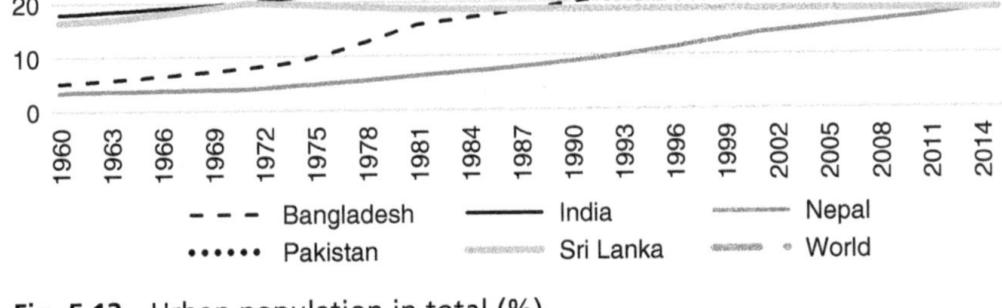

Fig. 5.13 Urban population in total (%)

include at least three other large components, trade, finance, and public administration. Let us now explore the data on trade, finance, and government.

Trade

Sri Lanka is sometimes seen as exceptional because it spent more money on welfare. In fact, Sri Lanka was offbeat because of its ability to fund welfare. This ability derived from the fact that it was a more open economy in the 1950s (Fig. 5.14). The colonial economic system made the whole region open to trade, investment, and migration. In Sri Lanka's case, trade was the main support for the economy, the key tradable was tea and other tree crops. British India exported grain, tea, and textiles. From these beginnings, the entire region seemed to converge in the 1960s towards a closed economy. Figure 5.14 (tracking foriegn trade in GDP) starts from a time when this first transition was nearly over and trade-GDP ratios were quite low in the region. Note that the Indian levels were the lowest throughout, until the recent years. I call this fall of trade 'trade repression' (see Chapter 8). In the 1980s, when

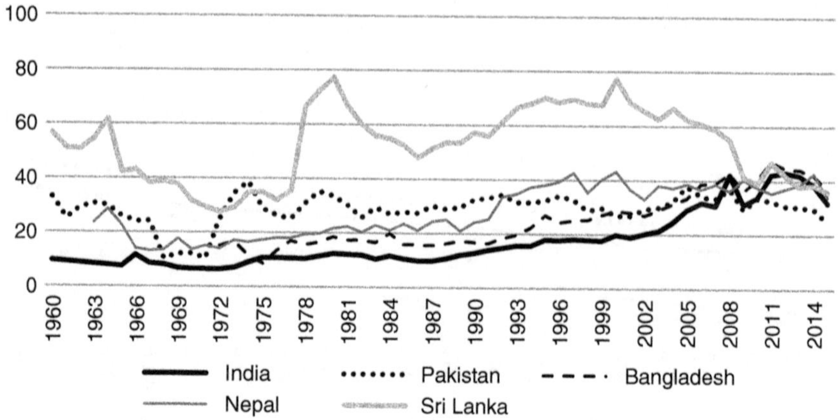

Fig. 5.14 Trade-GDP ratio (%) 1960–2015

Source: World Bank and World Trade Organization

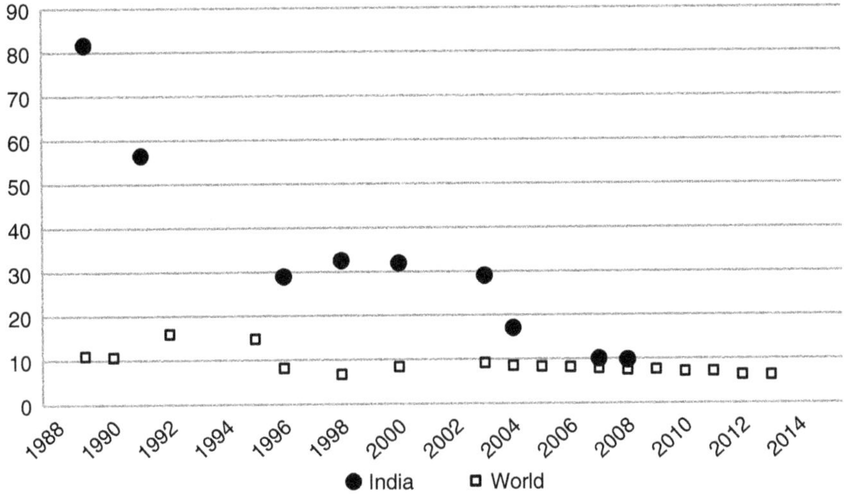

Fig. 5.15 Tariff rate (simple average) on all products (%). India and the world

industries like readymade garments started to export again, there was a divergence. The Sri Lankan economy responded to openness more strongly than did the rest of South Asia. As the liberalization process matured, the country ratios caught up with each other again.

A more direct measure of trade repression is average tariff rates. No matter how it is measured, the average tariff rates in all South Asian countries were many times that of the world average. Sri Lanka had lower figures than the South Asian average, and India well above the average. Figure 5.15 shows the more recent convergence of tariff rates between India and the world. The convergence was a universal phenomenon in the region.

Finance and Remittance

Growth needs investment, and investment needs to be financed. A comparison of the role of banks in their economies (Fig. 5.16) shows that banking maintained a slow and unsteady growth until about 2000. These years had seen nationalization of banks, and a regulated financial

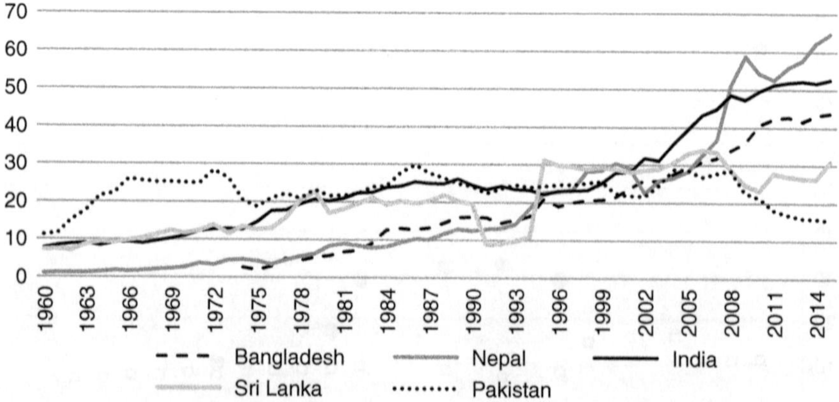

Fig. 5.16 Bank credit in GDP (%)

sector that was often forced to make credit available to the poor and the politically connected at subsidized rates. From the early 2000s, regulations were eased off throughout the region, some banks were privatized in Pakistan and Bangladesh, and private investors invited to start banks. The microfinance revolution unfolded in the 1990s, first in Bangladesh, and then in India (see Box 9.1, Chapter 9). In this phase, the relative importance of organized finance seemed to diverge. The difference remains unexplained in the book, because too little research appears to exist on why banking performed in an uneven way under the impetus of capitalist forces. A plausible speculation is that the convergence of banking and microfinance shored up credit performance in Bangladesh and India. At least, bank penetration into local areas is greater in these countries. In India the penetration was achieved during the regulatory era. In Nepal, quite a different factor, inward remittance, may have stimulated saving, and in turn, banking.

Whether via banks or directly, inward remittances have gone into private consumption and investment on a staggering scale in South Asia. One of the key features of the recent globalization is an enormous increase in the demand for labour services, within the region (between Nepal and India, for example; and unofficial migration between Bangladesh and India) as well as outside the region (all five countries).

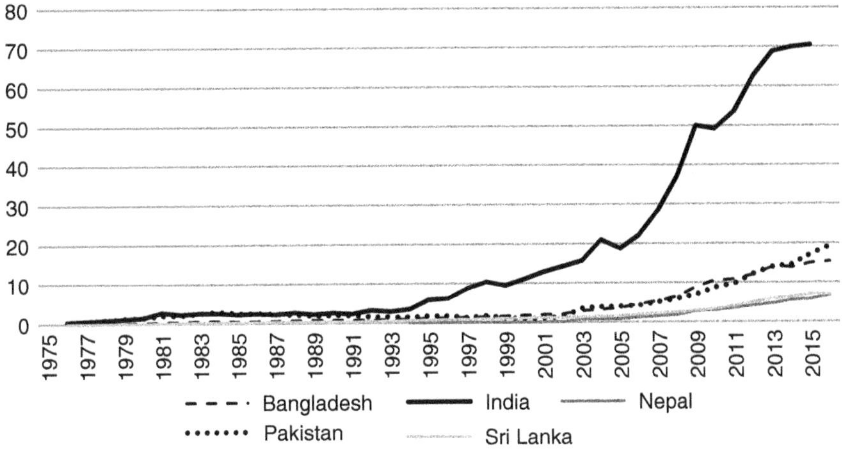

Fig. 5.17 Inward remittance (billion US$)

The extent of the increase was much more impressive than the growth of trade or industrialization.

The remittance revolution touched the five countries differently. There were two distinct peaks, one of these occurred during the 1970s and 1980s due to exploding demand for people in the Persian Gulf states (Figs. 5.17–5.19, especially Fig. 5.18), and the other occurred in the 2000s when the export of labour-intensive services (software, tourism, small businesses) made a part of the workforce more mobile than before. In Pakistan and Bangladesh, the Gulf boom had dramatic effect, the second boom by contrast was a more muted one. India by contrast was a follower in the first boom but a leader in the second one.

The interesting exception is Nepal. Limited data do not permit drawing any conclusion of the effect of the Gulf boom on Nepal. Nepal did take part in the second upswing, and sent out a large number of people outside the region. It is likely that the enormous surge in remittances in relation to the size of the economy was an effect of migration within the South Asia region. Be that as it may, there is little doubt on the significance of this exchange earning for consumption, government operation, and investment in Nepal, now the subject of a large literature (see Fig. 5.19).

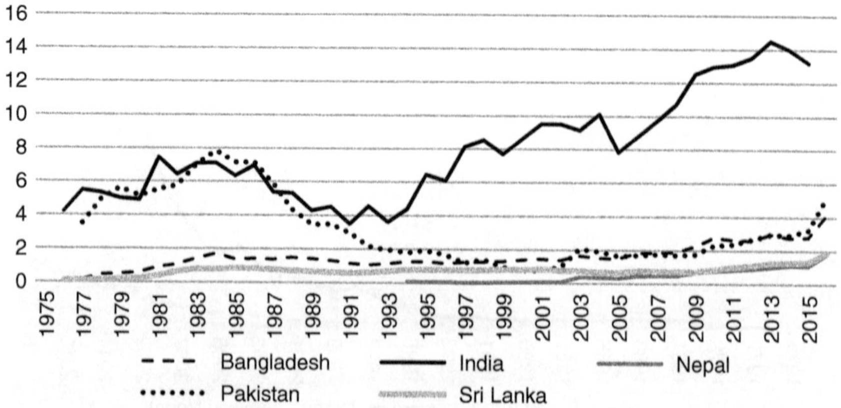

Fig. 5.18 Inward remittance (% of world)

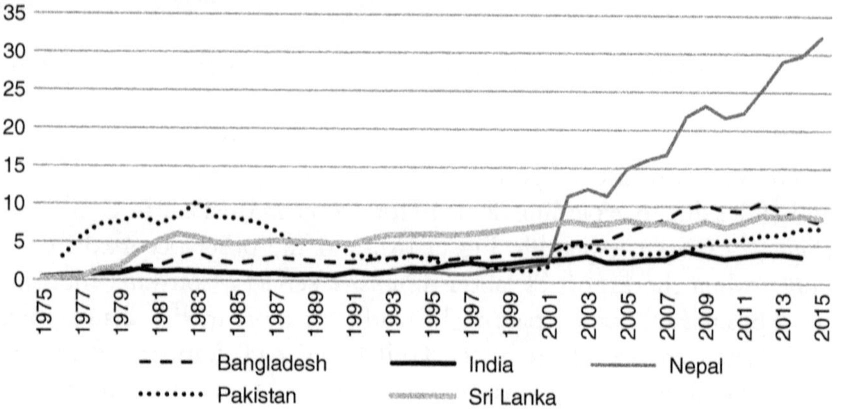

Fig. 5.19 remittance/GDP (%)

The effect of the remittance shows up in Fig. 5.20, which tracks the external balance of goods and services as a percentage of GDP, simple average over five countries. The numbers differed between countries, but there was a broadly similar trend. In the 1960s and the 1970s, there was a steady fall in the balance, and in the 1980s and 1990s a steady rise. The fall occurred due to rise in import commitments and weak exports. The reversal in the 1980s, however, did not occur because of better trade

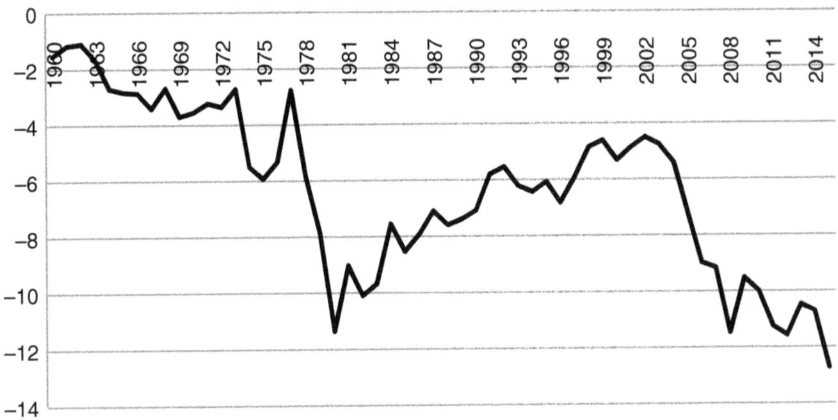

Fig. 5.20 External balance of goods and services (% of GDP, simple average of five countries)

performance. It was due to remittances to begin with, which export of textiles and other labour-intensive goods reinforced later. The more recent fall is not researched enough, and probably reflects the joint effect of openness and import of capital goods.

State

The state matters to economic development because it invests in public goods, infrastructure, and provides protection to the lives and consumption of the poor and the vulnerable sections of the population. In South Asia, the state did more than this, it nationalized businesses, and started new ones. From the 1980s, the second role of the state has receded, both in practice and in the realm of ideology, and the first role as guarantor of welfare was maintained, in no small measure due to increased income from taxing enterprise and consumption.

As far as we can measure, the size of the government in relation to the economy increased throughout the region from the end of colonialism until the mid- to late 1980s, and, on average, fell thereafter. Nepal is an exception, in that the size of its state was small throughout, and began to

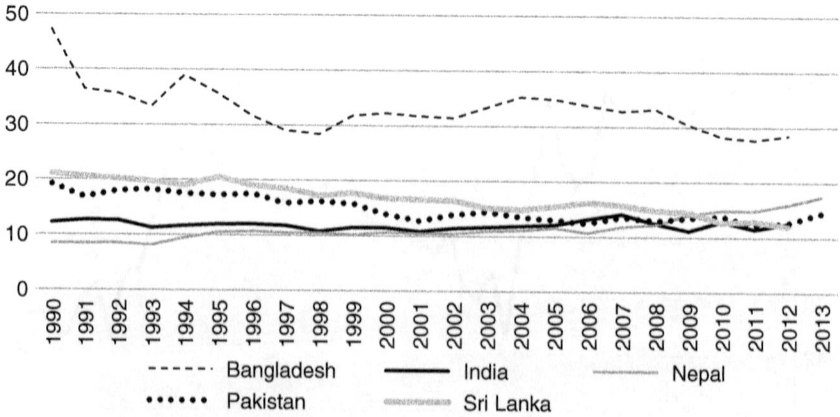

Fig. 5.21 Government revenue to GDP (%)

rise from 1990 (Fig. 5.21). In India, the earlier rise was the bigger one (see Chapter 7). After 1982, government size did not continue to rise as rapidly as before. Nor was there a fall. In Pakistan and Bangladesh, a small increase in government until about 1972 was followed by a steep increase thanks to nationalization of businesses. The subsequent fall was a result of privatization.

Does the size of the state bear any connection with the levels of development and levels of poverty? In principle, if the provision of public goods and welfare are the main influences behind human development and reduction in poverty, we would expect the period when the state grew in size to show an improvement in HDI and fall in poverty, and the years when the government size started to fall show a decline in HDI and rise in poverty. This inference cannot be tested because the data do not stretch sufficiently far backward. Based on the Indian experience of poverty, the relationship goes the other way. Poverty was high and persistent in the 1960s and 1970s when the state expanded, and fell in the more recent years when the size of the state stabilized. The correlation can be seen as evidence that private earnings, not public expenditure, matters more to improvements in HDI and poverty. But the evidence is inferential, relies on the controversial headcount data, and relevant for India alone.

Sri Lanka is perhaps the best candidate to test the relationship between state and development. Sri Lanka was the richer nation to begin with, and spent more money on welfare and development (see Chapter 4). Despite fiscal difficulties in the 1970s brought on by statist-protectionist policies, the government size remained large because of these expenditure commitments. After the statist policy was abandoned in the 1980s, government size first stabilized and then started to fall. Sri Lanka's high achievements in development did not suffer a setback thereafter. Sri Lanka, therefore, seems to confirm the conclusion that more public expenditure is not the only way, nor perhaps the most efficient way, to deliver more development.

Sustainable economic growth needs good institutions, ones that create incentives for people to invest, save, and hire, without having to pay bribes at every step. Where does South Asia stand in the world on institutional quality?

Institutions and Entrepreneurship

Economists sometimes suggest that in the presence of weak institutions that create incentives for rent-seeking, expropriation, and opportunism, economic growth should not happen or should not be sustainable. This is so because '[t]he demand for entrepreneurs is limited by poorly developed institutions (constitutions, law, regulations, enforcement, informal constraints) and poor governance.'[25] A persuasive critique already exists of this position, indeed of the faith that institutions are necessary preconditions for sustained economic growth.[26] South Asia appears as another anomaly for those who believe in the importance of institutions.

[25] E. Wayne Nafziger, 'Entrepreneurship and Development,' in A.K. Dutt and Jaime Ros, eds., *International Handbook of Development Economics*, Volumes 1, Cheltenham: Edward Elgar, 2008, 371–87. Cited text appears in p. 377.

[26] Ha-Joon Chang, *Kicking Away the Ladder: Development Strategy in Historical Perspective*, London: Anthem Press, 2007.

Table 5.3 South Asia against the world on institutional quality and growth performance

	Forbes 'Best Country for Business' rank among 144 countries, 2015	World Bank 'Ease of Doing Business' rank among 189 countries, 2015	GDP growth rate in 2014–2015	
			Actual	Multiple of world
Bangladesh	121	174	6.3	2.1
India	97	130	7.3	2.4
Pakistan	103	138	4.0	1.3
Nepal	118	99	5.4	1.8
Sri Lanka	91	107	7.4	2.5

Note: http://www.forbes.com/best-countries-for-business/list/3/#tab:overall (accessed 5 August 2016). http://www.doingbusiness.org/rankings (accessed 16 August 2016).

If measurable institutional quality is a predictor, the economy of the region should have seen a great deal less growth and entrepreneurship than it in fact did. Table 5.3 shows that South Asia is one of the world's worst places for doing business, measured in institutional quality.[27] The region remains behind the world in such matters as legal regulations for investor protection, contract and intellectual property rights enforcement, and employment laws outside the shrinking organized industrial sector. And yet, the average rate of GDP growth in South Asia is more than double that of the world GDP growth rate in the last 20 years.

Of course, institutional quality does matter to development, and with a better record of performance, South Asia could possibly grow even faster, though there is no way to know. Institutions that allow opportunism, corruption, patronage, and fraud are pervasive in the region and do distort the process of economic change. Still, the anomaly between

[27] The 'best country for business' index reported in the Table is a composite of all of these attributes. It includes measures of Trade Freedom, Monetary Freedom, Property Rights, Innovation, Technology, Red Tape, Investor Protection, Corruption, Personal Freedom, Tax Burden, and Market Performance. Of these benchmarks, on investor protection, India and Pakistan score well (8 and 25, respectively). On all other benchmarks, all countries in South Asia lie nearer the bottom of the world ranking.

institutional quality and growth suggests that we need to be open-minded about what causes growth and what obstructs growth in emerging economies, where institutions and organizations usually change more slowly than market opportunities. The states in charge of legal and other types of reforms sometimes wake up late to discover that unprecedented scale of investment has begun in unexpected fields, causing discords and disputes, before a regulatory or institutional intervention occurs. Think of digital media as an example. If institutions can explain the *origin* of economic growth (the club of countries that experienced origin has only one member, Britain), it does not explain the *emergence* of growth in poorer countries.

Conclusion

South Asia has done well on GDP growth in the last 20 years, and has performed not worse than, perhaps better than the world average on poverty, inequality, and HDI. All five countries are in the process of moving away from dependence on agricultural livelihoods. The Green Revolution slowed that process, but did not reverse it.

Are these countries industrializing, as politicians and economists hoped they would in 1950? They are not, with the partial exception of Bangladesh. Some industries did well no doubt, but overall the recent economic experience of South Asia cannot be called industrialization. The region did not emerge from liberalization as a manufacturing powerhouse in the way China did. Instead, the most dramatic field of change is services. This mixed group includes trade, finance, and migration. The labour-intensive industries, which have been successful in exports, grew for the same reasons that services did. The finding suggests that the major failure of the pre-reform regime was not the choice of industrialization strategy, but trade repression.

Trade will be taken up in Chapter 7. The next two chapters will deal with the most obvious dimension of livelihood change, agriculture, beginning with the land reform experience.

6

Land Reforms

When British colonial rule ended in the region, the new nation states faced a similar set of challenges with agriculture. Land provided livelihood to the majority of the working people. Productivity of land was low and had remained almost unchanged in the previous half a century. Population growth from the 1920s had created the spectre of depressed wages and rising poverty. Even though agriculture was ailing, theories of industrialization required that resources necessary for the process – saving, raw material, food for urban workers – would have to come from agriculture. If, as in India, the industrialization was to be capital-intensive, even more savings would be necessary. There was a contradiction here. How could a poor agriculture support an expensive industrialization? Taxation of the peasants was out of the question. In fact, the tax-income ratio in agriculture had been falling continuously from the late nineteenth century (excluding plantations). In 1947, it was low throughout the region. Was agriculture, then, to be an aid or an obstacle to the development process? How could it be an aid?

A decade into nationhood, the larger countries were in the process of implementing two types of change that would address these issues. The first one was land reform. This would mean one of two things, grant of

T. Roy, *The Economy of South Asia*, Palgrave Studies in Economic History, DOI 10.1007/978-3-319-54720-6_6

security to peasant property right, and redistribution of land from large to small farms. The case for redistribution was based on an observation that small farms tended to be more productive than large farms, so that redistribution should serve two aims at once, improving equity and increasing efficiency. The second type of intervention occurred in the sphere of trade. Export of agricultural goods came to be regulated and was virtually prohibited in India. Given that the region had a comparative advantage in agricultural production, the closure of export in effect depressed prices and gave the urban occupations an implicit subsidy.

Redistributive land reform was not a great success in any of the five countries. In India, scholars see the failure of redistribution as a failure of the political system. Others consider that there was not enough good land to redistribute in the first place. In Pakistan, land reform was caught up in a political contest. In Sri Lanka, the rhetoric of land reform was used to drive out foreign plantation estates. In Bangladesh, redistribution had to face the absurdity that the so-called large farms were too poor themselves. While land reforms did not work as expected, trade repression weakened the peasants' incentive to invest in land.

What was the aim of the programme? Why did it not deliver? Was the fault with the means, or the aim, of the policy? The rest of the chapter will explore these questions, first with country-specific evidence and, in the concluding section, with some comparative lessons.

India

Initial Conditions

In 1947, there were two independent discourses on Indian agriculture. One of these, conducted by academic economists, held that the most important problem of agriculture was slow growth, low productivity, and therefore, increasing poverty. Parts of the Indo-Gangetic Basin, they believed, were desperately land-scarce. In this scenario population growth and extension of cultivation had led to diminishing returns. In the dry rainfed areas, extension prospects were strictly limited in the first place because of water shortage. These experts pointed at the low yield by international comparison, and obstacles to the optimum use of land, such as fragmentation of holdings into separate plots.[1]

A second discourse, conducted within political circles, held that the priority for the new nation state should be to address inequality in landholding. Peasant property right, more than resource endowments or technology, was the problem that needed fixing. Who were the agricultural classes then? They were peasant proprietors in western and southern India and in the Punjab, collective proprietors or kinship groups in the Haryana area, cultivating landlords in northern Pakistan, occupancy tenants (or tenants with secure legal user right) and 'absentee' or city-dwelling landlords in the Bengal delta, and tenants-at-will almost everywhere. From before independence, the political mobilization programme pursued by the Congress tried to bring the peasant-proprietors and tenants to one political platform. Success in this endeavour was more likely when the party defined a common enemy of the peasant, the 'zamindar' or the rentier landlord. The political programme then promised reducing the holdings and the power of the landlords. This strategy would not work so easily in Pakistan. The Muslim League, which had ties with the cultivating landlords, adopted only a diluted version of the programme.

Who were the rentier landlords? India had inherited from the British a property rights system consisting of two types of landowners. In 1793, the East India Company then ruling Bengal conferred secure ownership right to zamindars, a category of rural magnates who had been tax collectors during the pre-British revenue system (see also Chapter 2). Between 1820 and 1840, in southern and western India, ownership titles were handed to peasant cultivators, at least those who could prove continued use of land. Variations of peasant proprietorship were introduced in many regions of India thereafter, an important variant being rights of kinship groups on village land. In the late nineteenth century, tenancy reforms in Bengal conferred occupancy rights to long-held tenancies, pushing a range of other types of tenancies to the status of

[1] Tirthankar Roy, 'Agrarian Crisis in Interwar India: Retrieving a Narrative,' *Economic and Political Weekly*, 41(52), 2007, 5389–5400.

tenants-at-will. Internal committees of the Congress identified 'feudal' relations and 'landlordism' to be the main problem of agriculture, and advocated land reforms in order to redress what was seen as a historic injustice done by the British towards the cultivators. The injustice was that in the zamindari areas, peasant rights were weak by law, and in the proprietary areas, peasant rights were often mortgaged to moneylenders.

These two challenges – protecting the peasant and raising productivity – were often seen as a single problem amenable to one solution. 'What should be the objectives of land policy?' The First Five-Year Plan document asked, and answered that it should contain the following elements: 'increased agricultural output,' and reduced 'disparities,' end of exploitation, and security to tenants. 'The first aspect is the subject of land management legislation, the second of land reform legislation. Land policy should include both elements.'[2] The Plan document did not set out a theoretical relationship between land management and land reform, but left implicit the belief that land management was in poor state because land control was in the hands of rent-seeking 'intermediaries' like the zamindars. The missing link emerged a little later in a scholarship that contended that small farms were more efficient than large farms (Box 6.1).

Land Reforms

The first and dramatically successful move was the abolition of zamindari right (1950). Ironically, the zamindars as a group had been growing poorer for many decades, thanks to their own incompetence as agriculturists and to tenancy regulation introduced in 1859 and tightened in 1885. In 1950, they were a shadow of their eighteenth century glory. With the exception of a few local areas, where the zamindars had already become cultivators and could reassign land in their names, other went down meekly and without protest.

---

[2] India, *First Five Year Plan*, Delhi: Planning Commission, 1953, 88.

Having killed this paper tiger, the Indian states concentrated on two other types of land reforms after 1950. The first type was redistribution of land, or seizure of land above a ceiling from large farmers and giving the seized land to the landless workers, tenants, and small peasants. In 1971, the revised land ceiling in India was 10–18 acres of irrigated land per family, and 54 acres of dry land. The second type consisted of making the property right of the cultivator more secure than before, where the cultivator was a tenant farmer.

In spite of strong sponsorship, the redistribution drive ended in a whimper. Too little land was taken over and redistributed. The overall extent of land redistributed by the state until 1992 did not exceed 1.3 per cent of all operational holdings.[3] The proportion varied from state to state, and it was somewhat higher in states like West Bengal and Kerala, where the radical left movement was strong. These were also states with high population pressure on land, so that beneficiaries got tiny entitlements. Adjusted for the quality of land, the proportion of redistributed land was even smaller, for the landlords gave up their worse lands.[4] In numerous cases, redistribution was obstructed and defeated by landholders by illegal and clandestine means, such as transfer of title to relatives. The legal obstacles in the way of land redistribution were considerable, because property rights were poorly recorded and regionally variable. In short, institutional obstacles to enforcement were formidable. Wolf Ladejinsky, an international expert on land reforms who made a significant contribution to the land reform programmes in Taiwan and Japan, and who more or less gave up on the reforms in India, voiced his frustration in a series of writings that focused on these enforcement failures.[5]

It was not all enforcement failure, however. There was another big obstacle to land reforms, one related to resources. Where was there land

[3] P.S. Appu, *Land Reforms in India: A Survey of Policy Legislation and Implementation*, New Delhi: Vikas Publishing House, 1996.

[4] Pranab Bardhan and Dilip Mookherjee, 'Subsidized Farm Input Programs and Agricultural Performance: A Farm-Level Analysis of West Bengal's Green Revolution, 1982–1995,' *American Economic Journal: Applied Economics*, 3(4), 2011, 186–214.

[5] Wolf Ladejinsky, 'Agrarian Reform in Asia,' *Foreign Affairs*, 42(3), 1964 445–460.

to redistribute? A committee headed by the economist Raj Krishna estimated that government reports tended to be overoptimistic about the extent of surplus that was available. The correct figure was between 4 and 5 million acres of landholding, the quantity that could be taken away from the so-called large farmers under ceiling laws. Small farming households – those owning 2.5 acres of land or less on average – numbered well over 40 million in 1960.[6] The number would be much higher if the so-called middle peasants – farmers who managed to earn a living in good seasons, but faced severe stress during bad seasons – were included among claimants to redistributed land.

State-level data showed a similarly depressing picture.[7] The small quantity of surplus indicated that few farms had land above the legal ceiling anywhere, and that the so-called large farms were large only in the imagination of economists. Inequality in landholding tended to be high everywhere (see below), but even farms in the highest brackets made ends meet with considerable difficulty. Simple arithmetic showed that redistribution would weaken the larger farms without benefiting the smaller ones.[8] Furthermore, it was not at all clear that redistribution of land to smallholders was the answer to low and stagnant productivity.

Another intervention would involve making user rights more secure. Indeed, this type of reform had a more successful career than did redistribution. The critics of zamindari tenure knew for a long time that the zamindari system made the tenant unwilling and unable to improve land. In the 1970s, a further argument was developed by economists to show why *the landlord* might not want to invest in improving land. A theory of the rural economy pictured a landlord as one who hired tenants on fixed share and supplied credit and other

[6] India, *Report of the Committee on Land Reforms*, New Delhi: Government Press, 1978.

[7] For example, in Tamil Nadu in 1970, The Land Revenue Reforms Committee estimated that 1.25 million acres was 'surplus' or potentially available for takeover and redistribution. At the same time, 14.7 million people or roughly 3.7 million families were either landless or in possession of plots of land that left them wage dependent. S.A. Kosalram, 'Political Economy of Agriculture in Tamil Nadu,' *Social Scientist*, 1(12), 1973, 3–21.

[8] That redistribution was an unattainable dream all along is demonstrated in more recent popular discourse on land reforms that advocate reduction in the ceiling to unrealistically low levels so as to make land reform work.

inputs to them, thus earning both rent and interest from the transaction. The theory then claimed that a fixed-share tenancy reduced the landlord's incentive to invest, because the improvement could make the tenant less dependent on loans. A different view on tenancy argued that if innovations were profitable, the landlord would eliminate the tenants, consolidate plots of land, and become a capitalist farmer instead.[9] Whether or not the landlord would invest and innovate depended also on the type of innovation in question. Some forms of technology, such as tractors or harvesters, carry economies of scale and might encourage consolidation and owner-cultivation. Others, such as biological innovations like new seeds, do not necessarily carry economies of scale and might not lead to elimination of the tenant.

If tenancy was inequality inducing as well as bad for economic growth, there was a strong case to regulate or outlaw tenancy. Many states did take that road, but enforcement of tenancy regulation again was generally slack.

Crisis in Agriculture

With institutional intervention not amounting to much, agricultural growth remained tied to growth in area rather than growth in productivity in the first two decades after independence. By an identity, the increase in production between any 2 years is a product of change in area of cultivation and change in productivity. For the major agricultural regions in India that we have data for, the first decade after independence (1950–1960) saw an increase in production driven by growth in area under cultivation, and the subsequent 7 years (1960–1966) saw a slowdown in production because growth in area slowed down. Throughout, productivity growth played a relatively small role in driving production.

[9] A useful survey of the debate can be found in Alice Thorner, 'Semi-Feudalism or Capitalism? Contemporary Debate on Classes and Modes of Production in India,' *Economic and Political Weekly*, 17(49–51), 1982. A spinoff of the tenancy debate was a theory that the large farmer exploited the small by interlocking land, commodity, and credit markets.

During 1950–1965, agricultural production had grown at an average rate of 3.1 per cent per year, nearly half of that growth coming from expansion in area under cultivation. The picture varied somewhat between regions. Everywhere, the basic elements remained the same – growth was land-using, productivity changed little, population grew rapidly, and expansion in the 1950s led to a slowdown in the 1960s.[10]

The pattern was quite similar to the pattern of agricultural change in the colonial period. Agricultural growth was *land-using* rather than *land-saving* throughout. Land-using growth was usually driven by state irrigation investment. The postcolonial state gave an impetus to canal irrigation just as the colonial state had done between 1880 and 1910. In both times, the focus of the intervention fell in areas with perennial rivers, mainly the Indo-Gangetic Basin. Population growth ensured that real wages of agricultural labourers and agricultural earning rose little in 1950–1960, and in some regions fell in 1960–1970.

There is some evidence that inequality in landholding increased in these years, though the extent of the increase was small.[11] A small set of cultivating landowners were wealthy, not necessarily because they owned vast quantities of land, but they owned non-land capital such as irrigation wells and implements, most peasants experienced a fall or a stagnation in average landholding and increasing wage dependence in the

[10] A government report on Tamil Nadu showed that the area under food-grains increased at the annual average rate of 2.3 per cent in the 1950s and 0.2 per cent in the 1960s, production at the rates of 5.3 and 2.7 per cent respectively, and productivity at 3 per cent in the 1950s. Madras, *The Perspective Plan for Tamil Nadu: Towards A Greener Revolution, Report of the Task Force on Agriculture, 1972–1984*, Vols I and II, Madras: State Planning Commission, 1972, and Kosalram, 'Political Economy.' The 1960s average productivity growth was not reported, but in individual crops, and especially in the commonly consumed millets such as cholam and cumbu, there was a fall in the 1960s. The West Bengal picture was bleaker. In the 1960s, the area under cultivation of rice increased at the compound growth rate of 0.6 per cent per year, whereas the growth rates for production and productivity were negative. K.M.B. Rahim, D. Majumder and R.K. Biswas, 'Determinants of Stagnation in Productivity of Important Crops in West Bengal,' Santiniketan: Agro-Economic Research Centre Visva-Bharati, 2011. In the same decade, population growth rate in the state exceeded 3 per cent per year, and an industrial stagnation had set in. The state was ready for an outbreak of political violence, which occurred both in the cities and the impoverished rural areas around the turn of the 1970s.

[11] H.R. Sharma, 'Distribution of Landholdings in Rural India, 1953–1954 to 1981–1982: Implications for Land Reforms,' *Economic and Political Weekly*, 29(13), 1994, A12–A25.

1960s. Some leftist economists thought this was classic 'polarization' as the rich grabbed more land pushing the middle peasants to join the proletariat. Measures of inequality in landholding do not bear this out. More likely, with population growth, the middle peasants felt pressure because they had to share little land, and low-quality land, among larger numbers. The rich were not getting richer, but the middle was getting poorer.

India faced famine in 1965. When the mid-1960s harvest failure occurred, it was clear to some people in the government that institutional intervention did not deliver. New varieties of the wheat plant that yielded a larger output under suitable applications of water and fertilizers became available for wider use in 1965–1966. These were introduced in India by a group of officials, with the help of the Ford Foundation, and state-level agricultural extension workers. Before the economists noticed what was happening, the Green Revolution was on its way (Chapter 7).

But this was a wheat phenomenon. What about paddy-growing regions?

Tenancy Reform in West Bengal

The appeal of land reforms never totally receded among academic economists. Even during the heyday of the Green Revolution the dominant discourse on transforming traditional agriculture was a Marxist one. It was Marxist in two senses. First, it was particularly interested in the distribution of land, and interested in the so-called polarization of peasants into landed and landless classes. And second, it weighed the possibilities of mobilizing small peasants, tenants, and agricultural workers into a political movement, even a revolutionary one. The Marxist analysis of Indian agriculture has been summed up into three key propositions.[12] First, 'Indian agriculture [is] largely

[12] Venkatesh B. Athreya, Goran Djurfeldt, and Staffan Lindberg, *Barriers Broken: Production Relations and Agrarian Change in Tamil Nadu*, New Delhi: Sage, 1990. I have found the review essay by Murray J. Leaf, 'Indian Agriculture and Agrarian Communities: Two Studies,' *Economic Development and Cultural Change*, 42(3), 1994, 647–653, helpful.

stagnating due to a paralyzing grip of landlordism and merchant/usurious capital.' Second, the state worked for 'the preservation of the existing relations of production.'[13] And third, technological change like the Green Revolution favoured the rich and deprived the poor, making the distribution of land and income more unequal, and increasing the political power of the landlords and creditors.

Although redistributive land reform had failed, the sentiment against 'landlordism' supplied a broad justification for empowering the tenant farmers. One way to do that was to convert tenant rights into an effective ownership right, at least a shared ownership right. This prescription was in fact adopted in West Bengal in the late 1970s as we shall see. In most states, tenancy was outlawed or regulated, with laws and enforcement procedures that were at best half-hearted.

By and large, like redistribution, tenancy also receded from public discourse in the 1980s. One of the factors that made it obsolete was the Green Revolution in Punjab, which gave rise to a category of tenants that the economists participating in this debate had not foreseen and found it hard to explain with the help of Marxist categories. Large landlords began to lease in land from smaller landlords. 'With the introduction of new technology, "old" landless and small owner tenants are giving way to the relatively better placed "new" tenants.'[14] This tendency did not make the theoretical insights on tenancy obsolete, but revealed a differentiation among tenants, and among landlords, which contemporary theory was unable to handle.

The only significant field of tenancy reform occurred in West Bengal. When the Communist Party of India (Marxist) formed a government in the state in 1977, it quickly set in motion laws to secure the rights of more than a million tenants, a move that saw nearly 8 per cent of operated area vested in the state and redistributed to the new title holders. Known as the Operation Barga, and possibly the most radical institutional reform in agriculture in independent

---

[13] Athreya, Djurfledt, Lindberg, *Barriers Broken*, 313–4.

[14] Iqbal Singh, 'Reverse Tenancy in Punjab Agriculture: Impact of Technological Change,' *Economic and Political Weekly*, 24(25), 1989, A86–A92.

India, this step was later seen as a necessary precondition for wage increase and poverty reduction, and increased private investment as well.[15]

Such claims are doubtful and hard to test, because the Operation Barga occurred at the same time that dwarf rice varieties capable of high yields with suitable application of water and fertilizer came into usage in Eastern India. Security of property might have been important. It is impossible to dismiss the counterfactual that status quo in property rights would deliver the same outcome by encouraging landlords to take advantage of the new technology, and what was crucial in Bengal, invest in tube wells in order to do so. If one set of economists insist that radical land reform made the most difference, another set claims 'that the emergence of the private groundwater irrigation has been instrumental in the agricultural growth of West Bengal.'[16]

Box 6.1 The farm size and productivity debate

In a 1962 article, Amartya Sen observed that there was a negative association between farm size and land productivity. If robust, the finding would justify redistributive land reform. Redistribution would then be the solution to two problems at once – inequality and stagnation. The finding was read to mean that the small farms applied labour more intensively, because labour service was supplied by the family and was not priced. The finding confirmed a prediction of the Russian economist A.V. Chayanov that, under certain conditions, the family farm would employ labour more intensively than the capitalist farm. Sociological studies of the village also occasionally drew similar conclusions (e.g., Joan Mencher on Tamil Nadu).

[15] T. Besley and R. Burgess, 'Land Reform, Poverty Reduction, and Growth: Evidence from India,' *Quarterly Journal of Economics*, 115(2), 2000, 389–430; A. Banerjee, P. Gertler and M. Ghatak, 'Empowerment and Efficiency: Tenancy Reform in West Bengal,' *Journal of Political Economy*, 110, 2002, 239–80.

[16] Bhaswar Moitra and Pranab Kumar Das, 'Private investment in groundwater irrigation: Do the public institutions matter?' paper for South Asia Network for Economic Research Institutions, 2006.

Later, disagreements emerged on the interpretation of the negative relationship. An early test using village data concluded that 'there may be many reasons to expect some sort of an association, but none whatsoever for any linear relation' (Ashok Rudra). After the Green Revolution, the inverse relationship was tested with better statistical methodology. Some studies found that the strength of the association depended on soil quality, the larger farms contained a bigger share of poorer and variable grades of soil, and that an earlier inverse relationship tended to disappear in some of the Green Revolution regions. In Punjab, the inverse relation held in two of four agro-ecological regions in the mid-1980s, whereas in one of the four regions, an initial inverse relation turned into a positive one. In short, Green Revolution created economies of scale that were not present before. The larger farms had more diversified cropping pattern than the smaller subsistence-oriented and mainly grain-producing farms, which made comparisons between them more difficult. Sen, in a restatement written with one of his critics Rudra, stressed the importance of non-labour inputs.

In 2011, Chand et al. conclude that '[a]dvances in technology and the scale factor in production did not dilute the superior performance of lower size holdings.' However, opposite conclusions were also drawn in some surveys, and with historical data, leading to the idea that capital market imperfections allowed the larger farms to access more inputs and apply more inputs per acre especially during technological transformation. Long before this date, the use of the inverse relation in advocacy of redistribution had ceased.

Readings: Ramesh Chand, P.A. Lakshmi Prasanna, Aruna Singh, 'Farm Size and Productivity: Understanding the Strengths of Smallholders and Improving their Livelihoods,' *Economic and Political Weekly*, 46(26–27), 2011, 5–11; G.D. Dyer, 'Farm Size and Productivity: A New Look at the Old Debate Revisited,' *Economic and Political Weekly*, 33(26), 1998, A113–116; A.V. Swamy, 'Factor Markets and Resource Allocation in Colonial Punjab,' *Journal of Development Studies*, 34(3), 1998, 97–115; Amartya Sen, 'An Aspect of Indian Agriculture,' *The Economic Weekly*, 1962, 243–46; G.K. Chadha, *The State and Rural Economic Transformation: The Case of Punjab, 1950–85*, New Delhi: Sage Publications, 1986; Ashok Rudra, 'Farm Size and Yield per Acre,' *Economic and Political Weekly*, 3(26/28), 1968, 1041–44; Ashok Rudra and Amartya Sen, 'Farm Size and Labour Use: Analysis and Policy,' *Economic and Political Weekly*, 15(5/7), 1980, 391–394; Joan P. Mencher, *Agriculture and Social Structure in Tamil Nadu: Past Origins, Present Trans formations and Future Prospects*, Durham, N.C.: Carolina Academic Press, 1978.

Pakistan

Two quite distinct types of agricultural property rights existed in Pakistan in 1947. Huge areas in Punjab and Sind provinces, extending into the large princely state of Bahawalpur, contained irrigated agricultural land that produced valuable commercial crops in 1947. The farms were large by Indian standards. The proprietors who owned them were called landlords, especially when they cultivated with tenant farmers, as in Sind. They were not 'absentees' like the Bengali zamindars. There were also many freeholder peasants.

In the North West Frontier Province in Pakistan, landholding pattern differed from the Punjab and Sind plains. Under the tribal land law, which prevailed here, private property was recognized but not the right of the owners to sell land. The superstructure of local property right consisted of communal rights to a territory, so that sale of the local right contradicted the legal right of tribes to settle and rule a territory. The expansion of imperial states such as the Mughal Empire and the unified Sikh state, and attempts to create a revenue system by co-opting the clan leaders did intensify hierarchy but did not lead towards alienable property right. The dependence of these states, which formed of outsiders, on the local clan chiefs was too great for the revenue system to impart any deep effect.[17]

The British Raj was interested in establishing alienable property rights. This was an easy matter in the Punjab canal colonies where property rights were created from scratch, and in Sind, where landlords cultivated their estates with tenant farmers. Elsewhere, such as the North West Frontier Province, they found land ownership and land use rights too mixed up for alienable ownership to be defined. In these regions, they nominally recognized alienable property of the tax collecting landlords. Many landlords were absentees in their estates. The British also legally recognized the force of custom and joint rights, so that in effect peasant rights remained a user right and not one easily saleable. From

[17] Feroz Ahmed, 'Transformation of Agrarian Structure in the North-West Frontier Province of Pakistan,' *Journal of Contemporary Asia*, 14(1), 1984, 5–47.

time to time tenancy reforms tried to convert tenants into owners of the plots of land that they cultivated, without significant effect.

Land Reform

Like in India in the 1950s, in Pakistan too, one of the tenets of the new development policy was that 'the replacement of the unproductive landed gentry by a landowning class actively interested in farming appeared to be one of the most important pre-conditions for agricultural progress.'[18] As in India, the precise causal connection between institutional reform and agricultural growth was left undefined. The political will to implement a ceiling law, however, was weaker in Pakistan. Although land reform was made a point of discussion in the Muslim League's Agrarian Committee, formed in the same year (1949) as its Congress counterpart, the Agrarian Reforms Committee, the large landholders were too powerful within the party for a radical programme to emerge. In Gunnar Myrdal's words, 'the upper class status of those who stepped into power . . . weighted heavily towards the landlord class.'[19]

Some analysts, including Myrdal, believed that compared to the Parliamentary rule in the early days of Pakistan, the military dictatorship under Mohammad Ayub Khan (1958–1969) was less beholden to landlords. The characterization may apply to military regimes of Pakistan in general. A land reform programme did start in 1959, though it was of a different kind from the Indian counterpart. First of all, in keeping with much higher land-person ratio in West Pakistan, the ceiling was set many times higher than the ceiling in India. In 1971, the revised land ceiling in India was 10–18 acres of irrigated land per family, and 54 acres of dry land. In Pakistan, the 1959 ceiling was 500 acres of irrigated and 1000 acres of dry lands per person. In principle, a family could retain greater quantities of land than these limits. Further, the application of

[18] P.C. Joshi, 'Land Reform and Agrarian Change in India and Pakistan since 1947,' *Journal of Peasant Studies*, 1(2), 1973, 164–185

[19] Gunnar Myrdal, *Asian Drama*, vol. 1 of 3 vols., London: Allen Lane, 1968, p. 311.

the ceiling was made dependent on the value of the productive capacity of land measured in Produce Index Units, which encouraged under-reporting of land yield. In the end, the quantity of land taken over by the government did not amount to much, 1.9 million acres, or 6 per cent of the 28–30 million acres of cultivated land area.

It was also clear that the state was less concerned than the state in India about the quantity of land held. The focus of the legislation instead was on regulating the relationship between the landlord and the tenant, since tenancy was much more extensive in West Pakistan and some of the tenants were magnates in their own right. The ideological elevation of the owner-cultivator that one would encounter in India was missing in West Pakistan. This difference left tenancy a more open, more visible, and more contractual system in Pakistan than it was in India. It also meant that it was easier for the Pakistani owner-landlord to move money from land into industry and services, join politics, become an 'absentee,' and remain an absentee, without drawing adverse attention from the economists.

The second land reform introduced in 1972 during Zulfikar Ali Bhutto's rule was of a different order. Although Bhutto himself was a landowner, his regime tried to be harsher on the landlord, consistent with its socialist leaning. The ceilings were reduced to 150 acres of irrigated land and 300 acres of dry land. A bonus holding, however, was allowed based on the Produce Index Units to owners of tractors or tube wells. Since the productivity was based on a 1940s estimate, the bonus was inflated, leaving the actual effective ceilings at 466 and 560 acres respectively, which could again be bypassed by misreporting ownership. The 0.6 million acres the government could get hold of in 1972 made even less of a difference than the reforms of 1959.[20]

Already by then, the Green Revolution had begun and landlords with medium-sized holdings started resuming cultivation from tenants on an extensive scale. One of the classic arguments for land reforms that the landlords were not entrepreneurial enough because they earned easy money from rent no longer had much force. The pattern of inequality

[20] Akmal Hussain, 'Pakistan: Land Reforms Reconsidered,' in Hamza Alavi and John Harriss., ed., *South Asia*, London: Macmillan, 1989.

in landholding changed. There is some evidence, though the evidence may be hard to read because of evasion of ceiling laws, that inequality declined in the 1960s. On the other hand, between 1972 and 1980, notwithstanding a more radical land reform, inequality increased, and there emerged a 'positive relationship between agricultural development and inequalities.' The relationship was mediated by access to water, especially canal water, which favoured the larger farms and was a pre-condition for the adoption of high-yielding seeds.[21]

Incidentally, tests of the farm size and productivity relationship posed a bigger problem for Pakistan than in India. The larger farms of Pakistan were really large, sufficiently so to be differentiated in soil quality and irrigation ratio. A simple aggregation of all land would not make any sense in that case. Building on this difficulty, one contribution to the debate made the important point that the standard practice of defining large and small farms with reference to the extent of land they owned rather than the water resources they could command carried little meaning when so much of the production possibility depended on water.[22] The farm size and productivity debate was measuring the wrong variable.

Bangladesh

In 1947, the then East Pakistan, the largest delta in the world, was at the limits of expansion in cultivation. It was also one of the most densely populated parts of South Asia. For decades, a Malthusian scenario was a very real prospect here. Agricultural output per worker had fallen in the first half of the twentieth century, and a famine in 1943 carried off a section of the rural poor already made vulnerable by increasing poverty. What was to be the solution? The West Pakistan experience had little relevance in East Pakistan.

[21] Muhammad Sarfraz Anwer and Rajan K. Sampath, 'Inequalities in Land Distribution In Pakistan,' *Pakistan Economic And Social Review*, 34(2), 1996, 119–143.

[22] Waqar A. Jehangir and Rajan K. Sampath, 'Farm Size and Land Use Efficiency in Pakistan's Agriculture,' *Pakistan Development Review*, 30(3), 1991, 263–274.

In 1940, the Bengal Land Revenue Commission, popularly known as the Floud Commission after its Chairman Francis Floud, estimated that half of the agricultural families in the eastern delta possessed less than 2 acres of land and 23 per cent possessed land over 5 acres. The Floud Commission recommended that the zamindars be abolished, a suggestion for which it became famous. This was the easiest thing to do. The zamindars were already impoverished, as we have seen. They suffered from the long-term decline in output-per-worker along with their tenants. Beyond this cosmetic step, not much more was done until 1971 either in the sphere of institutional reform or the technological one.

In 1971, when Bangladesh was born, there were 1000 persons per square mile, population was growing at the rate of 3 per cent per year, and the land-per-person ratio was a mere half an acre. The interfluvial districts had fertile soil and plenty of groundwater, and recorded some of the highest paddy yields in the world. Paddy cultivation was monsoon dependent, and faced a great threat from floods during the monsoon. A diversification in the crop mix could in principle improve both food security and output per worker. But the technological options either to improve crop choice or mitigate flood risk were limited. In the 1950s, the major thrust of state intervention was flood control, with spill-over benefits in the form of water diversion into irrigation schemes. The expected effects on cropping pattern of the large gravity irrigation schemes were uncertain. When irrigation development did accelerate, in the 1970s, the canals turned out to be a less important asset than newly constructed private tube wells.

Soon after 1971, land reform re-entered the development discourse of independent Bangladesh. The case for land reforms rested, as elsewhere, on the assumption that small farms were more productive than large farms. Research studies that replicated the methods followed in the Indian studies found the relationship to hold.[23] Recent studies on the size-productivity relationship also confirm the negative relationship, while

[23] M.A. Taslim, 'Redistributive Land and Tenancy Reform in Bangladesh Agriculture,' *Journal of Developing Areas*, 27(3), 1993, 341–376.

explaining it with reference to supervision costs. The wage-labour-dependent larger farms, in this view, faced tighter labour markets and higher supervision costs compared with the more numerous family farms.[24]

Notwithstanding such endorsement, calculations based on alternative ceilings showed that a redistributive land reforms would be an absurdity given the farm-size distribution in this region, an exercise that would be expensive in information needs and in the end 'cannot meet the requirements of any more than a tiny proportion of the farming population.'[25] Although ceiling laws did exist, they were not seriously applied, because there was no sensible way to do so. Bangladesh' demography defeated land reforms.

The case for land reform also depended upon the condition of legal insecurity faced by the large group of tenants-at-will. The controversial crop-share arrangement that later led to the Operation Barga in West Bengal was controversial in Bangladesh too. Still, studies done later would not agree on whether or not tenants and owners, secure tenancy and insecure tenancy, made for any difference in efficiency.[26] The dire picture of crop-share tenancy drawn by proponents of land reforms appeared either missing or irrelevant in Bangladesh, even though most contracts were of this type here. Before economists could come to one mind on this, the Green Revolution began, and all cultivators irrespective of institutional arrangement seemed to jump in. Surveys done in the 1980s revealed that the Green Revolution activated the lease market, to such an extent that ownership mattered little to production decisions.

Why did land reforms fail in Bangladesh? Although the size-productivity relationship was expectedly negative, the finding made little sense, because the large farms were themselves small. Further, here as elsewhere, productivity had more to do with ecology and water than with size.[27]

[24] Kazi Ali Toufique, 'Farm Size and Productivity in Bangladesh Agriculture: Role of Transaction Costs in Rural Labour Markets,' *Economic and Political Weekly*, 40(10), 2005, 988–992.

[25] Taslim, 'Redistributive Land and Tenancy Reform.'

[26] Ibid.

[27] Mushtaq Husain Khan, 'Power, Property Rights and the Issue of Land Reform: A General Case Illustrated with Reference to Bangladesh,' *Journal of Agrarian Change*, 4(1–2), 2004, 73–106.

Sri Lanka

As in the rest of South Asia, in Sri Lanka, the boundary between a high rainfall zone and a semi-arid dry zone is quite marked. The high rainfall wet zone consists of south-western coastal areas and the mountains, with different cropping pattern between them. The dry zone occurs in the southeast, east, and north. The wet zone gets annual rainfall above 250 cm, the dry zone rainfall ranges in 120–190 cm. The limited extent of land suitable for rice cultivation has always been a challenge for the Sri Lankan state, and led, in the 1920s, to the establishment of a research station that collected information on the dry zones. The push to expand rice cultivation in the dry zone was a policy driven both by necessity, and as we have seen in Chapter 4, by emotion. A serious effort, however, materialized only in the 1970s.

Sri Lanka had two types of property regimes in land, peasants and plantations. Although rice cultivation provided livelihood and subsistence to the peasants, and later emerged as a nationalist symbol, it was the European plantation system in the mountains that led capitalism in modern Sri Lanka. Soon after independence, the nationalist government set out to reduce the role of foreign capital in the economy. In this endeavour it adopted much the same strategy as the Indians did. Formally, the government kept the door open to foreign investment. In practice, it applied a heavy squeeze on the foreign firms through taxation, and restrictions on repatriation of profits. The threat of nationalization was always present, though outright nationalization did not happen until 1975. On the other hand, future extension of plantation area was to happen under the leadership of the State Plantation Corporation, established in 1957. Since foreign capital was engaged in plantation activities, the squeeze led to a process of 'Ceylonization' of land and estate ownership. Between 1948 and 1972, the percentage of land held by foreign companies fell from 69 to 30 in tea, from 38 to 13 in rubber, and 11 to 4 per cent in coconut.

Thereafter, nationalization of plantation land was introduced through the backdoor via a land reform programme. Although the argument for land reforms had been made from at least the 1920s, the discourse was often mixed up with the ethnic nationalist agenda. When Sri Lanka Freedom Party won the 1956 elections, land reform was back on the table. The Paddy Lands Act of 1958 provided security of tenure to tenant farmers in paddy lands and reduced the crop-share going to the landlords. A cheap credit scheme was introduced in 1967, a price support scheme in 1974, and a crop insurance scheme implemented around 1970.[28] In 1972, Sri Lanka embarked on a more radical land reform, including the acquisition of land above ceiling and its redistribution to small-holders. The ceilings were set at 25 acres in the case of paddy land and 50 acres in the case of other agricultural land. The ceilings applied to tenants and lessors too. Within 2 years, the ceilings were extended to company-held land, that is, the estates, thus forcing the companies either to leave or to fragment and sell estate land.

If the land reforms in India and Pakistan had yielded too little land for redistribution, in Sri Lanka there was dramatic success. The extent of acquired land in 1972 was half a million acres, which amounted to 10–12 per cent of total cultivated land area. In a second wave that occurred after 1975, a further 10 per cent of area was acquired.[29] The percentage acquired (20–22 of cultivated land area) was well above that in the mainland. The difference was due to the fact that the land acquired came from plantation estates. Almost no paddy land was touched. Sixty per cent of tea estate land, 30 per cent of rubber, and 10 per cent of coconut plantation area were taken over. The land reform became a success by attacking a soft target, foreign corporates. Some of the plantation land was thereafter owned and managed by the state, or leased out. In 1975, all company-owned plantations had been brought under direct state control. Apart from state ownership and management, the policy also favoured the formation of cooperatives.

In effect, the land reforms were trying to force an end to the supposed dualism between subsistence agriculture and capitalistic agriculture, or

---

[28] H.M. Gamini Herath, 'The Green Revolution in Rice: The Role of the Risk Factor with Special Reference to Sri Lanka,' *Asian Survey*, 21(6), 1981, 664–675.

[29] G.H. Peiris, 'Land Reform and Agrarian Change in Sri Lanka,' *Modern Asian Studies*, 12(4), 1978, 611–628.

the distance between the small-holding paddy growing peasants and the European plantations. Being confined to the non-rice and plantation land, the reform had unintended effects. If one of the expected aims of such programme was to strengthen the property right of the actual tiller, the Sri Lankan programme implied 'an unprecedented erosion of private property rights in agricultural land.'[30] It did not help the subsistence sector much, but it did weaken the foundations of capitalist agriculture, which had until then been the bread and butter of public welfare and private investment.

It is not clear if the inverse relationship between farm size and productivity, which influenced opinion in India and Bangladesh in favour of redistributive land reforms, had any role behind this disaster. It is known that along with pressures coming in from the leftist parties, the opinion of the Inter-Agency Mission of the International Labour Organization led by Dudley Seers influenced decisions. Other left-leaning British economists also joined the advocacy for land reforms in Sri Lanka.[31] Within the Sri Lankan land administration, a reaction against subdivision was present. There was support for the view that subdivision of estate land would reduce productivity. This was exactly what happened. With the sale of estates, landholdings tended to divide up into smaller fragments. 'An outcome of this transfer of control from sterling companies to Ceylonese ownership has often been a fall in their agricultural condition and output per acre.'[32] Throughout the 1970s, there was 'marked lowering of output in the major plantation industries.'[33] The land reforms killed the capacity of the most profitable economic activity to provide finance for development.

The redistributive land reforms were distortionary at two other levels. First, the decline of the capitalist plantation system reduced the prospect of the emergence of a wage-employed worker elite in independent Sri

---

[30] N. Sanderatne, cited by Vijaya Samaraweera, 'Land Reform in Sri Lanka,' *Third World Legal Studies*, 1982, 104–22.

[31] Samaraweera, 'Land Reform.'

[32] N. Ramachandran, *Foreign Plantation Investment in Ceylon 1889–1958*, Colombo: Central Bank of Ceylon, 1963, 169.

[33] Peiris, 'Land Reform.'

Lanka. The fact that the majority of these workers were Tamil migrants did little to salve the feeling of alienation among these people. On the other hand, the redistributive agenda was carried out in a manner so that 'the Indian-origin workers have been discriminated against in an undisguised fashion.'[34] The land reform hurt livelihoods while it did not recognize the right to compensation of those it was hurting. Secondly, the redistribution did not make much difference to the paddy growing peasants. Hardly 12 per cent of the acquired land was handed over to the peasants.

Nepal

Depending on altitude and agricultural prospects, the agro-ecological regions in Nepal can be classified into three general types, the Himalayan or Alpine, the Hills, and the Terai. The high altitude areas cannot sustain intensive cultivation. Livelihoods here combine some cereals with livestock rearing and transhumanism. The hills that dominate the landscape of the country contain extensive terrace cultivation. Much of this is monsoon dependent. The Hills also contain large water-deficit regions that sustain dryland agriculture. The Terai, being an extension of the Gangetic floodplains, contained well-irrigated land of sufficient extent to sustain rice cultivation. The Terai was forested until the early twentieth century, when forests began to be cleared for cultivation. Control of malaria helped the process.

Research done by Japanese scientists in Nepal in the 1970s produced a fourfold classification of agricultural regimes that corresponded to the altitude-based geographical zones – these were, going from low to high altitude, paddy dominant zone, maize-millet and paddy zone with or without tropical plants, maize and wheat zone, and potato and bitter buckwheat zone.[35] In the 1970s, when the Japanese agronomists did

[34] Samaraweera, 'Land Reform.'

[35] Yoshikazu Takaya and Yoshikazu Itoh, 'Vertical Zoning of Monsoon Asia by Agricultural Landuse: A Progress Report,' *South East Asian Studies,* 14(1), 1976, 99–122.

their survey, they found the higher altitudes overpopulated, running out of grazing and common lands, at the limits of their potential, and experiencing emigration. This regime has not changed much since the surveys were first done, except that irrigated high-yielding rice established itself in the Terai and the mid-Hills from the late 1970s.

Demographic and legal changes made competition for agricultural land fierce from the end of the nineteenth century. In the process, several ethnic minority groups of Tibeto-Burmese origin lost access to land to Hindu settlers. To reverse this process, land reform laws were introduced in 1964 and 1968, with a redistribution component added, as elsewhere in the region. The 1964 Lands Act abolished the intermediary tax collecting landlords who had so far controlled land in the lowlands, introduced a ceiling (of 8 acres) on landholding and introduced a redistribution scheme. Enforcement was weak, partly because of legal ambiguity as in India, and partly because the centre governed the regions with a light touch. 'The vast majority of landlords in Nepal have taken advantage of the loopholes in land reform legislation to retain ownership over all their original property.'[36] Further, the king was dependent on the local power that the landlords exercised. Therefore, the local magnates retained considerable control on land. Because of this failure, members of the ethnic minority groups were inclined to leave Nepal for India. In effect, the land reforms ended in no more than a 'rhetoric.'[37]

This was not surprising, nor a measure of failure. Of all the South Asian regions, Nepal was the most severely land scarce. In Bangladesh, scarcity stemmed from population pressure on land, in Nepal from the generally poor quality of land. Despite the presence of landlords, holdings were on average small. There are no reliable measures of the arable area in Nepal, but assuming about 20 per cent of the area (current proportion) or 2.94 million hectares are cultivable, the actual land area transferred – 22,000 hectares – was less than 1 per cent of the arable land. '[A]gricultural land,' a comparative study of Philippines and Nepal

---

[36] Thomas Cox, 'Land Rights and Ethnic Conflict in Nepal,' *Economic and Political Weekly*, 25(24/25), 1990, 1318–1320.

[37] Fraser Sugden, 'Pre-capitalist Reproduction on the Nepal Tarai: Semifeudal Agriculture in an Era of Globalisation,' *Journal of Contemporary Asia*, 43(3), 2013, 519–545.

states, 'is already fragmented into uneconomic parcels and overused. Thus, the problem of poverty is one of an aggregate shortage of resources rather than their redistribution . . . [In the Terai] more than half of holdings are now less than one hectare in size, and 45% are less than half a hectare . . . In the hills, 73% of holdings are less than a hectare, with 54% less than half a hectare in size. Nepal's very small farms cannot provide even a poverty line income for the majority of rural families.'[38]

The failure of land reforms in Nepal, no matter the source, contributed to insurgency in a direct fashion. The restored monarchy instituted some measure of decentralization. Notwithstanding panchayat rule, land distribution remained unequal in 1990, minority ethnic groups were disproportionately deprived of landholding and overrepresented among agricultural labourers, and indebtedness reinforced the effects of unequal land control. Over 20 years of steady migration of landless people from the hills to the Terai had turned competition for land fiercer, and Terai into a 'battle zone.' 'Caught in the middle of this tug-of-war between migrant peasants and the state are the Tarai's common lands and forests.'[39] Together with the fact that Nepal's population was dependent on agriculture, the situation was fraught with the risk of political collapse, or 'authoritarian recidivism.'[40] The rise of the Communist Party, Marxist, in the early 1990s owed to the attraction of 'land to the tiller' agenda. The electoral process was so dependent on elite power that the mainstream parties failed to deliver on the promise, or stem conflicts over limited land, leading to insurgency in the late 1990s.

[38] Wilfrido Cruz and Christopher Gibbs, 'Resource Policy Reform in the Context of Population Pressure: The Philippines and Nepal,' *American Journal of Agricultural Economics*, 72(5), 1990, 1264–1268.

[39] Nanda R. Shrestha, Dennis Conway and Keshav Bhattarai, 'Population Pressure and Land Resources in Nepal: A Revisit, Twenty Years Later,' *Journal of Developing Areas*, 33(2), 1999, 245–268.

[40] Madhav Joshi and T. David Mason, 'Land Tenure, Democracy, and Insurgency in Nepal: Peasant Support for Insurgency Versus Democracy,' *Asian Survey*, 47(3), 2007, 393–414.

Conclusion

Between 1950 and 1970, governments in South Asia formulated agrarian policy on the assumption that institutional reform would achieve two ends at the same time, rise in productivity of land, and reduction in rural inequality. The foremost area of institutional reform was redistribution of land, and redefinition of property right of the peasant. Other policies of minor importance were Community Development and promotion of cooperative credit. These policies by and large left little measurable impact on either productivity or equity.

Two contending views exist on this failure. In the 1980s, political scientists looking back at 30 years of deficient intervention saw it as a failure of politics. The aim was fine, the means were not up to the task. Notwithstanding attempts to empower the rural poor, the actual functioning of democracy and party politics involved reliance of the state on the locally powerful elite, including landlords and dominant peasants. When those left out of the redistributive project belonged in minority ethnic groups, there was double deprivation, and conditions were ripe for a mass rejection of electoral politics. There is much value in the interpretation. Maoist insurgency in Nepal, and in large areas of the forested uplands of India, seems to thrive in the backdrop of a double deprivation, that is, a combination of land inequality and ethnic marginalization.

But there is another view of the failure of redistributive land reform. The aim was unattainable; the means did not matter. There was not enough land available for redistribution. Of course, landlords might block redistribution. Still, their wealth and political power tend to be exaggerated. Areas where the failure of the land reform generated insurgency were areas where soil quality was poor, water was scarce, alternative opportunities of earning income were limited, and the landlords themselves earned a precarious livelihood. The poverty of the landowners reinforced the poverty of the landless. Redistribution was no solution to this problem, it would only redistribute poverty. In Sri Lanka, redistribution was an excuse to kill a profitable business.

Until recently, economists would often compare South Asia with East Asia, and attribute their unequal achievements to the greater success of land reforms in the latter. Land reform, this narrative went, raised demand for industry, generated savings, and yielded more taxes in Japan, Korea, and Taiwan.[41] Figure 5.12 (Chapter 5) suggests that this may be a false analogy. Differences in geography ensured a lower yield-per-hectare in South Asia compared with the world average. A hectare in India or Nepal gave an output that was a third or less than a third of Korea and Japan in 1960. Arable proportion was higher in East Asia. Population density was higher too, but a substantial disparity in yield per person remained. It is not obvious that East Asia proves a case for redistribution in South Asia. Their geographies are too different.

The geographical interpretation of the failure of land reforms would justify the Green Revolution, and it did, but only after the fact. In 1966, when the new technology was introduced, land reform had not been discredited. And if the new technology had not been available then, it is likely that the countries would have gone for more land reform with more determination than before. As it happened, new technology did come in, became a visible success, and hope shifted from institutions towards technology. In India and Pakistan, the Green Revolution changed the discourse of agricultural development. As average land productivity increased within a few years, economists began to turn away from the pessimistic predictions of Thomas Malthus, towards the more optimistic models of labour-intensive development popularized in the mid-twentieth century by writers like Ester Boserup, Shigeru Ishikawa, and Yujiro Hayami.

[41] See, for a statement of this narrative, J. Mohan Rao, review of Rizwanul Islam, ed., *Rural Industrialisation and Employment in Asia*, New Delhi: International Labour Organisation, 1987, *Economic Development and Cultural Change*, 40(2), 1992, 447–453.

7

The Green Revolution

If we are looking for overlapping experiences within South Asia, we should look no further than the Green Revolution. Most areas in the Indo-Gangetic Basin straddling four countries took part in the Green Revolution of the 1970s. The outcome was not identical everywhere. The same technology and similar ecology gave rise to larger gains in land yield in some parts and lower yield gains in others. What factors made the revolution possible? Why did the outcomes differ? The present chapter is an exploration into these questions.

The story can be told in three stages. Between 1947 and 1966, agricultural growth occurred by extending cultivation in India and Pakistan into newly irrigated areas. This was becoming unsustainable by the mid-1960s in India. The semi-dwarf wheat and rice plants revived growth, and defined the next stage of agricultural change when land yield was the main source of growth, and it was driven by increased application of fertilizer and water. The resultant revolution in agriculture encouraged investment in industry, services, and infrastructure, and thus became the catalyst in a process of structural change.

T. Roy, *The Economy of South Asia*, Palgrave Studies in Economic History, DOI 10.1007/978-3-319-54720-6_7

The time span best suited for studying the structural change is 1966–1985. A further wave of Green Revolution continued beyond 1985, though the years after 1985 should be appropriately called 'post-green-revolution,' because in these years the costs of the strategy in the shape of diminishing returns and ecological stress showed up more clearly than before. I will remark on this phase in the concluding section of the chapter.

The Geography of Production Possibility

The vast Indo-Gangetic Basin spanning an area of 700,000 square kilometres spread over India, Pakistan, Bangladesh, and Nepal presents farming with a more or less similar set of challenges and opportunities. Being situated on the Tropic of Cancer, the region receives excessive heat. Agriculture is possible at all because the land also receives moisture from the monsoons. The distribution of the moisture is uneven seasonally and regionally. Dry seasons are long, and cultivation during the dry seasons demands human intervention on a large scale.

The eastern parts of the Basin get plenty of monsoon rains, and the western part, though deficient in rainfall, can access surface water from the perennial Himalayan rivers and sustain intensive cultivation. These sources cannot be controlled easily, nor diverted and redistributed without heavy expenditure. They enable grain production on traditional methods. The traditional method did not seem capable of sustaining the growing population of South Asia in the twentieth century. The Basin has another resource that could provide a solution to the problem, underground aquifers. From the 1960s, when the Green Revolution established roots in the Basin, wells and canals were used as complementary resources, wells being used for the dwarf varieties of rice and wheat, as well as when the rains failed, during dry seasons, and when controlled application of water was necessary.

The contribution of the high-yielding variety seeds in combination with chemical fertilizers – the scientists' contribution to the Green Revolution – forms the centrepiece of a much-advertised narrative of how American science modernized the third world. The story refers to the experiments that Norman E. Borlaug and his team in the International Centre for the Improvement of Maize and Wheat, Mexico, conducted with hybrid plants. They were trying to develop a sturdy wheat plant based on the indigenous varieties available, which would be able to take in sufficient water and be responsive to chemical fertilizers. Similar experiments in the International Rice Research Institute in Manila produced a rice variety. While not berating the contribution of science, scholars have shown that the core of the agricultural revolution, in fact, was water.[1] Science was neither a necessary nor a sufficient condition for the Revolution. Water was both. The potential of indigenous seeds in the presence of more and controlled water tends to be underestimated in the seed-scientific explanations. Besides, water enabled shifts to more profitable traditional crops like sugarcane. Where water harvesting continued to be an expensive proposition, seed science did not deliver.

To a favourable combination of science and hydrology, national policy played a supportive role. In the early stages, officers of the government and agricultural universities did useful campaign and demonstration. Farmers needed to be shown how water, nitrogenous fertilizers and the new seeds should be combined. The impact of intervention may well have fallen once the initial gains were reaped, and it did slow in many areas. However, the state (at least in India) supported the process through subsidization of water, fertilizer, seeds, and credit ensuring that the level of input application would be sustained. The states supported the process also by investing in roads and electricity.

Still, the government had not 'planned' the revolution. It happened because of an almost accidental conjunction between private investment and new knowledge in the late 1960s. Once it took roots, the state tried to sustain it. In this effort, national policy differed somewhat.

[1] Kapil Subrahmanian, 'Revisiting the Green Revolution: Irrigation and Food Production in Twentieth Century India,' PhD Dissertation of King's College, London, 2015.

India

The regions where the Green Revolution was a notable success had relatively more groundwater to begin with. The Indian Punjab in 1950 had two significant differences with the rest of India; it had a higher irrigation intensity and a higher average farm size. The resource endowment condition was a great deal more favourable in Punjab. The farms were not only larger but also owner operated. The owners were market-oriented profit-seeking capitalists, rather than subsistence-seeking peasants. Another region where the technology succeeded was Tamil Nadu. With 41 per cent of the cultivable land irrigated, Tamil Nadu had a favourable resource endowment, even though the irrigated areas were concentrated in the main delta. In the 1960s, cultivable area expanded by using the so far underutilized capacity of two traditional sources of irrigation, tanks that stored both canal and rain water – there were about 37,000 of them in 1980 – and canals drawn from the perennial rivers. There was, however, no significant breakthrough either in the capacity of these systems or in devising new systems. If anything, siltation and decay of the tanks were a problem. In the 1960s, the momentum was running out, whereas large increase in the labour force depressed wages.[2] The Green Revolution arrived in time to avert a social crisis.

In Punjab, the initial spurt died about 1972, the year of a great drought, but a second spurt started around 1977. Initially, the Green Revolution was introduced with a great deal of knowledge support from state agricultural universities and extension departments. The second wave by contrast came to depend upon budgetary support. The support was at first offered as subsidized credit made available to Punjab farmers through cooperatives. One author attributes the success of the cooperatives to the farmers' ability to buy and use the technological package more than their counterparts in Pakistan Punjab, where the same knowledge package delivered a smaller gain in yield.[3] A slowdown in the cooperative machine,

[2] C.T. Kurien and Josef James. *Economic Change in Tamil Nadu: 1960–70 – A Regionally and Functionally Disaggregated Study* by, Delhi: Allied Publishers, 1979.

[3] Monohar Singh Gill, 'The Development of Punjab Agriculture, 1977–80,' *Asian Survey*, 23, 1983, 830–844.

according to the same study, explained why the drive slowed between 1972 and 1977. Thereafter direct input subsidy on fertilizer, electricity, and water, and price support sustained the application of inputs to agriculture.

Between 1970 and 1985, Punjab achieved near-total irrigation coverage. The High Yielding Variety (HYV) package was adopted in practically all farms in the state. The productivity of wheat and paddy was the highest in India, and not too far below the highest in the world around 1985. Irrigation growth had been achieved by means of tube wells and electric pumps, and the larger farm size ensured a high level of demand for tractors. By 1980, Punjab (divided in 1965 into Punjab and Haryana) had India's highest density of roads and electricity, per capita consumption, and average

Fig. 7.1. Harvesting grain in Punjab Province, Pakistan.

The Green Revolution occurred in a few regions of the subcontinent, where water could be harvested relatively easily. In Punjab (Indian and Pakistani Punjab), the process was also more reliant on mechanical equipment. © dbi-images/Alamy Stock Photo

state domestic product, all in all the biggest economic growth success story in postcolonial India.[4]

Real agricultural wages started to increase from about 1975, and as local supplies of wage workers slowed, migrants from Bihar filled the gap. The conditions in which the migrants worked were compared with the conditions of the indentured labourers in the tropical colonies of the nineteenth century. Many were paid less than the minimum wage, and were almost bonded to their employers.[5] And yet, like the nineteenth century indentured workers, both wages and bargaining power improved in the long run.

From the early 1980s, the Green Revolution momentum shifted eastward to West Bengal and Bihar and to varieties of summer paddy. The impetus came in a similar way as it had developed in Punjab or Tamil Nadu. Fertilizer-seed package was made available by the state, in this case in the form of 'minikit' distributed by extension officers. Cheap credit and electricity subsidy encouraged installation of tube wells and electric pumpset on an extensive scale. The annual rate of growth in food-grain production in West Bengal increased from 2.9 per cent in 1959–1978 to 4 per cent in 1979–1999. The acceleration was impressive (2 to 4.5) in the main food crop, rice.[6]

The effects of the revolution were subjects of several controversies.

Green Revolution and Rural Inequality

Almost as soon as the Green Revolution began, an academic discussion started on what it meant for inequality. The theoretical debate made the assumption that larger holdings had better access to non-labour inputs, and the Green Revolution benefited from the application of non-labour inputs. Furthermore, non-labour inputs carried state subsidy, so that larger holdings were entitled to greater quantum of state support. 'The

[4] Sukhpal Singh, 'Crisis in Punjab Agriculture,' *Economic and Political Weekly*, 35(23), 2000, 1889–1892.

[5] Manjit Singh, 'Uneven Development in Agriculture and Labour Migration: A Case of Bihar and Punjab,' Shimla: Indian Institute of Advanced Study, 1995.

[6] Ratan Khasnabis, 'The Economy of West Bengal,' *Economic and Political Weekly*, 43(52), 2008–9, 103–115.

direct benefit of subsidizing fertilizer and underpricing water and power goes mainly to fertilizer producers and high-income farmers while having negative effects on the environment and production, and even on the income of small farmers.'[7] Another factor that may contribute to inequality is imperfect capital market. 'The increased rate of return to land provides a strong incentive to accumulate more land, especially under the condition of an underdeveloped capital market, because alternative investment opportunities . . . are not easily available.'[8]

On the other hand, the biological input combination that produced the Green Revolution was neither expensive nor did it entail significant economies of scale. Small farmers could in principle access and implement the package as easily as the large ones. An active water market could distribute water evenly among users, irrespective of who owned a well. If that is the case, then the revolution should be scale-neutral. Of course, overall rural inequality may still increase because the revolution favours the landowners over the landless and the tenants. Even that may be temporary. Eventually, increasing productivity and scarcity of local labour should transmit the gains from landowners to wage-earners. Did the benefits 'trickle down' and 'percolate' in this manner?

At first, many economists stressed the inequality effect. The Punjab experience was later read in a way that the inequality argument was rejected and trickle down favoured.[9] The pattern of rural inequality measured by the Gini coefficient among landholders (excluding the landless workers) showed that the coefficient tended to be high on average (above 0.5), but that the Green Revolution made little change to it. The effect on inequality, it was found, depended on whether the main source of water was well or canal. Large farmers had better access to water from canal irrigation, and there was less of a trading opportunity with canal water. In Punjab, inequality increased in the 1950s, on account of new canal irrigation projects that brought new land under cultivation. The Green Revolution of the 1960s by

---

[7] Montek S. Ahluwalia, 'Economic Reforms in India since 1991: Has Gradualism Worked?', *The Journal of Economic Perspectives*, 16(3), 2002, 67–88.

[8] Yujiro Hayami, 'Induced Innovation, Green Revolution, and Income Distribution: Comment,' *Economic Development and Cultural Change*, 30(1), 1981, 169–176.

[9] Chadha, *State and Rural Economic Transformation.*

contrast left little or no impact on the level of inequality.[10] This effect of canal water on inequality had been noticed in the case of West Pakistan as well.

Regional inequality was a much less ambiguous thing. Here the revolution necessarily made regions more different than before. Cautious assessments of the new agricultural strategy stressed that 'the picture generally painted of the Green Revolution is brighter than is actually warranted: in less favoured regions conditions are grim.'[11] Why so?

Why Did It Not Happen Everywhere?

Those who took part in the surplus labour debate (Box 7.1) did not ask serious questions about the quality of natural resources available. They debated whether removing people or improving knowledge worked better in changing the conditions of the peasants. The truth is, neither would have any effect without sufficient supply of water. The Green Revolution depended on the complementary relationship between land and water. Subsidized exploration and mining of groundwater played a fundamental and a somewhat unsung role in the revolution. And because groundwater played such a critical role, the HYVs could not work their magic where aquifers were expensive to tap.[12] India's dry lands fall in this category. There is a well-known argument that the marginal returns from state investment should be higher in the dry areas compared with the more endowed irrigated areas.[13] And yet, the technological options that can have potential effect on returns from agriculture in the dry zones are limited, and not all can be pursued either under state direction (as in the first Green Revolution), or with reliance on the market (as with the second Green Revolution).

---

[10] Sharma, 'Distribution of Landholdings in Rural India'.

[11] Francesca Bray, citing B.H. Farmer, ed., *Green Revolution?*, London: Macmillan, 1977, reviewed in *Modern Asian Studies*, 13(4), 1979, 681–704.

[12] West Bengal, which witnessed a small-scale political revolution in 1969, was one example. The important role of water in the failure of agricultural process in this state is stressed in James Boyce, *Agrarian Impasse in Bengal: Agricultural Growth in Bangladesh and West Bengal 1949–1980*, Oxford: Oxford University Press, 1987.

[13] Shenggen Fan, Peter Hazell, T. Haque, 'Targeting Public Investments by Agro-ecological Zone to achieve Growth and Poverty Alleviation Goals in Rural India', *Food Policy*, 25, 2000, 411–428.

Box 7.1 The surplus labour debate

In the 1960s, the choice of agricultural policy became linked to an academic debate on surplus labour. The Caribbean-American economist W. Arthur Lewis defined as 'surplus' those labourers who could be removed from the production process without an adverse effect on production. Lewis claimed that surplus labour was present in many poor countries. Yet, this was good news rather than bad for those countries that wanted to industrialize. By tapping in a pool of wage labour that was content to get a wage equal to the average output in the subsistence sector, the employers would save on labour cost, and invest until 'the capitalist wage begins to be forced up.'

Indian economists drew two policy conclusions from the Lewis model. First, industrialization was the answer to low productivity in agriculture. Second, low productivity in agriculture stemmed from overpopulation and not from the capacity of land to produce crops. Did surplus labour exist in Indian agriculture? Did it owe to overpopulation?

Theodore Schultz of Yale University attempted to answer these questions on the basis of a natural experiment. He compared agricultural situations before and after the 1918–1919 influenza epidemic in India. The experiment showed that mass mortality reduced the area under cultivation. The doctrine of surplus labour was 'demonstrably false.' The problem of Indian agriculture was technology, not population, and the solution to the problem was new technology in agriculture, not industrialization. Schultz' book came a few years after Borlaug's experiments, and supplied a rationale for wide adoption of the new agricultural technology.

Further tests of the hypothesis produced conflicting results. The standard test involved estimating the labour input elasticity in a production function. A near-zero elasticity would suggest surplus labour. A marginal productivity less than the wage rate, presuming it is set by subsistence, would also suggest that too many people were employed for a job that could be done with fewer people. There was a conceptual confusion here between seasonal surplus and year-round surplus. Seasonal surplus labour was an outcome of the monsoons, but removing them would lower output by making labour scarce during the few weeks when sowing and harvesting tasks reached their peak. Some tests did yield low elasticity (0.25–0.4), but overall, the literature was marred by 'careless data handling and poor methodology' (Wellisz et al.).

Readings: Raj Krishna, 'Some Production Functions of Punjab,' *Indian Journal of Agricultural Economics*, 19, 1964, 87–97; Stanislaw Wellisz, Bernard Munk, T. Peter Mayhew and Carl Hemmer, 'Resource Allocation in Traditional Agriculture: A Study of Andhra Pradesh,' *Journal of Political Economy*, 78 (4), Part 1, 1970, 655–684; T.W. Schultz, *Transforming Traditional Agriculture*, New Haven: Yale University Press, 1964; W.A. Lewis, 'Economic Development with Unlimited Supplies of Labour.' *Manchester School*, 22(2), 1954, 139–91.

Therefore, even if the revolution was unjustly accused of increasing personal inequality, it did increase regional inequality. The differential in land yield between the best and the worst performing agricultural zones is more than seven.[14] The differential between 'irrigated' (more than half of cropped land receives irrigation) and 'rainfed' areas in respect of incidence of rural poverty remains wide, and the incidence correlates negatively with the percentage of cropped area irrigated.[15] The ratio of yields between irrigated crops, such as wheat and rice, and rainfed crops, such as sorghum, has diverged in the last 20 years. Rural poverty has remained entrenched in these regions. A recent article has shown that initial conditions in the shape of agro-ecological characteristics and endowments still influence the capacity of induced agricultural change to reduce poverty in India.[16] Land conservation efforts, upon which the future of the dry lands depends, involves a level of subsidization that cannot be extended to all farmers in the arid zones.[17] Finally, sustainable resource management strategies such as watershed development often involve trade-offs between successful conservation and increasing inequality between the landed and the landless.[18]

In those regions where the Green Revolution could not work and industrialization was a distant prospect, neither Schultz nor Lewis could offer much solace. There was no recipe for such 'agrarian impasse,' to quote the title of a book on Bengal. In 1970, the districts caught up in this trap included those in densely populated Eastern India, and the vast forested uplands in central India, where a violent Maoist insurgency continues today. In areas like these, small and medium farms were under

---

[14] Andrew D. Foster and Mark R. Rosenzweig, 'Agricultural Productivity Growth, Rural Economic Diversity, and Economic Reforms: India, 1970–2000', *Economic Development and Cultural Change*, 52(3), 2004, 509–542.

[15] Fan, Hazell, Haque, 'Targeting Public Investments'.

[16] R. Palmer-Jones, and K. Sen, 'What Has Luck Got To Do With It? A Regional Analysis of Poverty and Agricultural Growth in Rural India', *Journal of Development Studies*, 40(1), 2003, 1–31.

[17] John L. Pender and John M. Kerr, 'Determinants of Farmers' Indigenous Soil and Water Conservation Investments in Semi-arid India', *Agricultural Economics*, 19, 1998, 113–125.

[18] John Kerr, 'Watershed Development, Environmental Services, and Poverty Alleviation in India', *World Development*, 30(8), 2002, 1387–1400.

a great deal of stress. The proportion of cultivated area divided into small plots (less than 2 hectares) increased (by 6 per cent) in the 1970s, except in the Green Revolution areas, where the small farms fared better.[19] Rural poverty remained high and real wages in agriculture hardly moved throughout the 1970s.

The Green Revolution succeeded in raising the productivity of land *and* aggregate productivity under two different conditions, one relatively less labour-intensive and another relatively more. In Punjab and Haryana, in western Gujarat, and southern Karnataka, irrigation intensity, larger holdings, high level of fertilizer intensity, and medium population density delivered both high land yield and high labour productivity. In Tamil Nadu, coastal Andhra, and West Bengal, irrigation and fertilizer intensity combined with application of labour inputs delivered the gains. These were densely populated small-holding areas, where rise in land yield did not translate to similar rise in labour productivity. Low yield regions likewise fall in two patterns. In dry lands and uplands, irrigation intensity is smaller. In Bihar and eastern UP, holdings are too small, and as a result of this, fertilizer application is also low.[20]

Rural Industrialization

A new discourse on industrialization emerged from the experience of the Green Revolution. In a 1976 book, the economist John Mellor argued that a sharp improvement in agricultural production contained the possibility of an industrialization process that would make use of the demand for intermediate and capital goods in agriculture, supply of material to agro-processing activities, and increased consumption of manufactures among rural communities.[21] Some of these effects did follow in the core areas of the Green Revolution.

[19] D Bandyopadhyay, 'Land Reforms in India: An Analysis', *Economic and Political Weekly*, 21 (25–26), 1986, A-50-A56.

[20] Edison Dayal, 'Agricultural Productivity in India: A Spatial Analysis,' *Annals of the Association of American Geographers*, 74(1), 1984, 98–123.

[21] John W. Mellor, *The New Economics of Growth – A Strategy for India and the Developing World*, Ithaca: Cornell University Press, 1976.

Protection offered to small firms, and capital accumulation in the Green Revolution regions, made industrial entrepreneurship more diverse and broad-based than before. The merchant-banker communities were now joined by communities that had made their money in land, such as the Kammas of Andhra Pradesh, Patidars in Gujarat, and Gounders in Tamil Nadu.[22] Researchers found that within the regions that experienced significant change in land yield, agriculture had grown more reliant on manufactured inputs and urban services than before, induced higher wages in the secondary and the tertiary sectors, which raised demand for farm produce.[23] Continued low wages in the poorer areas was an attraction for small-scale factories, giving rise to a large increase in the 1990s in the share of non-farm income and reduced dependence on farm incomes in rural households.[24]

The expansion in rural nonfarm activity is a significant development of the recent decades. In some examples, agricultural growth and the growth of small-scale industry and services coincide in the same regions. The connection is seen in the machine parts and metal industry clusters that emerged initially to serve the equipment trade and repairs linked to agricultural demand. Coimbatore in Tamil Nadu and Batala in Punjab are examples of this type of industrialization. Tamil Nadu witnessed a robust small town growth around the small-scale semi-artisanal textile industry. Green Revolution, when it began to transform agriculture in parts of the state, also at the same time contributed to urbanization, electrification, and small-scale industry growth, near the same areas where the agricultural transformation was happening.[25]

But there are exceptions to that pattern too. Concluding a survey of long-term structural change in rural India, Foster and Rosenzweig

[22] Harish Damodaran, *India's New Capitalists: Caste, Business, and Industry in a Modern Nation*, Ranikhet: Permanent Black/New India Foundation, 2008.

[23] K.P. Kalirajan and U. Sankar, 'Agriculture in India's Economic Reform Program', *Journal of Asian Economics*, 12(4), 2001, 383–399.

[24] Foster and Rosenzweig, 'Agricultural Productivity Growth,' 509–542.

[25] Madras Institute of Development Studies, *The Tamilnadu Economy: Performance and Issues*, New Delhi: Oxford and IBH, 1988.

suggest that the rural nonfarm growth 'is not predicated on expansion of local agricultural productivity,' and that factory industry has in fact sought out low-wage areas 'that did not benefit from enhancement of local agricultural productivity growth.'[26] In other words, in terms of development policy choices, some rural nonfarm businesses can be an alternative to, rather than complementary to the Green Revolution.

After 1985

The peak of the Green Revolution did not last beyond 15 years, followed by diminishing returns. There is indication that between 1980 and 2005, the rate of growth in average grain yield was falling, in some cases to near-zero rates.[27] Among other factors, the diminishing returns occurred because of land degradation and over-extraction of groundwater. The exact scale of land degradation is a matter of dispute. An estimate suggests that of the 329 m ha of land area, anything between 121 m ha and 190 m ha is subject to levels of soil and wind erosion that can impair the productive power of land. The exact reasons for land degradation are open to interpretation. Population growth, agricultural expansion, and input-intensity have all shared some measure of the blame. Not all of the land degradation is a direct result of the Green Revolution. Some of it is a result of trying to replicate the Green Revolution in regions where resources are of poorer quality. Thus, in vulnerable environments, where soil quality and water supply are already low, land degradation is a bigger problem. About 70 per cent of the water used for irrigation and all the water put to non-agricultural use is extracted from underground. Groundwater extraction has led to fall in the underground water levels in many districts of India. A fifth of the population of India and a much larger proportion of the urban population are

[26] Foster and Rosenzweig, 'Agricultural Productivity Growth.'

[27] A.S. Mathur, S. Das, S. Sarkar, 'Agriculture in India: Trends and Prospects,' *Economic and Political Weekly*, 41(52), 2006–2007, 5327–5336.

expected to live under conditions of extreme water scarcity by 2050.[28] Again, agricultural expansion is not the only reason for the gathering crisis, but one of the main contributing factors.[29]

A different type of environmental stress occurs in rice cultivation regimes of West Bengal, Bangladesh, Bihar, and Nepal. It does not arise so much from land degradation as from arsenic poisoning. Arsenic occurs in shallow aquifers in the eastern regions of South Asia. They are recycled into food in two ways, irrigation water used in paddy cultivation and drinking water extracted from affected sources. In many districts, the reliance on these aquifers has reached a point where the level of arsenic intake exceeds prescribed tolerable limits by several times. The problem is a serious one because water extracted for irrigation cannot be treated economically. Drinking water can be and is treated, but this is a partial solution at best. The options available – switch to dryland crops, surface water, or deeper aquifers known to be unaffected – are not likely to be acceptable either to the producers or the consumers. Soil treatment may or may not have a lasting impact in the flood-prone delta regions.[30]

After 1985, the older Green Revolution regions like Punjab experienced a deceleration in agricultural growth. Agriculture no longer led general economic growth. The post-1990 economic reforms benefited industry and services more. The state support to farmers was not withdrawn, but earnings were higher outside agriculture and the gap was increasing. Somewhat later in West Bengal, the same thing happened.

In Punjab, which had not diversified enough either inside or outside agriculture, the slowing down meant the onset of a 'crisis,' on which a large literature now exists. Punjab remained a wheat-rice state. Here, the slowdown would mean that relative wealth characterized the big farmers,

---

[28] B. Venkateswarlu and J.V.S.N. Prasad, 'Carrying Capacity of Indian Agriculture: Issues related to Rainfed Agriculture,' *Current Science*, 102(6), 2012, 882–888.

[29] D. Byerlee, 'Technical Change, Productivity, and Sustainability in Irrigated Cropping Systems of South Asia: Emerging Issues in the Post-Green Revolution Era,' *Journal of International Development*, 4(4), 1992, 477–496.

[30] Hugh Brammer, 'Threat of Arsenic to Agriculture in India, Bangladesh and Nepal,' *Economic and Political Weekly*, 43(47), 2008, 79–84.

whereas the smallest farms experienced erosion of their capacity to hold on to the gains made in the previous two decades. Their retreat was illustrated in a spate of suicides by small farmers in the 1990s. There was persistence of poverty among a group of marginal landowners, a smaller proportion perhaps than in India as a whole, but large enough.[31] In this way, decades of the Green Revolution made the farming community divided in Punjab. The differentiation had significant political effects. 'Fragmentation of farmers' movement during the last decade or so,' Surinder Jodhka writes, 'cannot be understood without referring to the growing internal differentiation within the landowning classes/castes.'[32]

The Green Revolution was a fiscal burden, the true extent of which remains unknown. In the 1960s and the 1970s, direct investment in canal construction, rural infrastructure, research laboratories, and universities formed the main heads of public expenditure related to the effort. These were visible expenses that came out of the budget. Between 1980 and 2000, expenditure was more indirect in nature, and therefore less visible than before, and took the form of input subsidies and expenditure on the quasi-state agencies that administered them. Huge aid was doled out in the shape of subsidized water, electricity, fertilizers, credit write-offs, price-support, and zero taxes. Input subsidies increased from less than 1 per cent to more than 8 per cent of agricultural GDP between 1980 and 1999.[33] In the 1980s, the state granaries started buying a great deal of the grain output for public distribution. Although in its original aim the public distribution system was meant to serve poor consumers when food prices increased, an additional aim was to stabilize and shore up post-harvest prices when the harvest was good, in deference to powerful farm lobbies. Special-price shops then sold this food to card-holders at a subsidized price. The 1990s, the first decade of economic reforms, saw sustained conflict between the farm lobby and reformists over the scale of input subsidies. Conflicts such as

---

[31] Singh, 'Crisis.'

[32] Surinder S. Jodhka, 'Beyond 'Crises': Rethinking Contemporary Punjab Agriculture,' *Economic and Political* Weekly, 41(16), 2006, 1530–1537.

[33] Ashok Gulati and S. Narayanan, *The Subsidy Syndrome in Indian Agriculture*, Delhi: Oxford University Press, 2003.

these sharpened a diversity of interests of the farm and the non-farm sectors, which followed from their common dependence on public resources.

There were other conflicts too. Although the public distribution system contributed to stabilizing consumption by the poor, the costs of this enormous and unwieldy institution were large, and looked pointless when the prospect of basic shortages had disappeared. Even after the subsidies paid to maintain it, it was not clear that the policy helped the poor consumers more than it helped the rich farmers. While food disappeared from market channels to government storage, an inefficient and wasteful public storage system ensured that starvation persisted in the poorly endowed regions with inadequate communication infrastructure. Localized famines and starvation deaths persisted as grain rotted in public warehouses.[34] Under these criticisms, in the late 1990s, reforms designed to achieve better 'targeting' were introduced, though their impact on poverty is uncertain.

The economic reforms did not particularly help agriculture, because trade restrictions persist. Exports constitute not more than 15–18 per cent of agricultural output around 2010. It could potentially be much higher. Until 1995, export of agricultural goods was more or less prohibited. The critics of neo-liberal policy argued that openness would lead to a sustained rise in food prices, depression in wages, and worsening poverty.[35] Long-term estimates of competitive advantage suggest that a liberal trade regime should see India export its major grains without running into domestic stress.[36] Persuaded by this line of argument, the late 1990s did see a partial opening up of the borders.

In the Uruguay Round Agreement on Agriculture, tariffs in the developed markets were reduced by 35–45 per cent on fruits and

[34] On the costs of the public distribution system, see R. Radhakrishna and K. Subbarao, 'India's Public Distribution System', Washington DC: World Bank Discussion Paper 380, 1997.

[35] For a discussion, see Martin Ravallion, 'Prices, Wages and Poverty in Rural India: What Lessons do the Time Series Data hold for Policy?', *Food Policy*, 25(4), 2000, 351–364.

[36] Ashok Gulati, 'Indian Agriculture in a Globalizing World', *American Journal of Agricultural Economics*, 84(3), 2002, 754–761.

vegetables, flowers, and other agricultural products. Following this development, farmers and orchard owners in India began diversifying into non-traditional, high-value-added products such as fruits and flowers. Floriculture emerged as a money-spinner in Southern India. Other success stories included basmati rice and soybeans.[37] It is expected that the conversion of grain lands into orchards and tree crops is a trend that will continue into the future.

Pakistan

Compared with the rest of South Asia, Pakistan is an arid country. The agricultural geography of Pakistan is divided into four areas, canal-irrigated plains, 'rangelands' or the savannah that covers much of Baluchistan, mountains, and the submontane. The plains and submontane include sandy deserts in the west and 'barani' or rain-fed lands of north Punjab. Except in the canal-irrigated plains, prospects of significant gains in agricultural productivity anywhere is limited. The barani areas have been urbanized, and industrialized, but they also contain poor agricultural areas. Aridity means that any agricultural growth is bound to deepen regional inequality.

In the Indo-Gangetic Basin, especially the Indus basin in West Pakistan, water diversion and reallocation projects on a large scale were done during the British colonial times. The diversion was done initially in the form of canals. Canal water was diverted by means of channels that benefited farms in proximity to the canals. The Indus basin is also endowed with an extensive underground aquifer. Soon after independence, tube wells were used on a bigger scale than before to extract groundwater. Private investment in pump sets increased, and water from perennial sources were carried further.

[37] On the expected impact of rice trade liberalization on the Asian exporters, see Ashok Gulati and Sudha Narayanan, 'Rice Trade Liberalisation and Poverty', *Economic and Political Weekly*, 38(1), 2003, 45–51.

The Green Revolution stood on this combination of canals and wells, surface and groundwater, and horizontal and vertical drainage. The combination changed the rules of the game because 'the availability of supplemental ground water permits irrigation during periods when canal deliveries are relatively restricted, which in turn facilitates double cropping and growing high-value crops in situations where it would otherwise be infeasible.'[38] As the new cropping pattern and dependence on the irrigation regime took roots, a market for groundwater emerged. Once again, canals and wells were interdependent parts of a package. When canal water fell short, owners of tube wells sold well water to small farmers who did not own wells. When canal water was in excess, owners of wells again sold water.[39] Prices presumably cleared markets.

Agricultural growth was limited in the 1950s, and accelerated in the 1960s, at first due to aid-funded investment in infrastructure, and after 1965, due to the fertilizer-responsive plants. Within 4 years, 1966–1969, wheat production in West Pakistan increased by 79 per cent, and rice production by 61 per cent. Although government agencies played a role in introducing the new varieties, the scale of their adoption was not exactly a measure of the success of government campaign. The availability of wells was a more important factor. According to a 1968 survey of small industrial firms, 'government officials and economic planners in Pakistan have been unaware of the existence of... the thousands of tube wells installed by individual Punjabi farmers.'[40]

Despite the increase in land yield, the contribution of knowledge to the rise in production cannot be ascertained. Some studies find that the 'total factor productivity,' which is conventionally treated as a measure of the contribution of innovation, did reach internationally respectable

[38] Muhammed J. Khan and Robert A. Young, 'Farm Resource Productivities, Allocative Efficiencies and Development Policy in the Indus Basin, Pakistan,' *Land Economics*, 55(3), 1979, 388–396.

[39] Ruth Meinzen-Dick, 'Private Tubewell Development and Groundwater Markets in Pakistan: A District-level Analysis,' *Pakistan Development Review*, 33(4), 1994, 857–869.

[40] Frank C. Child and Hiromitsu Kaneda, 'Links to the Green Revolution: A Study of Small-Scale, Agriculturally Related Industry in the Pakistan Punjab,' *Economic Development and Cultural Change*, 23(2), 1975, 249–275.

levels, whereas others find that it did not.[41] These calculations are vitiated by the fact that the prices of inputs were regulated. For what these numbers are worth, the low factor productivity growth would suggest that the Green Revolution process was dependent, as in India, on input application to an unhealthy degree. Also, wheat and rice yields were higher in the Indian Punjab than in the Pakistan Punjab, even though the two regions share similar geographical features. While input application and diversification of crops improved in both regions, they improved more in Indian Punjab than in Pakistan Punjab.

These findings have led to an interesting question, does culture matter to productivity gains? In principle, culture could make a difference via the ability to make informed choices about quality of inputs and manner (such as the timing) of their application. Studies find that parallel to the India-Pakistan difference in productivity, there was a difference in the levels of 'human capital.' Within a region, informed choices are sensitive to schooling levels, though the relationship does not show up for low levels of school education.[42] A study of the export success, basmati rice, noted 'the crucial role of education in helping farmers adjust to fast-changing agricultural technologies,' and at the same time, the inadequate levels of access to schooling in the regions of cultivation.[43] The positive impact of human capital can be seen also in the value that the farmers themselves placed on education. In Pakistan, for example, 'attitudes towards education have begun to change in recent years in the Canal Colony Districts, especially among the prosperous big farmers. The revolution in mechanical technology and chemical technology which is now employed in agriculture is making new demands upon the capabilities of the farmers (see also Fig. 7.1). They are becoming increasingly aware of the value of education in terms of their own situation, namely for better

[41] Rinku Murgai, Mubarik Ali and Derek Byerlee, 'Productivity Growth and Sustainability in Post-Green Revolution Agriculture: The Case of the Indian and Pakistan Punjabs,' *World Bank Research Observer*, 16(2), 2001, 199–218.

[42] Rauf A. Azhar, 'Education and Technical Efficiency during the Green Revolution in Pakistan,' *Economic Development and Cultural Change*, 39(3), 1991, 651–665.

[43] Mubarik Ali, 'Institutional and Socioeconomic Constraints on the Second-Generation Green Revolution: A Case Study of Basmati Rice Production in Pakistan's Punjab,' *Economic Development and Cultural Change*, 43(4), 1995, 835–861.

farming and coping with the new technologies.'[44] A similar virtuous effect was the impact of the Green Revolution on fertility transition, The adoption of capital-intensive technology reduced the demand for children and enabled more investment in them.[45]

The inequality debate was as controversial in Pakistan as it was in India. One view, the mainstream across South Asia, was that the new technology was adopted to a greater extent and more profitably by the larger farmers. A minority view held that small farmers followed the example of the larger farmers and substituted chemical fertilizers for cheap local manure, achieving the same effect. A yet third view claimed that the small farmers did copy the practices, but after a lag and when the rate of return from specific innovations was already diminishing.[46] Thus, their gains were more modest.

Not only in Punjab and Sind, throughout Pakistan, wherever the new technology was adopted and land value increased, landowners tried to secure their hold over land. Absentees came back or took direct interest in land. In regions where tenants had been the main body of cultivators rather than the proprietors, there were numerous clashes. Emigration was an escape route from these conflicts. Many emigrants, in fact, did come from districts with a history of landlord-tenant clashes.

When landowners saw the value of their land go up because of productivity gains, they sometimes replaced tenants and labourers. In the larger farms of Pakistan, landowners did this by buying tractors as a substitute for draught animals. Tenants owned the bullocks in the old system. Tractorization, therefore, displaced tenants. Although tractors were welcome, the government restricted the import of combined harvesters, so that the harvest operation remained labour intensive.

[44] Hamza Alavi, 'The Rural Elite and Agricultural Development in Pakistan, *Pakistan Economic and Social Review*, 14(1/4), 1976, 173–210.

[45] Prem Bhandari, Dirgha Ghimire, 'Rural Agricultural Change and Fertility Transition in Nepal,' *Rural Sociology*, 78(2), 2013, 229–252.

[46] M. Ghaffar Chaudhry. 'Green Revolution and Redistribution of Rural Income: Pakistan's Experience,' *Pakistan Development Review*, vol. 21(3), 1982; Faiz Mohammad and Mian M. Aslam, 'Wealth Effects of the Green Revolution in Pakistan,' *Pakistan Development Review*, 25(4), 1986, 489–513.

Bangladesh

The Green Revolution in Bangladesh had an earlier beginning than that in West Bengal, but otherwise, it had many similarities with the latter. Between 1968 and 1992, fertilizer inputs grew from 8.8 kg of nutrients per hectare to 48.3 kg, and there was a similarly large rise in pesticide use. The area under irrigation rose from 8.2 per cent in 1968 to 23.7 per cent of cropped area in 1992.[47] The peak of the expansion occurred in the 1970s and the early 1980s. Between 1972 and 1985, the area irrigated increased by about a third, and the use of fertilizers three times. Between these years, total cropped area changed little, from 30 to 32 million acres. Land extension had reached an absolute barrier. As a result of access to water and fertilizer, crop mix changed, as it did elsewhere in South Asia.

Between 1980 and 2000, rice and wheat production increased at the rate of 3 per cent per year, though the pace of growth decelerated over time.[48] Growth in output was impressive across all varieties of rice, but especially in boro, or summer paddy cultivation. The dwarf plants cultivated in summer yielded more rice per acre, whereas the monsoon dependent paddy varieties presented limited scope for productivity growth. Further, the summer rice was produced for the market, whereas the monsoon rice was partly consumed in the household. Along with summer paddy, area and production in some of the other profitable and water-intensive crops increased, including sugarcane and wheat. As the fall in fertility set in there was sustained rise in output-per-worker in agriculture.[49]

The institutional foundations of the Green Revolution in Bangladesh were somewhat different from those in the rice growing regions of India. The Bangladesh Rice Research Institute together with the International

[47] Sanzidur Rahman, 'Regional Productivity and Convergence in Bangladesh Agriculture,' *Journal of Developing Areas*, 41(1), 2007, 221–223.

[48] Raisuddin Ahmed, 'Rice Economy of Bangladesh: Progress and Prospects,' *Economic and Political Weekly*, 39(36), 2004, 4043–4052.

[49] E. Dayal, 'Sources of Labor Productivity in Bangladesh Agriculture,' *GeoJournal*, 20(3), 1990, 293–299.

Rice Research Institute of Manila developed varieties of hybrid rice that were well adapted to the Bangladesh inland ecology. While grain trading was regulated in India, in Bangladesh it was deregulated in the late 1970s. Growth of private trade not only helped feed the growing population of Bangladesh, it also enabled legal or illegal grain export to India in years of surplus. Further, except for a few years, subsidization of inputs was not practiced on a serious scale, in sharp contrast with India, where production came to depend on subsidies more and more.

In common with the other nations, 'the scenario dramatically changed during post-green-revolution period (1985–1992).'[50] The rate of improvement in efficiency of agricultural production started to fall. Diminishing return was inevitable in all post-green-revolution societies, but the Bangladesh case was complicated by near monoculture. If rice was in crisis, everything else was in crisis. Options of a more attractive crop mix while staying within rice monoculture had more or less run out in the 1990s, though some improvements were still thought to be possible with better practices.

In contrast with India, Pakistan, and Bangladesh, in Sri Lanka and Nepal, the impact of the Green Revolution was limited, for different reasons.

Sri Lanka and Nepal

Sri Lankan cereal yields were already well above the South Asian average (Fig. 5.11), thanks to rainfall and irrigation potential available in the western, southern, and central areas. There was another factor, the availability of good indigenously developed hybrid rice plants. These seeds may not have pushed the country towards a trajectory of growth, but they may still have helped the country recover from occasional droughts. The dry lands of the east and north were another matter. A colonial research station in Kandy, now known as the Field Crops Research and Development Institute, located in the University of

[50] Rahman, 'Regional Productivity and Convergence.'

Peradeniya campus, did significant work in the 1950s on the dry zones. The results became useful when a major initiative was undertaken to push dryland cultivation in the 1960s and 1970s. In particular, experiments with indigenous rice seeds were more effective in this country than they were elsewhere in South Asia.[51]

Between 1965 and 1979, total crop output increased and import-dependence fell. These effects followed from extension of cultivation. Although the time span was the same as that of the Green Revolution in mainland South Asia, 'Sri Lanka's progress in the Green Revolution has been less than impressive.'[52] The success in raising output came from settlement of the dry areas along with a large investment in irrigation. While reducing expenditure on cheap food, the UNP government in the end of the 1970s introduced the Mahaweli Programme as a compensation to the poorer sections of society. The Programme involved resettlement of landless peasants in the dryland areas, and the provisioning of irrigation facilities in the same areas. The irrigation schemes were aid-funded. By 1984, the dry zones produced a considerable share of cereals under the high yielding varieties.

In Nepal, the Green Revolution was confined to the Terai more or less. The introduction of dwarf wheat in the mid-1960s encouraged double cropping with rice and wheat. Since then, the wheat seed changed a number of times, as farmers in the Terai drew on the resources and the knowledge of farmers in the contiguous areas in India.[53] Nepal's own investment in plant research and extension tended to be low among the Green Revolution countries. Although wheat area increased through intensive cropping, Nepal, especially the Terai, remained a rice growing area.

Figures 5.11 and 5.12 show that cereal yield gains were the smallest in Nepal, and adjusted for population, yield per person fell. The

[51] Adam Pain, 'Agricultural Research in Sri Lanka: An Historical Account,' *Modern Asian Studies*, 20(4), 1986, 755–778.

[52] H.M. Gamini Herath, 'The Green Revolution in Rice: The Role of the Risk Factor with Special Reference to Sri Lanka,' *Asian Survey*, 21(6), 1981, 664–675.

[53] Michael L. Morris, H.J. Dubin, Thaneswar Pokhrel, 'Returns to Wheat breeding Research in Nepal,' *Agricultural Economics*, 10(3), 1994, 269–282.

combination of fertile soil and controlled irrigation occurs in parts of the Terai, but rarely elsewhere in Nepal. Consumer preference ensured continued popularity of tall and fertilizer-invariant rice varieties.[54] Like in Bangladesh, rice dominated crop choices in Nepal, so that yield trend followed general rice yield. Overall, '[t]he Green Revolution did not "transfer" well to Nepal, with its diverse agro-climatic zones, limits to irrigation, and lack of inputs and credit.'[55]

The fact that a narrow geographical zone alone could use the new technology raised the prospect of regional inequality as the limited Green Revolution progressed. Good estimates of regional inequality are unavailable. Analyses of the regions where agricultural growth did take place reveal the presence of immigrant agricultural workers from the more impoverished regions. The existence of a pool of landless labourers within the lowlands and seasonal migration from the hills made efficiency gains shared more widely than previously thought.[56] How large the scale of the effect was in relation to the economy cannot be said.

Whatever the impetus – population growth or new technology – agricultural expansion took place at the expense of forests. A major issue with agricultural expansion in Nepal, therefore, was deforestation, and its potential effects on soil erosion, flooding, and decline in soil fertility. Foreign aid inflow has been influenced by impressions of the environmental impact, though cause and effect relationships are matters of controversy. Nepal, in this way, emerged into a kind of test case in the global discussions on environmental policy.[57]

---

[54] H.K. Upadhyay, C.C. David, G.G. Thapa, K. Otsuka, 'Adoption and Productivity Impact of Modern Rice Varieties in Nepal,' *Developing Economies*, 31(1), 1993, 122–37.

[55] Julie Guthman, 'Representing Crisis: The Theory of Himalayan Environmental Degradation and the Project of Development in Post-Rana Nepal,' *Development and Change*, 28(1), 1997, 45–69.

[56] '[T]he trade-off between efficiency and equity arising from differential technology adoption across production environments may not be as large as is commonly thought, owing to the presence of interregional adjustments in the labour market.' Hari K. Upadhyaya, Keijiro Otsuka and Cristina C. David, 'Differential Adoption of Modern Rice Technology and Regional Wage Differential in Nepal,' *Journal of Development Studies*, 26(3), 1990, 450–468.

[57] Guthman, 'Representing Crisis.'

Conclusion

Economists ask four types of question about the Green Revolution.

First, why did the farmers adopt new technology? Did they respond to market incentives, or respond to land reforms that made their property more secure than before? In view of the limited scale of the land reforms throughout South Asia, support for the second story cannot be strong. Equally, the market incentive story should be qualified too. Although in the first few years, the adoption of the technology on a large scale did happen because of market incentives, the revolution was flagging in the 1970s, and sustained thereafter – at least in India – by subsidization of inputs. Furthermore, by regulating trade, the governments of India and Pakistan ensured that market signals played a small role in farmers' decisions, and that food was available at a stable and below-the-world-market price. So, the correct answer to this question, in India, is markets between 1965 and 1980 and state support thereafter.

Second, what were the effects of the Green Revolution on rural society? Early investigations into this question predicted increased inequality. Later studies found ways in which efficiency gains were shared. One such mechanism was rise in wages, and immigration.[58] Another mechanism was industrialization. A third mechanism was an institutional one. Good infrastructure combined with high yield and capitalist farming encouraged new types of contracts between the peasants and large corporate farms. A yet fourth effect was that the Green Revolution directly or indirectly encouraged the fertility transition and investment in education.

Third, how does agriculture contribute to industrialization? 'Low agricultural commodity prices,' a paper on Pakistan says, 'have increasingly been used in Pakistan in the last two decades for immense resource transfers to the industrial sector, the government exchequer and the urban consumers.'[59] The statement was valid for India and Bangladesh

[58] Upadhyaya, Otsuka and David, 'Differential Adoption.'

[59] M. Ghaffar Chaudhry, 'Comments on 'The Agrarian Sector in Pakistan's Development Process – Historical Evidence and Implications for Policy and Theory'', *Pakistan Development Review*, 28(4), 1989, 526–8.

as well. In view of the regulation of prices and agricultural trades, the classic question of late development – can agriculture contribute – turns into a measurement problem. In the 1980s and 1990s research papers and books appeared on the subject. There were two particular measurement issues, terms of trade between agriculture and industry, and net resource flows. The two can be causally related when price policies shape resource flows. One study on resource flows found that a modest net flow towards agriculture in the 1950s reversed from the mid-1950s, that the drain from agriculture lasted until the Green Revolution was in full swing, and thereafter, the flow reversed again.[60] All this is pro-intuitive, even though later re-estimation of trading and financial incomes suggested some modification to the picture.

Finally, where is agriculture headed in South Asia? The Green Revolution is well past its peak, and it is time to count the costs. The environmental damages that it has caused are significant. Subsidized inputs led to the overuse of fertilizers and land, and degraded soil. Extraction of groundwater led to depletion of aquifers. To the extent the Green Revolution throughout South Asia was a tube well revolution, it shifted irrigation dependence from public sources towards private ones. At the same time, because of this shift, further investment in the system became dependent on the cost of complementary inputs, such as oil to run pump sets. When governments set their fuel prices to world market rates, farmers' risk goes up.[61] In short, the answer to the question is that agriculture is heading into a future where liberalization conflicts with sustainable agricultural growth.

The 1990s and beyond can be characterized as a post-green-revolution era that brings the negative externalities of the process into sharper relief. The Green Revolution was a water-intensive process of change. Vast productivity differences persisted between irrigated lands on the one hand, and rain-dependent lands on the other. Given the

[60] Sudipto Mundle, 'Inter-Sectoral Resource Flows in Post-Colonial India,' *Indian Economic Review*, 12(2), 1977, 151–167.

[61] Tushaar Shah, Mehmood ul Hassan, Muhammad Zubair Khattak, Parth Sarthi Banerjee, O.P. Singh, and Saeed Ur Rehman, 'Is Irrigation Water Free? A Reality Check in the Indo-Gangetic Basin,' *World Development*, 37(2), 2009, 422–434.

region's geography, the quantity of the latter type of land was greater. Even in irrigated areas, sustained application of chemical inputs and extraction of water exhausted soil and groundwater in large areas.

Regulation of trade, or what I will call in the rest of the book, trade repression, was an integral part of the strategy to make agriculture pay for industrialization. The story of trade and industry forms the subject of the next two chapters.

8

Trade and Industry I: India

The factor proportions theory of international trade predicts that a labour-abundant agricultural country will specialize in the production and export of labour-intensive and agricultural goods. If interest rates are high and capital markets thin, the country should import capital-intensive goods. This prediction fits the experience of pre-1947 South Asia, but fits it uneasily. While selling agricultural goods and labour services to the world, colonial India also developed a competitive factory industry. This anomaly suggests that entrepreneurs, especially those who made money in trade, need to play an explicit role in the economic history of South Asia.

In 1950, the states in the region inherited a large business world consisting of agricultural trade, with associated banking, insurance, storage, and transportation infrastructure. The trading firms, big banks, industrialists, and factory workers concentrated in a few cities – the ports Bombay, Calcutta, Madras, and Karachi, and Ahmedabad and Kanpur. More specialized than colonial India, Sri Lanka exported mainly plantation crops and Nepal exported mainly timber. The territories of Pakistan, India, and Bangladesh formed parts of a more or less integrated network of business in the colonial times.

T. Roy, *The Economy of South Asia*, Palgrave Studies in Economic History, DOI 10.1007/978-3-319-54720-6_8

Many economists in the mid-twentieth century and later believed that agricultural trade and finance were exploitative, and therefore, merchants and creditors needed to be restrained, even outlawed. Development economists in the 1950s were neither interested in nor knowledgeable about the commercial world of the countries that they were giving advice to. Business lobbies that did influence India's industrialization policy represented an interest group. Trading firms and foreign firms did not have political weight. In this backdrop, the government set out to repress trade to favour industry, with little opposition. The rest of South Asia had a more benign attitude to trade, but shared India's enthusiasm for industrialism.

This big turn, its varied manifestation, and eventual end form the subject matter of this and the next chapter. I study India in this chapter, because the literature is large, and because India pursued repression of trade further than the other countries. The next chapter will study the other four countries, including trade among the five countries.

Trade Repression

The onset of two big changes defines the mid-twentieth century – a relative fall in the role of trade within the economy, and enlargement of the government. Both these trends reversed from the last quarter of the twentieth century. Trade-GDP ratio reversed, and government expansion slowed (Figs. 8.1 and 8.2).

With foreign trade, the trade-GDP index is easily measurable, and shows a significant dip in the 1950s, 1960s, and the 1970s (Fig. 8.1). It is difficult to reconstruct domestic trade. The Indian National Accounts does not report trade data in sufficient detail. The figures are usually clubbed together with hotels; and show only retail trade. A great deal of the wholesale commodity trade took place under the direction of the government and para-statal agencies, for which no separate breakdown from general administrative income is available. The National Sample Surveys report a different set of numbers from the National Accounts. I have collated together the numbers that are available and created a graph that can be compared with Fig. 8.1. It is patchy, but tells a consistent story, the importance of domestic trade *in the private sector* experienced a relative decline in the 1950s, 1960s,

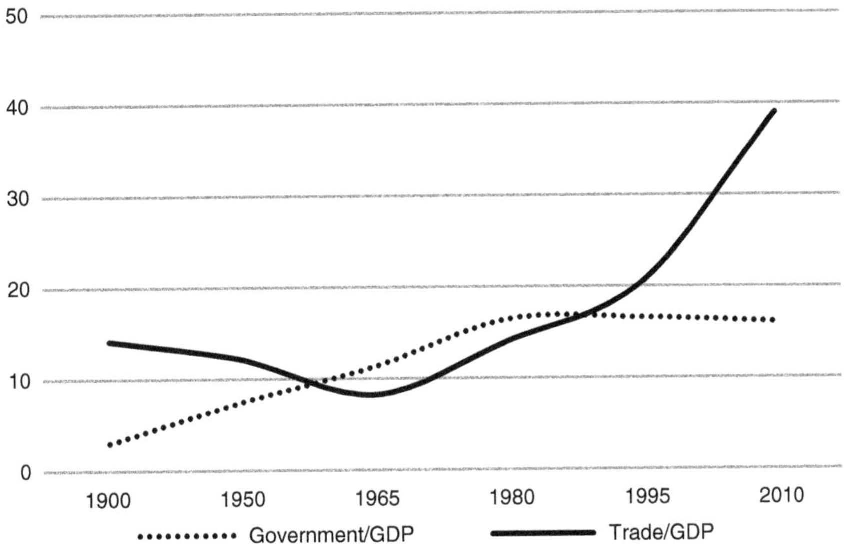

Fig. 8.1 Foreign trade and government expenditure in GDP (%) India 1900–2010

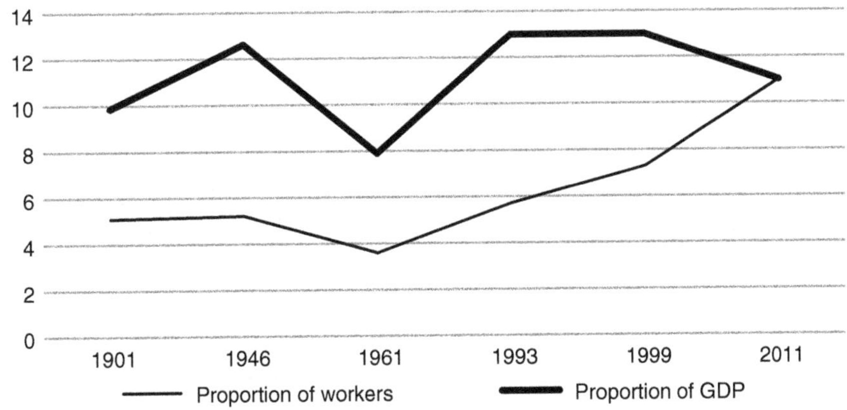

Fig. 8.2 Status of domestic trade in Indian economy (numbers are percentages)

Sources: S. Sivasubramonian, *National Income of India in the Twentieth Century*, New Delhi: Oxford University Press, 2000; J. Krishnamurty, 'Occupational Structure,' in Dharma Kumar, ed., *The Cambridge Economic History of India, vol. 2: c. 1750–c. 1970*, Cambridge: Cambridge University Press, 1983; India, *Economic Survey 2014–15*, Delhi: Government Press, 2015, volume 2. EPW Research Foundation, 'National Accounts Statistics of India - 1: Macro-Aggregates,' *Economic and Political Weekly*, 30 (46), 1995, 2955–2964; K. Sundaram, 'Employment and Poverty in India in the Nineteen Nineties.' Working Paper of CDE Delhi School of Economics, 2002

and possibly the 1970s (Fig. 8.2). There was no absolute decline, for growth rates of real GDP arising from trade remained positive throughout. The growth rate was small, and stayed marginally above the average GDP growth rate in these decades, speeding up only from the 1990s. More than a depression, this is a condition of *repressed* trade when compared with periods before or after.

Other figures confirm the conclusion. In the 1920s, half of India's highest income tax payers described themselves as traders.[1] In the 2000s, trading firms occupied barely 9–10 per cent of the private corporate sector.[2] The trade repression was accompanied with a decimation of corporate trading firms. Figure 8.2 supports that conclusion. The dip in the proportion of GDP was greater than the dip in the proportion of workers, which suggests that units that had higher labour productivity declined. An economic system containing organized and cosmopolitan commercial houses turned into one made up of neighbourhood shop-keepers in the mid-twentieth century. Where did this repression come from? What instruments were used to repress trade?

In India, there were separate regulations that had the effect of reducing the role of trading in the economy. Regulating imports in order to serve import-substituting industrialization was one part of this. The others were regulation on domestic and export trade in agricultural goods, fragmentation of intra-regional trade, and discouragement of foreign personnel recruitment in export-oriented foreign firms. The immediate impact of the Partition was adverse on firms engaged in rice trade, jute trade, and transportation operations between areas where hard borders came up, especially Bengal and Punjab. Large Indo-British firms engaged in running river steamers, the Indo-British firm Macneill-Barry for example, lost that business. Export-oriented industries like tea and jute faced higher costs.

Over the medium term, the government partly nationalized agricultural trade. Starting with the Essential Commodities Act of 1956, the government of India introduced bans on export of agricultural goods, on future markets,

[1] V.K.R.V. Rao, 'National Income of India,' *The Annals of the American Academy of Political and Social Science*, 233, 1944, 99–105.

[2] R. Nagaraj, 'Size and Structure of India's Private Corporate Sector: Implications for the New GDP Series,' *Economic and Political Weekly*, 50(45), 2015, 41–47.

on private trade, and on sale of agricultural goods except in approved sites. Most states (that is, provinces) first tolerated and then disallowed informal banking operations connected with agricultural finance. Earlier, foreign trade and domestic trade had a complementary relationship, because indigenous bankers financed both. With the fall of commodity export, and the link between foreign trade and domestic trade weakened, both trade and finance suffered. Leading communities that financed trade, such as the Marwaris, Multanis, Rohillas, and the Nattukottai Chettiars, had to shift money to retail businesses. Some left business.

In the export-oriented industries like jute and tea, trade repression involved a different set of instruments. Artificially overvalued exchange rate was bad for all commercial exports. The contribution of tea to total exports fell from over 20 per cent in 1947 to nearer 10 per cent at the end of the 1960s.[3] Tea was made to pay a hefty export tax. Exchange control meant restriction on imports of machinery. The tea industry turned to the home market, reduced investment, neglected stocks, and relaxed quality control. The export-production ratio declined from 70 per cent in 1950 to 27 per cent in 1991. In the jute industry, the regime imposed other kinds of cost. Jute packaging faced international competition from polypropylene from the 1960s.[4] But well before this competition became serious – the early 1970s – the one hundred odd jute textile mills of Calcutta had started going bankrupt (see Fig. 8.3). The immediate reason for their decline had little to do with the market. These companies, managed by British managing agency firms and part-owned by them and by the public, were targets of hostile takeovers by Indian upstarts who mismanaged these companies. In some cases, the former owners and managers gave up control. A string of British firms that specialized in the import of engineering goods and chemicals also were taken over by Indian families and subsequently mismanaged.

[3] I.S. Gulati, 'Competitiveness of India's Tea Exports,' *Economic and Political Weekly*, 3(7), 1968, 325–332.

[4] Synthetic substitute prices were approximately two-thirds that of comparable jute goods in the international market in the late 1960s. The ratio did not change very much, in fact marginally converged in the 1980s. The Government of India protected domestic consumption of jute. On relative price trends, Goutam K. Sarkar, 'The Fading Fabric-II: Jute Manufacturing Sector,' *Economic and Political Weekly*, 21(50), 1986, 2188–2197.

Fig. 8.3. Hastings Jute Mill

Migrant workers from Bihar turn raw jute into bolts of jute at the Hastings Jute Mill near Calcutta (Kolkata) city. The mill had a colourful history like many of the 200 odd jute mills near the city. The managing agency Andrew Yule operated Hastings Jute Mill, established in 1876 by Adam Birkmeyer. It was acquired by Bangur Brothers in 1946, became bankrupt, and was sold to Kajaria group (Murlidhar Ratanlal Exports) in Calcutta. © National Geographic/Alamy Stock Photo

When the management was unaffected, the government of India came down heavily on the transaction system that these firms relied on. These firms procured capital and technology from abroad, and recruited top management internationally. They were global firms, much more so than the multinationals that set up semi-autonomous branches within India, sold cosmetics, chemicals, cigarettes, or medicines to the Indians, and enjoyed the benefit of tariff protection. They did not trade much and did not export anything. The global firms did both, and because they did, they needed to maintain connections with marketing offices and partners abroad, and needed easy repatriation mechanisms. The nationalist state sharply erected capital controls and tariffs, informally banned foreign

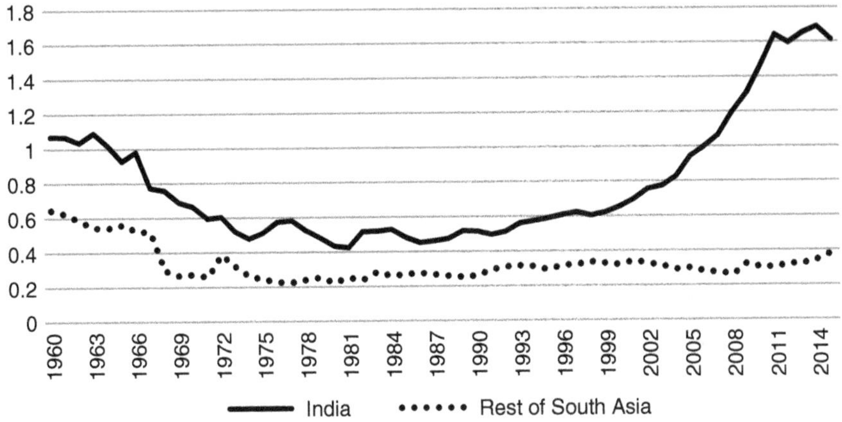

Fig. 8.4 Export as proportion of world export (%)

hiring, which made trading, repatriation, and recruitment abroad more difficult than before. Between 1950 and 1970, except a few multinationals selling goods to Indians, the British firms that were engaged in export-oriented trading and manufacturing were squeezed out of India.

The combined effect of trade repression was not only attrition of capital and enterprise in the domestic economy, but also retreat from world trade. As Fig. 8.4 shows, the extent of the retreat was dramatic for India, though the trend was shared with the other South Asian countries. The turnaround in the graph for India occurs around 1982–1983, long before any formal economic reforms. The only thing that had changed was the value of the Indian currency (Fig. 8.5).

Where did the anti-trade sentiment come from? It may have come from a vague sense that India, with its history of famines, needed to control food trade. A colonial sentiment also played a part. British provincial officers justified their benevolent rule by blaming Indian money-lenders for the poverty of the peasants. This stylized and politically motivated narrative was absorbed by the Indian nationalists, and reinforced by Indian Marxists. According to the latter, 'merchants enjoying monopoly position' in colonial India 'advanced money to needy peasants for growing cash crops, and in the process absorbed the entire profit themselves . . . To exploitation through taxes, rent and

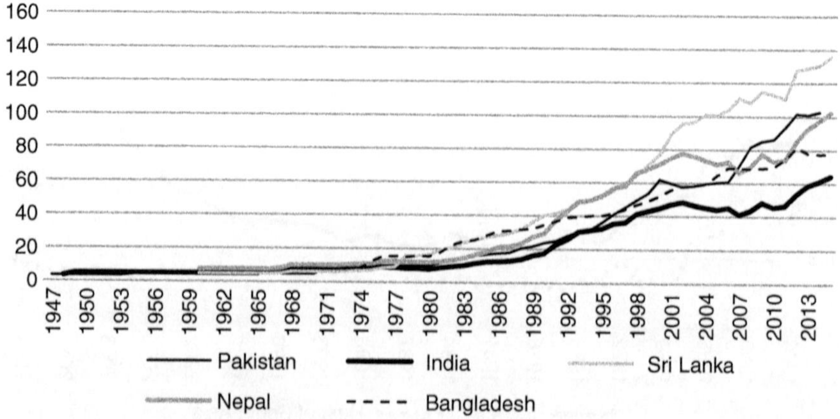

Fig. 8.5 Local currency/US$

Source: World Bank, World Development Indicators; and https://knoema.com/infographics/rygejhb/rupee-devaluation-against-dollar-1947-till-date (accessed 10 September 2016)

interest was added the exploitation by the merchant through the market. The nominally independent peasant became enmeshed and dominated by usurer's and merchant's capital.'[5] No statistics was supplied to show what proportion of the income from production was shared, and whether the income was large enough in the first place. But then serious evidence was not necessary. That all rural trade was exploitation and all rural finance was 'usurious' were matters of faith. No other narrative was considered. Therefore, state repression of trade and finance went ahead unchallenged, and from time to time, was endorsed by historians.[6]

The trade depression cost dear. In 1947, Japan and China were out of the reckoning in Asian trade, and India was by far the larger national economy in all of Asia. The Partition-related dislocation was severe, but not crippling. India still had a huge credit balance in the external

[5] Indian School of Social Sciences, 'Economic Crisis in India and the Fifth Five Year Plan', *Social Scientist*, 3(5), 1974, 61–88.

[6] For example, David Hardiman, *Feeding the Baniya: Peasants and Usurers in Western India*, Berkeley and Los Angeles: University of California Press, 1996; and essays in Sugata Bose, ed., *Credit, Markets, and the Agrarian Economy in Colonial India*, New Delhi: Oxford University Press, 1994.

accounts thanks to the sterling balances, and a diversified industrial base. The leadership expressed justifiable confidence that India would play a leading role in post-war Asian economic regeneration. The Indian statement in an Asian Relations Conference held in 1947 expressed this sentiment in no uncertain terms: 'India, of all the Asian countries, must do everything in her power to take the former place of Japan.'[7] As the 1950s progressed, something quite the opposite happened. Trade war broke out between India and Pakistan. Indian trading firms were in retreat, and export growth fell. By the 1960s, a re-emergent Japan ended any ambition India might have of leading the Asian market.[8]

Was this necessary? Was trade repression somehow a sacrifice that needed to be made for import-substituting industrialization and the prevention of famines? With hindsight, the answer must be negative. There is no analytical link between industrialization and repression of trade. Regulation of agricultural trade did not save the country from food shortages. The problem of food shortage lay in production, not marketing. A simpler solution to the threat of famines would have been for India to allow freer food trade with Pakistan. In other words, trade repression stemmed from politics and not from either economic theory or economic history.

There were occasions when the government came close to opening up foreign trade. The 1967 foreign exchange crisis was one of these (see Chapter 3). In the post-oil-shock years, when foreign exchange was in short supply and aid had nearly dried up, India avoided opening up trade by negotiating barter-based trade arrangement with the USSR, which made it possible to import oil without strains on exchange. Some saw the Indo-Soviet barter trade as a colonial dependent relationship, others saw it as a means to gain freedom from western hegemony. No matter the rhetoric, by 1975 a quarter of India's exports went into servicing debts to the USSR.

---

[7] Cited in Sumanta Banerjee, 'India and South Asia: Growing Economic Stake,' *Economic and Political Weekly*, 6(24), 1971, 1168–1169.

[8] By then, South Asian countries were competing against each other. Protectionist moves by Sri Lanka in the 1960s, for example, were read as a reaction to threats from the Indian textile industry.

When did trade repression ease? Before tariff policies and foreign investment policy changed, the Green Revolution led to a revival of local trade in agricultural commodities. The quantitative scale of the revival of commodity trade remains unmeasured. It was of significant order in the main states that benefited from new technology. A study on trade in North Arcot in Tamil Nadu, for example, has shown that local trade in agricultural produce and especially agricultural inputs, such as chemical fertilizers, revived as an effect of the Green Revolution. The revived trade, called commercial explosion in one work, made land-holding peasants take on a trading role. This is a contrast with the colonial era of commercialization, when agricultural growth attracted capital from professional bankers. The state being against capitalism in agriculture, 'the possibilities of private traders to concentrate capital through this kind of trade [was] limited.'[9] But there was a change no doubt.

Trade repression was absent throughout in manufactured consumer goods. Urban trade, especially in consumer goods and machinery, as well as urban food trade, were never seriously regulated by contrast with agriculture and foreign trade. The Green Revolution and the backdoor globalization (see below) of the 1980s revived trading in these fields. In the 2000s, foreign trade revived in all parts of South Asia. More surprisingly, intra-South-Asia trade, long obstructed by hard borders and hostile politics, started to increase. A lot of trade among South Asian countries is technically illegal so that estimates of revival are often wide apart from each other. Nevertheless, market integration within South Asia was big enough to be a talking point among economists who expected 'great economic benefits from a policy of deep regional integration.'[10]

Along with regulating trade, the nationalist regime also regulated the older industries. Jute and tea have been mentioned above. Cotton textiles deserve a longer discussion.

---

[9] Barbara Harriss-White, 'The Role of Agro-Commercial Capital in 'Rural Development' in South India,' *Social Scientist*, 7(7), 1979, 42–56.

[10] John Williamson, 'Pakistan and the World Economy,' *Pakistan Development Review*, 37(4), 1999, 181–201.

Cotton Textiles

The Mahalanobis model that charted India's industrial pathway after 1956 implied that the state should concern itself with producing capital goods, while leaving the consumer goods to the small firms and rural firms. The model did not specify a role for the export-oriented industries that had done so well in the colonial times, jute, tea, and textiles. The government decided that to allow the cotton mills to grow further would lock up foreign exchange and savings, and harm the interest of the small firms. In 1948, the Cotton Textiles (Control) Order froze mill capacity in weaving, taxed mill production of cloth more heavily than before and reserved goods for exclusive production in the handlooms.[11]After 1960, the industry retreated from export, ironically while East Asia was building its own industrialization upon textile export. The quality and range of cotton cloth fell. Not surprisingly, domestic consumption level also declined in the next decade. The 1970s were disastrous for the industry. The majority of the colonial-era mills were left with obsolete machines and too little money to buy new machines. Owners and managers stripped the assets of the firms that they felt would sink (Fig. 8.6). Some were nationalized and were mismanaged by the government officers.

Even as the cotton mills were sinking, the textile industry grew in capacity because fabric production shifted to small firms. This may sound like a success of the regulation favouring small-scale industry, but that was not quite the case. The small firms where fabric production moved were not the handlooms, where capacity could grow legally, but the technically illegal mechanized weaving factories called power-looms. Between 1960 and 2000, the number of power-looms expanded by almost a million. Most of these factories started with looms discarded by closed and modernizing mills, which machines were of limited capability. On an average a factory would have anything between 4 and 40 looms. The

[11] D. Mazumdar, D., 'The Issue of Small versus Large in the Indian Textile Industry', World Bank Staff Working Paper No. 645, Washington, DC, 1984; I.M.D., Little, D. Mazumdar, J. M. Page Jr., *Small Manufacturing Enterprises, a Comparative Analysis of India and Other Economies*, New York: Oxford University, 1987.

Fig. 8.6. Derelict cotton mill in Bombay

Dark factory floor with abandoned machinery was once a common sight in Bombay, symbol of the neglect of the cotton textile industry by a government keen to develop 'heavy' industry. The picture shows the interior of the Madhusudan Mills. © Kunal Ghevaria

quality of processing was poor. The illegality restricted the power-looms from raising bank loan for investment. After the Textile Policy ended in 1985 and power-looms became legal, some of the larger factories modernized themselves, but the smallest firms made profits when the market was good and closed down when the market turned bad.

How should we read the rise of the small-scale weaving factory? Mechanized spinning and weaving in South Asia started in the nineteenth century in the form of vertically integrated cotton textile mill that had a spinning unit, a weaving unit, and a processing unit all under one compound. The majority of the cotton mills of Bombay and Ahmedabad were vertically integrated production systems. After 1950, new entry into the textile industry occurred in the form of independent weaving factory, spinning factory, and processing factory, under different ownership. These firms clustered in small towns, and not in the big cities like Bombay and Ahmedabad. They formed a system of textile production based on market transactions, as opposed to one based on vertical integration and hierarchical management.

Undoubtedly, the power-looms were helped by regulation imposed upon the mills. But regulation was harsh for the power-looms too. So regulation alone cannot explain their rise. In the long run, power-looms had market forces on their side. The vertical integration model is an appropriate organizational choice when there are technological or other forms of interdependencies, and the costs of operating in markets are high.[12] These conditions were present in nineteenth-century India. In 1880, for example, a textile mill would need to procure machines from Manchester, and hire foremen and engineers from abroad. There were economies in this activity; it would make sense for the merchant contracting for spinning machines and engineers abroad, to do it for weaving and processing machines at the same time. Search cost for labour was high, and there were economies of scale in gathering wage labour in an urban site. Therefore, the cotton mills tended to be large and integrated. A hundred years later, migrant labour was available aplenty in small towns. Capital was available from local sources. Machines were locally purchased and repaired. Setting up a mechanized textile mill did not entail any particular advantage of integration. At the same time, large cotton mills located in Mumbai (Bombay) and Ahmedabad faced high urban charges.

Flexible specialization was another factor that favoured the small weaver. In the 1980s, worldwide, consumers of textiles reduced the habit of buying pieces of cloth, to be tailored, and switched to ready-made garments from department stores. In South Asia, the old habit

[12] See N. Lamoreaux, D.M.G. Raff and P. Temin, 'Beyond Markets and Hierarchies: Towards a New Synthesis of American Business History', *American Historical Review*, 108(2), 2003, 404–33, for an application and a survey. For other major contributions in application of theory to explain economic history, see O.E. Williamson, *Economic Institutions of Capitalism*, New York: Simon and Schuster, 1995; and several essays in C. Sabel and J. Zeitlin, eds., *World of Possibilities: Flexibility and Mass Production in Western Industrialization*, Cambridge: Cambridge University Press, 1997.

survived a little longer because cloth retailing did not happen in large stores yet. As the region started to export readymade garments abroad, a certain quantity of the export surplus reached the domestic retail market. From the 1990s, tailoring shifted to the factories that catered to both exports and home consumers. The rise of readymade garment production created a new need to differentiate products, which was possible if clothing makers dealt with suppliers of cloth in small lots. As a result of this shift, fabric brands ceased to matter, and large mills lost their brand image.

Although power-looms represented the decline of vertical integration in cotton textiles, the manner of their growth did not allow the majority of them to become high-quality manufacturers. After the old textile policy was abandoned in favour of a new one in 1985 and a liberal import regime was introduced, some Indian mills tried to reinvent themselves as producers of high-quality fabrics. Vertical integration still matters in certain lines of production. Denims, for example, require integration in spinning, weaving, and processing. Few old mills could adapt in this way, however. The main beneficiaries of the reforms were a small subset of weaving factories or power-looms and the knitwear industry.

By contrast with these stories of decline and depression, the most dynamic segment of large-scale industry in the 1950s was the public sector.

Public Enterprise

India's industrial policy pushed the government to start industries. These projects received foreign aid and technical assistance. Between 1955 and 1965, oil, gas, and heavy machinery were the three main fields to attract aid-funded public investment. Whereas half of US aid went into food and commodities, a quarter went to industrial projects started by the government, and another quarter to railways, power, and irrigation development, again under the government. West German, Soviet, and British aid went into industrial development. Foreign aid helped the government meet its two deficits, fiscal and foreign exchange, but did little to alleviate the shortage of foreign exchange for the private sector. A great deal of the aid money funded the government's purchase of technology.

Oil and steel were the first areas to receive government investment. By 1955, the government had signed agreements with Burmah-Shell, Esso, and Caltex for refinery expansion. The Assam Oil Company was an existing firm in crude oil production and refining. In a series of steps taken in the 1970s, these companies were nationalized to form Indian Oil Corporation. The government next acquired a partnership in explorations projects in Assam through a new joint venture called Oil India Ltd., and began to establish itself as the main agency for explorations in Gujarat through a department called Oil and Natural Gas Commission (ONGC). New refineries were set up, some with joint ownership, and some of them owned by the government.

In 1947, there were two large private sector integrated steel producers in India, the Tata Iron and Steel Company or TISCO, and the Indian Iron and Steel Company or IISCO. From early in the 1950s, the government decided to set up public sector units, while not stopping expansion in the private sector. The policy succeeded to the extent that by 1964, half of domestic production was coming from the new public sector units, and this proportion was projected to be 75 per cent by the early 1970s. All of the new capacity was dependent on foreign aid, and 84 per cent of aid into steel went into public sector capacity expansion. Of the first generation of public sector steel mills, Bhilai was established with Soviet assistance, Durgapur with British assistance, and Rourkela with German assistance. A fourth project in Bokaro was conceived in the 1960s, and negotiations began first with the US government for official assistance.

Foreign aid made it clear that political choices were a necessary condition for receiving aid. The USA did not like being an instrument of India's socialist experiment, and wanted to commit money to private enterprises instead. The dispute mattered not only to industrial policy, but also to American foreign policy. Financing of oil refinery and new steel plants were disfavoured by the donors because of conflicts of interest with multinationals. The government found it unpleasant to negotiate with the oil multinationals on profit margins and explorations. India, therefore, welcomed the emergence of the USSR as a large oil producer. Soviet aid began to enter state refinery projects from the late 1950s. As the Cold War warmed up in the 1970s, USSR turned into a major trade partner and a source of ideological support for public sector industrial production (see also Chapter 3).

After oil and steel, the government moved into heavy engineering, a field it had more or less preserved for itself. Three diversified companies were established. The first one of the three was Heavy Engineering Corporation, set up to make steel plant machines. The leading company in the manufacture of machines and components for the power utilities was Bharat Heavy Electrical or BHEL, which started in 1964. In the same year, Bharat Earth Movers Limited started making railway coaches and mining equipment. Earlier, in 1948, the Indian Telephone Industries was set up to make telecommunication equipment, and in 1953, the Hindustan Machine Tools was established to manufacture machine tools, though it later diversified into tractors and watches. Other engineering companies came into the government's hands through nationalization, for example, Bridge and Roof, an ailing British construction firm that had started in India in 1920.

Petrochemicals and fertilizers were the last major field to receive government investment from the 1960s. Petrochemicals started as an extension of the government owned oil refineries. Growth of petrochemical production was limited until 1980, and protected under high tariffs. Therefore, the use of plastics was also limited, for better or worse, compared with the rest of the world.

Import-Substituting Industrialization and Private Enterprise

In the private enterprise sector, the new policy had the effect of encouraging production expansion in cement, chemicals, machinery, machine tools, transport equipment, and tyres, among other industries. Encouragement would mean easier conditions for grant of investment license, and where relevant, import license. In return for the favour, the government controlled the prices of intermediate goods, including cement and steel. After 1992, both types of license were withdrawn. Price controls had ended earlier.

Industries that supplied material to construction activity, steel and cement, were a priority for the government. As we have seen, one of the two private steel firms, Tata, was left private. Tata Steel enjoyed a protected market that was growing thanks to large infrastructure projects. India has plenty of cement grade limestone. Cement production started during World War I. During the World War II, the government took over distribution and regulated prices. After independence, the price control stayed, and though controls were relaxed from time to time, prices continued to be regulated until around 1990. Again as in steel, the existing private producers were left untouched, but few new entry was allowed.

In the engineering industry, private companies made complete machines for traditional industries like textiles, cement, sugar, paper, mining, and rubber. The equipment for utilities like power and railways were reserved for the public sector. In automobiles, the government decided to retain the five existing main firms, disallowed new entry and competition, but allowed the incumbents to enter technical collaboration with foreign partners. An exception to the policy not to allow entry was two-wheeler manufacturing, where Bajaj and Royal Enfield entered.

The Indian chemical industry was large, but populated by small firms with limited technological capability. These firms served traditional users. The alkali chemicals manufacturers supplied caustic soda, chlorine and soda ash to paper, glass, aluminium, and soaps and detergents; inorganic chemicals manufacturers supplied sulphuric acid to fertilizers and batteries, among other users; carbon black went to tyres; calcium carbide to acetylene gas and fertilizers; and organic chemicals to food, glue, drugs, leather, among others. Two other large components were dyes and pesticides. In the 1970s, certain branches of the industry were extended the benefit of small-scale reservation (see Chapter 3).

The high tariff barrier had provided an opportunity to the world's leading producers of consumer goods and drugs, including Levers, Philips, Johnson and Johnson, Nestle, and Glaxo, to open branches in India. A range of technical collaboration agreements also brought in foreign participation in industry, especially engineering. Foreign partnership was rare outside the government sector, and subject to strict licensing control. An Indian firm could not just purchase machines abroad, nor could a foreign multinational enter India easily. Foreign technology was available to private firms via foreign collaboration agreement. This was licensed, and the licenses were hard to get. There were several high profile cases in the 1950s and 1960s of expansion plans being abandoned because the government delayed or denied collaboration license. One of these was a special steels project of TISCO, the private sector firm.

Towards the end of the 1960s, there were signs of a crisis in the making.

Industrial Stagnation and Recovery 1965–1985

In the late 1960s, industrial growth fell and stayed low until the end of the 1970s. Between 1955 and 1965, the growth rate of real GDP in manufacturing was 7 per cent per year, in the next 10 years, the rate was 4 per cent (the difference was smaller, from 6 to 4, if small industry is included). Economists offered quite different diagnoses. Marxists blamed under-consumption caused by poverty, inequality, and destitution.[13] They pointed at a fall in cotton textile purchase per head to illustrate the under-consumption. As a matter of fact, there was quite a lot of smuggled goods coming in from East Asia, from pens made in Taiwan to clothing made in Thailand, from the 1970s, suggesting that Indian quality rather than purchasing power may have fallen. According to non-Marxist economists, excessive government investment in projects that yielded low returns was responsible for the stagnation.[14]

In fact, there was a combination of factors behind the industrial stagnation. For example, in the older industries like textiles and engineering there was widespread bankruptcy. Tea survived an outright crisis but

[13] See essays in Deepak Nayyar, ed., *Industrial Growth and Stagnation: The Debate in India*, Delhi: Oxford University Press, 1994, on the extent of the industrial decline, and interpretations thereof.

[14] Pranab Bardhan, *The Political Economy of Development in India*, Oxford: Basil Blackwell, 1984; I.J. Ahluwalia, *Industrial Growth in India: Stagnation since the Mid-Sixties*, Delhi: Oxford University Press, 1985; J.N. Bhagwati and T.N. Srinivasan, *Foreign Trade Regime and Economic Development: India*, New York: Columbia University Press, 1975.

had to live with a slow-growing and low-quality market. In the new industries import substitution possibility was running out. Exchange crisis following the first oil shock of 1973 induced tighter import controls. In deference to the anti-multinational political mood, the Parliament took a hostile stand on foreign investment. In the 1970s, foreign firms were placed under the purview of two restrictive laws, the Monopolies and Restrictive Trade Practices Act (most multinational firms fell within the definition of a 'monopoly', which followed the benchmark of average size), and the Foreign Exchange Regulation Act, which made repatriation of profits difficult. Some of the multinationals left India. When cement, rubber, paper, and sugar, faced sluggish market, the companies making machines for them did too. The public sector industries made heavy losses, and had poor record on technical efficiency. In steel, for example, protection, discouragement to exports, and public sector dominance led to an inefficient pattern of growth that neither met demand nor utilized the resource advantage that India possessed. Assessments of foreign aid and aid-tied imports were negative, and alleged India's dependence upon foreigners.[15] A survey found ground to conclude that aid-tying led to inappropriate technological choices.[16]

The extreme form of protection practised in India hurt export. Inefficiency 'spilled over.' For example, the high cost of locally made machines raised the cost of goods made by using those machines. Comparative advantages were ignored. As resources were channelled into non-competitive capital goods, exportable labour-intensive manufactures were denied capital. Resources, thus, were made to move to sectors with lower return to capital and lower employment potential. The quality of light manufactures and consumer goods such as cotton textiles, despite a strong historical legacy, was poor by world standards and the producers of these goods faced bankruptcy.

Bankruptcy spread in the textile and engineering factories also because of militant unions. With the rise of regional political parties, trade

[15] See, for example, K.K. Subrahmanian, 'Role of Foreign Aid and Investment', *Social Scientist*, 1(6), 1973, 3–29.

[16] U. Lele and I. Nabi, 'The Role of Aid and Capital Flows in Economic Development', *American Journal of Agricultural Economics*, 73(3), 1991, 947–950.

unions, in their turn, were a field of contest between regional political parties and local leaders, many of whom tried to break the monopoly of recognized unions. These new dynamics engendered some of the largest and most violent industrial disputes, such as the Bombay Textile Strike (1982–1983).[17] From the mid-1950s, the industrial network based in Calcutta, one of the oldest and wealthiest in British India was falling behind the rest of India, and by the mid-1960s, urban unemployment was a serious problem here. Trade union violence played a particularly destructive role in this city.

The politics of large versus small added its own share of problems. In 1977, for the first time in independent India, a non-Congress party with a significant presence of Gandhians within its leadership, formed a government in Delhi. The experiment lasted a few years. It left a legacy in the shape of significant state aid to handicrafts and small firms, often at the expense of large firms. By the end of the 1980s, '[a]ny item that can be produced by small manufacturers is banned from production by any other means irrespective of cost effectiveness in production, technological progress, international competitiveness, and overall industrial health of the country.'[18] By means of a variety of instruments, implemented by a number of agencies and involving both fiscal support and quantitative restrictions, numerous product lines came to be reserved for production in small-scale industry.[19] In the 1980s, the number of such products exceeded 800.[20]

In the late 1970s, industrial growth picked up again. Between 1975 and 1985, the growth rate of real GDP in manufacturing increased from 4 per cent (1965–1975) to 6 per cent. Like the stagnation, the revival has no easy explanation. The old industries had reached a point where they could not fall any further. There were a few new growth areas,

---

[17] Hubert van Wersch, *The Bombay Textile Strike 1982–83*, Delhi: Oxford University Press, 1992.

[18] S. Guhathakurta, 'Economic Independence through Protection? Emerging Contradictions in India's Small-scale Policies Sector', *World Development*, 21(12), 1993, 2039–2054.

[19] S.P. Kashyap, 'Growth of Small-sized Enterprises in India: Its Nature and Content, *World Development*, 16(6), 1988, 667–681.

[20] J. C. Sandesara, 'Small-Scale Industrialisation: The Indian Experience', *Economic and Political Weekly*, 23(13), 1988, 640–654; M.H. Bala Subrahmanya, 'Reservation Policy for Small-Scale Industry: Has It Delivered the Goods?', *Economic and Political Weekly*, 30(21), 1995, M51–M54.

petrochemicals, manmade fibre textiles, and fertilizers, for example. In these fields, technical collaboration and foreign investment received encouragement, though on a case by case basis. What I later call 'backdoor' globalization enabled some offbeat enterprises, like the collaboration on automobiles between the government of India and Suzuki Motors. In 1983, the investment licensing policy was modestly liberalized. In 1985, a new Textile Policy shed the most controversial regulatory clauses.

Employers learnt how to avoid unions. The industry-wide strikes of 1981–1983 failed. But these left large employers more nervous than before. In new firms, employers avoided hiring. In the 1970s, labour laws were made more stringent than before. Unable to retrench or redeploy labour, the employers became reliant on casual labour, which carried an air of illegality and exploitation. In the 1980s, organized manufacturing saw 'jobless growth'. Production and investment picked up, but employment did not. Interestingly, real wages grew. Employers either successfully handled militancy and rewarded a smaller remaining workforce, or were forced by the protests to deliver more wages.[21]

Industrial investment recovered in the 1980s also because the government, instead of nationalizing more bankrupt businesses, made investments indirectly. State-owned financial companies began to give long-term loans to corporates. The principle of channelling public money into private companies was introduced with the nationalization of the

---

[21] For a selection of writings interpreting the 1980s 'jobless growth' in organized manufacturing, I.J. Ahluwalia, *Productivity and Growth in Indian Manufacturing*, Delhi: Oxford University Press, 1991; Ajit Ghose, 'Economic Restructuring, Employment and Safety Nets', ILO-ARTEP, *Social Dimensions of Structural Adjustment in India*, ILO, Delhi, 1995; R. Nagraj, 'Employment and Growth in Manufacturing Industries: Trends, Hypotheses and Evidence', *Economic and Political Weekly*, 29(4), 1994; S.R. Bhalotra, 'The Puzzle of Jobless Growth in Indian Manufacturing', *Oxford Bulletin of Economics and Statistics*, 60(1), 1998, 5–32; K.V. Ramaswamy, 'The Search for Flexibility in Indian Manufacturing: New Evidence on Outsourcing Activities', *Economic and Political Weekly*, 34(6), 1999, 363–368. For a survey of this literature and an interpretation of the 1990s, see B.N. Goldar, 'Employment Growth in Organized Manufacturing Growth in India', *Economic and Political Weekly*, 35(14), 2000, 1191–1195. On labour issues see Dabashish Bhattacharjee, 'Globalising Economy, Localising Labour', *Economic and Political Weekly*, 35 (42), 2000.

Life Insurance Corporation in 1955, and almost immediately ran into a corruption scandal. Allegation of corruption pursued the state-run financial system in the 1980s as well. Still, taxpayers' money had better chance of getting into a profitable investment.

Along with these changes, a bottom-up type of change had begun in the countryside. The Green Revolution gave a boost to both consumption and small-scale businesses. Rural wages were rising in areas that directly took part in the Green Revolution. Profits were to be made in farming. Rich peasants invested the profits in small-scale industry. This was noticed in Punjab. In small-scale textile production in the towns of Tamil Nadu, the presence of middle peasants as textile entrepreneurs was long established. That particular example of diversification originated before the Green Revolution, and was linked to transition in the handloom weaving industry in the region. It was reinforced by agricultural accumulation.[22]

The second process of change began around 1980.

Backdoor Globalization

The state allowed market forces to play a bigger role in industry, without announcing a liberalization, or even meaning to do so. The official policy stayed faithful to a closed and protectionist economy, but exchange control was relaxed. Why it was relaxed nobody knows for sure. The most obvious game-changer was the remittance from the Gulf. All we know is that for the first time in post-independence history, in 1980, oil shocks and the threat of exchange shortage did not lead to the imposition of tighter controls, but the opposite, the Rupee was allowed to float. There were also a move to involve scientists in framing an information technology policy (mid-1980s), a reform in the textile

[22] T. Roy, 'Growth and Recession in Small-scale Industry: A Study of Tamil Nadu Powerlooms', *Economic and Political Weekly*, 1999; H. Damodaran, *India's New Capitalists: Caste, Business, and Industry in a Modern Nation*, London: Palgrave Macmillan, 2008; Sharad Chari, *Fraternal Capital. Peasant-Workers, Self-Made Men, and Globalization in Provincial India*, Stanford: Stanford University Press, 2004.

policy as we have seen, and the joint venture in automobile manufacture. All of these steps were begun during the last days of Indira Gandhi's Prime Ministership (she was assassinated in 1984), which was otherwise known for hard socialist leanings.

It is more than likely that the five countries observed each other in relaxing exchange rate, as if in a closely coordinated move. The fact that between them they traded little (except India and Nepal), and that each government looked towards trade outside the region imparted a uniformity in their action (Fig. 8.5).

As soon as the Rupee started depreciating (Fig. 8.5), exports of three light industries, clothing including knitwear, leather goods, and cut gems, rose, and with the profits, these businesses started buying machines and tools abroad. The automobile joint venture between the government of India and Suzuki Motors turned into a powerful symbol of industrial modernization. The success of the lightweight cars it made underscored the conservatism of its Indian rivals, who had remained wedded to heavy and inefficient cars in small numbers. The enterprise encouraged auto ancillary production in India, and the entry of some keiretsu-affiliated Japanese firms in ancillary production. The presence of this component manufacturing complex attracted the next-generation auto manufacturers that came into India in the 1990s and beyond, such as, Toyota, Honda, and Mitsubishi.

Export success in industry, however, built on small-scale industry. The major examples were textiles and clothing, leather, gems and jewellery, processed food, plastics and plastic intermediates, machine tools, pharmaceuticals, and the handicrafts. In textiles and clothing, the reservation policy was helpful to the existing firms, whereas trade reforms enabled them to access technologies better than before. The quality of clothing produced from India improved as a result. Another export success story was the handicrafts. The world market for ethnic goods rediscovered Indian designs and products. In the process, a large number of new stakeholders – NGOs, private firms, innovative government departments, designers, design institutions – worked to promote the trade of modern goods made with traditional designs, and even fashioned a whole new discourse on the crafts, stressing their strengths and innovative ability rather than their weakness and traditionalism.

Notwithstanding export success, the general picture of the small firm was a mixed one. The overall growth rate of small firms decelerated in the 1990s.[23] No matter which industry they worked in, small firms were subject to harassment by corrupt tax and customs officers, and in the case of the handicrafts, by the tourism mafia of northern India.[24] The product reservation for the small firm created perverse incentives discouraging small firms from expanding or modernizing in a legal way. It created barriers for larger firms to enter the reserved areas. These down-the-scale biases led to poor technological effort, limited quality control and brand creation. Only in the early 2000s did this policy see serious reform. In current scholarship on small firms, the problems of technological backwardness and slow adaptation are stressed, and attributed to the weight of bad practice in the past, the low cost of labour, and the low skill component of the workers.[25]

Backdoor globalization, therefore, could only go so far. Tariffs remained high. Little had changed to industrial regulation. In 1991, there was fear of an exchange crisis because of poor export performance, import dependence, and the channelling of foreign currency into projects that did not create the capacity to repay in foreign currency. The end of the closed economy was introduced in 1992 with a sharp drop in the average tariff rates.

Full Liberalization

Industries that had been sheltered from international competition before, such as manufacture of machinery and machine tools, faced bankruptcy when trade policy was changed. There were closures in

---

[23] M.H. Bala Subrahmanya, 'Small Industry and Globalisation: Implications, Performance and Prospects,' *Economic and Political Weekly*, 2004, 1826–1834.

[24] Maureen Liebl and Tirthankar Roy, 'Handmade in India: Status Report on India's Artisans', *Economic and Political Weekly*, 38(51–2), 2003–4, 5366–5376.

[25] See, for example, several essays in Konosuke Odaka and Yukihiko Kiyokawa, eds., *Small and Medium Scale Industry in India and the Model of Japan*, New Delhi: Allied Publishers, 2008.

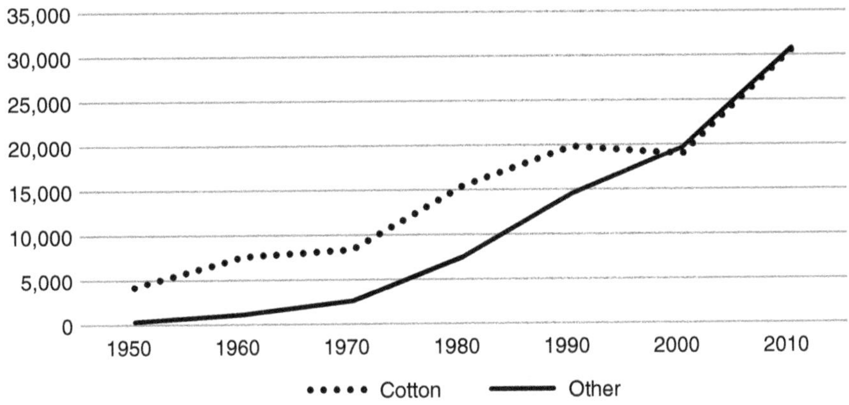

Fig. 8.7 Production of fabrics in India 1950–2010 (million sq. metres)

machinery and metallurgy. At the end of 2000, 1.9 million workers were on the rolls of factories that had registered themselves with agencies in charge of bankruptcy and liquidation. A little less than half of this figure was employed in textiles and engineering. Not all of these closures were an effect of the economic reform, some of it was a carryover of the bankruptcy that had happened before. Indian law did not permit closed units to be officially closed. At the same time, the reforms revived the fortune of tea to some extent. Through mergers and acquisitions, some old tea companies consolidated into a more efficient structure.

With rise in clothing export, the textile industry also turned around. India's share in the world trade in textiles and apparel rose from near-zero in 1970 to 5 per cent in 2015, in apparel alone the percentage was 12. For the last 20 years, the average growth rate in exports in value has been well above the rate of growth of world trade. Figure 8.7 suggests that the fabric production curves turned up in the 1970s. In the 1990s, cotton fabric production suffered somewhat, because by then India's cotton cloth had found a market among apparel exporters in East and Southeast Asia, and these markets experienced a recession. The recovery thereafter was impressive. Almost all of this growth occurred in small firms.

Diamond exports also did well. Rough diamonds were mined in Africa and Russia, first sent to Antwerp, and then to other countries for cutting and polishing. Bombay joined the polishing trade in the 1970s, not only because wages of skilled workers was low in India, but also, a significant part of the world trade in diamonds was in the hands of Palanpuri Jain merchants based in Antwerp and Bombay. As wages increased in Bombay, the industry moved to Surat. Under the liberal regime, it became easier to import better tools. From the mid-2000s, the capability in Surat had increased sufficiently for it to take up both simpler and complex tasks. The leather industry also had a brief export boom in the 1990s, because technological capability in finishing improved enough for some of the large firms to diversify into footwear and fashion articles. Finally, some of the handicrafts, mainly knotted carpets and printed and embroidered textiles, grew in scale, thanks to direct exports and to tourism demand.

These export successes occurred in light industry. In heavy industry, a different dynamic was set in motion. Foreign investment, mergers and acquisitions, led to consolidation of companies, more investment, and expansion. Their market was the Indian market. Few corporates exported on a significant scale. After 1992, cement attracted foreign investment. Some of the most regulated heavy industries experienced the most dramatic expansion. For example, cement production increased from 50 tonnes in 1992 to 220 in 2015, making India the second largest cement producer in the world. The greater part of this increase went to private housing, and had direct relationship with average income and private saving. Again thanks to foreign investment, the machine tools industry diversified and grew into a major player in Asia. The southern city of Bangalore is now known internationally as a software hub; it is in fact also the machine tools hub of the country. Although the industry is oriented to the large home market, it has forged close ties with East and Southeast Asian producers. For example, the major companies operating in the machine tools now include about half a dozen trading firms based in China, Singapore, Korea, and Taiwan, engaged in the import of tools. Petrochemicals was another impressive growth story. Along with it, plastics emerged as a huge new field of investment. The chemical multinationals already in the Indian market, mainly Bayer, diversified. India now exports a certain quantity of organic chemicals.

From the 1990s sporadically, and after 2000 systematically, the IT service business started to grow in India, becoming a phenomenal growth story. Firms developed software for export, captive software for user organizations, and performed business process for international clients. A whole set of professions and jobs were created since 2000, including in areas like software analysis and development, domain specialism, information security, database and network administration, communication, designing and architecture, data warehousing, semiconductor design, and more recently digital business. Through the 2000s, the workforce tended to be young and contained more women than in any manufacturing industries. In 2000, the number employed did not exceed a few hundred thousand; in 2006, the number was placed at 1 million; in 2010, estimated employment exceeded 3 million. Since then, employment seems to have stabilized, though good data are hard to come by. The companies are based in cities like Bangalore, Hyderabad, Pune, Trivandrum, and Gurgaon, but the workers tend to be trained in smaller towns.

IT services are labour-intensive and the relatively low salaries of India explains international competitiveness to some extent.[26] But there were other complementary explanations. In hardware, the trade regime relaxed in the 1980s, due to the influence and intervention of key technocrats. Specific government support measures such as help to foster 'software technology parks' were also important.[27] Satellite communication developed in India faster and earlier than in other poorer countries. A further factor was reverse brain drain from the US involving Indian IT professionals. Many came back to start new firms. A significant number were also hired as managers by the Indian large firms when they expanded their operations overseas.[28] The business changed the profile of entrepreneurship in India, as we shall see in Chapter 9.

[26] Discussed in Ramesh Subramanian, 'India and Information Technology: A Historical and Critical Perspective,' *Journal of Global Information Technology Management*, 9(4), 2006, 8–46.

[27] Murali Patibandla, Deepak Kapur, Bent Petersen, 'Import Substitution with Free Trade: Case of India's Software Industry,' *Economic and Political Weekly*, 35(15), 2000, 1263–1270.

[28] Elizabeth Chacko, 'From Brain Drain to Brain Gain: Reverse Migration to Bangalore and Hyderabad, India's Globalizing High Tech Cities,' *GeoJournal*, 68(2/3), 2007, 131–140.

There was dramatic growth in the supply of engineering education by private entrepreneurs. During the retreat from world trade, 1947–1980, engineering graduates per million persons increased from near-zero to 30. In the next 10 years, the number more than doubled to 75, and at the end of the next decade exceeded 300. Whereas the government institutions remained tied to a conventional course-offering dominated by mechanical and civil engineering, the thousands of new institutions offered specialized professional courses dominated by electrical engineering, electronics, and information technology. A whole education industry grew almost overnight in small towns bypassing the university system. Private institutes and in-house training met the need and thus demonstrated that the market rather than the state was a more efficient agent to supply vocational education. Industry insiders, however, complained that the quality of formal education did not improve at the same pace as the quantity of graduates being turned out.

Were the reforms a success?

An Assessment of the Liberal Reforms

It was not much of a success if we measure success by industrialization. '[P]ost-1991 industrial growth has not accelerated,' a 2006 assessment concluded. 'Manufacturing was an engine of growth in India in the 1970s and 1980s. Since the 1991 economic reform, it appears that the speed of the engine has slowed down.'[29] These conclusions are too sensitive to the cut-off years chosen to make the comparison, as well as the index itself. GDP and the Index of Industrial Production yield different results. Shifting the years even slightly could lead to the conclusion that the 1990s were a better time, but perhaps not a lot better.

Manufacturing industry was a rather sluggish engine. Ten years into the economic reforms, studies of Indian manufacturing reported big growth of production, great promise, but low levels of capability and

[29] K. Kalirajan and S. Bhide, 'The Post-reform Performance of the Manufacturing Sector in India', *Asian Economic Papers*, 3(2), 2005, 126–157.

scale compared with global counterparts. For example, a 2000 study found a wide gap in labour productivity between the best practice CNC machine tools producers in India and the minimum levels achieved by foreign firms selected for comparison. The study also found that India still retained an advantage thanks to an even wider gap in wages, and a record of speedy but less effective after-sale service.[30] A 2002 survey of the chemical industry found firms, long used to protected market for basic chemicals, struggling to deal with imports, high costs, research and development, and new technology.[31]

Manufactured exports come from small firms and light industry. Large companies of India were once successful as exporters. They left that legacy behind with the passing of the Empire. Import substituting industrialization killed that tradition. Huge growth, new investment, and technological modernization made the Indian companies grow bigger, but mainly in their own backyard. Except in IT, few Indian corporates succeeded, even tried, to establish a global brand. This was a failure no doubt. The failure was compounded by the fact that the small town manufacturer had to deal with poor institutions and infrastructure. They were sometimes far away from the ports, banks, and consumer markets. The ports in India were, and still are, backward by Asian standards. The small firms operated in a milieu in which transaction costs in doing business were large, which kept many of these firms outside the mainstream commercial infrastructure even as their goods globalized.

In large-scale industry, gains were distributed in an uneven fashion.[32] The re-integration with the world market drove weak and overcapitalized firms to the wall, in textiles, in machinery and metallurgy, chiefly ferrous metals. In synthetic textiles and engineering, decline owed to tariff reduction. On the other hand, deregulation of technology import

[30] John Sutton, 'Indian Machine Tools Industry: A Benchmarking Study', New Delhi: ICRIER, 2000.

[31] KPMG India, *Indian Chemical Industry: New Directions, New Hopes*, 2002. Available at http://www.in.kpmg.com/pdf/KPMG_Chemtech_Report.pdf (accessed 1 August 2016).

[32] Kwok Tong Soo, 'From Licence Raj to Market Forces: The Determinants of Industrial Structure in India after Reform', *Economica*, 75, 2008, 222–243.

offered a few firms that were better managed, more creditworthy, and already technologically advanced, the chance to modernize quickly. Thus, the reforms had the effect of a sharper inter-firm polarization. The dice was loaded for new firms in new industries located in new industrial clusters. New firms also had better access to foreign collaboration. In the 1990s, foreign branded firms re-entered India. After a brief time when partnerships between Indian and foreign firms was the norm, a series of mergers and acquisitions took place, and many Indian consumer brands suffered creative destruction.[33] One of the spill-over effects of foreign investment was the formation of a new paradigm of agricultural trade under contract with a dominant industrial monopsonist. PepsiCo in Punjab pioneered the model, which was later replicated elsewhere.[34]

Critics of the reforms argued that the growth of wages slowed in the 1990s, and employment did not rise fast enough. A slow jobs growth can be seen either as limited demand for labour or as a fall in the supply of labour, a result of demographic transition and increased enrolment of young adults in schools.[35] Interestingly, even though the labour-intensive and low-skilled goods did well in exports, skill premium increased after the reforms, and employment of skilled workers increased at some cost to unskilled and poorly paid workers.[36] Complementary interdependence between technology and skill might explain the pattern of wage change.[37]

Employment growth rate rose in large-scale industry after 1992, but the workers lost bargaining power. In the 2000s, some regional states

---

[33] Baldev Raj Nayar, 'Business and India's Economic Policy Reforms', *Economic and Political Weekly*, 1998, 2453–2468.

[34] Sukhpal Singh, 'Contracting Out Solutions: Political Economy of Contract Farming in the Indian Punjab', *World Development*, 30(9), 2002, 1621–1638.

[35] S.S. Bhalla and T. Das, 'Pre- and Post-reform India: A Revised Look at Employment, Wages, and Inequality', Delhi: India Policy Forum, 2006.

[36] This is counterintuitive. Economists often analyse such opening-up effects with the help of the Stolper-Samuelson model on the interaction between trade and factor markets. The prediction of the model is that the demand for the abundant factor and goods intensive in that factor, should rise after liberalization, and the demand for factors that had been scarce but protected before, should fall.

[37] R. Chamarbagwala, 'Economic Liberalization and Wage Inequality in India', *World Development*, 34(12), 2006, 1997–2015.

proceeded further than others in creating employer-friendly labour regimes. New policy instruments, such as special economic zones, played a role in pursuing the agenda. So did a series of pro-employer court judgements against the application of the old labour laws.[38] In few firms that started after 1992 was there a trade union. In the export processing zones, many workers were women, a trend that some authors attribute to the employers' desire for a non-unionized workforce.[39] There was, finally, the growth of a new mind-set. The legacy of nationalism that saw trade unions as 'weapons of the weak' was on the wane. Organized labour was seen in media as groups fighting for sectional interests, sometimes at the cost of national interest. The business press took a reformist stand on law. The government as well as the judiciary followed a non-interventionist role in respect of job-loss and enterprise restructuring. By means of voluntary retirement, contract labour law, and case laws, large corporates managed to subdue labour. They reduced their core, that is, the permanently employed and unionized labour force. The work done by the core workforce was outsourced to other firms or done by contract labour. In some cases, outsourcing and contract labour were identical strategies.

These somewhat negative assessments would apply with particular force to the first 10 years of formal reform (1992–2002). The next 15 years (2002–2016) were easier. The quality and productivity issues that plagued manufacturing then and plague it even now reduced in extent, which can be seen in the steady rise in exports of machine tools and chemicals, where capability had fallen behind in the former period. The problems did not disappear. An easy import and investment regime created options for the users to bypass limited domestic capability. For example, high cost of power and the legacy of the protectionist era still burden the pace of change in the chemical industry. Use remains import dependent. Varieties of speciality chemicals are imported rather than resourced at home by user industries that require them. Over half of

---

[38] A useful set of essays on changes in the labour regime can be found in Dipak Mazumdar and Sandip Sarkar, eds., *Globalization, Labor Markets and Inequality in India*, London: Routledge, 2008.

[39] Jayati Ghosh, 'Globalization, Export-Oriented Employment for Women and Social Policy: A Case Study of India', *Social Scientist*, 30(11/12), 2002, 17–60.

India's machine tool use is imported. In short, trade openness became a shock absorber of sorts, when quality problems were slow to resolve.

Conclusion

Interpretations of postcolonial Indian development fall in two types. Both focus on industrialization. First, the state expended too much effort on a wrong kind of industrialization between 1950 and 1990, sustained it with protection and regulation, and then, realizing the mistakes, removed protection and regulation and unshackled private enterprise. A second view is that industrial growth was higher before, and not after, the economic reforms, and therefore, the case for liberalization is not proven. At any rate, it is prone to exaggeration, whereas the statist model did deliver a lot of good.

Both these views overlook trade and other services. The story of non-agricultural enterprise in independent India was not just a story of failure to industrialize fast enough, but one of repression of trade and revival of trade. Further, both views misread the costs of the economic policy framework of postcolonial India. The costs cannot be measured by calculating industrial growth rates. The cost was the fading of accumulated comparative advantage in three fields. India was a trading economy before 1947, it lost a lot of the trading capital after 1947 thanks to regulation. India had a lot of foreign capital before 1947, it lost its position as a cosmopolitan business world after 1947. India was Asia's leading theatre of corporate business after World War II. It lost that position to East Asia, and then to Southeast Asia. I have shown that trade repression and xenophobic nationalism were responsible for the regression.

When the liberalization began, corporate capital revived, but there was no return to the old times. Large Indian companies gained, so did foreign capital, but unlike in the period before 1947, these companies made things for the home market and did not export a lot. The exporting businesses operated from smaller firms.

A similar trajectory can be found in the post-1950 history of trade and industry in the other South Asian nations as well.

9

Trade and Industry II: Pakistan, Bangladesh, Sri Lanka, and Nepal

Chapter 8 showed that agricultural trade, textile production, and Indo-British corporate groups formed three pillars of support for the non-agricultural economy of India in the colonial times. After 1950, trade, textiles, and foreign firms suffered decline due to government intervention. In Pakistan, Bangladesh, Nepal, and Sri Lanka, these initial conditions did not occur together. Commodity trade was important everywhere, and engaged indigenous merchants and bankers, but with some exceptions (mainly in Sri Lanka), few of them were industrial or big firms in 1950. Textile production was important in Pakistan and Bangladesh. Among these countries, foreign firms were prominent in Sri Lankan plantations.

The desire to industrialize was present everywhere, but the ingredients were limited when compared with the Indian Union. The countries were similar in their reliance on industrialization and faith in state intervention. Given the differences in initial conditions, the contents of policy had to be varied. This chapter will describe the mix of strategies and pathways that emerged in the other four countries with regard to trade and industry.

T. Roy, *The Economy of South Asia*, Palgrave Studies in Economic History, DOI 10.1007/978-3-319-54720-6_9

Pakistan

1947–1972

In 1947, there were few large-scale factories in Pakistan, and the East and the West Pakistan shared them almost equally. A series of federal initiatives led, in 1948, to an industrial policy statement that reserved a few areas such as armaments and hydroelectric power for the government and encouraged private investment in all other fields. Specific policies were designed and statements were made to meet aims like reduction of regional inequality, including the growing inequality between East and West Pakistan. Still, industrialization happened more or less on laissez-faire principles. Compared with India, industrialization was to be less capital-intensive, state regulation was half-hearted and limited, which may be the reason why for some years during 1950–1970, Pakistan experienced the fastest industrialization in the world after Japan. The state was by no means inactive. It rewarded the investors with tax holiday, subsidies, foreign exchange allowance, and cheap credit. These benefits were passed on to a small coterie of favoured business groups. Thus, large urban business groups took advantage of the new opportunities, so that industrialization had a large-factory and urban bias.

The most dynamic industry was cotton textiles. In Pakistan, mechanized textile production began in the shape of spinning mills before independence. After independence, the state encouraged vertical integration, that is, spinning mills were encouraged to expand into weaving and integrate production. This did occur in both West and East Pakistan. Despite this tendency, in the late twentieth century, the vertically integrated mill was in retreat, as it was in India.

There was no mention of power-looms (weaving factories) in official sources from Pakistan until the early 1960s. In 1975, there were about 70,000 such looms. According to one estimate, the number was about 100,000 in 1989, along with 10,000 looms in 'independent units,' that is, the larger-sized and technologically advanced weaving factories.[1] In 1995,

[1] Pakistan, *Pakistan Textile Statistics*, Karachi: Ministry of Industries, 1990.

the power-loom industry consisted of 200,000 shuttle looms and 13,000 shuttleless looms.[2] In 2010, the industry had polarized a lot, with an organized corporate segment that operated mainly shuttleless looms and a small factory segment that operated mainly shuttle looms. The exact estimates of the size of these two segments cannot be found. Rough estimates place the former at 175,000–250,000, and the latter at 295,000.[3]

The Green Revolution gave a boost to small firms. From the beginning of the 1960s, small-scale engineering firms making and repairing diesel engines, pump sets, strainers, and farming tools mushroomed in the small towns in Punjab province.[4] A few of these firms had begun operation before 1947, but most entered after 1961. The two clusters where this development started were Lahore, for more skilled work, and Daska (a small town near Sialkot), for ordinary work. The firms were family-owned and family-managed. They recruited workers with no prior experience, and trained them on the job. A polarization tendency soon developed; some of the larger firms were trying to emerge from obscurity, establish brands, made changes in design of pump sets, branched out into the manufacture of standardized spare parts and interchangeable ones, and try for bank loans. Many firms were also trying to market goods through trading firms, rather than work on contracts received from the user. A mid-1970s study explored the agriculture link and called the industrialization a 'microcosm of the development process: mobilization of resources, development of skills, diffusion of technology, and generation of income and employment.'[5]

[2] Q. Aziz, ed., *Working Conditions in the Textile Industry in Pakistan*, Karachi, 1992; *Asian Cotton Textile Outlook 1995–96*, Osaka: JTN, 1997.

[3] Noor Ahmed Memon, 'Pakistan Weaving Sector including Denim Holds the Highest Potential for Growth and Investment,' http://www.ptj.com.pk/Web-2010/06-10/June-2010-PDF/Dr.Noor-Ahmed-Memon.pdf (accessed 6 August 2016).

[4] Frank C. Child and Hiromitsu Kaneda, 'Links to the Green Revolution: A Study of Small-Scale, Agriculturally Related Industry in the Pakistan Punjab,' *Economic Development and Cultural Change*, 23(2), 1975, 249–275. See also Naved Hamid, 'Growth of Small Scale Industry in Pakistan,' *Pakistan Economic and Social Review*, 21(1/2), 1983, 37–76.

[5] Child and Kaneda, 'Links to the Green Revolution.'

Despite the offer of subsidy, the policies of the state created more obstacles than help. As with the Green Revolution, government policy and regulation did little to promote this private enterprise, and in fact, often worked against it. Employment size in the majority of the firms was below the limit necessary for registration under the Factory Act. Therefore, they were not eligible for assistance under government programmes. Nor did they have much link with the government polytechnics in the areas. The firms would have gained from access to western machine tools, but Pakistan's overvalued exchange system and aid-funded investment programmes combined to deliver subsidies to those, usually larger, firms, which were eligible to import equipment under these programmes and that could influence bureaucrats to obtain import licenses. The booming engineering and metallurgy businesses rarely applied for licenses, 'on the assumption that, even if technically qualified, their application would be entrapped by the bureaucratic morass and invitations to *bakshish* [gifts].'[6] A black market in Chinese machine tools was of more help than the government. The majority relied on traders, and with raw materials like pig iron for the foundry, on the black market.

Still, Pakistan's import license programme was more liberal than India's. This was so because Pakistan received, relative to its economy, larger volumes of aid and aid-tied import capacity.

1972–1977

In 1972 a radical phase of intervention started. In the first round of intervention, announced in January 1972, the management and control of all units in heavy engineering, heavy electrical, motor vehicles, tractors, basic chemicals, petrochemical, cement and electricity, and gas and oil refineries were nationalized. In the next round in 1973, bizarrely, flour and rice milling, and edible fat industries were taken over. In the same year, eight large banks were nationalized, including the pioneering

[6] Child and Kaneda, 'Links to the Green Revolution.'

Habib Bank and Muslim Commercial Bank. Nine shipping companies were taken over and merged under the Pakistan Shipping Corporation. Agricultural trade was nationalized or regulated.

The nationalization episode took a heavy toll on some industries, especially food processing, by driving capital away from industry into new and obscure fields, even to the Persian Gulf (see also Chapter 10), and by thrusting incompetent management on previously sound businesses. Despite nationalization, the 1970s turned out to be a good decade for industrial growth. The consolidation of the Green Revolution encouraged small enterprise in engineering. Throughout the 1970s, Pakistani nationals went abroad, mainly to the Gulf region, for employment, and back home, their remittance sustained a consumption boom. While the socialistic industrialization narrowed the opportunities of private investment in large factories, some of the potential investment flowed into consumer goods in small and medium firms.

These processes spilled over into the 1980s. By then, the number of emigrants had reached 2 million. The remittance they sent back home amounted to 10 per cent of national income. The remittance not only supported a large number of families back home but also increased demand for goods like plastics and garments. Punjab province led the interdependent processes of emigration, remittance, Green Revolution, and small industries, Sind coming a distant second. In the other larger provinces there was no more than a ripple effect.

1980 to the Present

From the end of the 1970s, regulation was relaxed, private investment invited back in, and nationalized firms were privatized. The privatization episode did not mend things smoothly. Several first generation business conglomerates never returned to their former glory, especially when they had lost asset in Bangladesh (see Chapter 10). In both Bangladesh and Pakistan, nationalized businesses were sold to private bidders from the late 1970s. The process in Pakistan was a more long-drawn one. The units were larger and formed a more diversified basket. There was also greater participation of international consultants in the process.

Nevertheless, the response rate to the equity sales by the government was not always high, dragging the process to more than 20 years.[7] Allegations of asset stripping by new owners occurred. The liberalization and privatization drives were almost inevitably accompanied by elements of crony capitalism. Army generals set up businesses, state patronage encouraged the emergence of new conglomerates, privatization and equity sales encouraged oligopolistic control as in the cement industry, cheap bank loans and other concessions led to over-leveraged industries in the 1990s. The rise of the Nawaz Sharif family and concessions to the sugar refining industry are sometimes seen as an example of favouritism as much as entrepreneurial acumen.[8]

A number of industries catering to the home market expanded from the 1990s. Foreign multinationals entered, and new business groups emerged (see also Chapter 10). However, in the traditional industrial segment, cotton textiles, there was disappointing growth, missed opportunity, and a 'failure to fulfil the historical mission.'[9] Unlike in East Asia, textiles in Pakistan failed to act as a catalyst of industrialization. The failure had many dimensions, from underinvestment to a neglect of learning to slow adoption of new technology. The failure may owe also to the fact that as a business, textiles had gone smaller in scale and failed to attract big capital. The syndrome reappears in India, though the brutality of India's Textile Policy was absent in Pakistan.

The garment industry in Pakistan had a later start than in Bangladesh. The industry experienced its biggest growth in the 1990s. The initial entrepreneurship came from the textile industry. Garment factories were started by spinning or weaving factory owners, but finding that garment manufacturing units were too labour intensive and required a different style of supervision, training, and management than in their

[7] Mushtaq A. Sajid and A.R. Chaudhary, 'Historical Development of Liberalization since 1947 In Pakistan,' *Pakistan Economic and Social Review*, 34(2), 1996, 179–192.

[8] Imran Ali and Adeel Malik, 'The Political Economy of Industrial Development in Pakistan: A Long-Term Perspective,' *The Lahore Journal of Economics*, 14(1), 2009, 29–50.

[9] Matthew McCartney, 'The Political Economy of Industrial Policy: A Comparative Study of the Textiles Industry in Pakistan,' *The Lahore Journal of Economics*, 19, 2014, 105–134.

own factories, they outsourced management of these factories to subcontractors.[10] Later, these intermediaries started as entrepreneurs in their own right.

Bangladesh

1947–1972

The first cotton mill, Mohini Mills, had been established in 1908. But large-scale textile production in the region that later became East Pakistan really grew under tariff protection in the 1920s. Between 1930 and 1947, over a hundred thousand spindles and 2700 looms were installed, many of these near Dhaka and Narayanganj. After 1947, the government gave active encouragement to expansion in capacity, and spindles increased to nearly a million in 1976. Looms also grew in number, but on a less impressive scale. In other words, a lot of the growth had happened in the form of independent spinning mills. These mills supplied yarn not only to the mechanized weaving factories but also to the handloom weavers. Therefore, the largest concentrations of handloom weavers occurred near the mill towns, mainly Dhaka.[11]

Between 1947 and 1970, the two Pakistans presented a contrast in the levels and speed of industrial growth. By 1970, there was concern and frustration with the slow transformation in East Pakistan, and the tone of scholarly exchange on the economic development of East Pakistan was turning impatient. A book by Stephen Lewis concluded an assessment of development policy in the country by saying that policy had had limited influence in promoting growth and even less on reducing regional inequality, but policy did not make things worse, and some

[10] Momeo Makino, 'Pakistan: Challenges for Women's Labour Force Participation,' in Takahiro Fukunishi and Tatsufumi Yamagata, eds., *The Garment Industry in Low Income Countries*, London: Palgrave Macmillan, 2014, 132–176.

[11] Nuimuddin Chowdhury, 'Growth and Structural Change in Large-Scale Cotton Textile Industry of Bangladesh, 1947–76,' *Bangladesh Development Studies*, 5(4), 1977, 393–41.

inequality between the East and the West was to be expected given their initial conditions.[12]

As a matter of fact, macroeconomic policy did considerable damage to industry in East Pakistan. Overvalued exchange, an instrument used to subsidize imports, hurt industries with export potential, and jute was prominent in the list. This effect was present in both Bangladesh and India. In both cases, export-oriented Bengal subsidized an industrialization policy designed far away, without getting anything back. And in both cases, the feeling of being short-changed grew among the Bengali population. This burden was reduced somewhat by an export subsidy scheme in the 1960s, but the West had a privileged position in the issue of export licenses and more lobbying power.

The cotton spinning mills were the backbone of the large-scale industrial sector in 1971. These mills mainly sold yarn to the handloom weaving industry. The government set up institutions, including cooperatives of artisans and trading agencies, to ensure smooth supplies of yarn to the handlooms. The industry was protected by high tariffs and taxes on imported textiles, though smuggling from India defeated the regulation to some extent.

After 1971 and the birth of Bangladesh, Pakistani entrepreneurs left the country, and 544 large and small manufacturing firms were nationalized. Many of these were jute and cotton textile firms. The industries nationalized in the 1970s had a large proportion of textile units that had already been burdened with old machines. The nationalized firms performed poorly also because the officers who managed these ran a 'clientelist' system. They hired white collar workers excessively.[13] There were other types of corruption as well.

[12] Stephen R. Lewis Jr., *Pakistan: Industrialization and Trade Policies*, Don Mills: Oxford University Press, 1970; reviewed in *Pacific Affairs*, 44(3), 1971, 457–458. Reviewing the book, the Oxford scholar Keith Griffin wrote, unkindly, that 'the illiterate masses in East Bengal evidently have a better understanding of what is going on in their country than the scholarly professor from Williams College.'

[13] V. Bhaskar and Mushtaq Khan, 'Privatization and Employment: A Study of the Jute Industry in Bangladesh,' *American Economic Review*, 85(1), 1995, 267–273.

1977–1990

In 1982 a comprehensive privatization was undertaken. Not surprisingly, the privatization in the 1980s did not seem to improve operations at all, at least not in the textiles. Moreover, exchange shortages and unsteady electricity supplies made any serious modernization effort unlikely. The new owners were not necessarily competent to push through a difficult revival strategy, and some may have indulged in asset stripping.

Tariffs started coming down quite sharply from the mid-1980s. The reform coincided with the onset of garment exports, which needed a stronger and revived textile sector. Intra-industry trade also started to grow. The large handloom weaving industry, for which lower Bengal delta was historically well-known, did not do badly either. In the 1980s, it grew at a rate above 2 per cent per year and was one of the main producers and suppliers of cloth to the rural population. It had also adapted successfully to market trends and new raw materials.[14] Growth of handloom production speeded up after 1975, though smuggled cloth from India makes it difficult to estimate the extent of the growth. It seems fair to conclude that 'domestic production has, at the margin, been the pivotal element in bringing about what may be regarded as a reasonably improved production performance in the post-liberation period.'

The employment pattern in handloom weaving industry changed. A significant development was the increase in the share of women wage workers, from 27 to 40 per cent between 1980 and 1988. Women's real earnings did not increase, suggesting an excess supply and low opportunity cost, but the finding is significant in view of the explosion in women's employment that started almost at the same time in the clothing industry. It would be interesting to explore the link, if there is any, between the two fields of women's employment. To my knowledge there is no study yet that do this.

[14] Nuimuddin Chowdhury, 'Bangladesh's Handloom Economy in Transition: A Case of Unequal Growth, Structural Adjustment and Economic Mobility amid Laissez-Faire Markets: A Synthesis,' *Bangladesh Development Studies*, 17(1/2), 1989, 1–22.

New capacity added in weaving occurred mainly in the power-looms, as it did in Pakistan and India. As electricity connection spread to rural areas, power-looms were started by the handloom weavers. A sample survey done in the late 1980s found that the industry had become extremely heterogenous, 'subsuming fairly large textile-weaving factories, on the one hand, and small, cottage-level powered weaving, on the other. The former tends to be urban and the latter rural, in location.'[15] Younger entrepreneurs with experience in wholesale cloth trade started factories in the towns. The growth of and conversion into power-looms was predicated on two almost simultaneous changes. One of these was the adoption of improved handlooms on a large scale. Changing the energy source to run a faster loom was the next step to changing from a slow to a fast loom. The second factor was the switch to polyester yarn, which suited the power-looms better than the hand-looms.

Garment Export, 1990 to the Present

The rapid growth of the garment export industry in Bangladesh is a story that has been told and retold so many times that only a brief account here should be enough. In 1979, a joint venture between the South Korean conglomerate Daewoo and a company called Desh began to produce garments on behalf of the Korean firm. The background to the joint venture was the quota set by the Multifibre Arrangement, from which Bangladesh was exempt being a small exporter, but to which Korea was subject. The Desh-Daewoo enterprise became famous because the majority of the over 100 Desh employees who were trained in Korea on production, marketing, and management left the enterprise to start their own trading firms.[16] These firms led a boom in the 1980s, during which the number of factories increased from less than a hundred to over a

[15] N. Chowdhury, 'Intermediate Power-loom Industry in Bangladesh: Interpretive Account and its Economic Characteristics,' Dhaka: Bangladesh Institute of Development Studies Research Report 86, 1989, 3.

[16] Yung Whee Rhee, 'The Catalyst Model of Development: Lessons from Bangladesh's Success with Garment Exports,' *World Development*, 18(2), 1990, 333–46.

thousand (1981–1991), employment from less than 40,000 to over half a million, and export value from less than US$30 million to over 1 billion US dollars.

There followed a rapid proliferation of trading and manufacturing firms. Other Asian garment exporters entered the market to form trade deals. Between 1991 and 2011, the industry and trade maintained steady growth, and became the most important private employer outside agriculture and a significant exchange earner. Along with growth in numbers, there were significant advancement in learning to deliver better quality, larger volumes of production, in scheduled time. So quick was the advancement in capability that most local manufacturing firms switched from serving Asian clients via local traders, to serving western retail chains directly. As the workforce expanded – the garment manufacturing workforce is around three and a half million at present – garment industry also emerged as the largest employer of women outside agriculture. Activists and analysts sometimes complained about the difficult conditions of work, absence of unions, and the relatively low and almost stagnant wages. Still, by creating hundreds of thousand women-headed households, the industry was also laying the foundation for a social revolution.

The astonishing thing about the garment export business is not the scale and speed of expansion, but the fact that the economists had missed noticing the potential of the business when it started. Not the government, nor the donors, nor the intellectuals had any inkling in 1979 that garment export would one day be an engine of growth. The boom was set in motion entirely by traders connected with the world markets. It was a product of domestic trading acumen joining hands with globalization of the textile market. It was only after the business took off that there emerged an industry in research and analysis. What are the issues?

The speed of the expansion has generated researchers' interest in 'knowledge spill over' between global and local players, trader and manufacturers.[17] One study that explores the profile of the local

[17] William Easterly, *The Elusive Quest for Growth: Economists' Adventures and Misadventures in the Tropics*, Cambridge, MA: MIT Press, 2002.

traders suggests the industry's ability to attract educated middle class persons. It would be difficult to imagine that the boom could be sustained on the scale in which it happened without the middle class responding positively to it. 'A characteristic of this industry is the high average education,' the study notes. 'Presumably, this is because manufacturers have to upgrade their skills and know-how continuously in order to survive the intense competition in the world garment market and because the high levels of the general human capital of the entrepreneur are needed to manage an increasing number of managers and experts.'[18]

At the same time, a prominent area of concern has been the mode of employment of women workers in the industry. When Desh sent 14 women for training abroad in 1979, 'tradition had precluded women from working in the factories.'[19] Forty years later, there are three million women wage earners in the garment industry. Surveys done in the 1990s revealed that paid work empowered women by making them more mobile and increasing their spending power and choices. The vast majority came from poor farming families or urban slums, where the alternatives in earning money had been to work as maids for lower wages. One study of 1996 found that 15 per cent of the women workers were also the sole earners in their families.[20] Thanks to the garment industry boom, 'women are more mobile, with a stronger presence in public space and a higher level of representation in formal paid labour.'[21] But the work added additional hours to the hours that they already devoted to household tasks, and this was taking a toll on

[18] Khondoker Abdul Mottaleb and Tetsushi Sonobe, 'An Inquiry into the Rapid Growth of the Garment Industry in Bangladesh,' *Economic Development and Cultural Change*, 60(1), 2011, 67–89.

[19] Salma Chaudhuri Zohir, 'Social Impact of the Growth of Garment Industry in Bangladesh,' *Bangladesh Development Studies*, 27(4), 2001, 41–80.

[20] Rumana Jamaly and Ebel Wickramanayake, 'Women Workers in the Garment Industry in Dhaka, Bangladesh,' *Development in Practice*, 6(2), 1996, 156–161.

[21] David Lewis, *Bangladesh: Politics, Economy, and Civil Society*, Cambridge: Cambridge University Press, 2011, 15.

their health.[22] There were also reports of harassment. Few jobs entailed a legal contract, and the female workforce was almost completely unorganized (see also Box 9.2).

Garment manufacture came as an opportunity for spinning and weaving as well. From about 1990, spinners were also catering to the knitwear manufacturers. Thereafter, spinning capacity fell behind weaving, and weaving capacity behind clothing. The garment manufacturing industry came to rely on import of fabrics, whereas the large production capacity in the spinning industry has encouraged a rapid expansion in knitwear.

In the last 20 years, employment and investment in three other organized large-scale private enterprises grew to be quite large. One of these was pharmaceuticals production. The origin of this was a medicines trade that emerged soon after independence. Low wages and relaxed health and safety regulations sustain the other large industry, which is the dismantling and scrapping of ships. Called by the *National Geographic* 'the world's most dangerous job,' ship breaking industry shuns the media and public attention, which makes good data on the work hard to come by. Conservatively a few hundred thousand people are said to be doing this work. The number can go up significantly on account of the 2016 depression in world shipping. Lastly, a revolution in financial intermediation unfolded in the last 30 years in Bangladesh, on the back of innovative NGO programmes (see Box 9.1 on microfinance) (see also Figs. 9.1 and 9.2).

Box 9.1 Microfinance

The poor tend to lose out on opportunities the market offers them because of insufficient access to credit, and in turn, the absence of collateral. Microcredit, pioneered by the Grameen Bank of Bangladesh (formally acknowledged as a bank in 1983), started as a way to get round this problem. The idea was to advance small loans without collateral to

[22] Pratima Paul-Majumder, 'Health Impact of Women's Wage Employment: A Case Study of the Garment Industry of Bangladesh,' *Bangladesh Development Studies*, 24(1/2), 1996, 59–102.

members of voluntarily formed groups, so that peer pressure ensured repayment. Although not all microcredit programmes now use this joint liability rule, most do. As the idea succeeded within Bangladesh, and then beyond, significant externalities came to be associated with microcredit – encouragement to self-employment, enterprise by women, non-governmental organizations, operation of banking with low transaction and fiscal costs (both were high in the formal state-controlled banking in South Asia), and the tie-up of training and skill building projects with financial ones.

Between 1995 and 2005, many papers and books assessed the claims of microcredit to deliver higher income, gender justice and empowerment, sustainability of the creditor bodies, and other goals, and came to mixed conclusions. The consensus was that microcredit worked, that it was a great idea, and it was flexible enough to be modified to suit local conditions, but the extent of the benefits as claimed were exaggerated. Assessments of the success of microcredit suffer from a basic identification problem. Credit is not everything that matters in making entrepreneurs out of people of small means. Opportunities are shaped also by policies, markets, and institutions.

South Asian countries differ in the way they developed microfinance. For example, in India, state-owned banks, and the semi-government body NABARD set up to oversee rural credit, wanted a part of the action. This intervention popularized the 'self-help groups' tool. The mainly saving group is offered affiliation with a bank once it grows to a certain size. The modification builds on the point that whereas banks incur high transaction cost, cannot monitor the small borrowers well enough, and offer low flexibility, they have one strength, which is the capacity to absorb losses better than the micro-creditors. In Pakistan, there has been a convergence between microfinance and Islamic banking, that is, banking that charges an administration fee and is conducted by charitable bodies. In Sri Lanka and Nepal, microfinance penetration has been limited.

The outlook for microfinance is changing. If one of its key strengths was to reduce transaction and monitoring costs, banks can match that to some extent with mobile phones. There is a great deal of scepticism over the expectation/claim that microfinance would create entrepreneurship 'below.' Micro-insurance is a current growth area, because the poor are vulnerable to shocks like natural disasters. But insurance requires different information and a bigger risk-absorption capacity than credit.

Readings: Joanna Ledgerwood, ed. *The New Microfinance Handbook*, Washington D.C.: The World Bank, 2013; Madhura Swaminathan, 'The Microcredit Alternative?' *Economic and Political Weekly*, 42(13), 2007, 1171–1175.

Fig. 9.1 Bangladesh garment factory

Workers in Beximco textile factory produce Jeans for export to western department stores. See Chapter 10 on Beximco group. © Joerg Boethling/Alamy Stock Photo

Fig. 9.2 Partially broken down ships in Bangladesh

Described as the world's most dangerous profession, ship-breaking is a low profile but a major activity in South Asia. © Shutterstock

Sri Lanka

Compared with the other countries of South Asia, Sri Lanka was more export-oriented, less agricultural, therefore with a smaller component of grain trading and associated banking, and less diversified in terms of the economic structure. Throughout the 1950s and the 1960s, the mainstay of the economy, the plantation sector performed indifferently. In a rather similar way as India, the government repressed the foreign firms that ran the plantations economy, eventually driving them out of the country (see Chapter 10). A limited form of import substituting industrialization occurred (see also Chapter 10), but it did not contribute much to GDP after 1970.

Just as the South Korean firm Daewoo's decision to source clothing from Bangladesh in order to bypass quotas started a garment industry in Bangladesh, the Sri Lankan garment industry took off because of an interest from traders and manufacturers from Hong Kong. As in Bangladesh, they hoped to bypass quotas by contracting work to Sri Lanka. The strategy delivered growth in clothing manufacturing capacity in a short time. The share of manufactured exports in total export increased from 13 per cent in 1977 to 48 in 1988, led by garments. Until the end of the 1980s, textiles and clothing dominated industrial growth.

In 1983, Sri Lanka's clothing export was big enough to attract quotas. The industry began to diversify into articles that did not invite import restrictions. In all cases, the opening of two doors – foreign trade and foreign capital – made for the speed with which manufactured exports could grow. The link between commodity trade and factor markets became closer, which link enabled easier transmission of knowhow and improved market access at the same time. In different ways, both Bangladesh and Sri Lanka showed that '[i]nternationalisation of production through FDI participation has been central to the rapid integration of developing countries in the global manufactured goods trade system.'[23]

---

[23] Prema-chandra Athukorala, 'Export Response to Liberalisation: The Sri Lankan Experience,' *Hitotsubashi Journal of Economics*, 39(1), 1998, 49–65.

In terms of scale, the industry in Sri Lanka is one of the smaller ones in the region, but in the context of the domestic economy, the industry is enormously important. At present it employs 300,000 directly, and 600,000 indirectly.[24] About a third of the workers are women. The industry is all privately owned, and like its Bangladesh counterpart, supplies clothing directly to retail chains throughout the world. It is concentrated in the Export Processing Zones. In Sri Lanka, labour market was remarkably flexible, which facilitated industrial adjustment under market-oriented policy reforms. This was a feature of the business environment and not an outcome of a well-conceived labour market reform process.[25]

Nepal

Two things are commonly said about trade in Nepal, that its land-locked situation and open borders with India restrict its option to pursue an independent trade policy, and that its position between China and India makes it a potential conduit for illicit trade into India. The prospect of gold import, illegal in India, through Nepal is a persistent issue in trade negotiations.[26] The free trade treaty was surely an asset in some ways, but it also thrust India's mistakes upon Nepal. Still views that highlight Nepal's tragedy, and blame India for it, are exaggerated. More than regulatory autonomy, what matters to prospects of trading in Nepal are simple trade costs, which, before recent highway building projects, were high.

Soon after colonial rule ended in the region, a valuable overland trade came to an end, or at least, was much reduced in scale. For centuries,

---

[24] http://www.srilankaexpo.com/index.php/products-a-services/industrial-products/garments (accessed 17 July 2016).

[25] Prema-Chandra Athukorala and Sarath Rajapatirana, 'Liberalization and Industrial Transformation: Lessons from the Sri Lankan Experience,' *Economic Development and Cultural Change*, 48(3), 2000, 543–572.

[26] Kishor Sharma, 'Trade Policymaking in a Land-locked Developing Country: The WTO Review of Nepal,' *World Economy*, 2015. 1335–1349.

communities on the Himalayan borderlands carried on caravan trade with Tibet, Central Asia, and Afghanistan, exporting a variety of goods produced in the plains of India for wool and silk. Nepal gained from the trans-Himalayan trade because some of the routes passed over Nepal or fed its markets. Quantitatively, the trade was nowhere near as large as maritime trade. But it gave livelihoods to many people, sustained the capital of the Newar people of Kathmandu, and carried valuable material. The British Empire valued this trade. The trade dwindled after China, India, and Pakistan made their borders difficult to cross.

From 1956, Nepal introduced an import-substituting industrialization regime, with high levels of protection.[27] Export was repressed by regulations that made it mandatory for exporters to sell a part of the goods to government-owned export firms in rice and jute. The regime remained in place for 30 years, and was dismantled under IMF pressure in 1986. While some capital goods industries did get established by the state in response to the policy, they remained concentrated in the richer zones. 'The very low absolute scale of industries in the "public" sector' has been observed.[28] The scale probably shows not lack of commitment but limited fiscal resources. One interesting episode during this phase reveals how India's choices hurt Nepal's trading and manufacturing prospects. In the late 1960s, Nepal imported raw materials for steel utensils and synthetic textiles from Japan and Hong Kong at a small duty, processed these and re-exported them to India. In India, both were highly protected, in short supply, and of poor quality. However, 'the vigilant sealing of Indian market for Nepalese manufactures based on third-country raw materials' put paid to these moves.[29]

Import substitution did encourage domestic private investment. Firms that processed natural resources for the home market, mainly food, beverage and tobacco, had room for growth (see Chapter 10).

[27] Kishor Sharma, 'Development Policy, Inequity and Civil war in Nepal,' *Journal of International Development*, 18, 553–569.

[28] Baburam Bhattarai, *The Nature of Underdevelopment and Regional structure of Nepal: A Marxist Analysis*, Delhi: Adroit Publishers, 2003, 202.

[29] Bhattarai, *Nature of Underdevelopment*, 248.

After the economic liberalization in the late 1980s, export-oriented industries increased their share. These consisted of textiles and clothing, carpets, and leather goods.[30] A number of these new enterprises were formed of joint ventures between Nepali and Indian capital. In clothing, the joint ventures started to evade export quotas imposed on India.

Since the economic reforms in India in the early 1990s, the scale of trade between Nepal and India has grown by a large extent, and the Indian share of Nepal's total trade has increased from 34 to 64 per cent between 1988 and 2015.[31]

Box 9.2 Women workers in the garment industry: Welfare and empowerment

The growth of labour-intensive industry under the impetus of globalization of the late twentieth century has led to new debates centred on the issue of workers' rights and welfare. The majority of the workers in garments are women, and poorly unionized. The limited success of trade unions in this milieu owed to several factors. The industries tend to be concentrated in the Export Processing Zones where standard labour laws do not apply. The factories are owned by small firms, and are often small in terms of the workforce under one roof. Whatever the reason, export of labour-intensive manufactures has become synonymous with flexible labour markets and female workforce.

Employment of women on such a scale is a revolution in its own right, in view of the unimpressive record of the region in creating non-agricultural employment in the past, and the appalling record of creating female wage-employment. Non-agricultural wage-work is overwhelmingly male-biased in this region. Migration adds to the bias because most migrants tend to be males. Worksites that internationally employ mainly women, such as textile factories, hotels and offices, tend to be filled with men in India, Bangladesh, and Pakistan. Gender equality standards are poor in mainland South Asia. Labour force participation rate for women (15–24) is around 30 per cent in South Asia in 2015, and 50 in the world.

[30] Kishor Sharma, 'Impact of Policy Reforms on Manufacturing Growth in Nepal,' *Asian Survey*, 37(6), 1997, 550–560.

[31] Nepal Rastra Bank data, cited by *Kathmandu Post*, http://kathmandupost.ekantipur.com/news/2015-12-02/lets-review-why-we-failed-to-diversify-trade-finmin.html (accessed 10 September 2016).

Similar imbalances exist in terms of most other measures of economic opportunity and participation. In 2000 the gap was bigger. The prospect of women running households with their own money, therefore, is a huge change.

Because the initial conditions were so abysmal, many women workers who came out of homes for the first time, faced bullying, brutal hours, sexual harassment, and poor facilities at work place. Women-headed households, far from empowering women, sometimes made the men take it easy. The evidence on how extensive these practices are, and how they are changing, remains conflicting, because studies tend to use small samples and case-studies. One large-scale study of Sri Lanka came to the conclusion that a binary framework that recognizes only better or worse conditions, more exploited or less exploited, empowered or not empowered would not do justice to reality. Paid work made the lives of women more complex rather than worse.

Readings: Peter Hancock, Sharon Middleton and Jamie Moore, 'Gender, globalisation and empowerment: a study of women who work in Sri Lanka's Export Processing Zones,' *Work Organisation, Labour & Globalisation*, 6(1), 2012, 131–146.

Trade Within South Asia

Since the economic liberalization began, anti-trade sentiment has weakened, and at the same time, trade within the region has shown sign of revival, as one would expect with growth and diversification of the South Asian economies themselves. The change is small and has occurred at a glacial speed. One estimate places intra-South-Asian official trade at 5 per cent of total foreign trade in 1998.[32] The figure for 2006 was 6 per cent. At the same time, there was considerable 'informal' trade between these countries, informal in the double sense that trade was conducted by unregistered entities, and sometimes involved prohibited or restricted goods, the scale of which was not known. Informal trade has grown between most partners. A study finds that well over half of the trade that went on between India and Sri Lanka was 'informal,' that is, without

[32] Nisha Taneja and Sanjib Pohit, 'India's Informal Trade with Nepal,' *Economic and Political Weekly*, 36(25), 2001, 2263–2269.

formal contracts and reliant on personal information exchange, and involved a variety of strategies, including payment of bribes, to minimize transaction costs and paperwork.[33] In 2004, the scale of informal trade was double that of formal trade, or well above 10 per cent of total external trade of the region.[34] Research on informal trade showed that India was a net exporter of goods to most countries (except Nepal). It might be expected that India would be net importer of services in turn, which it is.

The effect of regulation on informality can be illustrated with an example. The 1998 survey found that India's exports in the informal network consisted of conventional items like food and textiles, but India's imports consisted of East Asian electronics and other consumer articles. Given that Nepal's main transportation access was through India, these goods entered Nepal through India as legitimate imports into Nepal but were then sent back to India, a pattern of transaction called 'trade deflection.'[35]

A South Asian Trade Agreement came into being between 1993 and 1995, was renegotiated from time to time, a full operationalization was expected in 2016. Why was progress on such a vital initiative so slow? Apart from political obstacles (see Box 9.3) India's size caused anxiety among other countries. On the other hand, the range of Indian capability encourages individual countries to enter separate trade treaties with India, for example, the Indo-Sri-Lanka free trade treaty of 1999, which is believed to have taken some wind off the sail of the free trade zone. Between 2005 and 2010, India-Pakistan trade grew at a surprisingly rapid pace, mainly due to a fourfold increase in India's exports, which included metals, drugs, IT services, and a few consumer goods.[36] The free trade agreement is expected to consolidate these tendencies.

---

[33] Nisha Taneja, Muttukrishna Sarvananthan and Sanjib Pohit, 'India-Sri Lanka Trade: Transacting Environments in Formal and Informal Trading,' *Economic and Political Weekly*, 38(29), 2003, 3094–3098.

[34] Nisha Taneja, 'Informal Trade in the SAARC Region: Implications for FTAs,' *Economic and Political Weekly*, 39(51), 2004, 5367–5371.

[35] Taneja and Pohit, 'India's Informal Trade with Nepal.'

[36] Ishrat Husain, 'Prospects and Challenges for Increasing India-Pakistan Trade,' Washington, DC: Atlantic Council, 2011.

Box 9.3 SAARC

In 1985, the South Asian Association for Regional Cooperation (SAARC) was established by the heads of state of Bangladesh, Bhutan, India, Maldives, Nepal, Pakistan, and Sri Lanka. Kathmandu is the headquarters of SAARC. The aim was to achieve cooperation in areas of common economic interest. Whereas the big examples before SAARC (ASEAN or EU) formed of countries that shared two ideals, free trade and collective management of common security concerns, in SAARC the second aim had to take a minor place because of territorial disputes between India and Pakistan. In fact, the dispute was serious enough to undermine effective cooperation on trade. Subject to this qualification, SAARC has fostered some cooperation on agriculture and rural development; health; women, youth, and children; environment and forestry; science and technology; meteorology; human resources development; transport; information technology; biotechnology, intellectual property rights; tourism; and energy.

For two decades after it was established, SAARC had little more than symbolic value. On several occasions, meetings were postponed or cancelled in response to an immediate point of conflict. Dialogue on economic integration was often acrimonious and involved trading charges on non-tariff barriers. In its 30-year history, SAARC could organize few summit meetings. Negotiations were often protracted and endless.

Business demand for economic cooperation has grown louder. There are at least four types of motivating factor. First, there is untapped potential in intra-industry trade, say, in textiles. Second, India's lead in software and information technology processes is a potentially useful resource for the entire region, because these skills aid a range of businesses. Third, unofficial trade has grown notwithstanding barriers to official trade. And fourth, unofficial migration has grown, India being the main destination.

Readings: A. Mukherjee-Reed, 'Regionalization in South Asia: Theory and Praxis,' *Pacific Affairs*, 70(2), 1997, 235–251; SAARC website at http://www.saarc-sec.org/

Conclusion

In India trade repression forced many foreign firms to the wall, and at the same time, eased the way for Indian groups to shift from trade to manufacturing biased towards capital goods. The same story cannot be told with equal force for Pakistan, Bangladesh, and Nepal. While many indigenous groups (I include Indian capitalists in Nepal in this set) moved into manufacturing after 1950, the capital goods bias was absent. Industry continued to be dominated by textiles. The cotton textile mill industry was nurtured rather than repressed as it was in India. A friendlier policy, however, did not stop small firms from taking over the business of the cotton mills.

In Pakistan, Bangladesh, and Sri Lanka, a distinct feature of recent history is the socialist phase of the 1970s, followed rather quickly by openness and privatization. The interregnum affected corporate groups that had grown under the import-substitution regime. After 1980, privatization of nationalized businesses and cautious liberalization encouraged diversification and encouraged the growth of export capacity in manufacturing and services.

The two preceding chapters suggested that the industrialization drive, as well as the reforms, changed the rules of doing business in the region. How did the corporate world adapt to these changes? The next chapter explores the question.

10

Business

At the time of independence, there were 127 large companies in India. A set, consisting of 58 companies, was foreign-owned. The majority of the companies and almost all of the foreign ones belonged in diversified zaibatsu-like conglomerates that dominated the business world of Calcutta city. The groups included Andrew Yule, Bird and Heilgers, and McLeod.[1] Some of these conglomerates had their main interest in tea plantations. These tea companies operated in Sri Lanka and Bangladesh as well as India. Outside these conglomerates, there were numerous textile, trading, and financial companies, mainly owned by Indian business families. The prominent families were Birla, Singhania, Tata, Wadia, and Godrej. Tata was offbeat in the set as it owned one of the largest steel mills in Asia.

Corporate growth occurred on the foundation of indigenous and Indian Ocean trade. A well-developed framework of corporate law that encouraged investment in company shares and the share markets, and elements of

[1] For a full list of companies under some of the largest groups in 1951 and 1958, see R.K. Hazari, *The Structure of the Corporate Private Sector. A Study of Concentration, Ownership and Control*, London: Asia Publishing, 1966, pp. 377–400.

T. Roy, *The Economy of South Asia*, Palgrave Studies
in Economic History, DOI 10.1007/978-3-319-54720-6_10

which were copied by other parts of the Empire, also helped. In turn, the legacy of joint stock business went back to the history of the East India Company, and the many European and Indian firms that grew under the direct or indirect sponsorship of the Company in the nineteenth century.

How did this world change during the state-led development phase, 1950–1980? In the colonial times, business was more or less on its own, and the state took little interest or made few commitments to private enterprise except working on commercial and corporate law. This 'clean slate' as it were would mean that the relationship was designed only during the nationalist movement or after independence. Who designed it? The politicians or the businesses? There can be two positions on the questions, for India in particular. In one, import substituting industrialization empowered indigenous industrialists enough so that they could resist attempts by the state to regulate or discipline them. In another view, too much regulation shackled indigenous industrialists, until the reforms liberated them.[2]

This chapter complicates the narratives. I suggest that business history in the postcolonial times cannot be studied as a linear trajectory of either progressive empowerment or confinement. Corporate world was differentiated in 1950, and the states helped some and repressed others. For example, trading firms and exporting foreign firms suffered in India and Sri Lanka, possibly East Pakistan as well. Politicians' relationship with indigenous industrialists was more cordial, if still fraught with tensions. Further, the regulatory regime made a number of sudden turns. The composition of corporates before and after every one of these was different.

Still, some long-term processes can be discerned through these episodes. Trade, textiles, foreign investment, and a small indigenous industrial group were the foundations of corporate enterprise in South Asia until 1950. The industrialization policy did a great deal of damage to these fundamentals. Trading firms, textile mills, and British capital, declined, whereas the small indigenous industrial class gained. After the

[2] Variants of these theses we will meet in the discussions on business-politics relationship in the next section, where citations will appear.

liberal reforms, trade, textiles, and foreign investment revived too, but the link with the corporate sector had reduced. Trade and textiles are organized by small firms mainly. Foreign capital targets domestic market rather than export market. Foreign does not mean European or American exclusively, as in 1950, but also Arab, Malaysian, Japanese, and Korean. Indigenous corporates went through a golden age in the 1950s and 1960s, suffered bankruptcies thereafter, and revived after the reforms to invest in technology-intensive (including information technology or IT) industries. Except IT, big companies are not the export leaders in any of the five countries. Instead, they import technology to bring goods and services within reach of domestic consumers. In the last decade or so, they diversified from a manufacturing base to services including telecom, education, health care, hotels, department store, construction, and real estate.

The Indian case dominates the story, which is a reflection of the relative size of the corporate sector there (Table 10.1). All five countries share similarities as well, including a corporate revival, even emergence (Table 10.2). I will suggest that there are overlaps in the manner in which this emergence happened.

India

Foreign Firms: 1950–1980

Trade repression and import-substituting industrialization made gainers and losers in the corporate world. Indigenous industrialists were gainers on the whole, foreign firms included more losers than gainers. On foreign capital there was at first a difference between the tolerant stance of Prime Minister Nehru and the xenophobic stance of some of the business lobbies close to the Congress. Infighting within the Indian chambers of commerce reflected these divisions in politics.

In actual action, direct restraints on foreign firms could not be either strict or sustained in the 1950s because many of these firms exported and

Table 10.1 Market capitalization of listed companies

	US$ billion	% of GDP
Bangladesh (2012)	20	15
India (2015)	1516	73
Nepal (2012)	4	22
Pakistan (2012)	44	19
Sri Lanka (2015)	21	26

http://www.tradingeconomics.com/ (accessed 1 September 2016) and http://data.worldbank.org/indicator/ (accessed 1 September 2016)

Table 10.2 Change in corporate capital in relation to GDP (%) 1990–2015

	Market capitalization		Value of stocks traded	
	1990	2012–15	1990	2010–15
Bangladesh	1	15	0	15.0
India	12	73	6.9	62.7
Nepal	14 (2000)	22	0.6	0.6
Pakistan	7	19	0.6	7.3
Sri Lanka	11	26	0.5	6.7

Source: See Table 10.1

there was shortage of exchange.[3] Some multinational companies came in, though not because the government was particularly friendly, but the multinationals wanted to jump the tariff wall and sell goods to Indians. A certain number of technical collaborations were signed in these years. Government-approved technical collaboration agreement was the only way that technology was allowed to come in. Consumer good and drug manufacturing firms such as Hindustan Levers, Philips, Johnson and Johnson, Nestle, Coca-Cola, and Glaxo entered India or expanded business, and chemical producer Du Pont set up a base.

A few of the British multinationals had entered India in the interwar period. The Indian subsidiary of the food processing firm

[3] Kamal Mitra Chinoy, 'Industrial Policy and Multinationals in India,' *Social Scientist*, 13(3), 1985, 15–31.

Unilever was an example. The pharmaceutical and baby-food firm Glaxo (now GlaxoSmithKline) started a trading unit in India in 1924, became a manufacturer, and continued as a subsidiary of the multinational. The household chemicals firm Reckitt and Colman started a trading unit in India in the 1920s. One of the four constituent companies of the speciality chemicals manufacturer Imperial Chemical Industries or ICI, Brunner Mond, opened a trading office in India in 1911, and converted into a manufacturing firm in the 1950s, with its main plant located near Calcutta. All of these older multinationals had to shed any remaining link with trading, and turned into manufacturing entities.

British trading firms from Coventry and Birmingham had also entered India in the interwar period, and started manufacturing on the side. A few of these firms, such as Richardson and Cruddas, suffered hostile takeover, asset-stripping, and bankruptcy in the hands of Indian owners. Others continued while shedding their trading operation. The packaging manufacturer Metal Box Company (incorporated in 1930) started an Indian subsidiary in 1933, with its main plant near Calcutta. The Birmingham engineering firm Guest, Keen and Nettlefolds started a subsidiary in India, with its main manufacturing unit located in and near Calcutta, known as Guest Keen Williams. The Manchester engineering firm Mather and Platt started an Indian subsidiary in 1913, with a plant manufacturing electrical pumps in Calcutta. These firms gained from import substitution, for them it was a change of role from a manufacturer in England to a trader in India to a manufacturer in India.

On the other hand, policies discriminated against the old British firms who either exported their own products or were mainly trading. It was increasingly difficult, almost impossible, to buy machines and hire engineers, managers, or scientists from the world market, which was easy enough to do around 1900. These firms relied crucially on a flexible and global factor market, because their export interests required partnership with marketing firms abroad. Colonial India was a large buyer of foreign services. Many types of jobs, from administrative officers to teacher, engineers, and company executives, attracted expatriates. From the late 1950s, the Indian state practically banned such recruitment. The exporting British firms were disturbed by the new tax laws, capital controls, and forced Indianization of management. In this vulnerable condition, they were taken over and mismanaged by incompetent and frequently corrupt Indian business houses. Although policy towards foreign capital was not formally discriminatory, the effect of this indirect squeeze was an exodus and destruction of capital. Foreign direct investment as a proportion of capital stock was nearer 10 per cent before World War II, dropped sharply to 2 per cent after independence, remained depressed, and regained the interwar level around 2002 or 2003.[4]

The brunt of this downfall was borne by Calcutta city.

Downfall of Capitalism: A Business History of Calcutta

The global reach of the port cities, especially Calcutta, was consolidated from the late nineteenth century through the enterprise of a number of trading and shipping firms that established bases there, and then diversified into the jute textile industry, mining, tea and coffee plantations, inland navigation, coastal and transoceanic shipping, banks, insurance, engineering, oil, and utilities (tramways, electricity). With a few exceptions, the control of all were transferred to Indian owners from the 1940s, and with few exceptions, all went bankrupt between 1950 and 1970, some even earlier.[5]

A few examples of the origins of these firms may be in order. Andrew Yule (1834–1902), merchant and industrialist started or managed jute, coal and tea companies in Calcutta. The group's London associates were George Yule and later Yule, Catto. Bird and Co started in 1863 in labour contract business. After Ernest Cable (1859–1927) became a partner in 1886, Bird diversified into jute and coal. F.W Heilgers, a German firm with interest in paper, jute, and coal teamed up with Bird. Gillanders Arbuthnot was founded in Calcutta in 1833 by John

[4] M. Twomey, *A Century of Foreign Investment in the Third World,* Abingdon: Routledge, 2000, p 118 for the earlier estimates.

[5] Tirthankar Roy, 'Transfer of Economic Power in Corporate Calcutta 1950–1970.' *Business History Review*, 91(1), 2017, 3–29.

Gladstone, trading in textiles and indigo. His grandson Henry Gladstone led diversification into jute around 1880. British India Corporation was the product of a collaboration between five Kanpur merchants, George Allen, W.E. Cooper, Bevan Petman, J. Condon, and Gavin Jones, who, between 1876 and 1894, started woollen mills, cotton mills, and leather factories in the city. Jardine Skinner formed in Bombay in 1825, and reconstituted in Calcutta in 1844. It had common ancestry with the east Asian conglomerate Jardine Matheson, founded by the China traders William Jardine and James Matheson. Jardine Skinner started in jute and later diversified to tea. George Henderson was a Calcutta merchant who founded one of the earliest jute mills of Calcutta (Baranagar, 1857). Thomas Duff came to Calcutta after a stint with the Borneo Company in the 1870s, and set up some of the largest jute factories of the world. Turner Morrison was a shipping firm established by Alfred Turner (c. 1860) as an extension of the Liverpool trading house Turner and Co. Charles McLeod was first a jute trader (1880s) and later the manager-owner of the McLeod group of jute mills.

There were three stages in the transfer of control of these companies. The first stage occurred between 1947 and 1965. Stock market raids and panic sales were behind the transfer of individual companies, and even whole conglomerates like McLeod and Octavius Steel (to Surajmal-Nagarmal), Kettelewell Bullen (to Mugneeram Bangur), British India Corporation (to Haridas Mundhra), Begg Dunlop/Begg Sutherland (to Dalmia-Jain), and Jardine Skinner/George Henderson/Jardine Henderson (to Giridharilal Mehta). Government directive on compulsory divestment up to 25 per cent of the share-holding induced some firms to recruit Indian partners in a hurry. The jute and engineering conglomerates including Bird-Heilgers, Thomas Duff and Andrew Yule lost key companies to raiders. Little documentary information can now be found on the first stage, and resources for oral history are more or less lost.

The second stage can be dated in 1965–1975, when the surviving conglomerates became bankrupt and closed doors. The examples of Bird and Andrew Yule are prominent ones. Jute began to face competition from synthetic substitutes, but the competition does not explain why the firms did not diversify, reinvest in new fields, or even modernize within jute. Tougher regulatory and business conditions affected these firms particularly. But the collapse of management was a more serious factor. For example, the government had forced an Indianization of the top management of these firms, with the result that the transfer of managerial decision-making went to individuals who were either not ready for that role, or not competent or willing to perform it. A generation of Bengalis jumped up the executive ladder of Indo-British firms, with or without adequate experience or competence. At the time of their downfall, conglomerates like Bird were run by individuals who had little entrepreneurial experience.[6] Other than incompetence of the management, predatory behaviour was quite common. Allegations of asset striping were rife, and in some cases proven.

A third stage occurred in tea plantations. Most tea companies were listed in London and escaped stock market predators of India. Not many foreign tea firms survived the 1970s, when tea was in depression. However, on several occasions the transfer of control occurred in a negotiated way in the form of piecemeal sale of gardens. Two important examples of negotiated transfer were Williamson Magor and its affiliates (to Khaitan), and James Finlay (to Tata). In the 1970s, some of the tea estate companies of South India changed ownership. Kannan Devan plantations in South India was sold by James Finlay to the Tata group. Harrisons and Crosfield was acquired by the Goenkas, who were already established in tea thanks to an earlier acquisition of Duncan. A number of smaller companies in South India were acquired by individuals of limited means and no previous experience in tea growing.[7]

At present, more than half the jute mills are closed. The rest are owned by obscure business families, as well as the government, and depending on business conditions, earn profits only occasionally. Neither the owners nor the firms have the resources to make investment commitments. Tea business has revived, however, and Calcutta remains one of the centres of the global tea trade.

It was quite a different story with the indigenous groups.

---

[6] Roy, 'Transfer of Economic Power.'

[7] K. Ravi Raman, *Global Capital and Peripheral Labour: The History and Political Economy of Plantation Workers in India*, London and New York: Routledge, 2010, 149–150.

Industrial Licensing and Changes in the Corporate Sector

The takeovers of British firms by upstart Indian traders pushed a few Indian groups (prominent among them being Surajmal-Nagarmal, Bangur, Haridas Mundhra, and Sahu-Jain) into the list of the big industrial conglomerates. This dramatic transition happened almost overnight in the 1950s.

A series of government reports in the 1960s suggest that the top twenty indigenous business groups, including the traders-turned-industrialists mentioned before, experienced three types of change. First, they diversified into a number of fields including banks (the average was four or five unrelated areas per group), forming conglomerates like the zaibatsu in pre-war Japan. Second, these groups used the process of application for licenses to pre-empt investment by others, rather like pre-emptive domain-name registration now. Birlas were known for playing the game, and were found to hold, around 1970, close to 60 unimplemented licenses. And third, control over a large number of companies unrelated in their lines of business was maintained by means of an investment trust company, which was privately and fully owned by a family. The trust invested in some group companies, which then invested in other group companies, and so on.

The licensing system came both as a help and a hindrance for the large corporate groups of indigenous origin. Were they, then, partners of the politicians or victims of repression? Marxist writers believed that there was a state-business alliance. They qualified the idea by saying that Indian industrial capitalism was too immature, too 'financial' in orientation in comparison with the corporate capitalism of the West, to go it alone. They needed the state. The Soviet author A.I. Levkovsky and the French Marxist Charles Bettelheim expressed such views.[8] An Indian Marxist preferred the term 'tycoon capitalism.'[9] A recent book

[8] Quoted by Asim Chaudhuri, 'Conglomerate Big Business Groups in India: Some Traits of Tycoon Capitalism,' *Social Scientist*, 8(7), 1980, 38–51.

[9] Ibid.

suggests that the Indian capitalists had sufficient influence on the policies to resist attempts by the state to discipline them.[10] The investment licensing system may not have been to the liking of the industrialists, but they did not complain, because they did gain significant advantage from it.

Critics of the view of an alliance, even cronyism, would point out that the regime also made collective action by industrial capitalists more difficult than before. The major chambers of commerce lost considerable influence on policy-making, even though these bodies often successfully fought over minor provisions of policy. Bodies mainly populated by traders, such as the Indian Merchants Chamber, became relatively obscure. The chambers were platforms for huge infighting during much of their history.[11] Business and state relationship was splintered into numerous instances of 'particularistic lobbying' by individual businesspersons with individual ministers and bureaucrats.[12] Some post-reform writings go so far as to suggest that capitalists had been shackled by the state.[13]

Stanley Kochanek, in some of his writings, suggests that the corporates grew weaker and not stronger after 1950. He has a different interpretation for it. He shows how divided in scale, capability, and interests the private corporate sector was at all times.[14] In the 1980s, the large industry segment was dominated by the public sector, whose political effect was undermined by bureaucratic intervention. The remaining large businesses were geared to the home market and would not have cared for an open economy. The exporting businesses were small firms that did not have a lot of lobbying power. Thanks to

[10] V. Chibber, *Locked in Place: State-Building and Late Industrialization in India*, Princeton: Princeton University Press. 2003.

[11] Stanley A. Kochanek, 'The Transformation of Interest Politics in India,' *Pacific Affairs*, 68(4), 1995–1996, 529–550.

[12] S. Kochanek, 'Liberalisation and Business Lobbying in India,' *Journal of Commonwealth and Comparative Politics*, 34(3), 2008, 155–173.

[13] For one example, Swaminathan S.A. Aiyer, *Escape from the Benevolent Zookeepers*, Mumbai: Times Group Books, 2008.

[14] See Stanley A. Kochanek, 'Briefcase Politics in India: The Congress Party and the Business Elite,' *Asian Survey*, 27(12), 1987, 1278–1301.

government policy, the small firms in general contained many ghost firms that existed to take advantage of licenses and cheap loans; and thanks to years of brutal trade repression, the trading firms had become dwarfed family units that would not have agreed to a cosmopolitan trading order dominated by corporate players. It was because of this divided order that individual entrepreneurs could wield a great deal of influence through the backdoors of power.

What did the rising corporate groups make? While heavy engineering (equipment for steel, oil, utilities) was taken over by public sector firms, the major new fields left open for private enterprise were machine tools, chemicals, transport equipment, engineering (machines for traditional industries like textiles, sugar, paper), and cement. In steel, the Tata Steel was spared nationalization, but all new capacity came up in the public sector. Between 1947 and 1990, production of cement grew from about 4 metric tons to 50 tons. A small set of domestic firms, the biggest among them being the consortium Associated Cement Company, led this growth. The emerging player in cement was the Birla conglomerate. In engineering, indigenous Indian businesses had little expertise before 1947.

On an informal-personal level, the majority of the indigenous corporate leaders were close to politicians in New Delhi and received encouragement and favours, the most common form of favour was the permission to enter a technological collaboration. The exceptions perhaps were the people who had entered industry by taking over British firms. The case of the automobile industry is an example of close partnership. In the automobile industry, the government decided to retain the existing main firms, and allowed these to enter technical collaboration with foreign partners. Four of the companies were carmakers. The Birla group company Hindustan Motors of Calcutta (1941) produced cars with designs from Morris, Premier Automobiles of Bombay produced cars with designs from Chrysler, Standard Motors of Madras produced cars with designs from Standard Triumph, and Mahindra and Mahindra manufactured Jeeps under an agreement with Willys. Tata Engineering and Locomotive Company (TELCO) made engines collaborating with Mercedes-Benz, and Ashok Leyland of Madras made trucks and buses.

In almost all of these cases, key figures in the government took personal interest in the enterprise. A famous case was Raghunandan Saran. He had a car assembly plant earlier. With Nehru's encouragement, Saran and the British Leyland Motors jointly started Ashok Leyland in 1954. Before the negotiations ended, Saran died in an air crash. With government oversight and Leyland management, the firm continued. Another Madras firm, Simpsons, was taken over by an Indian in 1945 and produced tractors. Bajaj, a two-wheeler trader, set up a two-wheeler production plant in 1959, which diversified into three-wheelers in the 1960s. Kamalnayan Bajaj, the head of the conglomerate, was close to politics. Finally, Royal Enfield was licensed to produce motorcycles in the 1950s.

The spirit of partnership between politicians and industrialists stayed intact during Nehru's lifetime. It soured around 1965 and turned into mutual hostility in the 1970s. Indira Gandhi was afraid of corporate power turning against her. Her pro-socialist position would not have gone down well with the corporates either. The hostility waned again in the 1980s as the East Asian miracle rekindled faith in private enterprise.

The 1970s

When the industrial stagnation set in, and a section of the leftist intelligentsia blamed 'monopoly capital' for it, industrial regulation directed more energy to reducing the level of concentration in organized industry. A tighter licensing policy was introduced in 1970. Firms and business houses in possession of assets amounting to more than a stipulated level had to register themselves with the newly created Monopolies and Restrictive Trade Practices Commission, and seek approvals for expansion or diversification. Non-registration could invite penalties. The concerned department spent a lot of time enforcing registration. In the 1970s, several troubled private firms were nationalized to protect employment.

Did anti-monopoly steps and nationalization reduce concentration? They did not. The share of the top twenty business houses in total assets increased in the 1970s. The paradox suggests that the departmental powers to regulate private business were not used systematically, but with discretion. Permission could be traded for financial or political consideration. Businesses learnt to play by the rules of the game, and continued to expand with some window-dressing. As a former head of the monopolies commission explained in 1982, when the commission's powers had already been curbed, 'the political and bureaucratic authorities wield very large powers . . . These discretionary powers are the cause of the largest business in Delhi and in the state capitals, viz., lobbying by various industrial, trading and other economic interests.'[15] The monopolistic character of the industrial system, therefore, was artificially created by licensing itself.

Another target for the government was foreign capital, which faced a hostile repatriation and ownership regulation in 1973. Consumer good and drug manufacturing firms such as Hindustan Levers, Philips, Johnson and Johnson, Nestle, and Glaxo, continued to do business in India under diluted holding. A few others, including Coca-Cola and Dupont, had a presence before 1973, and left India thereafter. The real cost of the policy cannot be estimated by those who left India, but by those who stayed away. It is likely that a large number of those that stayed away were specialized firms in possession of niche technologies, tools, and processes.

Corporate Revival and Backdoor Globalization: 1980s

From the mid-1970s, the situation improved with growth in a few new areas. In the 1970s, new firms started in fertilizer production, petrochemicals and derivatives like manmade fibres, cables, and pipes. Fertilizers and associated chemicals had a boost from the Green Revolution. Another important growth industry was synthetic textiles, and in turn, petrochemicals. Private enterprise in petrochemical production is linked with the life story of the legendary entrepreneur Dhirubhai Ambani, the founder of the largest business house in India now. In early life a textile trader, Ambani

---

[15] H.K. Paranjape, 'The Vanishing MRTP Act: Will Only the Grin Remain?', *Economic and Political Weekly*, 17(23), 1982, 955–961.

established a successful textile manufacturing firm. The brand name 'Vimal' was the only fabric brand to emerge in the bleak 1970s, and the last one. The textile plant used synthetic fibres. In 1980, a joint venture with Du Pont started producing polyester filament yarn. Polyester production was regulated by investment license and import license, which applied to the raw material. Licenses were rationed, but Ambani's capacity managed to grow at a dramatic pace through the 1980s. His rivals attributed the growth to political connections. As one interested party was to rue later, 'you had to manage the system for all licences.'[16] The company was beginning to backward integrate into petrochemicals, and in 1992, with the economic reforms around the corner, commissioned a petrochemical complex. In the 2000s, the company discovered offshore oilfield in the Krishna-Godavari basin, and set up the largest refinery in the world.

In the second half of the 1980s, globalization was creeping back in. During Rajiv Gandhi's Prime Ministership (1985–1991), politics seemed to be torn between reform, that is, less state intervention than before, and strengthening equity, that is, more state intervention than before. A few significant steps were taken to deregulate private investment. For example, the Textile Policy was reformed, and investment limits imposed in 1969 upon 'monopoly' groups were relaxed. How large the total impact was cannot be ascertained. 'Since the Indian regulatory system is extremely complex and overlapping, it is difficult to change one part of the system without creating inequities in other parts of the system.'[17]

Nevertheless, the backdoor globalization did have lasting effects. The Maruti automobile enterprise, a joint venture between the government and Suzuki Motors, was an example. It spawned a sophisticated ancillary machine tools industry, which supported the foreign auto manufacturers that entered India in the 1990s. Joint ventures like Maruti were to become a popular way to attract technology, in the absence of a formal relaxation of the foreign investment rules. Several joint ventures were

---

[16] http://www.firstpost.com/business/nusli-wadia-explains-his-loss-to-ambani-in-polyester-war-514427.html (accessed 6 May 2015).

[17] Stanley A. Kochanek, 'Regulation and Liberalization Theology in India,' *Asian Survey*, 26(12), 1986, 1284–1308.

established, though few survived beyond 1990.[18] Studies on the failure of joint ventures found a fundamental flaw in the design of these ecollaborations, the foreign partner was more capable and had deeper pockets than the Indian partner. In many cases, the inequality in technical or financial capability was outweighed by the fact that the Indian partner was the politician's favoured child.

The liberalization reduced tariffs, and opened the field for foreign direct investment except in the services. None of this was an unmixed good news for capital and labour. There is no evidence that the top corporate houses had either a role in or even anticipated the dramatic tariff reforms of 1992, and the subsequent removal of barriers for foreign direct investment. If anything, the reaction of indigenous business was a mixture of fear, apprehension, and anger directed at reformers.

Domestic Firms After Reforms

How did tariff reform change Indian companies? Synthetic fibres is a useful case study, with Reliance again playing a large role in it. Import tariffs on the major manmade fibres and raw materials were brought down, step by step, from their peak level of 185 per cent in 1991–92 to 30 per cent in 1997–98. This dealt a blow to manmade fibre manufacturers. Between 1995 and 1999, world prices of polyester staple fibre and filament yarn crashed due to excess supply from East Asia. The majority of the firms in India making these products lost money after 1996. Less vulnerable were firms like Reliance, which commanded more assured long-term contracts and went for vertical integration. Reliance's expansion itself put further pressure on other polyester producers. By 1996, the synthetic fibre industry had too much capacity located in too many units operating at an average scale below the world norm. Between 1990 and 1996, JCT, Baroda Rayon, J.K. Synthetics, Sanghi Polyester, and Garware Nylon were among the list of manmade fibre

[18] Nirmalya Kumar, 'Indian Companies as Customers, Competitors and Collaborators,' *Indian Journal of Industrial Relations*, 45(1), 2009, 148–159.

manufacturers that came to the doors of the government agency in charge of reviving bankrupt firms, without much success.

Baroda Rayon, a medium-scale firm engaged in rayon, nylon, and polyester, faced problems throughout the 1990s. By 1997, burdened by unsustainable debts it tried several revival packages that included failed attempts to sell its plants to larger producers. In 1999, its polyester unit began operation under different management, and the rayon unit shut down. From the end of 1999, the company began defaulting on salaries, leading to a spate of protests and rallies from its 4,500 strong work-force. The textile operations of J.K. Synthetics, the main company of the G.H. Singhania group, was another casualty of adverse market conditions. In 1997, faced with massive debt (for some time, the company was the leader among private sector bad debtors to the banks), the company closed eight units in Kota and Jhalawar. The unemployment of 5,000 workers had a traumatic impact on the local economy, and numerous small firms ancillary to these plants also closed. In all these cases of closure, there was little resistance from workers.[19] Studies of textile mill closure in Gujarat and press reports from Rajasthan both underscore a point highlighted in some recent assessments of trade union response to closure, the non-interventionist attitude of some states in respect of closure and large-scale disputes.

In automobiles too, there was a shakeout. All of the original six companies did well until the end of the 1980s. The first major casualty of the Maruti-Suzuki phenomenon was Standard Motors, which had long been known to produce one of the least efficient cars in the world. After 1975, Leyland had more or less withdrawn from the management of Ashok Leyland. Its stake in the company was purchased by the Britain-based Hinduja group. After India opened its doors to foreign

[19] 'Secretary for Industries NS Sisodia, does not dispute [that the closure was a result of liberalization], saying it could be a possible reason but then, he adds, no one can dispute this right of the industrialist. He, however, said it was family dispute between the Singhanias which led to the crisis.' Quoted in Rajesh Sinha, 'Units Closing in on the Life of Rajasthan', The Indian Express Online, 3 December 1997.

investment in automobiles, Premier and Hindustan Motors went bankrupt, though their eventual closure was delayed because taxi contracts in Bombay and Calcutta favoured these two companies for some time.

The companies and groups that survived needed to reform themselves.

Intra-Firm Changes

Since the 1990s, large Indian business groups reformed their own houses by divesting businesses unrelated to their core advantage, expansion within the core areas, induction of non-family professional managers, decentralization of top management, and fragmentation of family assets.[20] And they did all this sometimes with the help of professional consultants in a planned manner. These processes have implications for the corporate economy as a whole. Of course, the changes going on in the top ten or fifteen groups have a demonstration effect on others. More than that, the changes imply the emergence of a top-end managerial labour market, and a bigger role for paid consultants in family firms.

The concept of the family firm underwent a change, from extended families to individualistic ones, even as the prominence of the family as such as owner-cum-manager remained intact. As far as we can tell, leadership succession was not guided by family structure in the British managing agencies in the 1940s. In that time, both the Indian-owned and the foreign-owned firms had family-ownership, but in the case of the British firms, the owner had a small controlling stake, was often physically distant from the day-to-day working of the company, and had a notional involvement in management. This was far from the case with the Indian firms, where the families had firm control on leadership succession. Between then and 1990, the role of families in deciding succession increased.

And yet, this was only the statistical picture. Inside some of the biggest families, the pressure to divide assets between siblings had grown after the death of the founder. Between 1952 and 2000, almost

[20] S. Manikutty, 'Family Business Groups in India: A Resource-Based View of the Emerging Trends,' *Family Business Review*, 13(4), 2000, 279–292.

all of the major business groups split, usually among brothers, and not always in a friendly fashion. In the colonial era, fewer cases of succession disputes and splits can be found. It is not impossible that more cases in the recent past were publicized than in the earlier era, but it is worth considering how economic policy played a part. Import-substituting industrialization, for example, by encouraging groups to hold licenses in unrelated businesses may have encouraged division and specialization within the family. A Marwari businessperson tells me that the concerns of the patriarch of a business family was often to settle the sons in *unrelated* businesses so that they would not fight each other for the rest of their lives. This social ethic would find the government's licensing system a useful tool to keep peace in the family. But when the tool did not work or the group was too big, like the Birla, a formal division of estate was inevitable.

The economic reforms pushed the tendency in a different way. Increasing competition made some firms vulnerable and some succeed, which would also encourage a parting of the ways between brothers who experienced different fortunes. Still, the end of the licensing system removed the need to diversify unnecessarily and pre-empt rivals.[21] Studies find that after split, businesses tended to increase the stake of the owner or family in the firms they now controlled. Eighty per cent of India's Fortune-500 companies in 1994 were still family-owned. Whether the aggregate trend should be called continuity or dissolution of the family firms, time will tell.

Foreign Firms, Mergers, Diversification

After the reforms, leading foreign firms including Bayer, Gillette, Goodyear, Datacraft, EMI, Sprint, Suzuki, Merrill Lynch, Xerox, and Vodafone, which had entered India through a joint venture, started independent operations. In a few cases, one notable example being the

[21] Ashok Punjwani, Vijay Aggarwal, Nand Dhameja, 'Family Business: Yesterday, Today, Tomorrow,' *Indian Journal of Industrial relations*, 44(2), 2008, 272–291; Sudipta Dutta, *Family Business in India*, Delhi: Response Books, 1997.

Britannia Industries, the separation was acrimonious, politically charged, and costly for the foreign partner. In another case, NOCIL, which was a joint venture between Shell and an old textile family Mafatlal, Shell breakaway occurred amidst bitterness in the course of negotiations to bring in new patented technology.

Two tendencies – foreign entry and ailing Indian brand – jointly led to a spate of acquisitions and mergers. One set of mergers happened between foreign firms in possession of global brands and Indian firms, such as Coca-Cola buying up a Bombay-based soft drink manufacturer Parle, or Lever buying up the Indian food brand Kissan. A second set of mergers occurred between Indian firms, desiring to restructure and develop areas of core competence and their weaker competitors, for example, Shri Ram Fibres or SRF, a tyre chord maker, buying the tyre cord division of CEAT tyres, and big cement companies buying regional cement companies. As a component of the same process, there were also de-mergers. Diversified groups like the Tatas shed non-core businesses like soaps and oils.

One legacy of the protected era had been the emergence of Indian consumer brands in soft drinks (Parle's Campa Cola, Rasna), consumer electronics and white goods (Videocon, BPL in TV and radio sets), watches (HMT, a government firm), cars (Ambassador of the Birla-owned Hindustan Motors), and machine tools. Few of these survived the 2000s, whereas Korean and Japanese brand names swept the consumer market in cars, white goods, and electronics. The sinking of Indian brands did not sink a company, but sometimes led to a move away from finished goods to component manufacture (Videocon, for example, from TV sets to tubes). Why Indian brands failed to become global remains a mystery. Was the key failure in advertising, in quality control and R and D, after-sale service, or more simply, was nationalistic branding an unsustainable business idea in a globalized world?[22]

Whereas Bombay, Pune, Madras, Hyderabad, and Bangalore were the cities where the corporate restructuring centred, Calcutta was losing

[22] S.L. Rao, 'Indian Companies in an Open Economy,' *Economic and Political Weekly*, 36(5/6), 2001, 457–461.

wealth. The British multinationals that operated from Calcutta were targets of leftist trade unions, suffered disturbed industrial relations, with disastrous consequences. Around 2008, ICI was bought up by Akzo Nobel, and its Indian subsidiaries merged to form Akzo Nobel India. By then, the manufacturing capacity had shifted out of Calcutta. Metal Box had a steady good run until the early 1970s, but faced difficulties thereafter, compounded by a crippling labour dispute in 1984–1985. The firm sold some of its assets to Tata and other companies, stopped production and wound up in the early 2000s. The GKW factories suffered steady losses and labour disputes in the 1990s, and closed down. GKN divested from the Indian subsidiary in 1994. The Indian company, GKW, exists as a small consultancy firm based in Bombay. In 1978, the parent company of Mather and Platt divested its interests. Mather and Platt India is now a subsidiary of Wilo AG. Its main manufacturing centres are Pune and Kolhapur in western India, no information is available on the Calcutta plant in the company's website. The Birmingham company Dunlop Rubber had a rather similar history to some of the older managing agencies. Its main manufacturing facility was based in Calcutta. It experienced a transfer of control to Indian owners, and suffered a rapid downfall thereafter. Allegations of wilful mismanagement have been made against some of the past owners of the firm.

British multinationals that had stayed away from Calcutta or divested from the city in time fared better. The transformers maker Crompton Parkinson sold its Indian subsidiary to the Thapar group, the company being renamed as Crompton Greaves. The ITC Limited, which originated as a subsidiary of the British American Tobacco company and is still owned by BAT, is a diversified firm registered in Calcutta but assets located elsewhere in India. The household chemicals firm Reckitt and Colman started a trading unit in India in the 1920s. Its manufacturing subsidiary in India is now known as RB, and a unit of the global firm formed of Reckitt and Colman, and Benckiser. These firms were left unscathed by the deindustrialization and extremely violent trade union movement of Calcutta, because their manufacturing facility was located away from the West Bengal state of which Calcutta city was the capital. In the 1990s, liberalization of foreign investment rules allowed some of these firms to strengthen their bonds with the parent multinational.

The attraction of a large home market eager to consume state-of-the-art goods has brought in multinational firms into India since the 1990s. Probably the most important cluster by provenance is Japanese investment in automobiles. Japanese investment took place both as subsidiaries and in joint ventures, such as those between Maruti and Suzuki, Telco and Hitachi, Yamaha and Escorts in tractors. In Southeast Asia and China, foreign investment led to growth in export capacity.[23] It is well-known that this effect was modest if not missing in India.

In the years since 2000, the main new entry into the corporate big leagues were the IT firms. Unlike manufacturing, where Indians failed to create global brands, in IT a few Indian firms emerged to lead global business.

Companies 2000–2015

Some idea of the current composition of big firms can be obtained from global lists. In 2015, 56 Indian firms figured in *Forbes Global 2000* list (Table 10.3). The number is small, measured in market capitalization the aggregate is smaller still, but the number is growing. In 2007, it was 34. The major cluster of big firms consists of government banks and oil and gas utilities. In the private sector, the main companies in the list can be called 'knowledge-based', that is, IT and pharmaceuticals. The most surprising development in the post-liberalization business world was the growth of the information technology (IT)-related services. In this one field, Indian capability and scale shaped global capability. And in turn, IT was not just another industry in India, but one that shaped a new middle class with commitment to openness and cosmopolitanism. This cultural effect of IT is perhaps its most revolutionary aspect.

Among the companies figuring in the list, Reliance Industries is diversified, but its major interest now is in energy. Only two government

[23] Geethanjali Nataraj, 'Japanese Investment in India: Trends and Prospects,' *Economic and Political Weekly*, 45(10), 2010, 20–23.

Table 10.3 Indian companies in Forbes Global 2000 list, 2015

Companies	Number of companies	Global rank	Market capitalization, $ b
Reliance Industries		142	43
IT			
Tata Consultancy Services		485	80
Infosys		672	40
Wipro		811	25
HCL		1007	21
Telecom			
Bharti		506	26
Idea		1512	11
MTNL (government)		1717	0.2
Pharmaceuticals			
Sun		1225	39
Lupin		1580	15
Dr. Reddy's		1946	10
Government utilities and energy firms	10		154
Government banks	14		57
Others	21		342
All	56		863

Source: http://www.forbes.com/global2000/list/ (accessed 7 May 2015)

firms, Bharat Heavy Electricals and Steel Authority of India, are market leaders in some sense and can be called the children of import substituting industrialization. These metallurgical and equipment making giants were started by the government from the 1950s. Nearly all of the privately owned firms experienced their greatest growth and diversification, and acquired their present shape after 2000. Pharmaceutical production was helped by the import-substituting state via a protective patent regime, but the three firms that figure in the Forbes list expanded after that regime had ended.

Among some of the firms that figure in the Forbes list, there is a trend in increasing overseas investment. Indians expanded the scale of asset holdings abroad between 1948 and 1982, though a precise division of these assets into private industrial and other types is unavailable.[24] In any case the scale of the recent increase dwarfs the older outflow. The recent outflow is industrial and reflects a globalization of Indian corporate capital. How large is this tendency? And what does it mean? Despite the rising scale of overseas investment from India, at least until 2008 when the flow began to drop, the relative scale of Indian investment is not really large enough to be excited about, not nearly so in comparison with the counterpart investment flow from China or South Korea. It is harder to answer the second question because outflows are influenced by factors that are specific to industries and individual firms. Overseas collaborations and acquisitions by three automotive firms (Tata, Mahindra, and Bajaj) have received attention, but what lessons these cases have for overseas investment in general is not clear.[25]

Nevertheless, the existence and visibility of Indian multinational has spawned a scholarship. It overturns common prediction that foreign investment should flow from capital-rich to capital-scarce regions. In one interpretation, favoured by the leftist economists in India especially, the overseas expansion represents the success of import-substitution, when India 'learnt to industrialize.'[26] But as we see from the preceding paragraph, very few private sector firms of the import substitution era appear in the list. Another contribution makes use of the 'varieties of capitalism' literature to suggest that large firms in emerging markets tend to be state-dependent, showing this with reference to the investment by state-owned financial institutions in large corporates.[27] The evidence does not explain the decision to invest overseas. Public sector banks have opened more services abroad, responding to more relaxed rules about non-resident Indian investment in India. Quantitatively speaking, this is a small outflow since Indian banks are small fry in the global financial

[24] Sebastian Morris, 'Trends in Foreign Direct Investment from India (1950–1982),' *Economic and Political Weekly*, 22(45), 1987, 1909–1918.

[25] Sunil Mani, 'Outward Foreign Direct Investment from India and Knowledge Flows, the case of three automotive firms', *Asian Journal of Technology Innovation*, 2013, 21(sup1), 25–38.

[26] Deepak Nayyar, 'The Internationalization of Firms From India: Investment, Mergers and Acquisitions,' *Oxford Development Studies*, 36(1), 2008, 111–131.

[27] Lawrence Sáez and Crystal Chang, 'The Political Economy of Global Firms from India and China, *Contemporary Politics*, 15(3), 2009, 265–286.

market. Overall, it remains difficult to explain overseas investment as a single process.

Companies and Entrepreneurship in IT Business

The literature on the origins of the industry has paid rather little attention to entrepreneurship and firm capability. A few Indian-owned firms, Tata Consultancy, which had existed from 1968, Infosys, Wipro, Satyam, and National Institute of Information Technology, laid the foundation for the export industry in the 1990s. The Y2K challenge, cheap call centres, and consultancy spurred another round of growth in 1990s, now in small firms. By 2000, all major global companies – including Sun Microsystems, Microsoft, Lucent, IBM, Adobe, Accenture, and Oracle – had set up subsidiaries in India.

The representative firm, however, is still small. Moreover, these firms and the people who started them and now manage them do not fit the traditional entrepreneurial stereotype. They do not come from business families. They accumulate wealth by using skills rather than tangible assets. They work in a world that involves a great deal of firm-to-firm and person-to-person interaction, a world of collaboration and frequent exchange of tacit knowledge, rather than one of competition. They tend to be more cosmopolitan than the traditional business family representatives were before liberalization. Caste and community matter little in this world in forging relationships, though caste is still relevant as a predictor of higher, especially scientific and technological education.[28]

The software entrepreneurs, in other words, see themselves as members of the 'middle class,' their story is that of middle-class capitalism in an integrated world. The life story of key entrepreneurs (especially that of the Infosys co-founder N.R. Narayana Murthy) became a symbol of this narrative of a new kind of capitalism in India that had no link with the old capitalism, and was even at odds with it. That story of the making of

[28] C.J. Fuller and Haripriya Narasimhan, 'From Landlords to Software Engineers: Migration and Urbanization among Tamil Brahmans,' *Comparative Studies in Society and History*, 50(1), 2008, 170–196.

capitalism is tied to another story, that of a responsible and ethical capitalism that these new entrepreneurs believe they lead.[29] The new cosmopolitan capitalism has faced challenges, such as in the IT hub Bangalore, where regional politics tended to project the IT industry as an imposition by outsiders. It has also proved robust enough to become a part of the remaking of India into a cosmopolitan business destination.

Even though the vast majority of the software workers came from private technical schools, many of the leading entrepreneurs and firms were set up by the graduates of the Indian Institutes of Technology sponsored by the state. In the previous decades, the institutes of technology served two aims, that of producing technical manpower needed by domestic industrial firms, and as a finishing school for doctoral candidates in American universities. As the outflow of doctorate hopefuls surged, the government railed in public about the 'brain drain' at the cost of the Indian taxpayer. No one knew what should be done about it. Meanwhile, engineers formed a large component of the Indian diaspora in the USA. Some of them invested money in starting firms in the Silicon Valley. Some of the others worked in the existing firms. The Indian workforce pool was familiar to these individuals, and recruits could in principle receive training and mentoring from them.[30] A relationship that began in this way matured in the late 2000s as many companies, irrespective of the ethnicity of ownership or management, purchased services and products made by India-based ones.

Other Services

Globalization has changed the corporate sector. Still, it will be a mistake to overlook how insular the Indian economy remains. For example, the service sector is protected both by investment regulation and the general

[29] Carol Upadhya, 'Imagining India: Software and the ideology of liberalisation,' *South African Review of Sociology*, 40(1), 2012, 76–93.

[30] Abhishek Pandey, Alok Aggarwal, Richard Devane, Yevgeny Kuznetsov, 'India's Transformation to Knowledge-based Economy – Evolving Role of the Indian Diaspora', online report available from Evalueserve, 2004.

unattractiveness of India as an expatriate destination. Key services from retail trade, to health care, hotels, print media, tourism, banking and finance, education and films, which together contribute about half of the Gross Domestic Product, have grown in scale but not much improved in the quality that they deliver.[31] Being labour intensive, they should gain from skilled immigration. India, however, receives negligible number of skilled immigrant workers. Since these businesses do not compete in the world market, few economists and politicians seem worried about the poor quality of output. India-watchers believe that a bolder opening up is unlikely in these protected areas, because political sentiment against it is too strong.[32] A media debate in 2012 about allowing Walmart in multi-brand retail showed how fierce nationalistic sentiment could be when it came to embracing openness in services.

Such sentiment is not special to India. It is rather odd in India's case because of the region's commercial heritage. Why should a people that engaged in globalization in the past be so afraid of globalization in the present? A tentative answer is that in the last 20 odd years a trading lobby has emerged in post-reform India that does not care for globalization in trade.

Business and Politics After the Reforms

Has Indian capitalists grown in political power in the last 20 years, or have they lost political power because there is more competition for them? The emergence of a stronger and larger private corporate sector in the recent years has indeed made lobbying for routine policy reform more institutionalized than before. Furthermore, political attitude changed. 'With the shift in government policy toward greater

[31] The World Health Organization ranks India 112th among 190 countries on the quality of its health care industry. Indian film industry, the largest in the world, does not produce films that can compete for international prizes. An HSBC index comparing expatriate lifestyle ranks India very low (20–30 among 34 countries) on health care, accommodation, utilities, finance, and ease of local travel.

[32] Sonal Pandya, 'Why foreign investment still polarizes India,' Washington Post blogs, 2014. http://www.washingtonpost.com/blogs/monkey-cage/wp/2014/09/30/why-foreign-investment-still-polarizes-india/ (accessed 1 April 2014).

emphasis on private sector development . . . government has become less suspicious of business demands and more willing to listen . . .'[33] The lobbying process in India involves, as before, corporates influencing party positions during legislation.[34] But the role of lobbying-by-bribery of the parties is less visible or discussed now than before. Contrast this with the 1980s, when '[t]he extraordinarily rapid growth of Reliance led to repeated charges in the press and by the opposition parties in Parliament that Ambani had received special treatment from Congress-led governments in return for secret contributions to the party.'[35] Having said that, the corporate sector remains as weak and divided as before in effecting paradigm shifts in government policy.

Pakistan, by contrast with India, inherited fewer large-scale firms in 1947, but gained from migration of capital.

Pakistan

Cities in the Punjab plains like Lahore and Multan were centres of trade, finance, and crafts in Mughal India. These cities depopulated in the eighteenth and nineteenth century during the decline of the Asian empires and the rise of Indo-European trade. Merchants and bankers left them for the new capital cities emerging in the successor states. Punjab remained a source of textile supplies into the Indo-European trade, but the main sources were nearer the coasts – Gujarat, Bengal, and Coromandel. From the middle of the nineteenth century, textiles ceased to be the main article of export in Indo-European trade, and grain and cotton increased in importance. A new link emerged between the port cities and the agricultural interior. The construction of canal colonies in late nineteenth century made Punjab plains once again central to long-distance trade,

[33] Kochanek, 'Transformation.'

[34] Vineeta Yadav, 'Business Lobbies and Policymaking in Developing Countries: The Contrasting Cases of India and China,' *Journal of Public Affairs*, 8(1), 2008, 67–82.

[35] Kochanek, 'Briefcase Politics.'

and stimulated an agriculture-based urbanization. Although not in the canal zones, Lahore and Multan gained from this prosperity and contributed to it by supplying trading and financial services. From the 1860s, Karachi grew in importance as one of the main ports to receive cargo sent from Punjab and Sind down the Indus. In this way, a new urban pattern emerged in the territory that became West Pakistan.

At the time of independence, Karachi and Lahore were both large and populous business towns. The majority of the businesses were owned by Hindus, Parsis, and Sikhs. With a small minority excepted, all of them left Pakistan for India in 1947. From the Indian side, Muslim businesses migrated to Pakistan. The transaction was unequal for Pakistan, and it is credible though not well established that the exodus of non-Muslims 'had a major disruptive effect on business development in the Pakistani areas.'[36] Industry yielded one per cent of national income, and was not doing well in 1947 despite a friendly government. Trading was much more profitable. Thereafter, the Korean War gave a large boost to trade. The profits accumulated during the 3 years of the war were reinvested in factories when the boom ended. Foreign exchange reserves built up during the war eased import of equipment. Although exchange controls were tightened soon after, investment in textile production took off.

The source of the investment was migrants from India.

1950–1972

From the Indian side members of the Halai Memon community of Gujarat, a trading group, migrated to Karachi and took over the textile trade. Other migrant merchants included the Ismaili Khojas from Bombay and East Africa, the Khojas who followed the Ithnā Ashari sect of Shiism, and the Dawoodi Bohras of western India. Chiniotis, a small group from Punjab (Chiniot) who had migrated to Calcutta and traded in leather, returned to their homelands and played a role in the

[36] Imran Ali and Adeel Malik, 'The Political Economy of Industrial Development in Pakistan: A Long-Term Perspective,' *The Lahore Journal of Economics*, 14(1), 2009, 29–50.

textile industry. A major destination of capital was the city of Faisalabad (then Lyallpur). Located in one of the canal colonies, Faisalabad always had plentiful supply of cotton. The nearby town of Chiniot, with an ancient heritage of craft and trade, was a source of entrepreneurship in trade and industry. Chinioti businesses were based in Calcutta, and some of them still live there.

Some of the most prominent firms were invited into Pakistan by the leadership on generous terms such as land grant. Later in the 1950s, these pioneer groups were also helped with bank loans and import licenses. Through this process, there emerged the famous twenty-odd business conglomerates of independent Pakistan, until the 1970s socialist drive decimated some of them. The history of these groups reveals a few invariant characteristics. Before the move, almost all of them were trading firms, with interest in tea, textile, leather, coastal shipping, and financial services. They were mobile and had bases of operation in many port cities of Asia. Some had their main offices in Calcutta. They were cosmopolitan as well as Muslim in their public profile.

Of the leading conglomerates, the Monnoo group based in Faisalabad, where they now own textile factories and other businesses, originated in a Calcutta-based Chinioti firm. The founder of the group exchanged a factory in Dhaka for assets in Calcutta in 1947, and then left Bangladesh in 1971 for Faisalabad. The Crescent Group also originated in a Chinioti family engaged in leather trade in Amritsar, which later shifted operation to Faisalabad. The Gujarati Memon firm known as Adamjee, and established by Adamjee Haji Dawood (1880–1948) started in general trade, specialized in jute trade, and established a jute mill near Calcutta in 1927. In the 1940s Adamjee was induced by M.A. Jinnah to campaign among the Memons to support the Muslim League and the demand for Pakistan. Adamjee established factories in both East and West Pakistan, but after his death, the group concentrated in the West. It is now one of the most diversified business groups in Pakistan. The Ispahani family of Bangladesh was started in the early nineteenth century as a trading firm in Bombay. Different branches of the family expanded in Madras, London, and Calcutta, before independence. The brothers Mirza Ahmed and Mirza Abol Hassan went to

Pakistan. Their operations were based in Dhaka and Chittagong. The second of the two brothers, who turned a prominent politician in later life, was a close associate of Jinnah.[37]

Another trading group to migrate from India were the Saigols. They were from Punjab, but had moved to Calcutta around 1890. Sayeed Saigol established a shoe shop in the city, and a rubber shoe factory called Kohinoor Rubber Works. During World War II, the factory prospered. Within a year after independence, Saigols moved from India to Faisalabad and set up a textile factory. With financial support from the government, the family diversified into sugar, chemicals, engineering, and edible oils.

Ahmed Dawood, from Kathiawar, set up an extensive trading operation in India in the interwar period. He shifted operation to East Pakistan in 1947, and owned some of the big factories of the province, including jute, cotton, and paper mills as well as a shipping firm. In 1971, Dawood group shifted to Pakistan, in the process losing assets on a large scale. The textile house Bawany originated in a Gujarati trading firm which had operations in Burma, before the shift to Pakistan. Similarly, Kassim Dada group, now a textile and investment house, originated in a Gujarati Memon firm which had operations in Burma and South Africa.

A different type of figure, Habib Ibrahim Rahimtoola was better known for his contributions to politics. His father, Ibrahim Rahimtoola (1862–1942), a member of the Khoja community of Bombay and the head of the family trading firm, gained fame as a politician in Bombay. Habib Ibrahim, when in his twenties, was inducted by Jinnah to join the Muslim League. His positions in the party helped him mediate between business and the government. In the 1950s he expanded the trading enterprise, and held senior managerial positions in banks and companies.

The trading firms that diversified usually owned banks as well. Some trading families that migrated to Pakistan from India established banks

[37] On the family's participation in interwar nationalist politics, see Joya Chatterji, *Bengal Divided: Hindu Communalism and Partition, 1932–1947*, Cambridge: Cambridge University Press, 1994, 80.

or were associated with the start of one. The Gujarati Ismaili Mohammed Ali Habib founded Pakistan's largest private bank, Habib Bank, and encouraged by Jinnah, shifted base from Gujarat to Karachi. Saigols headed the United Bank from 1959.

This stage in Pakistan's business history came to an end in 1971–1972. Some of the textile magnates who had invested in East Pakistan suffered loss of assets. Although the socialist phase (1972–1977) left the textile industry relatively unscathed by nationalization, most textile businesses had been diversified groups and these groups found some of their interest affected, and with finance in the hands of the state, found it harder to move savings between the branches. Prominent industrialists and business magnates lived in exile in the 1970s, having lost a lot during the socialist turn. The Saigols lost almost two-thirds of their assets to the nationalization drive. They expanded into construction in Saudi Arabia. Ahmed Dawood group, already affected by the exit from Bangladesh, suffered further loss during nationalization.

1980 to the Present

After the socialist phase ended, a long-drawn privatization process encouraged new entry. Textiles remained the mainstay of Pakistan manufacturing. The privatization led to considerable reshuffling among top groups. For example, a textile magnate, Mian Muhammad Mansha was a beneficiary of the privatization process. It enabled him take over the Adamjee group (insurance), a part of the Saigol group (cement), and importantly, a big private bank, Muslim Commercial Bank or MCB. In 2008, MCB was recapitalized by the sale of a substantial stake to a Malaysian interest. There were a few notable survivors. Sadruddin Hashwani's Hashoo group started in 1960 as a trading firm. In the 1970s it lost the trading business to the government and shifted to hotels. It is now a diversified entity, but its core business remains hotels and construction.

Growing business entities subsequently were built around a cluster of textile firms (example, Alkaram; Chenab group of Mian Muhammad Latif; Dewan Mushtaq; Gul Ahmed). Others, such as Atlas and Ghani group, started from trading and share-broking to move into manufacturing. A somewhat different profile is represented by the major private sector oil refinery operator, Attock, and its Saudi partner. The attraction of media, education, and real estate is strong for a number of these businesses that started first in trading and then moved to manufacturing. In common with the Indian counterparts, the Pakistani companies catered to the internal market.

Business and Politics in Pakistan

At the time of formation of Pakistan, big business chose to be apolitical. 'The fastest growing families were not the [politically visible] Isphahanis, Haroon, or Rahimtoola but Dawood, Saigol, Jalil (Amin), Shaikh, Fancy, Valika, Bawany, Bashir (Crescent), and Wazir Ali. Only the Adamjee family could be said to have played a major role in the Pakistan Movement . . .'[38] One could say that big business of Pakistan did not need to be political for the same reason as their Indian counterparts did. The latter had an enemy, foreign capital and foreign trade; they wanted the state to battle these enemies on their behalf. In West Pakistan, the corporate sector did not need to fight any such battle because foreign capital was insignificant. Business was taken on board by the regime. Many of them were trading firms, and therefore, the government did not introduce trade repressive regulations to the same extent as the Indian state did.

As the state started regulating the economy, business needed to take on a political role, all the more so because the bureaucracy took the landlords and the army more seriously than the corporate class. From about 1960, the corporate sector in Pakistan, by contrast with India, alternated between lobbying with individuals during the military regimes, and lobbying with parties during democratic ones. During Ayub Khan's regime, negotiations were direct and effective, but in popular sentiment, they represented self-interested transactions that

[38] Stanley A. Kochanek, *Interest Groups and Development: Business and Politics in Pakistan*, Delhi: Oxford University Press, 1983, p. 260.

had nothing to do with public interest, and therefore, were unpopular. The successor to the regime was almost driven to destroying corporate power in order to avoid the charge of being manipulated by it. And yet, businesses may have coordinated more during this time to defend its interests better.

Long after the end of the socialist experiment, the general character of the Pakistani corporate sector resembled the Indian one in key aspects. It was fragmented into different types of interest, fragmented by political loyalties, represented by weak chambers of commerce, and hardly visible beside the public sector. It is plausible that the 2000s saw a gradual paradigm shift. The capacity of big business to make themselves heard is greater than before not only because the top leaderships of the major rival parties are themselves from business, but also, some of the wealthiest Pakistani capitalists are expatriates. The expatriates can lobby key aspects of international relations better because lobbying is more institutionalized in the western world.[39] In both India and Pakistan, business is known to have taken advantage of the fact that banks are government owned, and are more susceptible to manipulations. In both countries, government banks carry a burden of bad debt. Is this corruption or institutional failure? Pakistan analysts argue that it is more of the former.[40]

Bangladesh

In 1947, East Pakistan had about 3000 factories. The majority of these were connected with jute and cotton textiles, small in scale, and owned by Bengalis. In terms of asset size, however, the Bengali share was small at 18 per cent. Three immigrant Gujarati Memon business groups,

[39] Mumtaz Anwar and Katharina Michaelowa, 'The Political Economy of US Aid to Pakistan,' *Review of Development Economics*, 10(2), 2006, 195–209.

[40] '[T]he positive and significant link between total leverage and political connections suggests that connected firms maintain higher leverage than nonconnected firms,' though the relationship works better for long-term leverage. Abubakr Saeed, Yacine Belghitar, Ephraim Clark, 'Political Connections and Leverage: Firm-level Evidence from Pakistan,' *Managerial and Decision Economics*, 36(4), 2015, 364–383.

Adamjee, Dawood, and Bawany, a Punjabi Chinioti group, Amin, and a Pakistani-Persian group Ispahani, owned the majority share, 47 per cent. The remaining part belonged to the government.[41] The Ispahanis and Adamjees, we have seen, were trading groups based in Calcutta long before the Partition. After Partition, they moved to the East and set up cotton and jute textile mills, along with sugar manufacture, tea plantations, banking, and insurance.

Among the non-Bengali groups, M.M. Ispahani, headed by Mirza Mehdy Ispahani, had interest in tea in Sylhet in eastern Bangladesh. Ispahani also owned jute and textile factories. Abdul Wahid Adamjee established a jute mill in East Pakistan, initially with government financial support, soon after independence. Ahmed Ebrahim Bawany, the founder of the Bawany group, was a trader and textile manufacturer in Burma, shifted base to Calcutta during World War II, and shifted again to East Pakistan after 1947. In the 1960s, Bawany group had extensive interest in jute, textiles, and chemicals. Ahmed Dawood, the founder of the Dawood group, had migrated from Gujarat to West Pakistan in 1948, and at the same time turned from a trader to an industrialist. The group owned cotton mills and insurance companies in West Pakistan, and paper, jute, rayon, chemicals, and shipping firms in East Pakistan.

Most Bengali groups operated in jute trade, baling, inland transport, tea trading, and tea production.[42] In the 1960s, members of the Bengali groups included Ranada Prasad Saha, who had taken over the assets of the Calcutta-based managing agency George Henderson. There were other examples of entry by this route, but a detailed history of transfer of British assets to Bangladeshi hands is unavailable. Abdul Kasem Khan, of what was to be known as the A.K. Khan group, had a trading firm based

---

[41] Stanley A. Kochanek, 'The Rise of Interest Politics in Bangladesh,' *Asian Survey*, 36(7), 1996, 704–722.

[42] Among other resources, I have used the information contained in websites to write this section, including http://archive.thedailystar.net/magazine/2012/05/04/cover.htm (on Latifur Rahman), http://kumudini.timdmp.com/main-blocks/our-income-generating-units.html (Kumudini Trust), http://www.beximco.com/#about (BEXIMCO), http://www.samsonchowdhury.com/en/timeline.php (Samson H. Chowdhury), http://www.midas-bd.com.bd/director/mr-mirza-ali-behrouze-ispahani/ and http://en.banglapedia.org/index.php?title=Ispahani_Family (M.M. Ispahani), http://www.dailynayadiganta.com/detail/news/106020 (Abdul Kasem Khan).

in Chittagong in 1945. After 1947 the firm diversified into manufacturing industry, including textiles, jute, and tannery, and established one of the big banks, Eastern Mercantile. The founder was a lawyer and judge in early life, a member of the constituent assemblies of both India and Pakistan, and a minister in 1958–1962.

Latifur Rahman belonged in a family that had been trading in tea since 1885, and from that base, entered tea production and jute mills. The brothers Ahmed Sohail Fasiur (A.S.F.) Rahman and Salman Fazlur Rahman inherited a family-owned jute mill while still students in the 1960s. Samson H. Chowdhury had a unusual biography. Son of a medical officer, Chowdhury was educated in Calcutta, joined the Royal Navy, took part in a naval mutiny in 1946, but was discharged honourably. He inherited a medical shop owned by his father in 1952, and with three friends, started a medical trading firm in 1958, named Square. In the 1960s, Square expanded as a trading firm.

The nationalization drive between 1972 and 1975 took over half of the abandoned assets of the larger groups, and the major part of the assets of the Bengali groups as well. Among major industries, tea was left alone but textile was nationalized. Thus, just when independence could have come in as an opportunity for the local entrepreneurs who were well placed to diversity, they lost that opportunity, and needed to move to newer fields. Two of these fields were real estate and trading. The Ispahani group stayed on in Bangladesh, but lost the jute and textile mills. Adamjee left Bangladesh, and the jute mill was nationalized. Bawany left too, lost assets to the government, and reinvented itself in Pakistan as a sugar manufacturer. Dawood lost 60 per cent of its assets to nationalization in Bangladesh. Latifur Rahman's jute mill was nationalized. While tea was left alone, regulations had made the export of tea difficult. A.S.F. Rahman group too lost the jute mill, and switched to trade in seafood and marine products. The group renamed itself as BEXIMCO. With exchange controls in place, the group, like Latifur Rahman in tea, engaged in barter-based trade with foreign partners. Medicines were an attractive import. Chowdhury's Square, a medicine trading entity, did not suffer nationalization.

Between 1975 and 1981, private enterprise was invited back in, and there was a limited attempt to privatize the smaller units. Amidst allegations of corruption and mismanagement, a new set of entrepreneurs became prominent by taking over privatized firms. One older group, Zahurul Islam, emerged from the socialist turmoil with more resources than before, having 'made a fortune on government contracts during the Mujib period.'[43] The Ispahanis regained some of their assets earlier lost to the government. The Saha business grew during this time. The A.K. Khan group also survived the crisis, thanks to diversified interest. Among new entry in this time, the real estate company Basundhara was significant, for the role it was to play in future.

In the 1980s Latifur Rahman regained control of the jute mill, took over a multinational pharmaceutical plant, invested in mass media, and from the 1990s, diversified into cement, cables, electronics, and food processing and distribution through the brand Transcom. With the barter trade experience behind them, BEXIMCO, which received its assets back, diversified into pharmaceutical production and trade. BEXIMCO partnered with the government in setting up the IFIC Bank in 1976. Square emerged as the leading pharmaceutical trading firm in the 1980s, diversifying as a licensed producer of international medicines, and then into chemicals. In the 2000s, Square also exported drugs and chemicals. Basundhara diversified from real estate to steel, cement, engineering, and paper.

In the 1990s, jute declined as a business. Adamjee jute mill never recovered from the shock of nationalization and mismanagement by the government. In 2002, it closed down. On the positive side, some of the survivors had already entered a new growth area, garments. In the case of BEXIMCO, garment production was integrated with existing textile production. The vertically integrated system contributed to making this group the largest in Bangladesh in terms of market capitalization. The A.K. Khan group set up joint ventures to expand in textiles. Garments also spawned a new set of business groups that had little prior contact in manufacturing. The Jamuna group established by an architect in the 1970s, the Nassa group that started with a knitwear factory in 1990, Hameem that started as a trading firm in 1981, and was

[43] Kochanek, 'Rise of Interest Politics.'

later a large producer of diversified range of clothing and textiles, are some examples.

We can draw three generalizations about the evolution of companies in Bangladesh in the last 40 years. First, the corporate growth story is not all about garments, but about pharmaceuticals, tea, construction, and services. Second, survival skills during civil war and military regimes sometimes worked as a business asset. In some cases, this was achieved by means of political connections. Political ties were not the most critical input in all cases, however. For example, the socialist era was a setback for most groups, with or without political ties. At the same time, socialism pushed some of the 1960s groups into foreign trade, which created new contacts that helped these groups redefine themselves from the 1980s. Third, groups tended to become conglomerates with diversified portfolio. In the long run, some of the groups display a progression from manufacturing (1960s) to trade (1970s) to manufacturing again (1980s and 1990s), and finally, to services (2000s). Almost all of the major corporate houses have expanded in services in the 2010s, the growth areas being universities (BEXIMCO and Ispahani), hospitals (Square), print and digital media (Latifur Rahman, BEXIMCO), financial services (Latifur Rahman), and shipping and inland transport (Ispahani, Kumudini Trust, the inheritor of the Ranada Prasad Saha businesses). In common with other countries of South Asia, telecom and IT services were another area of growth (A.K. Khan).

During military rule, the relationship between corporates and the government changed. On a personal level, individuals were known to be close to the regime, and gained from privatization. As a lobby, however, businesses lacked coordination and political power. 'Most past presidents [of the main chamber of commerce] were petty traders or drawn from the smaller business houses of Bangladesh, and were concerned with recognition and access to government to protect their own interests.'[44] This limited effect hurt businesses during a prolonged political deadlock (1993–1994). In a significant move at this point, Salman Rahman of BEXIMCO took over the main chamber of

[44] Kochanek, 'The Rise of Interest Politics in Bangladesh.'

commerce, not without a tough leadership battle, and played an effective lobbying role to break the deadlock.

Despite this example of institutionalized lobbying, the relationship between business and politics remained personal in the early 2000s. 'Businesspersons,' one author wrote in 2004, 'appear to have moved beyond party financing to invest in particular political persons who thereby became captives to the business agenda of their patrons.'[45] Some of the leading groups in this time were loyal to the Bangladesh Nationalist Party, led by the widow of Ziaur Rahman, and key ministers of the party were implicated in helping some businesspersons to deal with charges of fraud, corruption, and criminal conspiracy. At the same time, globalization reinforced a pro-business platform within mainstream politics, which brought the interests of the politicians and corporates more in line with one another, and made business negotiations more transparent. Whether or not this reduced the extent of 'commercialization of politics' is impossible to say.

Sri Lanka

Foreign Plantation Companies

In 1940, the Sri Lankan business sector consisted mainly of European plantations, and a large diverse set of Sinhalese and Indian firms engaged in trading. Tea and coffee plantations in the Sri Lankan highlands started in the early-to-mid-nineteenth century in the form of small estates owned and run by individual planters. A number of the pioneering coffee planters came from Scotland.[46] Towards the end of the century, London mercantile houses, called agency houses, formed

[45] Rehman Sobhan, 'Structural Dimensions of Malgovernance in Bangladesh,' *Economic and Political Weekly*, 39(36), 2004, 4101–4108.

[46] Ranald Michie, 'Aberdeen and Ceylon. Economic Links in the Nineteenth Century,' *Northern Scotland*, 4(1), 1981, 69–82.

partnership with the planters, and took charge of both the marketing and the finance sides of the business. A string of companies formed of these collaborations between agency houses and proprietary planters. Unable to sustain the business, impoverished planters sold land to London merchants. At the time of independence, British limited liability companies owned nearly 60 per cent of the tea estate land in Sri Lanka. A number of these, like Lipton or Finlay, were world market leaders. Thomas Lipton arrived in Colombo in 1890, and '[w]ithin three weeks he had become the largest individual estate owner in the island with estates totalling 2230 acres and warehouses and offices in Colombo.' Some of the larger trading firms that took over the plantations were multinationals, such as Finlay.[47]

The government of independent Sri Lanka (or Ceylon) did not outlaw foreign capital nor did it sequester assets of foreigners. Until 1960, tea estates still had significant foreign interest, even after suffering capital flight in the 1950s. However, the government decided to exploit and bully the business 'in the national interest.' It raised taxes, restrained repatriation, insisted on Ceylonization of management, and encouraged indigenous smallholders to grow tea, often within the same plantation areas. The government also made it impossible for legitimate sale of companies to go ahead. 'Ceylon has perhaps done more than any other country in the direction of regulating plantation activity.'[48] When the final nails, land reforms and nationalization, were driven, the business was a shadow of its former glory and the axis of world tea trade was shifting out of South Asia.

How large a loss was this? Interpretations of the economic value of the plantations have tended to be diametrically opposed. The Sri Lankan Marxists tend to dismiss the plantations as an exploitative business, controlled by British merchant capital, technologically primitive, and a business that left little positive legacy. A somewhat more balanced assessment, by Donald Snodgrass, still sees it as an 'enclave,' a business

[47] Geoffrey Jones and Judith Wale, 'Merchants as Business Groups: British Trading Companies in Asia before 1945,' *Business History Review*, 72(3), 1998, 367–408.

[48] George Beckford, *Persistent Poverty: Underdevelopment in Plantation Economies of the Third World*, Mona: University of West Indies Press, 1972, p. 218.

cluster formed of expatriate capital that exists to exploit local resources and delivers little direct or indirect benefit for the economy at large.[49] A classic leftist history of plantations by George Beckford also follows this line.

A sharply divergent view shows that these negative assessments were not just overdrawn, but wildly wrong. A series of statistical papers by Youngil Lim shows first of all that the export of plantation products carried a very high multiplier effect.[50] '[F]or every rupee's worth of exports, about 2.5 rupees of domestic income is created, a figure confirmed by other studies.' The multiplier arose not only because plantations contributed to fiscal and import capacity, but also, they contributed to growth of infrastructure. 'Ceylon has one of the best developed transportation systems in Southeast Asia. Surfaced roads and bus routes honeycomb the entire region of the plantation industry.' Lim goes on to attribute relatively developed port facilities, the foundations of an engineering industry, and banking development, to the demands of the plantations system. Not only capital, labour gained too. 'A substantial portion of total export receipts accrued to labour because of the large number of labourers employed on tea plantations.' The enclave thesis argues that export incomes do not have any impact on domestic market. Lim disagrees, 'contrary to the enclave thesis, the size of the domestic market seems to have expanded rapidly, as the volume of exports grew.' The decline of the plantation business, therefore, meant the loss of many of the qualities that had made Sri Lanka a more advanced economy in South Asia.

Indigenous Enterprise

'The first generation of Sinhala entrepreneurs accumulated their capital through the liquor trade and arrack renting as far back as the mid-nineteenth

---

[49] Donald R. Snodgrass, *Ceylon: An Export Economy in Transition*, Homewood, Illinois: Richard D. Irwin, 1966.

[50] Youngil Lim, 'Trade and Growth: The Case of Ceylon,' *Economic Development and Cultural Change*, 16(2), 1968, 245–260; Youngil Lim, 'Impact of the Tea Industry on the Growth of the Ceylonese Economy,' *Social and Economic Studies*, 17(4), 1968, 453–467.

century, and later invested their capital in graphite mining and coconut plantations.'[51] While tea was European owned, in coconut, rubber, and cinnamon, Ceylonese capitalists owned plantations. The nineteenth-century entrepreneur Jacob De Mel is an example. During World War II, some of these firms enjoyed an unprecedented opportunity. Richard Pieris started as a trading firm that specialized in plantation products and supplies. During World War II, the firm expanded its business by tapping into the war demand for repaired tyres. By then it was a public company. Cyril de Zoysa, more famous for his contributions to Buddhist institutions than the business house he owned, set up a similar enterprise in 1949, later known as AMW or Associated Motorways. The inheritor of tea, coconut, and rubber plantations owned by his family, and a trading firm, Ernest De Silva expanded his business by acquiring prime real estate in Colombo.

After 1948, there was a transfer of holdings of plantation capital from Europeans to groups like these. When independence came, there was an exodus of foreign firms. As in India, there were an indigenization of private enterprise, a retreat from cosmopolitan capitalism, and an attrition of capital. The true cost of this attrition has not been estimated. Between 1956 and 1977, Sri Lankan plantation interests were the main actors in the business world. The Richard Pieris and Company or Arpico integrated into rubber plantations, and later, tea. Jacob De Mel, likewise, left an inheritance of estates in tea, cinnamon, coconut, and plumbago. While representatives of these old houses were important public figures, the socialist spirit of the times restrained opportunities for investment, and in some cases, led to nationalization (Fig. 10.1).

During the period of import-substitution (1956–1977), some Sinhala entrepreneurs moved from trade to industry, such as processed food and garments, and built marketing ties with the Middle East, Europe and Asia. These opportunities were exhausted quickly. Furthermore, opportunities of accumulation of wealth by means of rubber, mining, or beverages were unavailable in the north and the east, where the ethnic

[51] Newton Gunasinghe, 'The Open Economy and its Impact on Ethnic Relations in Sri Lanka,' in Deborah Winslow and Michael D. Woost, eds., *Economy, Culture, and Civil War in Sri Lanka*, Bloomington: Indian University Press, 2004, 99–114.

Fig. 10.1. Nationalisation of the Port of Colombo (8 August 1958)

Prime Minister S.W.R.D. Bandaranaike formally announces the nationalization of the port. Exactly forty years later (1999), a major part of the port was privatized. Since then container traffic in Colombo port has grown at a faster pace compared with most ports of the region. © Keystone Pictures USA/Alamy Stock Photo

Tamil population lived, for several reasons. The UNP government, which took over power in 1977, invited private entrepreneurs to assume a bigger role. The older groups could now diversify. AMW participated in joint ventures with Japanese automotive firms to enter tyre manufacture and rubber plantations. Richard Pieris diversified into vinyl pipes and plastics. The more far-reaching effect of the pro-business stance of the government fell in two areas. First, the regime encouraged trading, which became a platform for a few groups to move first into manufacturing and then services. Second, the government privatized some nationalised firms, which served as a springboard for new groups.

One example that illustrates both these dynamics is Harry Jayawardena. In 1977 an employee of the state-owned trading corporation, he resigned to start a private tea trading company, Stassens. Stassens and Milford, two tea trading companies under Jayawardena's control, later acquired tea estates. One of the conglomerates to emerge from the privatization process was the Distilleries Company of Sri Lanka. In 1989 shares of the state owned Distilleries Corporation was sold to a consortium consisting of companies that belonged to Jayawardena, and the investment firm, Smith New Court. Since the acquisition, the company turned the bottled coconut arrack business into a marketing success, and diversified through another acquisition, into mobile telephony.

Besides privatization and trade, entry of foreign capital created a dynamic of business formation. In 1980, the Lanka Orix Leasing Company (LOLC) was established as a joint venture between Orix Corporation of Japan and institutional investors. In 2000, the family of Rajah Nanayakkara took over the majority stake in LOLC, leaving Orix holdings intact. Nanayakkara's main business then was import of used vehicles. LOLC is the largest nonbank financial company in Sri Lanka. After the end of the civil war, LOLC made speedy acquisitions in construction and hotels, anticipating a tourism and construction boom.

Two of the old-time groups reinvented themselves, in both cases, undergoing a change of ownership. One of the oldest Sinhalese conglomerates, Richard Pieris, was known to have fallen into a dormant state around 2002, when a hostile takeover bid by a UK-based entrepreneur took place, the bid succeeded but not before an expensive court battle. AMW entered joint ventures with India's R.P. Goenka, whose company owned the CEAT brand in India. In 2008, an UAE-based company acquired AMW.

The civil war imposed significant cost on the economy and the government. It also had the effect of increasing the speed of reforms in key areas. For example, the government in the 1990s sold the telecom monopoly, gas and power, banks, airline, and plantations in order to reduce budget deficit and yet finance military expenses. The process stimulated the stock exchange, and invited a great deal of Asian capital into Sri Lanka. The Air Lanka, for example, was sold to the Emirates, Colombo Dockyard to Sagawa, and Sri Lanka Telecom to Nippon Telephone and Telegraph. On the other hand, local entrepreneurs took the lead when the plantation units were privatized. The groups used that acquisition as a platform to diversify. Japanese, Korean, and Malaysian capital was involved in the private and joint ventures that came out of the process.

In the 2000s by contrast, business leadership came from multinationals and joint ventures, mobile phone providers, and services providers, often these roles combined in the operations of the larger conglomerates. The multinational companies that started operations in the last 20 years include the Ceylon Tobacco Company, a subsidiary of BAT, Sri Lanka Telecom, a joint venture between the government and Global Telecom Holding, which has interest in Pakistan and Bangladesh as well, Nestle, Chevron, and Dialog Axiata, also a mobile telephone provider. Axiata is a Malaysian firm. The Colombo Dockyard, similarly, is a joint venture between the government and Onimochi Dockyard of Japan. One of the shipbuilding firms of South Asia, Colombo Dockyard started in 1974 as a government company, and was in an indifferent state for almost 20 years. The contracts that changed the future shape of the company came in during the second half of the 2000s.

Another Japanese investment was the SG Group's acquisition of Expolanka Holding in 2014. Expolanka was a trading firm owned by Osman Kassim and his family. It began operations in 1978 in traditional export business, later diversifying into marine transportation, with special expertise in garments. SG shares similar expertise and has bases in East Asia. Softlogic Holdings started as a software development firm in 1991. In 2000s it partnered with Dialog Axiata in the mobile telephone business, providing GSM package to Dialog. In the 2000s, the group expanded in retail marketing, and acquired distributorship in a range of global brands.

In a distinct model of cross-border investment, Indian trading firms resettled in Nepal and played a part in industrial and commercial enterprise there.

Nepal

Three business houses of Indian Marwari origin have been prominent in Nepal. All originated in India-Nepal trade around the time of independence of India. The Chaudhary group, probably the biggest in Nepal, started in India-Nepal textile trade. In 1930s, the trader Bhuramull Chaudhary owned a textile shop in a prime Kathmandu street. His son inherited the business, and in the 1960s, with the help of two Marwari relations, established a spinning mill, a hosiery factory, and a metal working factory. Chaudhary retained its interest in trade. In fact, manufacturing almost anything in Nepal would mean relying on India for the raw material, machines, and sometimes market. Bhuramull's grandson Binod Chaudhary, however, took the business into another direction, processed food.[52] Another Indian Marwari enterprise, Sharda group originated in the early twentieth century in trade between India and Nepal. In 1948 it established a rice mill, and subsequently established a carpet manufacturing unit, and an edible oil plant. In 2006, the group set up a cement plant. Its main sources of growth seem to be trade in a diversified range of products, real estates, and the ownership of two banks. A third Marwari family, Khetan, specializes in mining and brewery.[53]

A fourth large group of companies, Vaidya, is an indigenous trading group engaged in export of tea, and the import of automobiles and consumer goods. Its business of importing Toyota vans took off when a large-scale construction of highways was under way. The most innovative side of the group is tea and medicinal plant production business. Nepal has emerged as a potential competitor to India in orthodox tea varieties, and the Vaidya group is playing a role in making this happen. The government of Nepal was a major intermediary in the 2000s in popularizing highland leaf tea in European markets, using the mountaineering community for the purpose.[54] The initiative requires the participation of large companies. Like the others, the Vaidya group also invested in construction, and education. Jyoti is another house of indigenous origin. Maniharsha Jyoti Kansakar operated a trading firm in the 1920s engaged in Nepal-Tibet trade. From the 1960s, the firm

---

[52] Binod K. Chaudhary, *Making It Big: The Inspiring Story of Nepal's First Billionaire in His Own Words*, London: Penguin, 2016.

[53] http://www.shardagroup.com/index.htm; http://www.khetan.com.np/intro.htm

[54] http://www.wipo.int/ipadvantage/en/details.jsp?id=3472

moved into the production of textile, steel, engineering, and automobile trading, and more recently, established itself in travel and transportation of cargo between Nepal and Indian ports.

Conclusion

We can draw five general conclusions based on the survey of corporate enterprise in this chapter.

First, it goes without saying that there was no linear pathway of enterprise development in these countries; rather the story is made up of a series of shocks. The earliest of the shocks led to the decimation of a substantial segment of foreign capital in India and Sri Lanka, more or less ending corporate leadership in exports. Later, introduction of hard socialism in India, Pakistan, Bangladesh, and Sri Lanka affected groups of indigenous capitalists. Finally, the sudden introduction of liberal reforms again acted like a shock. The second conclusion derives from the first. While a number of business groups survived socialism in Pakistan and Bangladesh, the shocks changed the composition of corporate groups.

Third, if we then ask, what was distinctive about the new corporate groups, at least a part of the answer will be the relationship forged between domestic business groups and foreign technology and investors. Ties with the Gulf, with Malaysia and Singapore, and with Japan and Korea contributed to the growth of some of the diversified conglomerates in South Asia. Some companies and groups went down after India opened its doors to trade and investment. Those that survived almost always did so by using foreign ties strategically.

Fourth, even as export of manufactured goods did take off after the liberal reforms, the leading business groups in the region do not export a lot (with the exception of IT). Exports come from small firms. Corporate enterprise instead focuses on consumption, strengthening home market brands, skill-building, and infrastructure. Whether this is a reflection of a fear of global markets, in turn a legacy of the autarkic regime, or the attraction of the home market we cannot say.

Fifth, as domestic consumers started consuming more services, a big change took place in the range of products and services that companies delivered from the 2000s. There is a distinct trend now to diversify from manufacturing to services. Services include education, retailing, real estate and construction, software support to finance or mobile telephony, transportation, hotels, and health care. The fact that the services tend to be still protected, contributes partly to the success of domestic firms in these activities.

The successful record of South Asia in services export has been mentioned. This leads us to the issue of migration.

11

Migration

According to United Nations data, sometime in the mid-1980s, the non-oil-exporting developing world began to experience a revolutionary change in their economic structure. From then on, the export of labour services and labour-intensive products created increasing capacity to import technology. The change was visible in the balance of payments and had two complementary parts. Merchandise trade volumes increased, imports increased faster than exports. In short, the trade expansion was linked to the accumulation of industrial capability. This was one half of the revolution. The other half occurred in services. The growth of trade and import of technology was paid for by selling labour services abroad.[1] In conventional account, a policy reform is held responsible for the whole movement. Liberalization of trading regimes by means of tariff reforms and exchange rate reforms were responsible for the trade boom. The causal link, however, cannot start with policy reform. It must start with the power to purchase technology, which grew

[1] Some of the other items in the balance of payments – other than trade and remittance – were individually smaller, moved erratically, and varied between countries. These included investment, foreign aid, non-labour services such as shipping and tourism.

T. Roy, *The Economy of South Asia*, Palgrave Studies in Economic History, DOI 10.1007/978-3-319-54720-6_11

with service income. That power began to grow from several years before the policy reforms started.

South Asia forms an important, if not the central, part of the global movement. The story began with emigration of millions of South Asians to the Persian Gulf. South Asians were no strangers to movements like these. Why do they move? With what effect? Why do destinations change? The chapter will explore these questions. Let us begin with a brief historical account.

Prehistory

As mentioned before, from the mid-nineteenth century, South Asians went to the tropical colonies in large numbers. This was economic migration, and the people who moved did earn somewhat higher wages than those who remained. Even so, coercion and misinformation played a significant role in creating these flows. Some of the more recent episodes of circulation of people from the region were forced. The Partition, the Sri Lankan civil war, the Bangladesh war, floods and disasters in Nepal, and the situation of Burmese Muslims, Tibetan Buddhists, Indo-Nepalese population groups, and Bangladeshi Chakmas pushed hundreds and thousands of people to cross borders and left some of them in a condition of statelessness.[2] A recent book shows that the majority of the Bengali migrants, who number in millions, resettled within the region but across international borders.[3] Most of these movements arose from violent ethnic conflicts or civil war situation, and as such, created diplomatic crises, at least impaired the diplomatic environment. At the same time, the biggest flows were economic in motivation. Migration of peasants from Bangladesh to Assam and population movements between India and Nepal were driven by livelihood choices rather than threats to life or property.

---

[2] Myron Weiner, 'Rejected Peoples and Unwanted Migrants in South Asia,' *Economic and Political Weekly*, 28(34), 1993, 1737–1746.

[3] Claire Alexander, Joya Chatterji, and Annu Jalais, *The Bengal Diaspora. Rethinking Muslim Migration*, London and New York: Routledge, 2016.

The types of migration that mattered most to the international economy were economic in nature and involved going to the West. From 1960, South Asian migrants to the United Kingdom and the USA, going abroad for work, business or education, surged. In 1961, people of South Asian origin formed 0.23 per cent of the population of United Kingdom. In 1991, the percentage was 3.04, and in 2016, 4.90, including a generation that was born in the United Kingdom.[4] In 1990, persons of Indian origin formed 0.3 per cent of the population of the USA. The corresponding figure for 2010 was 1 per cent. The total number of South Asians living in the United Kingdom and North America number between three and four million in 2014.

Large as the flow was, it was dwarfed by the flow of migration to the Persian Gulf, where annually, about 1.7 million people from South Asia go for work.

Persian Gulf Migration

The oil price shocks of 1973 and 1979 had contradictory effects on South Asia. The rise in import cost led to tighter exchange controls and a retreat from trading. On the other hand, labour export to the oil exporting countries soared to meet exploding demand for workers in construction, utility, and other services.[5] Between 1973 and 1975, 1.6 million persons went to work in Bahrain, Kuwait, Qatar, United Arab Emirates, Saudi Arabia, Oman, and Libya. The number rose to four million by 1985. In the smaller states, the proportion of foreign workers was well over half of the total population, and in Emirates, 90 per cent, in 1985.[6] Foreign workers came from many regions, including Southeast Asia, North Africa, and South Asia. South Asia dominated the flow.

---

[4] For the earlier percentages see Judith M. Brown, *Global South Asians. Introducing the Modern Diaspora*, Cambridge: Cambridge University Press, 2006, 40.

[5] http://asiancenturyinstitute.com/migration/194-asian-migration-to-the-gulf (accessed 15 October 2016).

[6] Jonathan Addleton, 'The Impact of International Migration on Economic Development in Pakistan,' *Asian Survey*, 24(5), 1984, 574–596.

Of 15 million expatriates in the Gulf region, about half the region's population, South Asians number about 9.5 million. In 2012, the International Labour Office data states that the total labour force of South Asia (including Maldives) was 656.4 million. The stock of people in the Gulf countries, nearly 10 million, forms a small 1.5 per cent of the labour force of South Asia. But, then, these people are situated at the better-paid end of the labour market. In South Asia, the rates of open unemployment were relatively low at 4 per cent, and youth unemployment at 10 per cent in 2012. But those employed were overwhelmingly concentrated in low-paid work, 24 per cent in daily earning of $1.25, and a staggering 62 per cent in $ 2 per day jobs. 'It is clear that working poverty is the major issue than open unemployment.'[7] In short, the Gulf employment did not have an effect on unemployment, but expanded opportunity for better quality and higher-wage work.

Consequently, the Gulf migration generated a relatively high remittance-to-income ratio. Well over half of the earning, and in some cases a higher proportion, were sent back home according to surveys done in the 1980s. The remittance intensity of migration had owed to the temporary nature of the flow, in turn, an effect of immigration rules in the Arab states that made obtaining citizenship practically impossible. Therefore, most migrants had an incentive to save for acquisition of property back home, which accounted for the money sent home. Regulations on the migration of dependents added to the incentive, while at the same time, made migration biased towards the young and the male.

The unbalanced sex ratio of migration is a prominent feature of the flow. 'Across the region, it is often male breadwinners who cross international boundaries,' with a corresponding 'feminisation of agriculture.'[8] Women constitute only 15 per cent of the total migrant workers from South Asia. If Sri Lanka, which sends out the maximum

[7] Piyasiri Wickramasekara, 'South Asian Gulf Migration to the Gulf: A Safety Valve or a Development Strategy?' *Migration and Development*, 5(1), 2016, 99–129.

[8] Sanjay Barbora, Susan Thieme, Karin Astrid Siegmann, Vineetha Menon and Ganesh Gurung, 'Migration Matters in South Asia: Commonalities and Critiques, *Economic and Political Weekly*, 43(24), 2008, 57–65.

number of women, is excluded, the percentage should fall significantly. Feminisation of agriculture has been observed to occur in Pakistan and in Nepal. The male-bias of migrants in South Asia stems from a social and cultural feature. This is, discouragement to women leaving home. A study on an earlier time attributed this to the relatively low average age at marriage of women.[9] The obvious long-term solution to this problem is for governments to encourage women migrants, and provide support that could facilitate such migration. However, governments often work in the opposite direction. In Nepal, the worry that women would become victims of sex trafficking led to restrictions on women migrants. Given the open borders between India and Nepal, it is easy to bypass the restriction. The effect of the restriction has been that more women enter unregistered and undocumented pools of migrants, increasing the chances of being exploited.

The pattern of Gulf migration has changed over time. The skill composition of migrants from Pakistan and India has steadily improved in the 2000s. The tendency matters for two reasons, skill composition should be a predictor of remittance per head, and higher skilled workers are less likely to be retrenched during recessions. A study on Pakistan found that remittance to Pakistan from the Gulf withstood the effects of the 2008 recession quite well, apparently because of rising proportion of skilled migrants.[10]

The externalities generated by the Gulf migration have been large and many-sided. Gulf migration changed the profile of business in South Asia. It gave rise to a huge business in recruitment agency, informal banking, insurance, transportation, and accommodation. Some of the richest corporate houses in the source countries of South Asia are recruitment agents. More than one of the top ten companies in Bangladesh are labour contracting companies. Given the rigidities of

[9] It is a historical observed pattern, and shows up indirectly in the British Indian census statistics between 1881 and 1931. See Tirthankar Roy, *Rethinking Economic Change in India: Labour and Livelihood*, London: Routledge, 2005, on age at marriage and feminization of agricultural workers.

[10] Udo Kock and Yan Sun, 'Remittances in Pakistan: Why They Have Gone Up and Why They Are Not Coming Down,' *Pakistan Development Review*, 50(3), 2011, 189–208.

formal banking, a great deal of the remittance occurs by alternative routes and stimulates informal banking.

Governments in the entire region reacted late to the migration to the Gulf, indeed to the whole issue of migration. Even today, official statistics are poor or missing on vital flows, for example, Nepali migration to India, or unofficial circulation of workers within South Asia. In the last few years, a new discourse has emerged on migration policy. Can or should governments play any role in the process? Of course, governments everywhere welcome emigration and would not want to regulate it. Key areas where bureaucracy once used to pose obstacles have seen market-friendly reform. Obtaining citizenship documents used to be a nightmare in India in the 1980s. It is now a considerably easier and speedier procedure. Beyond these facilitating roles, should governments regulate or monitor the process?

Encouraging flows directly by source countries, or asking destination countries to take in more, is a zero-sum game, because other source countries can play it just as well. However, recent experience suggests that governments do have a negotiating role, when ethnic employment laws (such as the *nitaqat* programme adopted by the Saudi Arabian government in 2011) that discriminate expatriates are introduced, or when recessions and oil price shocks lead to sudden waves of retrenchment. The Gulf in the last few years has seen such syndromes develop repeatedly. Two other areas, protecting the welfare and rights of workers, and channelling remittance money towards investment, are potentially appropriate for intervention.[11] The government, of course, can cause distortions too if, in the name of proper deployment of remittance, it tries to drive the flow of saving to its own banks. A key area of financial reform in India – deregulation of outward remittance – was introduced in response to the surge in inflow in the 2000s. This is an example of increased flexibility of the financial market engaged in remittance, which is a better policy approach to remittance deployment.

[11] Y Hamada, 'National Governance in International Labour Migration,' *Migration and Development*, 1(1), 2012, 50–71.

Why People Move

As the scale of migration grew, so did migration research, which deals with two broad themes – why do people move and why everyone does not move; and whether migration is a good thing or a bad thing for the place of origin. It is a truism that neither the attraction of better earning nor the 'push' of poverty automatically induces people to move. Not everyone in the same situation migrates. Those who do are usually a minority among those who are likely to do so. This selectiveness of migration is a puzzle to be explained. It can be explained with reference to a concept that one recent work calls 'mobility capital,' and includes in it contacts, connections, personal pre-histories, ties of affection and obligation, and skills and know-how.[12] No doubt, other elements can be added in this broad basket. In any case, the distribution of the capital is necessarily unequal.

Because migration is capital-intensive in this sense, every single act of migration is an inheritance bestowed on future or potential candidates for migration. The capital can be passed on. This feature relates to another remarkable characteristic, called migration persistence. 'Drawing on recent national survey data and unique census data at the district level,' a recent study finds, 'that for regions covering 20% of the population of India, poor *and* rich, mobility has been persistently high in magnitude and has been male-dominated, remittance based and circular in nature for well over a 100 years.' This stable historical relationship is called migration persistence.[13] A book on Bengali migration, similarly, argues that 'contemporary patterns of migration and resettlement… can best be understood by grasping the historical connections between places of origin and places of arrival.'[14]

At the risk of sounding a little far-fetched, migration persistence can be discerned in the Gulf phenomenon as well as in the Bengal example.

[12] Alexander, Chatterji, and Jalais, *The Bengal Diaspora,* 75.

[13] Chinmay Tumbe, 'Migration Persistence across Twentieth Century India,' *Migration and Development,* 1(1), 2012, 87–112.

[14] Alexander, Chatterji, and Jalais, *The Bengal Diaspora,* 3

India's Gulf connection, in fact, was centuries old. The Arabian Sea trade established links between the western coast of India and the Persian Gulf. Some Arab merchants settled in the Malabar coast. In the nineteenth century, Aden, which was administered from India, was home to Muslim and Parsi merchants and bankers with ties with India. The European colonial administration in West Asia recruited Indians in large numbers. India was also a major trading partner of the Gulf states. Migration analysts recognize that such past patterns of mobility can be extraordinarily durable, though drawing a direct line between past and present episodes can be difficult.

Migration and Development

Is migration a good thing or bad for the source country? The answer depends on how remittances are used, the externalities and institutional effects, and on labour market effects. Let us consider these in turn.

Remittance is driven by immediate motivations, including family maintenance, investment in capital, investment in education, a payment to a family member for looking after assets, and consumption smoothing, especially when remittance goes to agricultural households. Clearly, these motivations vary according to the economic profile of the source regions. There are plenty of studies that show that in poorer countries, migrant remittance contributes to expenditure at home on health care, education, and house construction. South Asia is no exception to this. The effects of remittances extend beyond these immediate expected gains. Remittances have stabilized economies otherwise dependent on imports. On the other hand, remittances could add to saving, stimulate domestic financial markets, encourage investment, including investment in education, industrialization, and entrepreneurship.

Migration, especially Gulf migration, has institutional effects. Two institutional features of migration are especially important for this discussion. First, whereas migration within the region is rarely contractual, migration from the region abroad usually is. The latter involves a large role for recruitment agents, who have the all-important rosters and who match skills with jobs. This is a crucial process involving scarce information, and therefore, costs money for the worker, the employer, and the agent. Agent-based migration resembles the nineteenth century indenture route, and as in that model, makes agency a powerful and profitable role. Secondly, and in an alternative model, migration happens via personal contact, that is, relations and friends already in the destination would sponsor new migrants until they get jobs. It is difficult to say how the balance between the two models has changed in the individual countries in question. What is clear is that both these routes favour those potential migrants who have money and who have contacts. Migration, in other words, creates inequality among potential migrants.[15]

Transnational migration is a more complex phenomenon than a set of financial flows. The use of remittances for consumption back home contributes to the making of a middle class, especially if the middle class can be identified with a consumer culture, such as demand for durables, education, better health care, and investment in property. Migration creates business and other contacts, transfers knowledge and values. Educational migration – that is, individuals who leave home to acquire education, and then settle abroad because the kind of education they receive yields value only in certain labour markets – involves 'social remittances,' that is, a transfer back of skills and values. This last effect occurs because educational migrants simultaneously receive training and work away from their places of origin. The migrants' desire to 'stay connected' with their homelands has been found to be surprisingly strong, which calls for a more nuanced understanding of the flow of benefits than a simple profit-and-loss approach. A counting of how many go and how many stay back says little about the legacy effects. The act of emigration changes *both* sets of people.

In theory, migration in the presence of surplus and underemployed labour is a good thing. It should raise total income, reduce unemployment, but not raise average incomes or wage cost for the employer. In

[15] Manohar P. Sharma, 'International Contract-Based Migration, Remittances, and Household Well-Being in the Western Province of Sri Lanka,' *International Migration*, 51(S1), 2013, e216-e248.

reverse, if wages do rise after migration, that could be a sign that underemployment was absent, and migration was a net loss for the society the migrants were coming from. In practice, it is hard to test these effects. The long-term effect depends partly on the skill composition of the workers who leave, and alternative opportunities available. Depending on the skills, the export could be seen as a 'brain drain,' a loss of potential resources for economic growth. One crude way to measure the effect would be to see if wages of skilled workers rise as labour exports grow, a rise might signal developing shortages as a result of export. But because demand for migrants tends to be occupation-specific, aggregate trends in wages can be ambiguous.

In the rest of this chapter, a few country-specific features and statistics are discussed.

Pakistan and Bangladesh

In 1970, inward remittance into Pakistan formed US$50 million, much of it from Pakistanis living in the United Kingdom. Between 1973 and 1984, 1 million Pakistanis migrated to the Gulf. By then, remittance size grew 60 times, and most of it came from the Gulf. In the 1960s, remittances formed about 1 per cent of national income. In 1982, the percentage was nine. Remittances stimulated consumption to a large extent, investment to a smaller extent, and added to the capacity to import.[16] Since imports consisted of mainly oil and machinery, remittance funded industrialization and general economic capability.

Pakistani migrants to the Gulf consisted of both skilled and semi-skilled types. The former consisted of doctors and managers. The latter consisted of service workers and artisans. In the 1970s, most migrants were skilled craftsmen like welders, machinists, electricians, and carpenters from Punjab. Some adverse impact on local artisanal skills cannot be

[16] These effects were tested and found to have the expected sign in Mohammed Nishat and Nighat Bilgrami, 'The Impact of Migrant Worker's Remittances on Pakistan Economy, *Pakistan Economic and Social Review*, 29(1), 1991 21–41.

discounted, thought the evidence is limited. Later, skilled services grew in scale. Like all big transition points, the government finally woke up to help or regulate the process. Overall the government welcomed the trend, but there were areas where it needed to intervene. One of these areas was the mechanism of remittance, which remained informal for a long time. In Pakistan Pushtun moneylenders organized the hundi network that was used to transfer a great deal of the money.

Migration to the West from the eastern Bengal delta dates back to the nineteenth century. During colonial times, sailors from the Bengal seaboard, mainly Noakhali and Chittagong districts, enlisted in British merchant marine. Later peasants from the inland district Sylhet also joined merchant marine. Some of the Sylheti sailors settled down in the United Kingdom. London's Brick Lane, a street now famous for Bangladeshi food, grew as a settlement of mariners. There was also considerable migration from the nineteenth century from the present Bangladesh region to Assam and Burma.

Bangladesh joined the 'Great Rush' to the Persian Gulf around the same time as the rest of the region, though the numbers were small to begin with.[17] By the late 1970s, the flow of Bangladeshi migration abroad was dominated by the Gulf migration. An early survey of the migration found a high remittance-income ratio, 65–75 per cent. This, considering that the ratio of earning abroad and potential earning at home was high (estimated at ten to one), made the remittance, though still small in volume, of great future importance as a component of national income. A recent study based on surveys of villages with a large proportion of the population abroad finds that 'households with migrants overseas were better off in terms of wealth scores in comparison to other households,' as well as better off in terms of welfare indices.[18]

[17] I borrow the phrase from Wahiduddin Mahmud and S.R. Osmani, 'Impact of Emigrant Workers' Remittances on the Bangladesh Economy,' *Bangladesh Development Studies*, 8(3), 1980, 1–28.

[18] Mausumi Mahapatro, 'Migration, Development and Welfare: Findings from a Household Survey in Two Selected Villages in Bangladesh,' *Migration and Development*, 2015, 1–17.

Nepal

Possibly the largest migration in Nepal occurs within the country: 'migration of people from west to east through the Himalayas, as well as from south (the plains) to north (the hills), from north to south (to settle the plains), and even (as in the tharus fleeing land appropriation) from east to west.'[19] However, the proportions have changed quite dramatically since the mid-1990s as the total numbers increased, a rise driven by migration of several hundred thousand people to the Persian Gulf.[20] Surveys done in the recent years show that more than half the households in Nepal have at least one member who lives outside Nepal. In terms of remittance-GDP ratio, Nepal's economy displays critical levels of dependence on remittance income.[21]

An important stage in the history of long-distance migration from Nepal occurred in the late nineteenth century when somewhere around a hundred thousand Gurkhas were recruited into the British Indian army. Many more were already working in a diverse range of services in India. In 1900, 5 per cent of Nepal's population was believed to be living in British India. Retired soldiers were given land in Northeast India, which encouraged migration of peasants to Northeast India. Between the India-Nepal Treaty of 1950 and 1970, hundreds of thousand Indians migrated to Nepal, and a similarly large number came to India for work. In 1970, there were an estimated 1.5 million Nepalese in India, over 10 per cent of the population of Nepal.[22] Migration on such scale created anxieties. The Land Reform Act of 1964 outlawed unlicensed land transactions between citizens and foreigners. At the same

[19] David N. Gellner, 'Caste, Ethnicity and Inequality in Nepal,' *Economic and Political Weekly*, 42 (20), 2007, 1823–1828.

[20] Bijaya Shrestha, 'Contribution of Foreign Employment and Remittances to Nepalese Economy,' *Economic Review: Occasional Paper* (Nepal Rastra Bank), 20, 2008, 1–15.

[21] Jhalak Sharma Sapkota, 'Protecting the Wellbeing of Nepalese Migrant Workers: The Nature and Extent of Interventions by the Government of Nepal,' *Asia Pacific Journal of Public Administration*, 37(2), 2015, 115–127.

[22] Srikant Dutt, 'Migration and Development: The Nepalese in Northeast,' *Economic and Political Weekly*, 16(24), 1981, 1053–1055.

time, government jobs were restricted to Nepali citizens, and citizenship rules were tightened.

All estimates of Indo-Nepalese population movements are impressionistic. If the above figure is correct, the proportion of Nepalese residents abroad (about 1 million) in a population of 28 million (2008) may have fallen in comparison with 1970. At the same time, the remittance sent home per head increased. The change suggests more skilled and education migration to India as well as abroad in the recent years. Educational migration is on the rise, which is connected with the growth of the middle class, and increased opportunities.[23] These individuals are often the first generation to leave home for a distant location, and how they perceive migration and connections depend on a complex mixture of family-oriented and work-oriented concerns. With women, these considerations complicate further by how they perceive the balance between family and work in their own lives.

All five countries of South Asia experienced an explosive growth of income from labour export in the 2000s, but in Nepal, the dependence of the economy on remittances was the greatest. The trend in labour export from Nepal and Indian economic prospects were interdependent, though an increasing proportion of the Nepalese remittances came from outside the region in the late 2000s.

Did Nepalese emigration have an impact on domestic wages and labour markets? There is a positive association between emigration and wages, but the interpretation remains open. The link between remittance and wage is never a direct one. Considerable financial market effects have been found to occur in Nepal. Even as remittances did encourage businesses like construction, the flow did not seem to have any effect on industrialization.[24] But of course some of the expected gains may not show up in the span of a decade or so.

[23] Jytte Agergaard & Ditte Broegger, 'Returning Home: Migrant Connections and Visions for Local Development in Rural Nepal,' *Geografisk Tidsskrift – Danish Journal of Geography*, 116(1), 2016, 71–81.

[24] Prakash Dahal, 'The Impact of Remittances on Economic Growth in Nepal: An Analysis of a Significant Basis of Development,' *Asia Pacific Journal of Public Administration*, 36(4), 2014, 261–282.

India

British India was one of the largest exporters of workers in the nineteenth century, sending labourers, professionals, and traders to the tropical regions directly or indirectly affiliated to the British Empire. India continued to be a large exporter of workers in the post-war world. Between 1950 and 1970, Gujaratis went to North America in search of business opportunities, doctors came to Britain, and a large number of student migrants went to both Britain and North America. The late twentieth century pattern was quite different. The majority of the recent migrants moved into Asian countries, and not the industrial West. The post-war western demand for blue collar workers, while it did attract some migration from South Asia, produced a smaller outflow than the small-scale capitalists who went to long-familiar East and Southeast Asian countries. The Persian Gulf of course dominated this trend.

The numbers of Indians who moved were larger than that in the colonial times. In 1980, a study published in a Canadian journal reported that Indian-origin persons numbered 3.8 million in Nepal, 1.4 million in Sri Lanka, 1.3 million in Malaysia, 500,000 in the United Kingdom, 475,000 in North America, and about eight million in Mauritius, Fiji, Guyana, and Trinidad and Tobago. These were the destinations of nineteenth-century emigration. There was a great deal of guesswork behind these figures, but the figures for Nepal, Sri Lanka, Malaysia, and the United Kingdom were considered by others to be reliable. Apart from these large Indian diaspora, there were at least a dozen countries where the number of Indian origin persons exceeded 10,000, the prominent ones being Nigeria, Indonesia, Madagascar, Malawi, Hong Kong, Thailand, Jamaica, Zimbabwe, and New Zealand. With a few exceptions, in all of these cases, Indians went into small business and skilled professions. The total number of people living in these smaller settlements was about 400,000. The number of Indian origin persons abroad was estimated to have doubled between 1970 and 1980. In 1980, 'the population of overseas Indians is about half of that of overseas Chinese, and about eight times more than that of overseas Pakistani.'[25]

Persons of Indian origin living outside India is now estimated at close to five million, of which less than a quarter lives in the former tropical colonies that received Indian workers in the nineteenth century. Along with numbers, the destinations changed. The older pattern of circulation within the formerly colonial areas of the tropics ended. The major post-war flows went to the Persian Gulf, USA (possibly two million Indian origin residents in the USA) and Britain (one to two million). The motivations changed too. Migration contributed to the post-war reconstruction of Europe, and sustained the steady growth of the western economies, educational migration worldwide, and running the oil economies.

Demand for workers being diversified along a whole spectrum of skilled services, migrants tended to be of diverse profiles. Labour intensive service industries, such as retailing, hotels, and restaurants, received more migrant workers than wage-employment in agriculture or industry as before. Britain received Indian doctors, and USA received Indian engineers. Many of the skilled migrants and educational migrants were retrained in the USA. Within one generation, the worker-migrants had produced a substantial number of entrepreneurs, again rooted in the same industries where migrant workers predominated.

Despite the differences, there were also some similarities between the postcolonial and the colonial migrations. Perhaps the most important one was the presence of and systematic use of ethnicity in constructing labour relations. In many businesses, older migrants owned the firm and newer migrants worked as employees. Special labour relations developed in situations where employers and the employees belonged in the same social set. The shared ties offered security to the newcomers, especially after migration restrictions made their legal status more contingent, and offered peaceful and predictable industrial relations to the employers. And yet, dependence could be perceived as exploitation, and where

[25] Prakash C. Jain, 'Indians Abroad: A Current Population Estimate,' *Economic and Political Weekly*, 17(8), 1982, 299–304.

dependence joined with illegality, the scope of exploitation increased. Ethnicity in the work-place, therefore, was an unreliable form of glue. On that point too, colonial and postcolonial migrations might share similarities.

Diaspora ties between India and Britain took over as the main driver of a relationship earlier mediated by goods, capital, and labour. By 1980, the Indian diaspora in Britain formed a differentiated population, and yet the different segments or communities within it displayed common patterns in the way they adapted their Indianness to their presence in Britain. These processes of transformation-transplantation became the subject of a large and growing literature in the 1990s, of which travel, mixed identities, displacement, and nostalgia were the major themes. Indian fiction writers in English explored such themes for a while.

As elsewhere, with the Persian Gulf, the Indian government moved in late and with some confusion over what its role should be. Diplomatic negotiations with the Western destinations have a longer history. Immigration controls in Britain were half-hearted and partially effective until the early 1970s, but they became stringent from 1973. Twenty years later, when migration from Europe had been made easier compared to migration from the former colonies, Britain's economic realignment away from its former colonies was complete. European integration and immigration controls weakened the relative importance for Britain of the poorer nations in the Commonwealth as partners in trade, investment, and labour exchange.

Conclusion

Just as the American dream could push migrants to the New World to work hard, the South Asian dream is to go abroad and make it big. This drive has been pivotal in the formation of an intra-Asian labour market since the last quarter of the twentieth century. It has changed the pattern of global flows of people, and in turn, South Asian economies have gained stability, and the capacity to import technology and consumer goods.

Export of people, like the export of textiles, is a crucial ingredient in sustaining globalization.

The most recent tendency in the labour market is growing transactions within South Asia. South Asian markets are now more integrated than during 1950–1990. If we take only the officially registered cross-border trade, the assessment that 'south Asia remains the least integrated region in the world' is probably right.[26] But unofficial or informal trade has grown for some time, if in an unsteady way. Nowhere is the tendency more evident than in population movements. The costs of crossing borders in this region have always been relatively low, a reflection partly of the rushed way borders were drawn at the time of Partition. The international borders do not coincide with significant geographical barriers, except the Palk Straits that separates Sri Lanka from India, but even that crossing is an easy one. On both sides of the borders societies share more similarities than differences. It is not surprising, then, that short- and long-distance migration would be such a regular feature of the recent history of the region.

[26] Shantayanan Devarajan and Ijaz Nabi, 'Economic Growth in South Asia: Promising, Unequalising, Sustainable?' *Economic and Political Weekly*, 41(33), 2006, 3573–3580.

12

Summary and Conclusion

Divergence and Convergence

The book began with an observation. South Asian economies fell behind the world between 1950 and 1980, and were catching up since then. How do we explain the falling behind, the catching up, and the turnaround?

Theories of comparative economic growth are not very helpful. An endogenous growth account might explain the divergence with reference to institutional weaknesses, but that would not immediately suggest why the convergence occurred, or the turnaround. Barriers to capital mobility were high during the divergence phase, compromising capital accumulation, and came down during the convergence phase. But South Asia's turnaround began before barriers to capital mobility eased. Political economy models that suggest why the 'elites' turned growth oriented from the 1980s tend to be India-centric, and exaggerate the agency of the elites while leaving the definition of the interest groups quite vague.

T. Roy, *The Economy of South Asia*, Palgrave Studies in Economic History, DOI 10.1007/978-3-319-54720-6_12

The alternative story offered in the book recognizes that South Asia began with certain endowments. These endowments the development policy did not utilize well, was at odds with, and partly destroyed, leading to a variety of crisis. In 1950, conditions in the region consisted of a mix of strengths and weaknesses. Strengths were South Asia's industrial lead, commercial heritage, entrepreneurship, port cities, and the institutional and military infrastructure left behind by the British Empire. The weaknesses were its geography and consequently high trade cost and difficult agricultural conditions outside the Indo-Gangetic Basin, and the poor quality of human capital. Development policy in all five countries, but especially India, failed to build on the strengths, and underestimated the weaknesses.

In their eagerness to speed up industrialization, the states weakened even destroyed a number of the advantages, the most important one being openness in commodity and factor markets. Instead of the cosmopolitan business world being profitably used, neglect and adverse regulation let the advantage dissipate. From this mess, South Asia could turn around thanks to the revival of exports, on this occasion, export of labour services. A 1970s surge in international migration was the moment of transition in the recent economic history of the region, one that enabled a qualified return to the open economy.

In a way, my story follows a simple factor accumulation account of comparative economic growth. Whereas the standard accumulation models focus on land, labour, and capital, the story in this book takes business enterprise seriously. The period 1950–1980 was a time in the region's history when inherited entrepreneurial capability was reshuffled and partly destroyed during a process that can be described as de-globalization. Present-day South Asia has recovered a great deal from the effects of that phase, if not completely.

The story needs to be qualified according to the specific situation of the countries in question. What was common and what was different in their experience?

The Narrative

In the 1950s, mainland South Asia consisting of India and Pakistan, and Sri Lanka or Ceylon could count on an administrative structure inherited from British colonial rule, a basic legislative framework, and a cosmopolitan capitalist tradition. The states believed that they could use some of these resources to address poverty and inequality, which was a justifiable goal in view of the long neglect of welfare during the rule of the Empire, and the confidence with which they set about that task came from the availability of some of these resources. The shared goal was rapid industrialization, in India industrialization with a capital goods bias. With limited technological capability, the countries relied on aid, capital control, and foreign exchange rationing to import the needed technology. Nepal was the exception in this set, because its geographical situation imposed limits on the capacity of the state and because of a free trade treaty with India.

The book identifies two areas where the states misjudged their capacity. They underestimated geographical constraints, especially the problems of transforming agricultural productivity. The method adopted, land reform, did little to redress the problem of low yield of land, and consequently, did nothing to alleviate low wage and mass poverty in agriculture. More damagingly, the states mistakenly assumed that they could manipulate their relationship with the world economy, and turn it into a tool of industrialization. Closing their economies to trade and factor movements – which all five countries pursued in different time spans – was a bad move at many levels. India favoured industry by suppressing trade. Ethnic repression of trade and investment was present wherever foreign capital had a significant presence before. Both India and Sri Lanka favoured indigenous business over existing international businesses. In this process, exports fell, just when industrialization, being depended on foreign technology, required higher import capacity.

These choices were not new in the post-war world. Other developing countries took the same road and encountered similar obstacles. Yet there was something distinct about South Asia. It had more resources to begin with. British India and colonial Sri Lanka had a larger corporate and industrial base than most developing countries did in the 1950s. The missed opportunity to use these to advantage is starker here.

Roughly between 1965 and 1975, the world economy got the better of South Asia, as harvest failure, oil shocks, and warfare caused severe shortage of foreign exchange. Remarkably, the strategy was sustained. In the 1970s, all five countries strengthened the hold of the state on the economy. A number of things may have contributed to it, the rise of the global left, the Cold War, and the agreement of the USSR to help. No matter the source, the political leadership tried to conserve exchange by more regulation on trade and investment.

There is no evidence that the crisis ended because economists, politicians, and foreign donors played an active role to end it. The crisis ended because the world economy turned benign. Economists did not write the script of South Asian economic resurgence. Labour markets did, at least initially. The oil shock of 1973 had contributed to the crisis to a significant degree. The Gulf oil boom helped end it. Hundreds and thousands of South Asians travelled to the Persian Gulf states in search of jobs from the late 1970s. The surge in inward remittance enabled the governments to allow import of technology by private buyers, and as wealth accumulated in unexpected quarters, a fuller liberalization became inevitable. The Green Revolution was another factor that aided the relaxation. Until the 1960s, sudden need to import food to meet harvest failure was a common occurrence in the region. The Green Revolution obviated that need from the late 1970s.

There was no return to the pre-1972 world. The crisis phase had removed some indigenous business groups that had gained from the first burst of industrialization. In turn, the exchange policy softening in India and privatization in the rest of South Asia invited new entry, like the Reliance in India. The relaxed exchange regime encouraged small firms making garments for the export market with imported machines.

In the more recent years, in all countries, the corporate sector has bifurcated. The state retreated from ownership of businesses, and growth is driven by private investment rather than the taxpayers' money. This growth has two distinct dimensions. On the one hand, small firms, service export, and emigration sustain exchange inflow and the ability of the rest of the economy to buy from the world market. On the other hand, big

Fig. 12.1. Neon lights of Thamel, Kathmandu

The enormous economic power of the middle class in the region manifests in a consumption boom. The spinoffs for retail trade are huge. Corporate groups and foreign investors in South Asia try to share in the boom, usually by importing technology to make goods and services for the domestic market. © robertharding/Alamy Stock Photo

corporate houses, with or without foreign partners, adapt foreign technology to serve domestic consumers and infrastructure redevelopment (see Fig. 12.1). Export is a success story for the small firm, whereas the home market is the field of operation for the big business.

Underneath the shared pathway, there were differences between the countries.

Differences

The most obvious differences were to be found in the initial conditions of Sri Lanka and Nepal. Sri Lanka was an island economy specializing in lucrative export crops, which accounted for a higher tax-per-head and higher welfare spending-per-head. In short, its colonial legacy differed somewhat from that of mainland South Asia, but differed because of a distinct economic geography. If Sri Lanka was blessed by geography, Nepal, the poorest country in the set, was cursed by geography. The landscape did not permit extensive and cheap trading, especially inter-regional trade within the country, confining much of the modern economy as well as governance to narrow valleys, leaving the rest exposed to the worst effects of population growth, land extension, and ecological degradation. Governments had little means to soften the impact; land reform was a dead dream. Nepal's economy was so deeply integrated with India's that protectionism has a different meaning for Nepal. What did come in to the rescue of the economy were tourism and emigration, to India and beyond.

The geography of the Green Revolution increased regional inequality. The proximate factor behind the Green Revolution was a new seed-fertilizer technology, but that technology would mean nothing without groundwater. The Indo-Gangetic Basin offered favourable conditions. So did a few other patches of land near the coasts or on river valleys. Conditions in the rest of the mainland depended a lot on conditions of the non-agricultural livelihoods. Where these were of poor quality, economic stress was extreme. On this point the hills of Nepal and the hills of Jharkhand or Andhra Pradesh were basically similar, despite being located in different nations. Both were witnesses to Maoist insurgency from the late-twentieth century.

Finally, some differences can be traced to the way nationalism emerged in the former colonies. In British India, the Congress had popularized a particular brand of economic nationalism as a weapon in its political battle for self-government. This narrative, which told the believer that foreign rule had impoverished Indians, neither the Muslim League nor the main contesting parties in Sri Lanka subscribed to. This fact alone shows how differently colonialism was perceived within South Asia. The desire to drive out foreigners, especially foreign traders, because of the damage they had allegedly inflicted under colonial sponsorship, was a peculiarly Indian desire. This was a constructed discourse like many other political narratives, and had little relation with historical reality. It served the interests of a business lobby. It took a heavy toll anyway.

The Future

Where is South Asia headed in the next 20 years? The answer depends at least partly on how we read political tendencies, after the states lost control of economic change. The post-state order ruled by markets, regional interests, and new types of organization will shape the future.

The state and the political elite lost control over the some of the biggest processes of change in private enterprise from the 1980s. On a number of occasions in the last 20 years, the government woke up late to endorse and regulate a trend that had begun without its knowledge. A formal manpower policy regarding Gulf migration came years after the migration started.[1] Agricultural price support and input subsidy took shape after the Green Revolution had taken roots, and then showed signs of slowing down. Software export and information technology services exploded in India in the absence of a definite policy framework. Private education expanded to supply trained workers to these businesses before a serious debate on the merits of private education even started. Clothing, cut gems, and leather goods exports initiated a strong revival in labour-intensive industry, in the presence of limited formal concessions to these industries. Mobile telephony and cable television are other examples where the government allowed the market to grow by doing little. In none of these cases did the states and their advisers planned the process, designed it, and even understood what was happening, before the trend became too big to stop. Some of the most dramatic changes in the region have happened because private entrepreneurs proved smarter than the economists and moved faster than them. These entrepreneurs were labour recruiting agents and companies, cable TV operators, software developers, designers, artisans, garment exporters, and peddlers of technical education.

As wealth accumulated in unexpected quarters, the definition of the elite has undergone a deep change. Bureaucrats, lawyers, landlords, and

[1] 'Official interest in expanding technical training opportunities came more than five years after skilled tradesmen had already begun migrating in large numbers and also lagged behind the private sector's response.' Jonathan Addleton, 'The Impact of International Migration on Economic Development in Pakistan,' *Asian Survey*, 24(5), 1984, 574–596.

industrialists formed the traditional elite, who made policies and fought nationalist battles in the 1940s. They dominated the post-1947 politics in India, Pakistan, Sri Lanka, and Nepal. From the 1970s, accumulation of wealth 'below' the bureaucrats, landlords, professionals, and industrialists reduced the power of the traditional elite and unleashed new political forces. The Green Revolution consolidated the capitalist farmer and reduced the role of the landlord class in Pakistan. Top industrial groups suffered in the 1970s due to the socialist drive in Pakistan. After India's liberalization in the 1990s, several industrial groups faced bankruptcy and decline. At the same time, labour-intensive small industry gained.

As a result of these bottom-up processes, there was regionalization of politics in India and Pakistan. Business lobbies in provinces gained a lot from exports of labour-intensive industry, gained in political power, and sometimes funded or allied with regional politicians. The technically illegal power-loom factories in cotton textiles grew by leaps and bounds in India because local authorities looked the other way.

As the growth momentum has decentralized, contradictory pulls and pressures have developed at the same time. For example, the peasants may want more state subsidies, whereas businesses may resent the underfunding of urban infrastructure because the state is over-committed to subsidizing the peasants. India's foreign investment policy wanted Walmart to enter the country, but its millions of petty traders did not. The Indian states disagree a lot on major areas of economic reforms, though in some respects, they have shown an ability to coordinate. The most recent example of coordination was post-2004 fiscal reform of the states. The stage where these battles are fought in India is the provincial one. The Congress in India morphed from a national to a regional party in the 1980s. The communist parties had been subjected to the same trend from much earlier. Beyond influencing regional politics, it does not appear that the new middle classes, such as small businesses, managers, capitalist farmers, either share much economic interest or have direct influence on national policy-making. Yet, national policy-making cannot ignore these groups. Likewise in Pakistan, Bangladesh, Nepal, and Sri Lanka, groups with capital have emerged with conflicting interest and limited lobbying power. This transition may seem to contain potential for instability. However, economic growth imparts a certain stability to the transition process, because it increases everyone's stake in market-led growth.

Yet, the retreat of the state is not necessarily good news for the sustainability of the South Asian economic miracle. The miracle has happened on the back of cheap resources. Sustaining the momentum in the presence of poor quality of institutions can be difficult. Too often one hears in casual conversations the statement that business success in small towns in India or Pakistan depends on political connections. Such sentiment is confirmed in all metrics measuring institutional quality in South Asia, which are among the worst in the world. Since political connections can be bought, poor institutions are not necessarily an obstacle to private investment. It is a tax nevertheless, a barrier to entry for some, and potentially damaging in the longer run. The sustainability of the convergence process will depend less on celebratory rhetoric and more on intervention in improving conditions for investment.

Bibliography

Acemoglu, Daron, Simon Johnson, and James Robinson (2001), 'The Colonial Origins of Comparative Development: An Empirical Investigation,' *American Economic Review*, 91(5), 1369–1401.

Adams, J. (1971), 'The Institutional Economics of Mahadev Govinda Ranade,' *Journal of Economic Issues*, 5(1), 80–92.

Addleton, Jonathan (1984), 'The Impact of International Migration on Economic Development in Pakistan,' *Asian Survey*, 24(5), 574–596.

Agergaard, Jytte and Ditte Broegger (2016), 'Returning Home: Migrant Connections and Visions for Local Development in Rural Nepal, *Geografisk Tidsskrift - Danish Journal of Geography*, 116(1), 71–81.

Aghion, Philippe, Robin Burgess, Stephen J. Redding and Fabrizio Zilibotti (2008), 'The Unequal Effects of Liberalization: Evidence from Dismantling the License Raj in India', *American Economic Review*, 98(4), 1397–1412.

Aghion, Philippe and Steven Durlauf, eds. (2013), *Handbook of Economic Growth*, Amsterdam: Elsevier (North-Holland), vol. 2.

Ahluwalia, I.J. (1985), *Industrial Growth in India: Stagnation since the Mid-Sixties*, Delhi: Oxford University Press.

Ahluwalia, I.J. (1991), *Productivity and Growth in Indian Manufacturing*, Delhi: Oxford University Press.

Ahluwalia, Isher J. and John Williamson, ed. (2003), *The South Asian Experience with Growth*, New Delhi: Oxford University Press.

T. Roy, *The Economy of South Asia*, Palgrave Studies in Economic History, DOI 10.1007/978-3-319-54720-6

Ahluwalia, Montek S. (2002), 'Economic Reforms in India since 1991: Has Gradualism Worked?', *The Journal of Economic Perspectives*, 16(3), 67–88.

Ahmed, Feroz (1984), 'Transformation of Agrarian Structure in the North-West Frontier Province of Pakistan,' *Journal of Contemporary Asia*, 14(1), 5–47.

Ahmed, Masood (1980), 'Import Substitution as a Strategy of Industrialization in Pakistan—A Review,' *Pakistan Economic and Social Review*, 18(1/2), 56–64.

Ahmed, Raisuddin (2004), 'Rice Economy of Bangladesh: Progress and Prospects,' *Economic and Political Weekly*, 39(36), 4043–4052.

Aiyer, Swaminathan S.A. (2008), *Escape from the Benevolent Zookeepers*, Mumbai: Times Group Books.

Alauddin, Mohammad (2005), 'Recent Developments in the Bangladesh Economy,' in Jha, ed., *Economic Growth*, 11–27.

Alavi, Hamza (1976), 'The Rural Elite and Agricultural Development in Pakistan, *Pakistan Economic and Social Review*, 14(1/4), 173–210.

Alexander, Claire, Joya Chatterji, and Annu Jalais (2016), *The Bengal Diaspora. Rethinking Muslim Migration*, London and New York: Routledge.

Ali, Imran and Adeel Malik (2009), 'The Political Economy of Industrial Development in Pakistan: A Long-Term Perspective,' *The Lahore Journal of Economics*, 14(1), 29–50.

Ali, Mubarik (1995), 'Institutional and Socioeconomic Constraints on the Second-Generation Green Revolution: A Case Study of Basmati Rice Production in Pakistan's Punjab,' *Economic Development and Cultural Change*, 43(4), 835–861.

Anwar, Mumtaz and Katharina Michaelowa (2006), 'The Political Economy of US Aid to Pakistan,' *Review of Development Economics*, 10(2), 195–209.

Anwar, Talat (2005), 'Recent Macroeconomic Developments and Implications for Poverty and Employment in Pakistan, in Jha, ed., *Economic Growth*, 76–101.

Anwer, Muhammad Sarfraz and Rajan K. Sampath (1996), 'Inequalities in Land Distribution in Pakistan,' *Pakistan Economic and Social Review*, 34(2), 119–143.

Appu, P.S. (1996), *Land Reforms in India: A Survey of Policy Legislation and Implementation*, New Delhi: Vikas Publishing House.

Athreya, Venkatesh B., Goran Djurfeldt, and Staffan Lindberg (1990), *Barriers Broken: Production Relations and Agrarian Change in Tamil Nadu*, New Delhi: Sage.

Athukorala, Prema-chandra (1998), 'Export Response to Liberalisation: The Sri Lankan Experience,' *Hitotsubashi Journal of Economics*, 39(1), 49–65.

Athukorala, Prema-Chandra (2007), 'Outward-Oriented Policy Reforms and Industrialisation in Sri Lanka,' *Economic Papers*, 26(4), 372–391.

Athukorala, Prema-Chandra and Sarath Rajapatirana (2000), 'Liberalization and Industrial Transformation: Lessons from the Sri Lankan Experience,' *Economic Development and Cultural Change*, 48(3), 543–572.

Athukorala, Prema-chandra and Sisira Jayasuriya (2005), 'Liberalisation and Industrial Growth: lessons from Sri Lanka,' in Jha, ed., *Economic Growth*, 102–118.

Athukorala, Prema-Chandra and Sarath Rajapatirana (2000), *Liberalization and Industrial Transformation: Sri Lanka in International Perspective*, New York: Oxford University Press.

Azhar, Rauf A. (1991), 'Education and Technical Efficiency During the Green Revolution in Pakistan,' *Economic Development and Cultural Change*, 39(3), 651–665.

Aziz, Q. ed. (1997), *Working Conditions in the Textile Industry in Pakistan*, Karachi, 1992; *Asian Cotton Textile Outlook 1995-96*, Osaka, JTN.

Baer, W. (1972), 'Import Substitution and Industrialization in Latin America: Experiences and Interpretations,' *Latin American Research Review*, 7(1), 95–122.

Bagchi, A.K. (1972), *Private Investment in India 1900-1939*, Cambridge: Cambridge University Press.

Bala Subrahmanya, M.H. (1995), 'Reservation Policy for Small-Scale Industry: Has It Delivered the Goods?', *Economic and Political Weekly*, 30(21), M51–M54.

Bala Subrahmanya, M.H. (2004), 'Small Industry and Globalisation: Implications, Performance and Prospects, *Economic and Political Weekly*, 1826–1834.

Bandarage, Asoka (1983), *Colonialism in Sri Lanka: The Political Economy of the Kandyan Highlands, 1833-1886*, Berlin: Mouton.

Bandyopadhyay, D. (1986), 'Land Reforms in India: An Analysis', *Economic and Political Weekly*, 21(25–26), A50–A56.

Banerjee, A., P. Gertler and M. Ghatak (2002), 'Empowerment and Efficiency: Tenancy Reform in West Bengal', *Journal of Political Economy*, 110, 239–280.

Banerjee, Abhijit and Rohini Somanathan (2007), 'The Political Economy of Public Goods: Some Evidence from India', *Journal of Development Economics*, 82(3), 287–314.

Banerjee, Sumanta (1971), 'India and South Asia: Growing Economic Stake,' *Economic and Political Weekly*, 6(24), 1168–1169.

Barbora, Sanjay, Susan Thieme, Karin Astrid Siegmann, Vineetha Menon and Ganesh Gurung (2008), 'Migration Matters in South Asia: Commonalities and Critiques, *Economic and Political Weekly*, 43(24), 57–65.

Bardhan, Pranab (1984), *The Political Economy of Development in India*, Oxford: Basil Blackwell.

Bardhan, Pranab and Dilip Mookherjee (2011), 'Subsidized Farm Input Programs and Agricultural Performance: A Farm-Level Analysis of West Bengal's Green Revolution, 1982–1995,' *American Economic Journal: Applied Economics*, 3(4), 186–214.

Barnds, William J. (1973), 'India and America at Odds', *International Affairs*, 49(3), 371–384.

Batra, Amita (2007), 'South Asia's Free Trade Agreement: Strategies and Options,' *Economic and Political Weekly*, 42(38), 3878–3885.

Beckford, George (1972), *Persistent Poverty: Underdevelopment in Plantation Economies of the Third World*, Mona: University of West Indies Press.

Bell, Clive and Peter L. Rousseau (2001), 'Post-independence India: A Case of Finance-led Industrialization?', *Journal of Development Economics*, 65(2), 153–175.

Besley, T. and R. Burgess (2000), 'Land Reform, Poverty Reduction, and Growth: Evidence from India', *Quarterly Journal of Economics*, 115(2), 389–430.

Bhagwati, J.N. and Padma Desai (1970), *India: Planning for Industrialization*, Oxford and New York: Oxford University Press.

Bhagwati, J.N. and T.N. Srinivasan (1975), *Foreign Trade Regime and Economic Development: India*, New York: Columbia University Press.

Bhalla, S.S. and T. Das (2006), 'Pre- and Post-reform India: A Revised Look at Employment, Wages, and Inequality', Delhi: India Policy Forum.

Bhalla, Surjit S. and Paul Glewwe (1986), 'Growth and Equity in Developing Countries: A Reinterpretation of the Sri Lankan Experience,' *World Bank Economic Review*, 1(1), 35–63.

Bhalotra, S.R. (1998), 'The Puzzle of Jobless Growth in Indian Manufacturing', *Oxford Bulletin of Economics and Statistics*, 60(1), 5–32.

Bhandari, Prem, Dirgha Ghimire (2013), 'Rural Agricultural Change and Fertility Transition in Nepal,' Rural Sociology, 78(2), 229–252.

Bhaskar, V. and Mushtaq Khan (1995), 'Privatization and Employment: A Study of the Jute Industry in Bangladesh,' *American Economic Review*, 85(1), 267–273.

Bhatta, Pramod (2011), 'Aid Agency Influence in National Education Policymaking: A Case from Nepal's 'Education For All' Movement,' *Globalisation, Societies and Education*, 9(1), 11–26.

Bhattacharjee, Dabashish (2000), 'Globalising Economy, Localising Labour', *Economic and Political Weekly*, 35(42), 3758–3764.

Bhattarai, Baburam (2003), *The Nature of Underdevelopment and Regional structure of Nepal: A Marxist Analysis*, Delhi: Adroit Publishers.

Bose, Sugata, ed. (1994), *Credit, Markets, and the Agrarian Economy in Colonial India*, New Delhi: Oxford University Press.

Boyce, James (1987), *Agrarian Impasse in Bengal: Agricultural Growth in Bangladesh and West Bengal 1949-1980*, Oxford: Oxford University Press.

Brammer, Hugh (2008), 'Threat of Arsenic to Agriculture in India, Bangladesh and Nepal,' *Economic and Political Weekly*, 43(47), 79–84.

Bray, Francesca (1979), Review of B.H. Farmer, ed., *Green Revolution?*, London: Macmillan, 1977 in *Modern Asian Studies*, 13(4), 681–04.

Brown, Judith M. (2006), *Global South Asians. Introducing the Modern Diaspora*, Cambridge: Cambridge University Press.

Burki, S.J. (1976), 'Development of West Pakistan's Agriculture,' in R.I. Stevens, Hamza Alavi and P. Bertocci, eds., *Rural Development in Bangladesh and Pakistan*, Honolulu: University of Hawaii Press.

Burki, Shahid Javed (1981), 'Pakistan's Development: An Overview,' *World Development*, 9(3), 301–314.

Byerlee, D. (1992), 'Technical Change, Productivity, and Sustainability in Irrigated Cropping Systems of South Asia: Emerging Issues in the Post-Green Revolution Era,' *Journal of International Development*, 4(4), 477–496.

Caldwell, John (c. 1998) 'The Global Fertility Transition and Nepal,' The Tibetan Himalayan Library (online resource), http://www.thlib.org/static/reprints/contributions/CNAS_25_sp_01.pdf (accessed 9 September 2016).

Chacko, Elizabeth (2007), 'From Brain Drain to Brain Gain: Reverse Migration to Bangalore and Hyderabad, India's Globalizing High Tech Cities,' *GeoJournal*, 68(2/3), 131–140.

Chadha, G.K. (1986), *State and Rural Economic Transformation: The Case of Punjab 1950-85*, New Delhi: Sage.

Chakrabarty, Bidyut (1992) 'Jawaharlal Nehru and Planning, 1938–41: India at the Crossroads', *Modern Asian Studies*, 26(2), 275–228.

Chamarbagwala, R. (2006), 'Economic Liberalization and Wage Inequality in India', *World Development*, 34(12), 1997–2015.

Chand, Ramesh, P.A. Lakshmi Prasanna, Aruna Singh (2011), 'Farm Size and Productivity: Understanding the Strengths of Smallholders and Improving their Livelihoods,' *Economic and Political Weekly*, 46(26–27), 5–11.

Chandra, Bipan (2010), *The Rise and Growth of Economic Nationalism in India: Economic Policies of Indian National Leadership, 1880-1905*, Delhi: Har-Anand Publications.

Chandra, Nirmal (1973), 'Western Imperialism and India Today, I and II', *Economic and Political Weekly*, 17(221–244), 403–408.

Chandra, Nirmal (1977), 'Monopoly Legislation and Policy in India', *Economic and Political Weekly*, 12(33–34), 1405–1418.

Chang, Ha-Joon (2007), *Kicking Away the Ladder: Development Strategy in Historical Perspective*, London: Anthem Press.

Chari, Sharad (2004), *Fraternal Capital. Peasant-Workers, Self-Made Men, and Globalization in Provincial India*, Stanford: Stanford University Press.

Chatterji, Basudev (1992), *Trade, Tariffs, and Empire: Lancashire and British Policy in India 1919-1939*, Delhi: Oxford University Press.

Chatterji, Joya (1994), *Bengal Divided: Hindu Communalism and Partition, 1932-1947*, Cambridge: Cambridge University Press.

Chaudhary, Binod K. (2016), *Making It Big: The Inspiring Story of Nepal's First Billionaire in His Own Words*, London: Penguin.

Chaudhry, M. Ghaffar (1982), 'Green Revolution and Redistribution of Rural Income: Pakistan's Experience,' *Pakistan Development Review*, vol. 21(3), 173–205.

Chaudhry, M. Ghaffar (1989), 'Comments on 'The Agrarian Sector in Pakistan's Development Process - Historical Evidence and Implications for Policy and Theory", *Pakistan Development Review*, 28(4), 526–528.

Chaudhuri, Asim (1980), 'Conglomerate Big Business Groups in India: Some Traits of Tycoon Capitalism,' *Social Scientist*, 8(7), 1980, 38–51.

Chenery, H.B. and A. Strout (1966), 'Foreign Assistance and Economic Development', *American Economic Review*, 56(4), 679–733.

Chibber, Vivek (2003), *Locked in Place: State-Building and Late Industrialization in India*, Princeton: Princeton University Press.

Child, Frank C. and Hiromitsu Kaneda (1975), 'Links to the Green Revolution: A Study of Small-Scale, Agriculturally Related Industry in the Pakistan Punjab,' *Economic Development and Cultural Change*, 23(2), 249–275.

Chinoy, Kamal Mitra (1985), 'Industrial Policy and Multinationals in India,' *Social Scientist*, 13(3), 15–31.

Chowdhury, Nuimuddin (1977), 'Growth and Structural Change in Large-Scale Cotton Textile Industry of Bangladesh, 1947-76,' *Bangladesh Development Studies*, 5(4), 393–341.

Chowdhury, Nuimuddin (1989), 'Bangladesh's Handloom Economy in Transition: A Case of Unequal Growth, Structural Adjustment and Economic Mobility Amid Laissez-Faire Markets: A Synthesis,' *Bangladesh Development Studies*, 17(1/2), 1–22.

Chowdhury, N. (1989) 'Intermediate Power-loom Industry in Bangladesh: Interpretive Account and its Economic Characteristics', Dhaka: Bangladesh Institute of Development Studies Research Report 86, 3.

Clemens, M.A. and J.G. Williamson (2002), 'Why did the Tariff-Growth Correlation Reverse after 1950?,' NBER Working Paper No. 9181.

Cox, Thomas (1990), 'Land Rights and Ethnic Conflict in Nepal,' *Economic and Political Weekly*, 25(24/25), 1318–1320.

Cruz, Wilfrido and Christopher Gibbs (1990), 'Resource Policy Reform in the Context of Population Pressure: The Philippines and Nepal,' *American Journal of Agricultural Economics*, 72(5), 1264–1268.

Dahal, Prakash (2014), 'The Impact of Remittances on Economic Growth in Nepal: An Analysis of a Significant Basis of Development,' *Asia Pacific Journal of Public Administration*, 36(4), 261–282.

Damodaran, Harish (2008), *India's New Capitalists: Caste, Business, and Industry in a Modern Nation*, Ranikhet: Permanent Black/New India Foundation.

Dayal, Edison (1984), 'Agricultural Productivity in India: A Spatial Analysis,' *Annals of the Association of American Geographers*, 74(1), 98–123.

Dayal, E. (1990), 'Sources of Labor Productivity in Bangladesh Agriculture,' *GeoJournal*, 20(3), 293–299.

Deaton, Angus and Jean Drèze (2002), 'Poverty and Inequality in India: A Re-Examination,' *Economic and Political Weekly*, 37(36), 3729–3748.

Demetriades, P.O. and K.B. Luintel (1997), 'The Direct Costs of Financial Repression: Evidence from India, *Review of Economics and Statistics*, 79(3), 311–320.

Desai, Meghnad (2005), *Development and Nationhood. Essays in the Political Economy of South Asia*, New Delhi: Oxford University Press.

Devarajan, Shantayanan and Ijaz Nabi (2006), 'Economic Growth in South Asia: Promising, Unequalising, Sustainable?' *Economic and Political Weekly*, 41(33), 3573–3580.

Dias, Sriyani (1991), 'Economic Liberalization and the Development of Manufacturing in Sri Lanka,' *Asian Survey*, 31(7), 613–629.

Dossani, Sameer (2008), 'Power and Patronage: The Political Economy of Pakistan,' *Middle East Report*, 246, 16–21.

Drèze, Jean and Amartya Sen (2002), *India: Development and Participation*, New York: Oxford University Press.

Drèze, Jean and Amartya Sen (2013), *An Uncertain Glory: India and its Contradictions*, Princeton: Princeton University Press.

Dunham, David and Sisira Jayasuriya (2000), 'Equity, Growth and Insurrection: Liberalization and the Welfare Debate in Contemporary Sri Lanka,' *Oxford Development Studies*, 28(1), 97–110.

Dutt, Srikant (1981), 'Migration and Development: The Nepalese in Northeast,' *Economic and Political Weekly*, 16(24), 1053–1055.

Dutta, Sudipta (1997), *Family Business in India*, Delhi: Response Books.

Dyer, G.D. (1998), 'Farm Size and Productivity: A New Look at the Old Debate Revisited', *Economic and Political Weekly*, 33(26), A113–A116.

Easterly, William (2001), 'The Political Economy of Growth Without Development: A Case Study of Pakistan,' Cambridge Mass.: Harvard University (Kennedy School of Government).

Easterly, William (2002), *The Elusive Quest for Growth: Economists' Adventures and Misadventures in the Tropics*, Cambridge, MA: MIT Press.

Edirisinghe, Neville (1987), *The Food Stamp Scheme in Sri Lanka: Costs, Benefits, and Options for Modification*, Washington, D.C.: International Food Policy Research Institute.

Eichengreen, B. and D.A. Irwin (2009), 'The Slide to Protectionism in the Great Depression: Who Succumbed and Why?' NBER Working Paper No. 15142. Cambridge, MA: NBER.

EPW Research Foundation (1995), 'National Accounts Statistics of India - 1: Macro-Aggregates,' *Economic and Political Weekly*, 30(46), 2955–2964.

Family Planning Association of Pakistan (c. 2006), Demographic Transition in Pakistan, Lahore, http://www.aspiringminds.com/research-reports?page=1 (accessed 9 September 2016).

Fan, Shenggen, Peter Hazell, T. Haque (2000), 'Targeting Public Investments by Agro-ecological Zone to achieve Growth and Poverty Alleviation Goals in Rural India', *Food Policy*, 25, 411–428.

Federico, Giovanni (2010), *Feeding the World: An Economic History of Agriculture, 1800–2000*, Princeton: Princeton University Press.

Feeney, Griffith, Shyam Thapa, and Keshav R. Sharma (2001), 'One and a Half Centuries of Demographic Transition in Nepal,' *Journal of Health, Population, and Nutrition*, 19(3), 160–66.

Feinstein, C.H., R.C.O. Matthews, J. Odling-Smee (1982) *British Economic Growth 1856–1973*, Oxford: Clarendon Press, 1982.

Foster, Andrew D. and Mark R. Rosenzweig (2004), 'Agricultural Productivity Growth, Rural Economic Diversity, and Economic Reforms: India, 1970–2000', *Economic Development and Cultural Change*, 52(3), 509–542.

Frank, A.G. (1966), 'The Development of Underdevelopment', *Monthly Review*, 18(4), 17–31.

Frankema, Ewout (2010, 'Raising Revenue in the British Empire, 1870–1940: How Extractive were Colonial Taxes?,' *Journal of Global History*, 5(3), 447–477.

Fuller, C.J. and Haripriya Narasimhan (2008), 'From Landlords to Software Engineers: Migration and Urbanization among Tamil Brahmans,' *Comparative Studies in Society and History*, 50(1), 170–196.

Furber, Holden (1951), 'The Unification of India, 1947–1951', *Pacific Affairs*, 24(4), 352–371.

Gallup, John Luke, Jeffrey D. Sachs, Andrew D. Mellinger (1998), 'Geography and Economic Development,' NBER Working Paper No. 6849, Washington DC.

Gellner, David ed. (2003), *Resistance and the State: Nepalese Experiences*, New Delhi: Social Science Press.

Gellner, David N. (2007), 'Caste, Ethnicity and Inequality in Nepal,' *Economic and Political Weekly*, 42(20), 1823–1828.

Ghani, Ejaz, ed. (2010), *The Poor Half Billion in South Asia: What Is Holding the Lagging Regions*, New Delhi: Oxford University Press.

Ghani, Ejaz, ed. (2010), *The Service Revolution in South Asia*, New York: Oxford University Press.

Ghani, Ejaz and Sadiq Ahmed, eds. (2009), *Accelerating Growth and Job Creation in South Asia*, New York: Oxford University Press.

Ghose, Ajit (1995), 'Economic Restructuring, Employment and Safety Nets', in ILO-ARTEP, *Social Dimensions of Structural Adjustment in India*, Delhi: ILO.

Ghosh, Jayati (2002), 'Globalization, Export-Oriented Employment for Women and Social Policy: A Case Study of India', *Social Scientist*, 30(11/12), 17–60.

Gill, Monohar Singh (1983), 'The Development of Punjab Agriculture, 1977–80,' *Asian Survey*, 23, 830–844.

Gilpin, R. (2001), *Global Political Economy*, Princeton, NJ: Princeton University Press.

Goldar, B.N. (2000), 'Employment Growth in Organized Manufacturing Growth in India', *Economic and Political Weekly*, 35(14), 1191–1195.

Goswami, Omkar (1985), 'The Indian Textile Industry, 1970–84: An Analysis of Supply and Demand', *Economic and Political Weekly*, 20(38), 1610–1612.

Goswami, Omkar (1990), 'Sickness and Growth in India's Textile Industry', *Economic and Political Weekly*, 25(44–45), 2429–40, 2496–2506.

Greif, Avner (2006), *Institutions and the Path to the Modern Economy: Lessons from Medieval Trade*, Cambridge: Cambridge University Press, 2006.

Griffin, K. (1971), Review of Stephen R. Lewis, *Pakistan: Industrialization and Trade Policies*, New York: Oxford University Press, 1970, Pacific Affairs, 44(3), 457–8.

Guha, Ramachandra (2007), *India After Gandhi: The History of the World's Largest Democracy*, London: MacMillan.

Guha, Ramachandra (2008), 'The Challenge of Contemporary History,' *Economic and Political Weekly*, 43(26/27), 192–200.

Guhathakurta, S. (1993), 'Economic Independence Through Protection? Emerging Contradictions in India's Small-scale Policies Sector', *World Development*, 21(12), 2039–2054.

Gulati, Ashok (2002), 'Indian Agriculture in a Globalizing World', *American Journal of Agricultural Economics*, 84(3), 754–761.

Gulati, Ashok and S. Narayanan (2003), *The Subsidy Syndrome in Indian Agriculture*, Delhi: Oxford University Press.

Gulati, Ashok and Sudha Narayanan (2003), 'Rice Trade Liberalisation and Poverty', *Economic and Political Weekly*, 38(1), 45–51.

Gulati, I.S. (1968), 'Competitiveness of India's Tea Exports,' *Economic and Political Weekly*, 3(7), 325–332.

Gunasinghe, Newton (2004), 'The Open Economy and Its Impact on Ethnic Relations in Sri Lanka,' in Deborah Winslow and Michael D. Woost, eds., *Economy, Culture, and Civil War in Sri Lanka*, Bloomington: Indian University Press, 99–114.

Guthman, Julie (1997), 'Representing Crisis: The Theory of Himalayan Environmental Degradation and the Project of Development in Post-Rana Nepal,' *Development and Change*, 28(1), 45–69.

Hamada, Y. (2012), 'National Governance in International Labour Migration,' *Migration and Development*, 1(1), 50–71.

Hamid, Naved (1983), 'Growth of Small Scale Industry in Pakistan,' *Pakistan Economic and Social Review*, 21(1/2), 37–76.

Hardiman, David (1996), *Feeding the Baniya: Peasants and Usurers in Western India*, Berkeley and Los Angeles: University of California Press, 1996.

Harriss-White, Barbara (1979), 'The Role of Agro-Commercial Capital in 'Rural Development' in South India,' *Social Scientist*, 7(7), 42–56.

Hasan, Parvez (2007), 'Role of the State in Pakistan's Economy: Assessing the Past and Exploring Future Challenges,' *Economic and Political Weekly*, 42(18), 1623–1630.

Hayami, Yujiro (1981), 'Induced Innovation, Green Revolution, and Income Distribution: Comment,' *Economic Development and Cultural Change*, 30(1), 169–176.

Hazari, R.K. (1966), *The Structure of the Corporate Private Sector. A Study of Concentration, Ownership and Control*, London: Asia Publishing.

Helleiner, E. (2002), 'Economic Nationalism as a Challenge to Economic Liberalism? Lessons from the 19th Century', *International Studies Quarterly*, 46(4), 307–329.

Herath, H.M. Gamini (1981), 'The Green Revolution in Rice: The Role of the Risk Factor with Special Reference to Sri Lanka,' *Asian Survey*, 21(6), 664–675.

Herring, Ronald J. (1983), *Land to the Tiller. The Political Economy of Agrarian Reform in South Asia*, New Haven: Yale University Press.

Herring, Ronald J. (1987), 'Economic Liberalisation Policies in Sri Lanka: International Pressures, Constraints and Supports,' *Economic and Political Weekly*, 22(8), 325–333.

Hoselitz, Bert (1960), *Sociological Aspects of Economic Growth*, Glencoe: The Free Press.

Howes, Stephen, Rinku Murgai and Marina Wes (2005), 'Expenditure Implications of India's State-Level Fiscal Crisis,' in Jha, ed., *Economic Growth*, 185–206.

Husain, Ishrat (2011), 'Prospects and Challenges for Increasing India-Pakistan Trade,' Washington DC: Atlantic Council.

Hussain, Akmal (1989) 'Pakistan: Land Reforms Reconsidered,' in Hamza Alavi and John Harriss, ed., *South Asia*, Macmillan, London.

Iimi, Atsushi (2004), 'Banking Sector Reforms in Pakistan: Economies of Scale and Scope, and Cost Complementarities,' *Journal of Asian Economics*, 15, 507–528.

India (1953), *First Five Year Plan*, Delhi: Planning Commission.

India (1978), *Report of the Committee on Land Reforms*, New Delhi: Government Press.

India (2015), *Economic Survey 2014-15*, Delhi: Government Press, volume 2.

Indian Council of Current Affairs (1968), *Foreign Aid: A Symposium, a Survey and an Appraisal*, Calcutta: Oxford Book and Stationery.

Indian School of Social Sciences (1974), 'Economic Crisis in India and the Fifth Five Year Plan', *Social Scientist*, 3(5), 61–88.

Islam, Md Rizwanul (2012), *Economic Integration in South Asia. Charting a Legal Roadmap*, Leiden: Martinus Nijhoff.

Islam, Nasir (1989), 'Colonial legacy, administrative reform and politics: Pakistan 1947–1987,' *Public Administration and Development*, 9(3), 271–285.

Islam, Nurul (1972), 'Foreign Assistance and Economic Development: The Case of Pakistan,' *Economic Journal*, 82(325), 502–530.

Iyer, Ramaswamy R. (2014), 'Indus Waters Treaty 1960: An Indian Perspective,' available at https://www.boell.de/en/2014/03/16/indus-waters-treaty-1960-indian-perspective (accessed 2 August 2016).

Iyer, Ramaswamy R. (2014), 'The Indus Waters Treaty', http://www.stimson.org/the-indus-waters-treaty (accessed 2 August 2016).

Jain, Prakash C. (1982), 'Indians Abroad: A Current Population Estimate,' *Economic and Political Weekly*, 17(8), 299–304.

Jalal, Ayesha (1995), *Democracy and Authoritarianism in South Asia: A Comparative and Historical Perspective*, New York: Cambridge University Press.

Jamaly, Rumana and Ebel Wickramanayake (1996), 'Women Workers in the Garment Industry in Dhaka, Bangladesh,' *Development in Practice*, 6(2), 156–161.

James, William, Seiji Naya and Gerald M. Meier (1989), *Asian Development: Economic Success and Policy Lessons*, Madison, WI: University of Wisconsin Press.

Jayal, Niraja G. ed. (2001), *Democracy in India*, New Delhi: Oxford University Press, 2001.

Jehangir, Waqar A. and Rajan K. Sampath (1991), 'Farm Size and Land Use Efficiency in Pakistan's Agriculture,' *Pakistan Development Review*, 30(3), 263–274.

Jha, Raghbendra, ed. (2005), *Economic Growth, Economic Performance, and Welfare in South Asia*, Basingstoke: Palgrave Macmillan.

Jimenez, Alberto Corsin (2008), 'Relations and Disproportions: The Labor of Scholarship in the Knowledge Economy', *American Ethnologist*, 35(2), 229–42.

Jodhka, Surinder S. (2006), 'Beyond 'Crises': Rethinking Contemporary Punjab Agriculture,' *Economic and Political* Weekly, 41(16), 1530–1537.

Jones, Geoffrey and Judith Wale (1998), 'Merchants as Business Groups: British Trading Companies in Asia before 1945,' *Business History Review*, 72(3), 367–408.

Joshi, Madhav and T. David Mason (2007), 'Land Tenure, Democracy, and Insurgency in Nepal: Peasant Support for Insurgency versus Democracy,' *Asian Survey*, 47(3), 393–414.

Joshi, P.C. (1973), 'Land Reform and Agrarian Change in India and Pakistan since 1947,' *Journal of Peasant Studies*, 1(2), 164–185.

Joshi, V. (1970), 'Savings and Foreign Exchange Constraints', in P. Streeten, ed., *Unfashionable Economics: Essays in honour of Thomas Balogh*, London: Weidenfield and Nicholson.

Kalirajan, K. and S. Bhide (2005), 'The Post-reform Performance of the Manufacturing Sector in India', *Asian Economic Papers*, 3(2), 126–157.

Kalirajan, K.P. and U. Sankar (2001), 'Agriculture in India's Economic Reform Program', *Journal of Asian Economics*, 12(4), 383–399.

Kashyap, S.P. (1988), 'Growth of Small-Sized Enterprises in India: Its Nature and Content, *World Development*, 16(6), 667–681.

Kearney, Robert N. (1985), 'Ethnic Conflict and the Tamil Separatist Movement in Sri Lanka,' *Asian Survey*, 25(9), 898–917.

Kelegama, Saman (2000), 'Development in Independent Sri Lanka: What Went Wrong?' *Economic and Political Weekly*, 35(17), 1477–1490.

Kelegama, Saman (2002), 'Sri Lankan Economy of War and Peace,' *Economic and Political Weekly*, 37(47), 4678–4685.

Kelegama, Saman and Kirit S. Parikh (2003), 'Political Economy of Growth and Reforms in South Asia,' in Ahluwalia and Williamson, eds., *The South Asian Experience with Growth*, 80–145.

Kerr, John (2002), 'Watershed Development, Environmental Services, and Poverty Alleviation in India', *World Development*, 30(8), 1387–1400.

Khan, Muhammed J. and Robert A. Young (1979), 'Farm Resource Productivities, Allocative Efficiencies and Development Policy in the Indus Basin, Pakistan,' *Land Economics*, 55(3), 388–396.

Khan, Mushtaq Husain (2004, 'Power, Property Rights and the Issue of Land Reform: A General Case Illustrated with Reference to Bangladesh,' *Journal of Agrarian Change*, 4(1–2), 73–106.

Khan, Mushtaq H. (no date), 'The Political Economy of Industrial Policy in Pakistan,' Working Paper of the School of Oriental and African Studies, London, https://www.soas.ac.uk/economics/research/workingpapers/file28876.pdf (accessed 1 September 2016).

Khasnabis, Ratan (2008–9), 'The Economy of West Bengal,' *Economic and Political Weekly*, 43(52), 103–115.

Kochanek, S. (2008), 'Liberalisation and Business Lobbying in India,' *Journal of Commonwealth and Comparative Politics*, 34(3), 155–173.

Kochanek, Stanley A. (1983), *Interest Groups and Development: Business and Politics in Pakistan*, Delhi: Oxford University Press.

Kochanek, Stanley A. (1986), 'Regulation and Liberalization Theology in India,' *Asian Survey*, 26(12), 1284–1308.

Kochanek, Stanley A. (1987), 'Briefcase Politics in India: The Congress Party and the Business Elite,' *Asian Survey*, 27(12), 1278–1301.

Kochanek, Stanley A. (1995–1996), 'The Transformation of Interest Politics in India,' *Pacific Affairs*, 68(4), 529–550.

Kochanek, Stanley A. (1996), 'The Rise of Interest Politics in Bangladesh,' *Asian Survey*, 36(7), 704–722.

Kock, Udo and Yan Sun (2011), 'Remittances in Pakistan: Why They Have Gone Up and Why They Are Not Coming Down,' *Pakistan Development Review*, 50(3), 189–208.

Kohli, Atul (1987), *The State and Poverty in India. The Politics of Reform*, Cambridge: Cambridge University Press.

Kohli, Atul (2006), 'Politics of Economic Growth in India, 1980–2005. Part II: The 1990s and Beyond', *Economic and Political Weekly*, 41(14), 1361–1370.

Kosalram, S.A. (1973), 'Political Economy of Agriculture in Tamil Nadu,' *Social Scientist*, 1(12), 3–21.

KPMG India (2002), Indian Chemical Industry: New Directions, New Hopes, 2002. Available at http://www.in.kpmg.com/pdf/KPMG_Chemtech_Report.pdf (accessed 1 August 2016).

Krishna, Raj (1964), 'Some Production Functions of Punjab,' *Indian Journal of Agricultural Economics*, 19, 87–97.

Krishnamurty, J. (1983), 'Occupational Structure,' in Dharma Kumar, ed., *The Cambridge Economic History of India, vol. 2: c. 1751–c. 1970,* Cambridge: Cambridge University Press.

Krueger, A.O., C. Michalopoulos, and V.W. Ruttan (1989), *Aid and Development*, Baltimore MD: Johns Hopkins University Press.

Kumar, Nirmalya (2009), 'Indian Companies as Customers, Competitors and Collaborators,' *Indian Journal of Industrial Relations*, 45(1), 148–159.

Kurien, C.T. and Josef James, (1972), *Economic Change in Tamil Nadu: 1960–70 - A Regionally and Functionally Disaggregated Study*, Delhi: Allied Publishers.

Ladejinsky, Wolf (1964), 'Agrarian Reform in Asia', *Foreign Affairs*, 43(2), 445–460.

Lakshman, W.D. (1985), 'The IMF-World Bank Intervention in Sri Lankan Economic Policy: Historical Trends and Patterns,' *Social Scientist*, 13(2), 3–29.

Lamoreaux, N., D.M.G. Raff and P. Temin (2003), 'Beyond Markets and Hierarchies: Towards a New Synthesis of American Business History', *American Historical Review*, 108(2), 404–433.

LaPorte, Robert Jr. (1969), 'Succession in Pakistan: Continuity and Change in a Garrison State,' *Asian Survey*, 9(11), 842–861.

Leaf, Murray J. (1994), 'Indian Agriculture and Agrarian Communities: Two Studies,' *Economic Development and Cultural Change*, 42(3), 647–653.

Lele U. and I. Nabi (1991), 'The Role of Aid and Capital Flows in Economic Development', *American Journal of Agricultural Economics*, 73(3), 947–950.

Lewis, David (2011), *Bangladesh: Politics, Economy, and Civil Society*, Cambridge: Cambridge University Press.

Lewis, Stephen R. (1969), *Economic Policy and Industrial Growth in Pakistan*, London: George Allen and Unwin.

Lewis, W.A. (1954), 'Economic Development with Unlimited Supplies of Labour.' *Manchester School*, 22(2), 139–191.

Lieberman, Samuel S. (1982), 'Demographic Perspectives on Pakistan's Development,' *Population and Development Review*, 8(1), 85–120.

Liebl, Maureen and Tirthankar Roy (2003–4), 'Handmade in India: Status Report on India's Artisans', *Economic and Political Weekly*, 38(51–2), 5366–5376.

Lieven, Anatol (2011), *Pakistan: A Hard Country*, New York: Public Affairs.

Lim, Youngil (1968a), 'Trade and Growth: The Case of Ceylon,' *Economic Development and Cultural Change*, 16(2), 245–260.

Lim, Youngil (1968b), 'Impact of the Tea Industry on the Growth of the Ceylonese Economy,' *Social and Economic Studies*, 17(4), 453–467.

Lindquist, Alan (1977), 'Military and Development in Bangladesh,' *IDS Bulletin*, 9(1), 10–18.

Little, I.M.D. and J.M. Clifford, *International Aid: A Discussion of the Flow of Public Resources from Rich to Poor Countries with particular reference to British Policy*, London: George Allen and Unwin, 1965.

Little, I.M.D., D. Mazumdar, J. M. Page Jr. (1987), *Small Manufacturing Enterprises, a Comparative Analysis of India and Other Economies*, New York: Oxford University.

Madras (1972), *The Perspective Plan for Tamil Nadu: Towards A Greener Revolution, Report of the Task Force on Agriculture, 1972–1984*, Vols I and II, Madras: State Planning Commission.

Madras Institute of Development Studies (1988), *The Tamilnadu Economy: Performance and Issues*, New Delhi: Oxford and IBH.

Mahapatro, Mausumi (2015), 'Migration, Development and Welfare: Findings from a Household Survey in Two Selected Villages in Bangladesh,' *Migration and Development*, 1–17.

Mahmood, Azhar (1997), 'The Role of Foreign Aid in Economic Development of Pakistan (1960–61 TO 1994–95),' *Pakistan Economic and Social Review*, 35(1), 57–90.

Mahmud, Wahiduddin and S.R. Osmani (1980), 'Impact of Emigrant Workers' Remittances on the Bangladesh Economy,' *Bangladesh Development Studies*, 8(3), 1–28.

Makino, Momeo (2014), 'Pakistan: Challenges for Women's Labour Force Participation,' in Takahiro Fukunishi and Tatsufumi Yamagata, eds., *The Garment Industry in Low Income Countries*, London: Palgrave Macmillan, 132–176.

Mani, Sunil (2013), 'Outward Foreign Direct Investment from India and Knowledge Flows, the case of three automotive firms', *Asian Journal of Technology Innovation*, 21(sup1), 25–38.

Manikutty, S. (2000), 'Family Business Groups in India: A Resource-Based View of the Emerging Trends,' *Family Business Review*, 13(4), 279–292.

Maniruzzaman, Talukder (1968), 'Development Administration in Pakistan,' *Public Administration*, 46(2), 171–184.

Maniruzzaman, Talukder (1975), 'Bangladesh in 1974: Economic Crisis and Political Polarization,' *Asian Survey*, 15(2), 117–128.

Mathur, A.S., S. Das, S. Sarkar (2006–7), 'Agriculture in India: Trends and Prospects,' *Economic and Political Weekly*, 41(52), 5327–5336.

Mazumdar, D. (1984) 'The Issue of Small versus Large in the Indian Textile Industry', World Bank Staff Working Paper No. 645, Washington D.C.

Mazumdar, Dipak and Sandip Sarkar, eds. (2008), *Globalization, Labor Markets and Inequality in India*, London: Routledge.

McCartney, Matthew (2010), Review of E. Ghani and S. Ahmed, eds., *Accelerating Growth and Job Creation in South Asia*, New York: Oxford University Press, 2010, in *Pacific Affairs*, 83(4),816–818.

McCartney, Matthew (2011), *Pakistan – The Political Economy of Growth, Stagnation and the State 1951-2008*, London: Routledge.

McCartney, Matthew (2014), 'The Political Economy of Industrial Policy: A Comparative Study of the Textiles Industry in Pakistan,' *The Lahore Journal of Economics*, 19, 105–134.

Meinzen-Dick, Ruth (1994), 'Private Tubewell Development and Groundwater Markets in Pakistan: A District-Level Analysis,' *Pakistan Development Review*, 33(4), 857–869.

Memon, Noor Ahmed (2010), 'Pakistan Weaving Sector including Denim Holds the Highest Potential for Growth and Investment,' http://www.ptj.com.pk/Web-2010/06-10/June-2010-PDF/Dr.Noor-Ahmed-Memon.pdf (accessed 6 August 2016).

Mencher, Joan P. (1978), *Agriculture and Social Structure in Tamil Nadu: Past Origins, Present Trans formations and Future Prospects*, Durham, N.C.: Carolina Academic Press.

Michie, Ranald (1981), 'Aberdeen and Ceylon. Economic Links in the Nineteenth Century,' *Northern Scotland*, 4(1), 69–82.

Mohammad, Faiz and Mian M. Aslam (1986), 'Wealth Effects of the Green Revolution in Pakistan,' *Pakistan Development Review*, 25(4), 489–513.

Mohan Rao, J. (1992), Review of Rizwanul Islam, ed., *Rural Industrialisation and Employment in Asia*, New Delhi: International Labour Organisation, 1987, *Economic Development and Cultural Change*, 40(2), 447–453.

Moitra, Bhaswar and Pranab Kumar Das (2006), 'Private investment in groundwater irrigation: Do the public institutions matter?' paper for South Asia Network for Economic Research Institutions.

Moorhouse, Geoffrey (1971), *Calcutta*, London: Weidenfield and Nicholson.

Morris, Michael L., H.J. Dubin, Thaneswar Pokhrel (1994), 'Returns to Wheat breeding Research in Nepal,' *Agricultural Economics*, 10(3), 269–282, 269–282.

Morris, Morris D. (1967), 'Values as an Obstacle to Economic Growth in South Asia: An Historical Survey', *Journal of Economic History*, 27(4), 588–607.

Morris, Morris D. (1980), 'The Physical Quality of Life Index (PQLI),' *Development digest*, 18 (1), 95–109.

Morris, Morris D. (1983), 'Growth of Large-scale Industry to 1947,' in Dharma Kumar, ed., *The Cambridge Economic History of India*, vol. 2, Cambridge: Cambridge University Press.

Morris, Morris D. (1997), Review of Mahbub ul Haq, *Human Development in South Asia, 1997*, New York: Oxford University Press, 1997, in *Economic Development and Cultural Change*, 48(2), 2000, 433–439.

Morris, Sebastian (1987), 'Trends in Foreign Direct Investment from India (1950–1982),' *Economic and Political Weekly*, 22(45), 1909–1918.

Mottaleb, Khondoker Abdul and Tetsushi Sonobe (2011), 'An Inquiry into the Rapid Growth of the Garment Industry in Bangladesh,' *Economic Development and Cultural Change*, 60(1), 67–89.

Muhammad, Anu (2006), 'Globalisation and Economic Transformation in a Peripheral Economy: The Bangladesh Experience,' *Economic and Political Weekly*, 41(15), 1459–1464.

Mukherjee, Aditya (2002), *Imperialism, Nationalism and the Making of the Indian Capitalist Class, 1920–1947,* New Delhi, Thousand Oaks and London: Sage Publications.

Mukherjee-Reed, A. (1997), 'Regionalization in South Asia: Theory and Praxis', *Pacific Affairs*, 70(2), 235–251.

Mukherji, Rahul (2000), 'India's Aborted Liberalization-1966', *Pacific Affairs*, 73(3), 375–392.

Mundle, Sudipto (1977), 'Inter-sectoral Resource Flows in Post-Colonial India,' *Indian Economic Review*, 12(2), 151–167.

Murgai, Rinku, Mubarik Ali and Derek Byerlee (2001), 'Productivity Growth and Sustainability in Post-Green Revolution Agriculture: The Case of the Indian and Pakistan Punjabs,' *World Bank Research Observer*, 16(2), 199–218.

Myrdal, Gunnar (1968), *Asian Drama*, vol. 1 of 3 vols., London: Allen Lane.

Nafziger, E. Wayne (2008), 'Entrepreneurship and Development,' in A.K. Dutt and Jaime Ros, eds., *International Handbook of Development Economics*, Volumes 1, Cheltenham: Edward Elgar, 371–387.

Nagaraj, R. (2015), 'Size and Structure of India's Private Corporate Sector: Implications for the New GDP Series,' *Economic and Political Weekly*, 50(45), 41–47.

Nagaraj, R. (1994), 'Employment and Wages in Manufacturing Industries: Trends, Hypotheses and Evidence', *Economic and Political Weekly*, 29(4), 177–186.

Nataraj, Geethanjali (2010), 'Japanese Investment in India: Trends and Prospects,' *Economic and Political Weekly*, 45(10), 20–23.

Nayar, Baldev Raj (1973), 'Treat India Seriously', *Foreign Policy*, 18, 1975, 133–154.

Nayar, Baldev Raj (1998), 'Business and India's Economic Policy Reforms', *Economic and Political Weekly*, 2453–2468.

Nayyar, Deepak, ed. (1994), *Industrial Growth and Stagnation: The Debate in India*, Delhi: Oxford University Press.

Nayyar, Deepak (2008), 'The Internationalization of Firms From India: Investment, Mergers and Acquisitions,' *Oxford Development Studies*, 36(1), 111–131.

Nepal, Apsara Karki (2016), 'The Impact of International Remittances on Child Outcomes and Household Expenditures in Nepal,' *Journal of Development Studies*, 52(6), 838–853,

Nishat, Mohammed and Nighat Bilgrami (1991), 'The Impact of Migrant Worker's Remittances on Pakistan Economy, *Pakistan Economic and Social Review*, 29(1), 21–41.

Nuruzzaman, Mohammed (2007), 'Neoliberal Economic Reforms, the Rich and the Poor in Bangladesh,' *Journal of Contemporary Asia*, 34(1), 2007, 33–54.

Odaka, Konosuke and Yukihiko Kiyokawa, eds. (2008), *Small and Medium Scale Industry in India and the Model of Japan*, New Delhi: Allied Publishers.

Oommen, Ginu Zacharia (2015), 'South Asia–Gulf Migratory Corridor: Emerging Patterns, Prospects and Challenges,' *Migration and Development*, 2015, 1–19.

Pain, Adam (1986), 'Agricultural Research in Sri Lanka: An Historical Account,' *Modern Asian Studies*, 20(4), 755–778.

Pakistan (1990), *Pakistan Textile Statistics*, Karachi, Ministry of Industries.

Palmer-Jones, R. and K. Sen (2003), 'What Has Luck Got To Do With It? A Regional Analysis of Poverty and Agricultural Growth in Rural India', *Journal of Development Studies*, 40(1), 1–31.

Panagariya, Arvind (2008), *India: The Emerging Giant*, New York: Oxford University Press.

Panchamukhi, V.R. (1977), *Trade Policies of India*, Delhi: Concept.

Pande, Aparna (2011), *Explaining Pakistan's Foreign Policy: Escaping India*, New York: Routledge.

Pandey, Abhishek, Alok Aggarwal, Richard Devane, Yevgeny Kuznetsov (2004), 'India's Transformation to Knowledge-based Economy – Evolving Role of the Indian Diaspora', online report available from Evalueserve.

Pandya, Sonal (2014) 'Why Foreign Investment Still Polarizes India,' Washington Post blogs. http://www.washingtonpost.com/blogs/monkey-cage/wp/2014/09/30/why-foreign-investment-still-polarizes-india/ (accessed 1 April 2014).

Papanek, Gustav F. (1962), 'The Development of Entrepreneurship,' *American Economic Review*, 52(2), 46–58.

Paranjape, H.K. (1982), 'The Vanishing MRTP Act: Will Only the Grin Remain?', *EPW*, 17(23), 955–961.

Pasha, Hafiz A. (1995), 'Political Economy of Higher Education: A Study of Pakistan,' *Pakistan Economic and Social Review*, 33(1/2), 19–36.

Patibandla, Murali, Deepak Kapur, Bent Petersen (2000), 'Import Substitution with Free Trade: Case of India's Software Industry,' *Economic and Political Weekly*, 35(15), 1263–1270.

Paul-Majumder, Pratima (1996), 'Health Impact of Women's Wage Employment: A Case Study of the Garment Industry of Bangladesh,' *Bangladesh Development Studies*, 24(1/2), 59–102.

Peebles, Patrick (1990), 'Colonization and Ethnic Conflict in the Dry Zone of Sri Lanka,' *Journal of Asian Studies*, 49(1), 30–55.

Peiris, G.H. (1978), 'Land Reform and Agrarian Change in Sri Lanka,' *Modern Asian Studies*, 12(4), 611–628.

Pender, John L. and John M. Kerr (1998), 'Determinants of Farmers' Indigenous Soil and Water Conservation Investments in Semi-arid India', *Agricultural Economics*, 19, 113–125.

Punjwani, Ashok, Vijay Aggarwal, Nand Dhameja (2008), 'Family Business: Yesterday, Today, Tomorrow,' *Indian Journal of Industrial relations*, 44(2), 272–291.

Radhakrishna, R. and K. Subbarao (1997), 'India's Public Distribution System', World Bank Discussion Paper 380, Washington, DC: World Bank.

Rahim, K.M.B., D. Majumder and R.K. Biswas (2011), 'Determinants of Stagnation in Productivity of Important Crops in West Bengal,' Santiniketan: Agro-Economic Research Centre Visva-Bharati.

Rahman, Sanzidur (2007), 'Regional Productivity and Convergence in Bangladesh Agriculture,' *Journal of Developing Areas*, 41(1), 221–23.

Ramachandran, N. (1963), *Foreign Plantation Investment in Ceylon 1889-1958*, Colombo: Central Bank of Ceylon.

Ramaswamy, K.V. (1999), 'The Search for Flexibility in Indian Manufacturing: New Evidence on Outsourcing Activities', *Economic and Political Weekly*, 34(6), 363–368.

Ranis, Gustav and Frances Stewart (1997), 'Growth and Human Development: Pakistan in Comparative Perspective,' *Pakistan Development Review*, 36(4), 333–352.

Rao, S.L. (2001), 'Indian Companies in an Open Economy,' *Economic and Political Weekly*, 36(5/6), 457–461.

Rao, V.K.R.V. (1944), 'National Income of India,' *The Annals of the American Academy of Political and Social Science*, 233, 99–105.

Ravallion, Martin (2000), 'Prices, Wages and Poverty in Rural India: What Lessons do the Time Series Data hold for Policy?', *Food Policy*, 25(4), 351–364.

Ravi Raman, K. (2010), *Global Capital and Peripheral Labour: The History and Political Economy of Plantation Workers in India*, London and New York: Routledge.

Ray, R.K. (1983), *Industrialization in India: Growth and Conflict in the Private Corporate Sector 1914–1947*, Delhi: Oxford University Press.

Rhee, Yung Whee (1990), 'The Catalyst Model of Development: Lessons from Bangladesh's Success with Garment Exports,' *World Development*, 18(2), 333–346.

Rothermund, Dietmar (1969), 'India and the Soviet Union', *Annals of the American Academy of Political and Social Science*, 386, 78–88.

Roy, T. (1996), 'The Role of the State in Initiating Development: A Study of Interwar South and Southeast Asia,' *Indian Economic and Social History Review*, 33(4), 374–401.

Roy, T. (1998), 'Development or Distortion? The Powerlooms in India, 1950–97', *Economic and Political Weekly*, 33(16), 897–911.

Roy, T. (1999), 'Growth and Recession in Small-scale Industry: A Study of Tamil Nadu Powerlooms', *Economic and Political Weekly*, 34(44), 3137–3145.

Roy, T. (2005), *Rethinking Economic Change in India: Labour and Livelihood*, London: Routledge.

Roy, T. (2007), 'Agrarian Crisis in Interwar India: Retrieving a Narrative,' *Economic and Political Weekly*, 41(52), 5389–5400.

Roy, T. (2012), *India in the World Economy from Antiquity to the Present*, Cambridge: Cambridge University Press.

Roy, T. (2014), 'The Rise and Fall of Indian Economic History,' *Economic History of Developing Regions*, 29(1), 15–41.

Roy, T. (2017), 'Transfer of Economic Power in Corporate Calcutta 1950–1970,' *Business History Review*, 91(1), 3–29.

Roy. T. (2017), 'The Origins of Import-Substituting Industrialization in India,' *Economic History of Developing Regions*, 32(1), 71–95.

Rudolph, Lloyd J. and Susanne H. Rudolph (1987), *In Pursuit of Lakshmi. The Political Economy of the Indian State*, Chicago: Chicago University Press.

Rudra, Ashok (1968), 'Farm Size and Yield per Acre,' *Economic and Political Weekly*, 3(26/28), 1968, 1041–1044.

Rudra, Ashok and Amartya Sen (1980), 'Farm Size and Labour Use: Analysis and Policy,' *Economic and Political Weekly*, 15(5/7), 391–394.

Sabel, C. and J. Zeitlin, eds. (1997), *World of Possibilities: Flexibility and Mass Production in Western Industrialization*, Cambridge: Cambridge University Press.

Saeed, Abubakr, Yacine Belghitar, Ephraim Clark (2015), 'Political Connections and Leverage: Firm-level Evidence from Pakistan,' *Managerial and Decision Economics*, 36(4), 364–383.

Sáez Lawrence and Crystal Chang (2009), 'The Political Economy of global Firms from India and China, *Contemporary Politics*, 15(3), 265–286.

Sajid Mushtaq A. and A.R. Chaudhary (1996), 'Historical Development of Liberalization since 1947 In Pakistan,' *Pakistan Economic and Social Review*, 34(2), 179–192.

Samaraweera, Vijaya (1981), 'Land, Labour, Capital and Sectional Interests in the National Politics of Sri Lanka,' *Modern Asian Studies*, 15(1), 127–162.

Samaraweera, Vijaya (1982), 'Land Reform in Sri Lanka,' *Third World Legal Studies*, 104–122.

Sandesara, J.C. (1988), 'Small-Scale Industrialisation: The Indian Experience', *Economic and Political Weekly*, 23(13), 640–654.

Sapkota, Jhalak Sharma (2015), 'Protecting the Wellbeing of Nepalese Migrant Workers: The Nature and Extent of Interventions by the Government of Nepal,' *Asia Pacific Journal of Public Administration*, 37(2), 115–127.

Sarkar, Goutam K. (1986), 'The Fading Fabric-II: Jute Manufacturing Sector,' *Economic and Political Weekly*, 21(50), 2188–2197.

Schultz, T.W. (1964). *Transforming Traditional Agriculture*, New Haven: Yale University Press.

Sen, Amartya (1962), 'An Aspect of Indian Agriculture,' *The Economic Weekly*, 1962.

Sen, A.K. (1981), 'Public Action and the Quality of Life in Developing Countries,' *Oxford Bulletin of Economics and Statistics*.

Sen, Pronab (1986), 'The 1966 Devaluation in India: A Reappraisal', *Economic and Political Weekly*, 21(30), 1322–1329.

Shah, Tushaar, Mehmood ul Hassan, Banerjee, O.P. Singh, and Saeed Ur Rehman (2009), 'Is Irrigation Water Free? A Reality Check in the Indo-Gangetic Basin,' *World Development*, 37(2), 422–434.

Sharma, H.R. (1994), 'Distribution of Landholdings in Rural India, 1953–54 to 1981–82: Implications for Land Reforms,' *Economic and Political Weekly*, 29(13), A12–A25.

Sharma, Kishor (1997), 'Impact of Policy Reforms on Manufacturing Growth in Nepal,' *Asian Survey*, 37(6), 550–560.

Sharma, Kishor (2006), Development Policy, Inequity and Civil war in Nepal,' *Journal of International Development*, 18, 553–569.

Sharma, Kishor (2015), 'Trade Policymaking in a Land-locked Developing Country: The WTO Review of Nepal,' *World Economy*, 1335–1349.

Sharma, Kishor and Badri Bhattarai (2013), 'Aid, Policy, and Growth: The Case of Nepal,' *Journal of Economic Issues*, 47(4), 895–910.

Sharma, Manohar P. (2013), 'International Contract-Based Migration, Remittances, and Household Well-Being in the Western Province of Sri Lanka,' *International Migration*, 51(S1), e216–e248.

Shrestha, Nanda R., Dennis Conway and Keshav Bhattarai (1999), 'Population Pressure and Land Resources in Nepal: A Revisit, Twenty Years Later,' *Journal of Developing Areas*, 33(2), 245–268.

Shrestha, Bijaya (2008), 'Contribution of Foreign Employment and Remittances to Nepalese Economy,' *Economic Review: Occasional Paper* (Nepal Rastra Bank), 20, 1–15.

Singh, Iqbal (1989), 'Reverse Tenancy in Punjab Agriculture: Impact of Technological Change,' *Economic and Political Weekly*, 24(25), A86–A92.

Singh, Manjit (1995), 'Uneven Development in Agriculture and Labour Migration: A Case of Bihar and Punjab,' Shimla: Indian Institute of Advanced Study.

Singh, Sukhpal (2000), 'Crisis in Punjab Agriculture,' *Economic and Political Weekly*, 35(23), 1889–1892.

Singh, Sukhpal (2002), 'Contracting Out Solutions: Political Economy of Contract Farming in the Indian Punjab', *World Development*, 30(9), 1621–1638.

Sinha, Rajesh (1997), 'Units Closing in on the Life of Rajasthan', *The Indian Express Online*, December 3.

Sivasundaram, Sujit (2010), 'Ethnicity, Indigeneity, and Migration in the Advent of British Rule to Sri Lanka,' *American Historical Review*, 115(2), 428–452.

Sivasubramonian, S. (2000), *National Income of India in the Twentieth Century*, New Delhi: Oxford University Press.

Snodgrass, Donald R. (1966), *Ceylon: An Export Economy in Transition*, Homewood, Illinois: Richard D. Irwin.

Sobhan, Rehman (2004), 'Structural Dimensions of Malgovernance in Bangladesh,' *Economic and Political Weekly*, 39(36), 4101–4108.

Soo, Kwok Tong (2008), 'From Licence Raj to Market Forces: The Determinants of Industrial Structure in India after Reform', *Economica*, 75, 222–243.

Subrahmanian, Kapil (2015), 'Revisiting the Green Revolution: Irrigation and Food Production in Twentieth Century India,' PhD Dissertation of King's College, London.

Subrahmanian, K.K. (1973), 'Role of Foreign Aid and Investment', *Social Scientist*, 1(6), 3–29.

Subramanian, Ramesh (2006), 'India and Information Technology: A Historical and Critical Perspective,' *Journal of Global Information Technology Management*, 9(4), 8–46.

Sugden, Fraser (2013), 'Pre-capitalist Reproduction on the Nepal Tarai: Semifeudal Agriculture in an Era of Globalisation,' *Journal of Contemporary Asia*, 43(3), 519–545.

Sundaram, K. (2002), 'Employment and Poverty in India in the Nineteen Nineties.' Working Paper of CDE Delhi School of Economics.

Sutton, John (2000), 'Indian Machine Tools Industry: A Benchmarking Study', New Delhi: ICRIER.

Swamy, A.V. (1998), 'Factor Markets and Resource Allocation in Colonial Punjab', *Journal of Development Studies*, 34(3), 97–115.

Symonds, Richard (1950), 'State-Making in Pakistan,' *Far Eastern Survey*, 19(5), 45–50.

Takaya, Yoshikazu and Yoshikazu Itoh (1976), 'Vertical Zoning of Monsoon Asia by Agricultural Landuse: A Progress Report,' *South East Asian Studies*, 14(1), 99–122.

Talbot, Ian and Gurharpal Singh (2009), *The Partition of India*, Cambridge: Cambridge University Press.

Tan, Tai Yong and Gyanesh Kudaisya (2000), *The Aftermath of Partition in South Asia*, Abington and New York: Routledge.

Taneja, Nisha (2004), 'Informal Trade in the SAARC Region: Implications for FTAs,' *Economic and Political Weekly*, 39(51), 5367–5371.

Taneja, Nisha and Sanjib Pohit (2001), 'India's Informal Trade with Nepal,' *Economic and Political Weekly*, 36(25), 2263–2269.

Taneja, Nisha, Muttukrishna Sarvananthan and Sanjib Pohit (2003), 'India-Sri Lanka Trade: Transacting Environments in Formal and Informal Trading,' *Economic and Political Weekly*, 38(29), 3094–3098.

Taslim, M.A. (1993), 'Redistributive Land and Tenancy Reform in Bangladesh Agriculture,' *Journal of Developing Areas*, 27(3), 341–376.

Thapa, Prem Jung and Shyamal Krishna Shrestha (2005), 'Economic Reforms in Nepal: Performance and Prospects,' in Jha, ed., *Economic Growth*, 52–75.

Thorner, Alice (1982), 'Semi-Feudalism or Capitalism? Contemporary Debate on Classes and Modes of Production in India,' *Economic and Political Weekly*, 17(49–51), 1961–1968, 1993–1999, 2061–2066.

Toufique, Kazi Ali (2005), 'Farm Size and Productivity in Bangladesh Agriculture: Role of Transaction Costs in Rural Labour Markets,' *Economic and Political Weekly*, 40(10), 988–992.

Tumbe, Chinmay (2012), 'Migration Persistence Across Twentieth Century India,' *Migration and Development*, 1(1), 87–112.

Twomey, M. (2000), *A Century of Foreign Investment in the Third World*, Abingdon: Routledge.

United States of America (no date), Foreign Relations of the United States 1964–1968, Volume XXV South Asia. Available at http://www.state.gov/www/about_state/history/vol_xxv/zb.html.

Upadhya, Carol (2012), 'Imagining India: Software and the Ideology of Liberalisation,' *South African Review of Sociology*, 40(1), 76–93.

Upadhyay, H.K., C.C. David, G.G. Thapa, K. Otsuka (1993), 'Adoption and Productivity Impact of Modern Rice Varieties in Nepal,' *Developing Economies*, 31(1), 122–137.

Upadhyaya, Hari K., Keijiro Otsuka and Cristina C. David (1990), 'Differential Adoption of Modern Rice Technology and Regional Wage Differential in Nepal,' *Journal of Development Studies*, 26(3), 450–468.

Van Schendel, Willem (2009), *A History of Bangladesh*, Cambridge: Cambridge University Press.

Van Wersch, Hubert (1992), *The Bombay Textile Strike 1982-83*, Delhi: Oxford University Press.

Venkateswarlu, B. and J.V.S.N. Prasad (2012), 'Carrying Capacity of Indian Agriculture: Issues related to Rainfed Agriculture,' *Current Science*, 102(6), 882–888.

Warr, Peter (2005), 'Poverty, Inequality and Economic Growth: India, 1957–1997,' in Jha, ed., *Economic Growth*, 343–368.

Waterbury, J. (1999), 'The Long Gestation and Brief Triumph of Import-Substituting Industrialization,' *World Development*, 27(2), 323–341.

Weiner, Myron (1993), 'Rejected Peoples and Unwanted Migrants in South Asia,' *Economic and Political Weekly*, 28(34), 1737–1746.

Wellisz, Stanislaw, Bernard Munk, T. Peter Mayhew and Carl Hemmer (1970), 'Resource Allocation in Traditional Agriculture: A Study of Andhra Pradesh,' *Journal of Political Economy*, 78(4), Part 1, 655–684.

Wells, Thomas (no date), 'Sen's Capability Approach,' The Internet Encyclopedia of Philosophy, http://www.iep.utm.edu/sen-cap/ (accessed 9 September 2016).

Wickramasekara, Piyasiri (2016), 'South Asian Gulf Migration to the Gulf: A Safety Valve or a Development Strategy?' *Migration and Development*, 5(1), 99–129.

Williamson, John (1999), 'Pakistan and the World Economy,' *Pakistan Development Review*, 37(4), 181–201.

Williamson, O.E., (1995), *The Economic Institutions of Capitalism*, New York: Simon and Schuster.

Wilson, John ed. (2009), *Pakistan: The Struggle Within*, New Delhi: Pearson-Longman.

Yadav, Vineeta (2008), 'Business Lobbies and Policymaking in Developing Countries: The Contrasting Cases of India and China,' *Journal of Public Affairs*, 8(1), 67–82.

Zaidi, S.Akbar (2005), 'State, Military and Social Transition. Improbable Future of Democracy in Pakistan,' *Economic and Political Weekly*, 5173–5181.

Zohir, Salma Chaudhuri (2001), 'Social Impact of the Growth of Garment Industry in Bangladesh,' *Bangladesh Development Studies*, 27(4), 41–80.

Index

T. Roy, *The Economy of South Asia*, Palgrave Studies in Economic History, DOI 10.1007/978-3-319-54720-6

M

N

CPSIA information can be obtained
at www.ICGtesting.com
Printed in the USA
BVHW08*1830280618
520354BV00007B/36/P

9 783319 547190